PRAISE FOR

How to Be a Movie Star

"An entertaining chronicle of the golden years of Hollywood crammed with celebrity gossip and inside info."

— *Washington Times*

"Mann's eminently yummy entry is pretty much everything you'd want in a Hollywood biography." — Salon.com

"With her elegance, ego, and extravagance, Elizabeth Taylor set a new standard for celebrity. Mann's alluring take skips tired anecdotes to focus on Liz's own obsession with fame. Delish."

— *Good Housekeeping*

"Mann digs pretty deep, with loads of interviews and context to show Taylor's steady, deliberate construction of her fame . . . [An] engaging and insightful study of celebrity."

— *Milwaukee Journal Sentinel*

"A revealing look at one of the biggest film stars of the post WWII era . . . Part biography and part meditation on the nature of fame, *How to Be a Movie Star* is also study of the culture of celebrity."

— *San Francisco Examiner*

"Wickedly entertaining . . . Mann cleverly forsakes a conventional biography and instead deconstructs a series of chapters of Taylor's life, deploying both well-known and freshly uncovered tales."

— *Sunday Times* (UK)

"A dazzling and sagacious red-carpet Technicolor guidebook to the lost art of stardom ... essential reading for aspiring love goddesses and mere mortals alike."

—Lee Server, author of
Ava Gardner: "Love is Nothing"

"Mann's smart, engaging, clear-eyed case study of Taylor's unique life in the spotlight locates the 'real' person somewhere between her private life and her public image. It's a fresh, unique, and wholly successful approach to a fascinating story."

—Mark Harris, author of
Pictures at a Revolution

"[Mann] has clearly done his research ... engrossing."

—*New York Times Book Review*

How to Be a
Movie Star

Books by
WILLIAM J. MANN

Wisecracker:
The Life and Times of William Haines

Behind the Screen:
How Gays and Lesbians Shaped Hollywood

Edge of Midnight:
The Life of John Schlesinger

Kate:
The Woman Who Was Hepburn

How to Be a Movie Star:
Elizabeth Taylor in Hollywood

WILLIAM J. MANN

How to Be a Movie Star

Elizabeth Taylor
in Hollywood

MARINER BOOKS
HOUGHTON MIFFLIN HARCOURT
BOSTON • NEW YORK

For Timothy Huber

First Mariner Books edition 2010
Copyright © 2009 by William J. Mann

ALL RIGHTS RESERVED

For information about permission
to reproduce selections from this book, write to
Permissions, Houghton Mifflin Harcourt Publishing Company,
215 Park Avenue South, New York, New York 10003.

www.hmhbooks.com

Library of Congress Cataloging-in-Publication Data
Mann, William J.
How to be a movie star : Elizabeth Taylor in Hollywood /
William J. Mann.
p. cm.
Includes bibliographical references and index.
ISBN 978-0-547-13464-2
1. Taylor, Elizabeth, 1932– 2. Motion picture actors
and actresses—United States—Biography. I. Title.
PN2287.T18M36 2009
791.4302'8092—dc22
[B]   2009013283

ISBN 978-0-547-38656-0 (pbk.)

Book design by Linda Lockowitz

Printed in the United States of America
DOC 10 9 8 7 6 5 4 3 2

*I don't pretend to be
an ordinary housewife.*

—Elizabeth Taylor

Contents

How to Be a
Movie Star

Prologue

How to Be a Movie Star

FOR ONCE THE SUN overhead was the brightest object around. On a warm morning in September 2006, Elizabeth Taylor, seventy-four, left the diamonds at home and boarded a sightseeing boat, the *Kainani,* off Oahu's North Shore. Wearing a baggy white T-shirt over a one-piece bathing suit, she gripped the arms of her black wheelchair tightly as the craft zipped out of Haleiwa Harbor. Slapping against the waves of the Pacific, the thirty-two–foot *Kainani* was a far cry from the *Kalizma,* the floating palace with six cabins and two staterooms on which Taylor had once navigated the world. But a leisurely cruise was not what the two-time Academy Award winner had in mind.

Three miles out to sea, the *Kainani* arrived at what its captain called "the shark grounds." On another excursion not long before, Elizabeth had sat forlornly while her friends dropped off the side of the boat in a Plexiglas cage to swim with Galapagos sharks. Alone on deck, she'd stewed; the sidelines had never been for her. So she'd insisted on another trip—and this time no one was going to stop her from going down.

In the months leading up to this day, the papers had been filled with tales of Elizabeth Taylor being "near death" or half-mad from Alzheimer's. She'd gone on *Larry King Live* to dispel the rumors, but she knew there were ways of making the point a bit more vividly. So, slowly and determinedly, she rose from that damn chair. Handed a mask, she followed the instructions to spit into it so that the plastic wouldn't fog up underwater. Then she slipped the thing on and bit down on the snorkel. Pushing aides aside, she stepped into the ten-by-six-foot cage. Lured by the engine, the sharks were already circling. With the pull of a lever and a wave from the star, the cage slid below the surface of the ocean.

Of course, this wasn't the first time Elizabeth Taylor had gone head-to-head with sharks. She'd tangled with lots of them: demanding studio heads, overbearing directors, bluenose columnists, greedy husbands. And she'd done so with a shrewdness and a keen understanding of just how a star went about getting what she wanted. "She was always in control," said her friend, photographer Gianni Bozzachi. "She did not seek fame but she knew how to use it. She was very smart. People don't know how smart." Some chroniclers, perhaps too dazzled by the violet eyes and the glittery melodrama of her life, have missed that salient point. Long before our own celebrity age, Elizabeth Taylor carved the template for how to be a movie star. So many of the tricks of the trade can be traced right back to her.

When the cage finally resurfaced, Taylor smiled at the photographer who was there to record the moment. Her scarlet nails, still perfectly manicured, sparkled in the sun. Getting into that shark cage, she later told columnist Liz Smith, was "the most exciting thing" she'd done—which, given her life, was saying a lot. "To be in that cage and watch the sharks get closer and closer," she told Ingrid Sischy in *Interview,* "I had no sense of fear." Of course not; sitting across from Louis B. Mayer had been far more unnerving. Within a short time, the photos and news of her adventure had zoomed around the world. Soon there was buzz about an eighth marriage and a possible lead in the film version of the musical *Sunset Boulevard.* So much for death's door, baby.

Movie stars—like automobiles, airplanes, and apple pies—are quintessentially American commodities. When we measure what we've given the world, the product of Personality—used to inspire, entertain, endorse, titillate, preach, stoke the flames of our imaginations, and sell, sell, sell—may prove more influential than even the Model T. Elizabeth Taylor—for her performances both good and bad, for her innocence, sexiness, rebellion, honesty, and sheer life force—has been called the greatest movie star of all. She has become a cultural artifact that transcends temporal value judgments and the hectoring of the moralists who plagued her career. Her life was made into art, soap opera, scandal, tragedy, and even a bit of myth—a transformation begun by the starmakers at Metro-Goldwyn-Mayer, the studio that launched her when she was twelve, and continued by agents and publicists like Kurt Frings, Bill Doll, John Springer, and Chen Sam, and given its final patina by the media, with which Taylor has always had a symbiotic relationship. A creature of newspaper headlines and telephoto images, Elizabeth enjoyed an unprecedented celebrity that made her into an icon of desire, of gusto, of appetites passionately sated, of candor, of courage, of never saying no to big bad life.

With her studio-instilled instinct for *presence* (not to mention her refusal to suffer even a moment of boredom), Elizabeth Taylor created the model for stardom and turned it into big business. Before "Liz," the paparazzi were just a bunch of aggressive Italian photographers; because of her, they became a worldwide phenomenon. Part engineering, part instinct, part fate, part simply the pursuit of good times, her fame continues to set the gold standard. Britney may break down; Angelina may steal Brad from Jen; Madonna may reinvent herself as saint, shepherdess, horsewoman, or action figure. But no one has done anything that Elizabeth Taylor didn't do first—and without the excess calculation.

Today's stars concoct their lives for public consumption: Was Britney really that crazy or was it just a quirky twenty-first-century way of staying in the headlines? So much in stars' lives is suspect today. Taylor, by contrast, was brought up to be a star; and while she certainly took advantage of every twist and turn in her epic life, she wasn't constantly configuring and reconfiguring her existence for maximum exposure—the way, for example, her first husband's grandniece, Paris Hilton, would do a couple of generations later. For Taylor, stardom came naturally. She had an affinity for the romance of life. Her fame was a roller coaster of spontaneity and strategy, and all the would-be icons who have followed her have attempted to retrace that pattern, manufacturing the kinds of developments that came to Taylor so extempore and that she (or those who worked for her) used so brilliantly to her advantage.

She also understood that riding the headlines was never enough; she knew that fame should be an exchange with the public. And so, for every cover of *Photoplay*, there was a *Giant* or a *Suddenly, Last Summer*. After all the hoopla over her affair with Richard Burton, she made sure there was a *Who's Afraid of Virginia Woolf?*

"I don't pretend to be an ordinary housewife," Elizabeth once declared, and that, in a simple sentence, is the secret of her appeal. Many of her contemporaries *did* pretend to be ordinary house-wives, succumbing to the dictum that stars should be like the rest of us. But Taylor stood apart, reveling in her ability to fascinate, to scandalize, to provoke. Swathed in mink, sailing aboard yachts, dis-carding husbands nearly as frequently as she changed her diamond earrings, Elizabeth dominated the headlines for three glittering decades, rewriting the rules as she went along, inverting paradigms, defying conventions, beating expectations, and in the course of it all laying down the yardstick by which celebrity has been measured ever since.

Part of her celebrity, of course, was inherent, magical, and un-quantifiable. "At her best, Elizabeth Taylor simply *is*," writes Ca-mille Paglia. "An electric, erotic charge vibrates the space between her face and the lens. It is an extrasensory, pagan phenomenon." Richard Burton, admittedly not an unbiased observer, thought that Elizabeth "emanated" something onscreen that he frankly didn't understand—a trait she shared with Brando, Clift, and Garbo.

But an equally large part of it was *craft:* Taylor grew up with the camera, after all, both the motion-picture variety and the pop-ping flashcubes of the press corps. By sheer instinct she knew how to position herself in a shot. One of her directors was amazed by her ability to determine the camera's location simply by the heat on her cheeks. She could also be a damn fine actress at times: Holly-wood historian Gavin Lambert thought that with the right di-rector, Taylor could "more than rise to the occasion," while Paglia declared her "the greatest actress in film history"—not for any proficiency in technique but for her mastery of the "liquid realm of emotion." That's the point: Of all the lessons Taylor learned so well at MGM, the most valuable had little to do with acting.

Consider this: In 1950, when she was eighteen and making *Father of the Bride,* the studio decided that Elizabeth should take a real-life trip down the aisle for the good of the box office. The marriage was a personal trauma for the sensitive young woman, but it also proved to be an instructive experience in the ways that stardom could be sold—and souls damaged. In such an ambitious and mercenary world, Taylor had to become tough and refuse to crumble like Judy Garland. Her triumph over the studio system meant that she would help lay the foundation for the industry and the ways of doing business that replaced it. She was the first female star to be paid a million dollars a picture *and* to take a share of the profits. When she was told a few years ago that Julia Roberts was making twenty million a picture, Elizabeth simply smiled and said, "I started it."

Some people even argue that she spurred the sexual revolution of the 1960s. One of the first big stars to pose nude for *Playboy* (though not fully) and to take off her clothes onscreen (discreetly), Taylor pushed the envelope on all things sexual. Her matrimonial adventures took the sting out of adultery. Her affair with the married Richard Burton—so notorious that it knocked John Glenn's historic space flight off the front page of some newspapers—occurred just as the public was "questioning old values and trying new ones on for size," the anthropologist George O'Neil observed; by its very prominence, O'Neil believed that the affair helped "speed up the revolution in moral standards." Slightly more than a decade earlier Hollywood had exiled the adulterous Ingrid Bergman, but in 1962 Elizabeth Taylor became the biggest star of the year after refusing to apologize for her love affair.

Writer Maureen Orth calls Taylor "the Madame Curie of fame extension." Indeed, from the sweet child of *National Velvet* who masqueraded as a jockey to win the Grand National, to the idealized young woman of *A Place in the Sun* who was worth whatever punishment Montgomery Clift risked on her behalf, to the fiery seductress of *Cat on a Hot Tin Roof* who slunk around in a revealing white slip, to the foul-mouthed shrew of *Who's Afraid of Virginia Woolf?* who tore everyone and everything around her to pieces, Taylor created characters in her four decades onscreen that were cannily layered onto her real-life persona. "That's how stars became great," said Hollywood agent Dick Clayton. "They had a little bit of everything for everyone."

But the best part she ever played was Elizabeth Taylor. Film theorist Richard Dyer has suggested that the alchemy of true stardom is produced by the reconciliation of contradictions. Certainly few other performers have exhibited as captivating a duality as Taylor. Watching her with Montgomery Clift in *A Place in the Sun*, critic Andrew Sarris decreed them "the most beautiful couple in the history of cinema," calling their gigantic close-ups "unnerving—sybaritic—like gorging on chocolate sundaes." And yet for all her movie-queen beauty, Taylor was also a good old gal who liked her fun and fried chicken. Stories about her 33.19-carat Krupp Diamond ("Big girls need big diamonds") were balanced by tales of the peanut butter and bacon sandwiches she carried in her bag.

It's exactly this kind of paradox, this melding of the ordinary and the extraordinary, that makes a personality memorable. Elizabeth was a smoldering siren who lured helpless men away from their wives, but she was also a bit of an oddball. Liz Smith recalled the time that the star was invited to dinner by a wealthy admirer. "Who is this person?" Elizabeth asked, insisting that she didn't visit people she didn't know. But when told that the man liked to "dress up in satin ball gowns and stick diamond tiaras over his bald spot," she had second thoughts. "Oh, why, he's one of us then," she said. "Of course I'll go."

She was a star without airs. Mike Nichols said that of all the people he'd worked with, Taylor had the "most democratic soul," treating electricians on the set the same way she would a Rothschild at a charity gala. After making *The Blue Bird* with the star in 1973, director George Cukor told Taylor that she possessed "that rarest of virtues—simple kindness." Tom Mankiewicz, the son of the man who directed her in *Suddenly, Last Summer* and *Cleopatra*, said Taylor could "spot a phony a mile away." In her own press she did her best to walk a careful line between hype and truth. "I try not to live a lie," she told one reporter at the height of the scandal with Burton, when no one was sure what it would do to her career. "I can't be that hypocritical [just] to protect my public."

Her authenticity, of course, became its own selling point. In 1966, while helping shape publicity for Taylor's film *Reflections in a Golden Eye,* no less than Gloria Steinem suggested a campaign featuring the star as the "movie queen with no ego." Despite Elizabeth's palatial dressing rooms and other luxuries, Steinem argued that Taylor set herself apart by being "expert at what she does, uncatty in her work relationships with other actresses, and pretty much willing to try whatever the director asks." After a decade of being known as Hollywood's home wrecker, it would be this more humane, bighearted view of Elizabeth Taylor that would prevail in people's minds. "She is the good-bad girl who gives the audience a sense of breaking the bonds of daily life without casting loose from all moorings," wrote the journalist (and Taylor's occasional lover) Max Lerner.

And what makes her unique in the Hollywood pantheon is that none of the images that spun around her circled too far from the truth. Garbo's supposed preference for being alone was simply part of a manufactured mystique. Katharine Hepburn's all-American public self (the "Creature," she called it) was crafted to disguise her unorthodoxy and ensure her legacy. But if "Kate" was largely fiction, "Liz" was real—no matter how much Taylor despised the press's ubiquitous nickname. Yet just because the product was more genuine than most doesn't mean that she was above merchandising it; every great star has to be a great peddler as well. Elizabeth knew how to make every scandal work for her and turn criticism on its head. "There's no deodorant like success," she once stated. Her grasp of the tricky business of fame meant that she'd out-shine other greats like Garbo and Monroe who never knew how to cope except when in front of the cameras. Elizabeth, by contrast, was equally at home on the soundstage or the world stage. Critic David Thomson once proclaimed Elizabeth "the most ambitious of them all."

True enough—but Taylor's ambition wasn't quite what one might expect. Certainly she knew how to play the game better than most; when her marriage to Eddie Fisher was crumbling, she distracted the press with a shopping spree in Paris, loading her-self down with boxes from Chanel, Dior, and Yves Saint Laurent. And even during her frequent hospital stays, the reports issued by her publicists were timed to have the maximum effect on pub-lic sympathy. Yet it was never about fame for fame's sake; stardom for Elizabeth was a means to an end. "Taylor seems more to co-exist with fame than to dwell within it," the writer Ethan Mordden observed.

Indeed, the primary function of her extraordinary celebrity was to enable the kind of rarefied lifestyle that she considered hers by birthright. The spotlight alone was never enough, the way it was for Hepburn or Joan Crawford. For Taylor fame was merely the currency that allowed her to do what she wanted when and where she wanted. Her friend, the producer Hank Moonjean, remem-bered being sent to Switzerland to look for a house for her. "Where the *fuck* are you?" the star demanded when she reached him on the phone. She wanted him back in time for a game of hearts she was setting up for the next day. Moonjean told her he'd found a house and that it cost $400,000 (a king's ransom then). "Buy it!" she com-manded. But didn't she need to see it? "No, just fucking buy it!" Should he try to negotiate down the price? "No," she cried, "just buy the damn thing so you can get back here and we can play fuck-ing hearts!" What was fame if she couldn't play cards when and with whom she wanted?

Elizabeth once remarked to Dominick Dunne—"without an iota of braggadocio"—that she couldn't remember a time when she wasn't famous. That's key to understanding her. Even though she didn't become a star until the age of twelve, her early entitlement sprang from a privileged childhood as the daughter of middle-class Americans who'd found the good life in British aristocratic circles and who, like MGM a few years later, indulged her every whim. Yet while she was always more a red-blooded broad than a blue-blooded dame (her designation as a Dame of the Order of the British Empire in 2000 notwithstanding), her love for the finer things would serve her well as a movie star.

Of course, such luxury meant that she never experienced "ordinary" life. Shooting a scene in *Butterfield 8,* director Daniel Mann handed his star a couple of eggs and told her to pretend to make breakfast as she stood at the stove. Taylor's eyes grew wide. Holding an egg out in each hand, she implored, "But what do I *do* with them?" She had never made breakfast in her life. Neither had she ever been to a baseball game or a school dance that wasn't arranged by the Metro publicity department. Yet studio press releases, cranked out on mimeograph machines, tried—not always successfully—to create the illusion that Elizabeth was just a simple girl with ordinary dreams.

This is the trap that biographers have sometimes fallen into, swayed by those long-ago press releases into chronicling Taylor's romances and marriages as simply the narrative of a passionate woman's heart. In most accounts, Elizabeth moves from Glenn Davis to Bill Pawley to Conrad "Nicky" Hilton (and beyond) without any other consideration than "love." Yet while Taylor's passion is undeniable, such an approach misses the far more interesting story of how these relationships were used by the studio and later by her own press agents to further her fame—and always with Elizabeth's compliance.

Indeed, the two central memes of Taylor's career—her marriages and her illnesses—were marketed for every last dollar of their commercial value. That doesn't mean they weren't real; it simply means that everyone involved understood the considerable gain that they promised to yield.

It is my job with this book to not only separate fact from fiction, but to also consider the ways in which they inform each other, and to document as best as possible the sometimes practical, sometimes mysterious ways in which Elizabeth Taylor became a movie star—and how she managed to stay on top for four magnificent decades.

How to Be a Movie Star is not a traditional biography. I do not cover every year of Taylor's life, or every film, or every up and down of every romance. There are plenty of other books that do that. I'm not here to repeat well-known anecdotes merely for form's sake. Instead I take instruction from the book's title. What intrigues me are those areas that haven't been fully investigated before: the mechanics of Taylor's fame and the alchemy that assured her enduring celebrity. By considering these, I hope to understand fame itself a little better. And for that, what better model than Elizabeth Taylor?

For my purposes, I concentrate on (to use Sarris's term) her "chocolate sundae" years, zooming in on key periods of Taylor's life that tell the larger story of her walk with fame: the campaign to be cast in *National Velvet;* the productions of *A Place in the Sun* and *Giant;* the jet-setting celebrity she enjoyed with Mike Todd (back when air travel was still a novelty to most people); the hysterical public reaction to her affair with Fisher; the transformative scandal with Burton; and the behind-the-scenes stories of *Cleopatra* and *Who's Afraid of Virginia Woolf?* I fade out with *The Little Foxes* and Elizabeth triumphantly taking her curtain calls on Broadway, basking in the affection of her public.

Her life went on from there, of course; her heartfelt advocacy on behalf of those with AIDS will likely be remembered as her greatest achievement. But after the late 1960s, Taylor ceased being a movie star, strictly speaking. Although she still made the occasional appearance in film or on TV, her fame was now carried along largely by the momentum of the previous forty years. And so grand and glamorous were those years that they could palliate the sometimes painful gaucheries of Taylor's later life: the trips to the Betty Ford Clinic, the marriage to construction worker Larry Fortensky, the friendship with Michael Jackson, *The Flintstones*.

To re-create Taylor's many different worlds, I have drawn from sources that were either never previously used or seriously underutilized, such as director George Stevens's personal papers for *A Place in the Sun* and *Giant*, which included Elizabeth's private medical records tucked away in one folder; the FBI files of Mike Todd; the business records of the Todd organization; the hundreds of letters Hedda Hopper received during the Eddie Fisher scandal; the studio marketing plans for *Butterfield 8*; the private letters between Burton and his former lover Claire Bloom; court depositions given by Taylor and Burton when Fox sued them over *Cleopatra*; the journal kept by producer Ernest Lehman during the making of *Who's Afraid of Virginia Woolf?*; and Taylor's working script for *The Little Foxes*, complete with her own handwritten notes. For the most part, the quotes I use come from fresh sources, such as transcripts of unpublished interviews with Elizabeth, Burton, George Stevens, Hedda Hopper, and others.

I also spoke with many of Taylor's friends, colleagues, and family, most of whom are here on the record. Only a few asked that their names not be used; I agreed to their anonymity because their proximity to Taylor offered valuable insight. Yet equally as important were those who, even if their connection to the star was tangential, offered commentary on the mechanics of her celebrity. Among these were publicists and agents who described for me the elaborate process of studio starmaking; Elizabeth's fellow contract players who shared their own experiences at the MGM lot and studio schoolhouse; and the original paparazzi who conveyed their unique perspective on the power and allure of fame.

If not the greatest star, Elizabeth Taylor is certainly the last. Her singular journey through the popular imagination tells us everything we need to know about fame and public life in the twentieth century. It also provides some telling insight into what it's become today. The old adage that they don't make stars like Elizabeth Taylor anymore is true. Even when they were making stars like her, she had few rivals. Some years ago, Elizabeth called herself "Mother Courage" and vowed she'd be dragging her sable coat behind her into old age. Whether sable or shark cages, Elizabeth Taylor has kept her word.

One

When in Rome

December 1961–April 1962

NEW YEAR'S EVE, 1961. People, ordinary and otherwise, were gathering along Rome's famed Via Veneto, a boulevard of blasphemy in the shadow of Vatican City. The atmosphere outside Bricktop's, the nightclub for the chic and the daring run by the cigar-smoking chanteuse who'd inspired Cole Porter's "Miss Otis Regrets," was feverish. The air was a blend of cigarette smoke and perfume. The holiday wasn't the only reason for the energy. Much of it came from rumors that somewhere inside Bricktop's the world's most famous woman was ringing out the old—not to mention the fairly recent—in her own lively fashion.

"Leez," the mob began to chant. "Leez!"

Within the smoky club, Elizabeth Taylor threw her head back in laughter, her cheeks rosy with champagne and revelry. The diamonds around her neck sparkled, and for a second her plunging neckline revealed even more soft cleavage than usual. Across from her, nearly as starstruck as the crowd outside, was Tom Mankiewicz, the nineteen-year-old son of the director who had brought Elizabeth to the Eternal City.

"It's impossible to exaggerate how beautiful Elizabeth Taylor was back then," Mankiewicz said. "She was so beautiful that my teeth hurt."

At twenty-nine, Elizabeth, the mother of three, still had the figure of a goddess—or at least the attitude and experience to convince just about everyone that her attributes were divine. Her beauty was real, but it was maximized by her performance: Her walk, her talk, her clothes, her jewels all announced, "I'm here. Aren't I grand?"—which would be followed by another eruption of ebullient laughter and a sip of something, then a flash of those magnificent eyes. Elizabeth Taylor made beauty warm and approachable—if expensive.

As just about everyone on the planet knew, she was in Italy to play Cleopatra, queen of the Nile. "It is important for Liz to know that Cleopatra was considered a goddess, directly divine, by herself as well as by the Egyptians," writer Paddy Chayefsky had advised the film's producers. The Egyptian queen, he said, was sensual, aristocratic, clever, and impulsive. Call it a match or a revision of history or just pure invention, but Cleopatra was becoming the latest incarnation of Elizabeth Taylor.

Now into its second year of production, having started and stopped any number of times in London and now in Rome, *Cleopatra* was on its way to becoming the most expensive production of its era. Part of the enormous budget—$20 million at that point, and it would later double—was because of its especially grand scale. The Alexandrian set was the largest ever built, spreading over thirty acres. And that was just the real estate. Wags joked, not without cause, that *Cleopatra* had the third largest navy in the world. But the real grandeur was Elizabeth; the hurricane of sex and glamour she stirred up didn't come cheap. Her $1 million salary was a landmark in 1961, and then there was her share of the profits. She stood to make a killing. But then—as this evening illustrated—she worked overtime.

In 1961 Elizabeth was the biggest star in the world. The annual exhibitors' poll had just confirmed her number one box-office status, largely due to her smash hit, *Butterfield 8*. She'd nabbed an Oscar for that one—though some people said that she'd really won for best performance in a real-life tragedy: her near-fatal (or fatal-ish) bout with pneumonia earlier that year. Six months later she was out of bed and causing a riot in Rome soon after she arrived with a neckline that plunged to her waist. Two thousand screaming fans broke through a ring of police when they spied her at the Sistina Theater, and she was lost among them for a moment. Scrambling into a parked car and locking the door behind her, Elizabeth waited until the police arrived to escort her to safety. Who said a million was so generous? And she played it all to the hilt.

Every day was more of the same: more outfits, more screams, more drama. Her life seemed concocted to create havoc and dispel boredom. Outside her hotel the street became a circus every time Elizabeth raised the blinds in her room. But what she was really doing was raising the curtain on the Era of Celebrity. Hundreds gathered daily, "thinking there might be a chance they'd see her walk in or out," Mankiewicz said. Her hold over the public and their dreams was like the caress of a steel vise. She had been trained in the all-American art of public living since girlhood, and she had elevated it to an almost Shakespearean level—with diamonds and disposable husbands.

Her training came courtesy of Metro-Goldwyn-Mayer, the studio that, more than any other, created the business of Hollywood and the cultivation of these things called stars. Trained by experts, Elizabeth had taken it all up a notch or two when given the opportunity. "No one—and I mean *no one*—has ever had that kind of fame quotient," Tom Mankiewicz said. "And no one has ever handled it quite so well."

Seated at Bricktop's on that New Year's Eve, Elizabeth glanced up to see a young United States marine in full-dress uniform approaching the table. "I'd like to ask you to dance," the young man said. Taylor's husband (number four), the singer Eddie Fisher, tried to shoo him away, but Elizabeth, her extraordinary blue eyes (the press routinely called them violet) filling with mischief, followed the kid onto the dance floor.

While Fisher brooded, the rest of the table admired how charming and ladylike Elizabeth was with the marine—even after just knocking back an Ivan the Terrible, a potent mix of vodka, grappa, and ouzo, on a dare from her costar, Richard Burton, who was there with his gracious, soft-spoken wife, Sybil. The Burtons were the official hosts of the party; Taylor and Fisher were the guests of honor. Among the entourage was Elizabeth's longtime pal Roddy McDowall, accompanied by his boyfriend, John Valva; the film's producer, Walter Wanger, in from Los Angeles; and director Joe Mankiewicz with his two sons, Tom and Chris, who were assisting on the film.

Once the marine had returned Elizabeth to the table, Eddie announced that they were calling it a night. "There isn't anything more important than the sleep and rest of Elizabeth Taylor," he often said. But someone had other plans. It wasn't even midnight yet, Elizabeth argued, arms akimbo, eyes flashing.

Burton egged her on. "You see here?" he asked, tapping Elizabeth's glass. "She hasn't even finished her champagne."

Several observers witnessed Burton switching his own glass with her empty one. His ruse continued for the next hour as he slid refills on the table and she drank them down eagerly. Fisher didn't catch on, but he knew something was happening. The increasing proximity of Elizabeth and Richard unnerved him. The others noticed it as well. "It was just a matter of time before they began an affair, if they hadn't already," Tom Mankiewicz said. "We were all just waiting for it to happen."

So be it. Movie people have affairs. It's part of the way business is done. Two years before, when he'd directed her in *Suddenly, Last Summer,* Joe Mankiewicz himself had taken up with Elizabeth. The *Cleopatra* publicists probably expected—perhaps even welcomed—a bit of behind-the-scenes with Taylor and Burton. But they had no idea of the earthquake that was about to hit.

The crowd outside was growing bolder, pushing against the red velvet ropes that cordoned off Bricktop's entrance. Photographers zipped up on their little Vespa motorbikes. One jumped off and shimmied up a streetlamp. Another crawled under the legs of the crowd to the nightclub's front door. But one man took the award for most enterprising performance.

Gilberto Petrucci, twenty-two and handsome enough to blend

in with the big names, dropped a few hundred lire into the palm of a doorman. Just as the clock struck twelve, he slipped inside the club, his camera discreetly covered by his coat. Smiling at his *buona fortuna,* he knew he'd have to act fast. Bricktop's bouncers would be on him at any moment to toss him out on his *natiche.* Unnoticed among all the noisemakers, Petrucci managed to get off a round of pictures, then dropped to his knees to change film.

"And I looked over," he said, "and I could see that under the table, Richard Burton and Elizabeth Taylor were holding hands."

Then he felt a hand on his shoulder—Bricktop's majordomo was putting an end to the impromptu photo session. As Petrucci left, he noticed Burton glance his way.

It was only then, apparently, that the *Cleopatra* company understood the commotion they were causing streetside. "We were told that we couldn't leave through the front door," Tom Mankiewicz said. "The Via Veneto was packed solid. Thousands of people were waiting out there for Elizabeth to come outside."

So they exited out the back under heavy escort, detouring through the warm kitchen smelling of garlic and oregano. On a side street they piled into two waiting cars. Someone caught sight of Elizabeth's black hair and sparkling dress, and shrieked, "There she is!" As the mob roared down the street, the cars sped off into the night. Elizabeth, undoubtedly, loved it; she liked a good chase scene. And one wonders if Burton might have acquired a taste for the thrill of it all himself that night.

Petrucci didn't pursue them. He had his photos and was developing them even as he wove his motorbike in and out of the snarl of traffic. "I invented a photo-processing lab right inside my Vespa, the only one in the world," Petrucci said. "This way I could process the pictures and get them in ahead of my rivals."

Magazines like *Oggi Illustrato, L'Europeo, Lo Specchio* and *Settimo Giorno* paid hefty sums for photos of celebrities. Petrucci was part of a roving band of freelance imagemakers who catered to this clientele. The term *paparazzi,* lifted from the Fellini film *La Dolce Vita,* had not yet become widespread, although it was along the glittery Via Veneto that photographers, stalking their subjects like prey, created what would become one of the celebrity circus's most controversial sideshows. It was here that Tony Franciosa, husband of Shelley Winters, went berserk after being snapped entering Bricktop's with Ava Gardner. It was also here that former King Farouk of Egypt hurled his considerable girth at a photographer after being caught with his mistress at the Café de Paris.

Though a tough breed, these "assault photographers" were far less aggressive than the paparazzi of today. Young men mostly, they dressed fashionably in coats and ties or cardigan sweaters that were sometimes complemented by colorful sashes. They traveled in packs, the heavy batteries of their Rolleiflexes slung over their shoulders. The best shots came when they worked together. One night while pursuing Ava Gardner, the photographers Tazio Secchiaroli and Elio Sorci came up with a plan. Secchiaroli would insinuate himself as close to Gardner as possible, then set off his flash directly in her face. When the time came, the actress's escort, actor Walter Chiari, took off after Secchiaroli just as they had hoped. Sorci, meanwhile, was snapping away. The resulting photos, published in *Settimo Giorno,* turned both young men into hotshots along the Via Veneto. "We discovered that by creating little incidents we could produce great features that earned us a lot of money," Secchiaroli said. Creating "little incidents" to produce dramatic reactions would become one of the signature arts of these photographers.

By 1961 the self-proclaimed king of the camera troops was a Russian expatriate, Ivan Kroscenko, who had declared that Elizabeth Taylor was the biggest "get" of all. Before Elizabeth's arrival in Rome, Kroscenko predicted that she would become a veritable cottage industry in Italy: "You'll see photographs of her—intimate ones—with some handsome actor, fascinating director, or patrician playboy." He spoke with such confidence because he'd heard murmurs that Fisher was fading out of the picture. And Kroscenko knew that stars in troubled marriages loved to let loose in Rome. "We can hardly wait," he said gleefully.

But the Taylor show had been subdued so far. If spotted, Elizabeth was always with her husband. She'd chosen a villa far out on the old Appian Way with walls so high that photographers couldn't see over them, even when perched in trees and armed with telephoto lenses. On the day she reported to Cinecittà Studios for costume tests, she flicked a finger at the mob of paparazzi and Joe Mankiewicz promptly ordered twelve guards at every gate.

Kroscenko's boasts led some people to suspect that he was planning to manipulate a shot with Taylor and a "lover," much as Secchiaroli and Sorci had done with Ava Gardner. If the star wouldn't give them an authentic love affair, the photographers might just hire some idle Italian nobleman to plant a kiss on her cheek. But on New Year's Day, Petrucci—Kroscenko's young protégé—brought news of what he'd spied inside Bricktop's. "And then it became the mission of all of us," Petrucci said, "to get the first photo of Burton and Taylor together."

Six thousand miles away, Hedda Hopper, widely syndicated columnist and notorious maker or breaker of Hollywood careers, took a call from one of her "leg men." Just days into the new year, Hedda was on to a story, and she'd told her spies to bring her the dirt. In the biz, these leg men were usually gay and enjoyed a wide swath of worldwide connections. This particular foot soldier had just gotten back from Rome, and he repeated what Hedda had been hearing for weeks: that as far as Elizabeth Taylor was concerned, Eddie Fisher was almost history. But he added a bit more juice. Sources on the set of *Cleopatra* reported lots of giggling and whispering between Elizabeth and her costar, the handsome Welshman, Mr. Burton. Just like Tom Mankiewicz, Hedda's spies considered an affair inevitable—if, in fact, one hadn't already begun.

Hedda seethed. She saw herself as more than a mere gossip columnist; she was the watchful mother and moral arbiter for an industry she loved deeply, even if she regarded it as often in need of chastisement. Long widowed, deeply lonely, approaching eighty, Hedda's whole world was her column and the vicarious view that it provided of other people's lives. Once she'd been more than just a fan of pretty little Elizabeth Taylor; she believed that she'd made the girl a star by promoting her in her column. But Taylor's marital adventures had always rankled Hedda, particularly the one that had brought Eddie Fisher into the picture. To Hedda's mind, Elizabeth had stolen Eddie away from sweet little Debbie Reynolds, and so she'd made it her job to instill that impression in the public's mind as well. Elizabeth's shameless actions had tarnished the industry's reputation, Hopper believed, damaging the movies as much as those horrible European directors and their damnable "realist" films. So she'd turned hard against her former protégé, and now that Elizabeth was at it again, she was about to turn harder. Like Fisher, Richard Burton was a married man with two children. In Hedda's view, "Hollywood's home wrecker" had to be stopped—as much for Sybil Burton as for the motion-picture business itself.

But for all her moral indignation and concern about the industry, Hedda also wanted to break the story before anyone else. Within days she'd drafted a column on the affair that claimed inside knowledge despite a lack of actual firsthand information. This was not the first time such techniques had been used in journalism, and Hedda had certainly printed rumor as fact before. Yet when her lawyer, Martin Gang, read the draft, he ordered her to kill the story. "You couldn't print that," he told her. "It would be very embarrassing for me to sue you." Not only did Gang represent Hedda, he also counted Elizabeth and Richard among his clients.

Hedda held back reluctantly, no doubt fretful that someone else might scoop her, but also livid that Elizabeth's bad behavior would proceed without censure. What added injury to insult in Hedda's mind was that *Cleopatra* was also bankrupting Fox. Many feared that the film's excess (which Hedda couldn't separate from Elizabeth's) would shutter Fox and put an end to the studio system. Ever since *Cleopatra* had started running over budget and behind schedule due to a change of director and Elizabeth's long recuperation from her pneumonia, Hedda had been offering snide assessments of the film's troubles. Miss Hopper had not extended any sympathy to Elizabeth over her near-death experience. While the entire world was waiting on edge to see if Taylor would pull through, Hedda scoffed to friends that it was all just a ruse so that Elizabeth could bleed more money from Fox. "Hedda had it in for Taylor," said one of her chief "spies," Robert Shaw. "She thought Elizabeth was destroying the Hollywood that she loved so well."

If she couldn't write directly about what was going on in Rome, Hedda made sure her words would still reek of reprobation. She implicitly attacked Elizabeth's grandiose lifestyle by telling readers how she'd walked by the star's first home in Beverly Hills, implying that it was modest (it was hardly that). "Now a palazza in Rome," Hedda sniffed, "with enough servants to take care of Cleopatra and her appendages." It was interesting wording, but whether coy or clueless, one could never be sure.

A few weeks later Hedda was cheering Jack Warner for calling off Elizabeth's next film after the star had failed to sign her contract on time. Privately, Hedda told Shaw that she was outraged that Taylor had agreed to appear nude (albeit discreetly) in *Cleopatra* and that she was equally irked at the Fishers for having the gall to adopt a baby girl from Germany when their marriage was floundering. "What's left for Liz but to go on repeating her mistakes?" Hedda asked. "What's to become of her? I'm not a prophet, but I have a terrible suspicion."

The new baby in the Taylor-Fisher villa was the least of Dick Hanley's problems. More than just Elizabeth's secretary, Dick was the gatekeeper, facilitator, ringmaster, therapist, and locator of errant gems. He made things happen when his employer snapped her fingers—or just snapped. The week after New Year's, Elizabeth—whose appetites included a dazzling array of culinary choices from caviar to hot dogs—developed a hankering for good old-fashioned American holiday fare, so Hanley placed a transatlantic call to Chasen's in Beverly Hills and ordered a thirty-pound roast turkey and two Virginia baked hams to be air expressed to Rome.

Dick had experience serving demanding bosses. He'd been Louis B. Mayer's secretary at MGM and then the assistant to Mike Todd, the flamboyant showman who was Elizabeth's third husband. Producers, directors, reporters, and husbands all knew the fastest way to Elizabeth was through Dick Hanley.

"He was the most important nobody in the universe because his job consisted of picking up Elizabeth Taylor's underpants," said Chris Mankiewicz. Dick could be shrill, brusque, and rude, but he was also fiercely loyal. Elizabeth trusted him more than anyone. Like most of her closest confidantes, Hanley was gay. He had taken a flat near Elizabeth's villa with his longtime lover, John Lee, with whom Elizabeth was also close.

Upon initial review, Hanley had been quite satisfied with the lavish, high-walled, fourteen-room (six baths) villa the studio had secured for the star, her husband, and her three (suddenly four) children. But when Elizabeth had pronounced it a dump, Hanley was on the phone shrieking to Fox. Elizabeth thought the place was "filthy," and claimed that the pantry was filled with rat droppings. A cleaning crew was quickly dispatched.

"It was one of the great old stone houses on the Appian Way," said Tom Mankiewicz. "It wasn't going to be pristine like a new house in Beverly Hills. But Elizabeth was a star, and she had certain standards."

In Roman times the Via Appia Antica was known as the "Queen of the Roads," winding its way from the imperial seat down to the heel of the Italian boot. The Apostle Paul had used the road to enter Rome; catacombs built by ancient Christians and Jews lay beneath the rocks on either side. Although Elizabeth's villa was actually located on Via Appia Pignatelli, a newer route jutting off to the north of the ancient highway, she was still smack-dab in the middle of history. Twice a day she passed under the Porta San Sebastiano, a gateway supported by two crenellated towers set into the old Aurelian Walls that had once protected the city from the threat of barbarian invaders.

But things antique held little appeal for Elizabeth unless they came bearing checkbooks. Dick Hanley understood her requirements, as well as her occasional need to misbehave and make the suits sweat a bit. "Life is different for her," he told friends who shared his more simple Midwestern upbringing. "A great star sees the world very differently than you or I. That's not good, that's not bad. It just is."

Charged with hiring staff for the villa, Hanley had managed to woo the French ambassador's Greek chef, who upon meeting Elizabeth declared, "You are the most beautiful of all the womans of the world." His new employer succumbed without hesitation. To serve as butler, Hanley hired an Italian with the incongruous name of Fred Oates, a tall man with "a beautifully cut white coat," whom Elizabeth found "dignified" and "charming." A painter, Oates flattered "Madame" by asking for permission to paint a portrait of her. She agreed.

But Oates was less enchanted when life interfered with art. Elizabeth smoked a pack of cigarettes a day and never used the same holder. Fresh ones—at least ten a day—always had to be at the ready, and they had to be color-coded. A green dress called for a matching holder—and Madame changed outfits quite frequently as her moods shifted. Every morning Oates prepared a box of cigarette holders based on what Elizabeth would be wearing throughout that day and evening, and not only did the holders have to match her outfits, they couldn't clash with the tablecloth.

Such regimens often befuddled new recruits, but Hanley saw it all as simply a matter of course. Taking care of Elizabeth's needs, no matter how frivolous, was his mission in life. Joe Mankiewicz was constantly revising *Cleopatra,* so Dick made sure Elizabeth's many scripts were always bound in her favorite Moroccan leather folders. Other chores also beckoned. When Elizabeth complained of cold tiles in her bathroom, Dick promptly produced white wool carpeting. And for Madame's baths, her faithful secretary always made sure that there were plenty of Murano votive candles on hand—not only because the power often went out along their remote road, but also because Elizabeth insisted her two daily baths, one at 7:30 A.M. and the other at 8:00 P.M., be taken by candlelight.

It was all routine for Hanley. He was used to Elizabethan mores. What he wasn't prepared for was the affair with Burton, which tilted everything toward the surreal. No one—except the two parties involved—can ever be absolutely sure when flirtation became fornication, but it's likely Hanley found out not long after the fact. (The best bet on when and where is early January in Burton's trailer.) If Elizabeth told anyone, it was Dick—her rock, her shoulder, her twice-daily candlelighter. But the problem was that Eddie Fisher trusted Dick too. After all, part of keeping Elizabeth happy had meant keeping Eddie happy—or at least content enough that he didn't complain overmuch. Elizabeth wouldn't be able to face the pressures on the set if her home life was tense, too.

The new baby was, as babies often are, a last-ditch attempt to salvage the controversial union, which had started so passionately and scandalously three and a half years earlier. After three difficult deliveries of children from two previous husbands, Elizabeth could no longer endure childbirth, so little Maria was adopted from an impoverished German family to fulfill Miss Taylor's wish to be a mother once more. But an adopted baby was also, then as now, a great public relations move, especially for a woman whose nonmaternal instincts had made so many headlines and for a couple rumored to be splitting up. Hanley made sure that he phoned Hedda himself to give her the news of Maria's entrance into the family. The columnist never printed a word about it, though she went on about it semiprivately to half of Los Angeles.

No doubt Hanley felt a great deal of sympathy for Eddie Fisher, who would always speak well of his wife's secretary, even after the marriage was over and Burton had done everything he could to win Hanley over. More than required, in fact. It was hard not to like Richard Burton. At thirty-six, a bit slouchy, craggy-faced, and pockmarked, he possessed an allure, a twinkle in his eyes, a lilt to his magnificently deep voice that drew people to him. Wry, dry, bombastic—sometimes all at once—and a master storyteller, Richard was the quickest wit on the lot and fiercely smart. Reacting to a typically grandiose Burton statement that no German had ever produced an original idea, the eager Yale student Tom Mankiewicz had shouted out a challenge. What about Goethe? Hegel? Marx? "Son of a gun," Mankiewicz said, "if he didn't trace every idea of theirs back to somebody else. He was an extremely literate man."

But the most appealing thing about Burton was the fact that he seemed unfazed by Elizabeth's great fame. Eddie bowed and scraped, but Richard called her "Lumpy." To her face. In public. Richard had a well-earned reputation for seducing his leading ladies, while his forbearing wife, to whom everyone knew he was devoted, turned a weary eye in the other direction. "Men wanted to be Richard, and women wanted to sleep with Richard," Mankiewicz said.

The difference between Taylor's once and future husbands was apparent. Burton was the diamond plucked from the Welsh coalmines who had become the most promising actor of his generation. While he was playing in *Cleopatra* (little more than a soap opera in his eyes) he was also writing to Christopher Fry in London, hoping to juggle the lead in a play by Sartre. Fisher, meanwhile, three years younger than Burton, had started out as a nightclub singer at Grossinger's, a Catskills resort. He'd enjoyed a string of pop successes such as "Oh! My Pa-Pa" until the rock-and-rollers banished him from the *Billboard* charts. Once a playboy who'd partied with the Rat Pack, Eddie had been reduced to the most pathetic of showbiz clichés: Husband to the Star.

What Burton and Fisher shared—apart from an interest in themselves and having sex with beautiful women—was liquor. Richard could go on notorious benders; for his first scene with Elizabeth in *Cleopatra,* he showed up suffering from a famously massive hangover. Eddie, uncharacteristically, was mostly sober in Rome, where his chief concern was keeping Elizabeth rested and happy—though he'd admit to having a few cocktails after he discovered his wife's affair, probably at the end of January. When he asked Elizabeth point-blank if she was carrying on with Burton, she admitted it. Yet Eddie refused to take the affair seriously. Nobody did at first. Dick Hanley told friends—and probably Eddie as well—that Richard would never leave Sybil. Elizabeth might be "an irresistible force," as the columnist Dorothy Kilgallen maintained, but Burton was "an immovable object."

Only Joe Mankiewicz had his doubts. "Elizabeth and Richard are two potential world-class destroyers," he said privately, "and poor Eddie is a singing waiter from Grossinger's."

Hanley advised Fisher to distract Elizabeth from the affair. "Take her shopping," Dick suggested. Eddie would later laugh in agreement: "To keep Elizabeth happy, you had to give her a diamond before breakfast every morning." So on February 5 Eddie and Elizabeth boarded a charter flight arranged by Hanley and headed to Paris, where the star told waiting reporters that she planned on buying a few "goodies." Her first stop was the salon of Yves Saint Laurent, who hid behind a curtain while the star selected several "vapourous" (his word) mousseline dresses. Next up was "a famous furrier" not far from the Elysée Palace, where Elizabeth checked out some "light" furs—chinchilla and pastel mink. Then on to Chanel, where a fashion show had just ended. But the models reapplied their war paint and stalked down the runway one more time for their illustrious guest. It was worth it. The grateful customer ordered three suits, two overcoats, and a couple of cocktail dresses. The buying spree concluded at Dior, where for $6,000 Elizabeth walked off with a fur coat described as Somali panther. All total, the afternoon cost twenty grand.

Though Eddie was depicted as the "checkbook-swinging husband" trailing after his wife, the money they spent was largely Elizabeth's. But what mattered was the absence of Burton from the picture. Although the Fishers made a point of ignoring reporters after they'd landed in Paris, they knew they were making headlines, and Dick Hanley was very happy to confirm all of their purchases to the press the next day. This wasn't simply a spoiled wife being coddled by a husband desperate to regain her affections. It was a movie star behaving as a movie star, upholding her end of the bargain with the public. Hedda Hopper could carp, lecture, and direct Miss Taylor to a pastor, but housewives swooned when they read about Elizabeth's shopping expedition. At least there was someone who wasn't stuck at home. Stories about impending divorce and scandal disappeared for a week or so, making the lives of everyone at Cinecitta Studios a little easier, if a little less interesting. For now the public was content with photos of Elizabeth in her Somali panther coat.

News always traveled fast along the Via Veneto. Sleeping during the day and living by night, the paparazzi heard everything before anyone else. On the night of Saturday, February 17, hours before the AP or UPI reporters got the word, the street photographers learned that Elizabeth Taylor, unhappy on the set, had attempted suicide by taking an overdose of sleeping pills. Shopping, it seemed, hadn't quite done the trick.

Hopping on his Vespa, Gilberto Petrucci hightailed it across town. Buzzing in and out of traffic, the photographer zipped along the Appian Way and under the Porta San Sebastiano, arriving at Salvator Mundi International Hospital only minutes after Elizabeth had been carried inside on a stretcher. Crowds were gathering as the ambulance driver, Paolo Renzini, snatched a few minutes of fame by recounting in detail how he'd carried an unconscious Elizabeth from her villa. A few minutes later Joe Mankiewicz was spotted hurrying into the hospital, and the newshounds took off in hot pursuit, cameras flashing. Questions flew. Would Richard Burton make an appearance? Where was Eddie Fisher? And would all this be wrapped up so that the film could finally be finished?

How different from the days at MGM, where studio publicity chief Howard Strickling would never have allowed such scandalous news to leak to the press. And stars and their publicists had not yet mastered the art of using scandal to their own advantage—although they were learning fast. The problem on the night of February 17 was that no one in Elizabeth's camp could get the story straight. For an organization known for its efficiency and for being on message and on time, this was a moment of panic. Awakened at 3 A.M. by a call from Reynolds Packard of the *New York Daily News*, Fox publicist Jack Brodsky offered no denials when asked if Taylor had suffered a throat hemorrhage related to her pneumonia and tracheotomy earlier in the year. Several news outlets ran with that story, which was apparently a wholesale invention of Packard's. News editors may have recalled how many papers that Elizabeth's pneumonia had sold for them. Meanwhile, completely out of the loop in Palm Springs, Elizabeth's agent, Kurt Frings, tried some damage control on his own, telling the press that the hospital stay was planned well in advance so the star could have a little rest.

By the following morning Brodsky and Walter Wanger had settled on the official line: food poisoning. Wanger announced that he'd also eaten the bully beef at Taylor's villa the day before and that he, too, felt sick. But they forgot one important thing: to check in with Dick Hanley. "Food poisoning?" Dick screeched when contacted by Reynolds Packard. "Where did that come from?" Taylor, he said, was just "tired out." No doubt a few urgent phone calls were hastily placed because Hanley was soon remembering that bloody beef. With the clout of a major movie studio behind them, the players and spinners were even able to get Elizabeth's doctors to back up the story. The eminent *Times* of London quoted the physician in charge of the case as saying Taylor suffered from "a stomach upset which might have been due to food poisoning." (Note the "might have been.") Breathing a sigh of relief, Brodsky wrote to his assistant Nat Weiss, "The food poisoning story . . . seemed to go over."

But what really happened was this: The affair with Burton hadn't ended, as Elizabeth had promised Eddie it would. She had fallen head over heels in love. And it wasn't all just a photo opportunity. When Burton had shown up with his hangover on their first day on the set, Elizabeth had helped steady him and, in the process, had looked down into his magnetic green eyes. "And it was like *here I am*," she said. No matter what it might do to her career or her carefully wrought public image, she couldn't contain her feelings for the volatile Welshman. No way could she end it. "They sneak off at night to an apartment [Dick Hanley's] and have matinees in her dressing room," Brodsky told Weiss. One day Brodsky was scheduled to meet Elizabeth and Eddie for lunch, but Elizabeth didn't show. It was obvious that she had snuck off with Burton. "It was very, very embarrassing to have to sit there with a man whose wife you know is off having an affair," Brodsky said.

Not long after this, Eddie paid a call on Sybil Burton in an attempt to enlist her aid in ending the affair. The smart, savvy Sybil listened politely and thanked Eddie for his concern. A huge row with Elizabeth ensued, with Roddy McDowall charging in and claiming that Eddie hadn't "behaved like a man." Soon the heartbroken Fisher was beating a hasty retreat to Switzerland, where he and Elizabeth had recently bought a house. Sybil, meanwhile, laid down the law, and Burton told Elizabeth that while it had been fun, it had to end.

Elizabeth was overcome. "This was a woman who had always, *always* gotten what she wanted," said her friend Hank Moonjean, the assistant director on *Butterfield 8* and Elizabeth's frequent companion in Rome. "You do not screw Elizabeth Taylor and then dump her. It just wasn't done. She didn't know how to process it in her mind."

On the afternoon of February 17, Walter Wanger had visited Elizabeth, finding her "upset about her life and future." She was also drinking heavily. She had surrounded herself with her usual group of acolytes: Hanley and John Lee, Roddy and John Valva, and the *Cleopatra* hairstylist, Vivienne Zavitz. She told Hanley that life without Richard gave her the feeling of "scenes missing"—a movie-making term referring to the intertitle SCENES MISSING placed in a rough cut of a film. Even in the most personal of crises, this child of the movies thought in cinematic terms.

Increasingly distraught, Elizabeth went up to bed early. When Wanger and Zavitz checked on her a while later and found her passed out cold, Zavitz shrieked, "She's taken pills!" Someone downstairs called an ambulance.

A suicide attempt? That's what Hollywood would believe. Most people laughed off the food poisoning story. Hedda Hopper conspicuously printed *not one word* about Taylor's hospitalization, even when the rest of the papers were filled with it. Certainly the accepted "truth" of that night has become this: Distraught over Burton, Elizabeth took some pills. But the suicide attempt story has never seemed to fit with the full picture of Elizabeth Taylor, the star who rallied from death and ill health so many times, who never gave up anything easily, who had a new baby in the house plus three other children. For a public inured to celebrity suicides, it's been easy to chalk up this episode as just one more failed attempt. But Elizabeth was never, ever Marilyn Monroe. She was never a victim.

When Joe Mankiewicz saw her that night at the hospital, he asked her how many pills she had taken. "Fourteen," she told him in a strong voice. "She'll be fine," Mankiewicz said. "If she can count them, she'll be fine."

Call it a tantrum with pharmaceutical overtones. This was an era, after all, when people routinely washed back handfuls of pills with shots of vodka if they wanted to blot out the world. Elizabeth—drunk and depressed—had made a great show of wondering how she could possibly go on without Richard. But an authentic suicide attempt? Joe Mankiewicz never thought so. "Dad's theory," said Tom Mankiewicz, "was that they could have stopped seventy-five percent of the accidental suicides in the world at that time if by law all sleeping pills had to be suppositories."

Two days after being admitted to the hospital, Elizabeth was discharged wearing a leopard-print fur coat and matching shoes. Eddie was there with Dick Hanley to pick her up in a black Cadillac. Photographers pursued them for the seven miles back to the villa, where Elizabeth graciously turned to face them in her doorway. Flashcubes popped all around. But Eddie refused to stop, slipping inside without looking back.

Far above these earthly dramas, John Glenn was piloting the first American manned flight to orbit the Earth. His landing later that day bumped the goings-on in Rome down a notch in the headlines, but some tabloids still went with Elizabeth on their front page. Leopard fur, they reasoned, sold better than a flight suit.

Meanwhile Richard Burton, seemingly stricken with guilt, put out a statement denying rumors of an affair, vowing "never [to] do anything to hurt [Elizabeth] personally and professionally." Yet the denial fizzled. So far no story had referred to anything more than troubles between Elizabeth and Eddie; Burton himself had not yet been mentioned. His denial, however, inserted his name into the story for the first time. That's not to say the press didn't know what was going on: Dorothy Kilgallen told her readers that "all the preliminary details have been burning on the Rome–New York grapevine for quite some time." Reporters were simply waiting for something concrete to tie Burton to Taylor, and unwittingly Burton had just given it to them. His publicist, Chris Hofer, had convinced his boss that a statement would end it all. But when the denial only ratcheted up the story, all that ended was Hofer's job. Peeved, the publicist told the press that he'd been made "the fall guy."

The gloves were now off. Paparazzi slapped ladders against the sides of Elizabeth's villa and scrambled over the walls. Dick Hanley and the servants had to beat them back with brooms and rakes. At Richard's villa, two-year-old Jessica Burton, soon to be diagnosed with autism, was so terrified by a photographer peering through a window that she screamed nonstop for hours. Ivan Kroscenko offered Jack Brodsky 100,000 lire for a negative of Burton and Taylor together that he could pass off as stolen from the studio. "The paparazzi were everywhere," Tom Mankiewicz said. "They were throwing themselves on the hoods of our cars."

Tom was dating Elizabeth's stand-in, Marie Devereux, a young English actress with an uncanny resemblance to the star. (The long shots of Cleopatra entering Rome on the Sphinx are actually of Devereux.) Whenever Tom and Marie took a stroll down the Via Veneto, they'd cause a sensation. Photographers would suddenly surround them with exploding flashes, only to turn away and curse in Italian when they realized Marie wasn't "Liz."

The real Elizabeth was still pining, though upright. Shooting scenes with Richard was pure agony, with the star often fleeing to her dressing room in tears. On the night of February 27, Elizabeth's thirtieth birthday, the star was feted in the Borgia Room of the fourteenth-century Hostaria dell'Orso by Eddie, Wanger, Joe Mankiewicz, Kurt Frings, and his wife, Ketti. Elizabeth's parents, Francis and Sara Taylor, had flown in from Los Angeles. Asked by Eddie to dance, Elizabeth gamely tried the twist, the latest dance craze. But she was miserable. Richard had sent flowers, but his card had been accidentally thrown away so she thought he'd forgotten the day. "Sheer horror," she called the night. "The worst [birthday] I've ever had."

Burton was equally moody and difficult. He'd lied to Elizabeth and to Sybil, his steadfast companion and chief booster for the last thirteen years. Suddenly it was all a terrible, heartbreaking scene, far more than he'd bargained for. Dark, angry binges were the result. One night Gilberto Petrucci spotted him leaving a nightclub, and star and photographer made eye contact. Whether Burton recognized him or not, Petrucci wasn't sure, but suddenly the drunken actor lifted one of the brass stands that held the rope cordoning off the door to the club and charged the photographer with it. Petrucci put up his arms to shield his face. Burton threw a sloppy punch. Petrucci just laughed and snapped a picture. "He was too drunk," the paparazzo said, "to make any difference."

Not long after that, still soused, Richard called Elizabeth, told her that he was on his way, and, in front of Eddie, made her choose between them. She chose Richard and ran out of the house in tears. Burton winked at Fisher. Time for Act Two.

• • •

In Hollywood Hedda Hopper finally found her tongue. (Not that it was ever lost for long.) Sitting at her old black Royal typewriter and freed from any constraints by Burton's PR debacle, she banged out a story that her lawyer could no longer obstruct. In her February 28 column, Hopper wrote: "By this time, Eddie might have started the long walk home." Musing over the photos of the couple returning from the hospital, Hedda remarked: "One look at Eddie's face and you can just skip all those denials about everybody being just dandy friends . . . The picture isn't finished but the honeymoon sure is over. Liz loves variety and the possibility that she might add Burton to her list is mighty amusing"—because, as Hedda insisted, Burton was not the type "to fetch and carry." The implication, of course, was that Eddie was.

Hopper's power was waning, but even as she approached her last reel, she could still rally America's conservative heartland. Her files, carefully organized by name and date, were stuffed with hundreds of letters from moviegoers outraged over how Elizabeth had broken up the supposedly happy home of Debbie Reynolds in 1958. For the rural and religious, who recalled Hedda's aggressive, flag-waving crusade against Communism, Miss Hopper was Mother Confessor. Her influence over Middle America guaranteed her continued power in Hollywood. When Elizabeth had failed to win the Oscar for *Cat on a Hot Tin Roof* and *The Eddie Fisher Show* had been canceled by NBC, some blamed Hedda's campaign against the couple. Now the old girl was gearing up for another whack, clutching a new batch of letters that expressed horror over the shenanigans in Rome. Hedda vowed to friends that this time she was going to "stop that hussy for good."

Yet studio executives were of two minds about the headlines being generated by "Liz and Dick," as the tabloids had begun calling the pair. Yes, they realized that the old guard, marshaled by Hopper and others, would no doubt call for boycotts of *Cleopatra*. Court documents, recently released, do reveal that many of the top brass at Fox were indeed anxious about their stars' behavior. But there was an emerging sense in this new post-studio Hollywood that perhaps there was no such thing as bad publicity. Joe Mankiewicz may have grown weary of the "sideshow" (his word) that *Cleopatra* had become. But among the film's publicists, a very different view was evolving.

In mid-February, Jack Brodsky still wanted to "bottle it up" as long as possible because the public would "crucify her and picket the theaters if she breaks up another family." Yet less than three weeks after making that dire prediction, Brodsky was "hoping and praying" that the sideshow didn't end before the picture was finished after he saw the enormous interest generated by the affair. He no longer denied to reporters the tales of the couple's clandestine meetings and may have even spread a few stories himself. A wire from the Fox front office affirmed the wisdom of the strategy: "We've been on page one of the *Daily News* and the *Mirror* for five days in a row. That's better than World War II!" Dorothy Kilgallen was certain that Fox must "appreciate the invaluable publicity Liz gets every time her private life explodes onto the front pages." Even Mankiewicz came around. A framed newspaper cartoon on his wall said it all. Two suburbanites are standing on a train platform in front of a poster advertising *Cleopatra*. "What really annoys me the most," one says, "is that I know I'm going to see it."

But they all still understood the risk. The final impact of the affair on the film remained a big unknown. The world was changing, but that much? Would the public really come out to see an adulterous couple flaunt their lovemaking on the screen?

Walter Wanger, who years before had shot his wife's lover in the testicles, suggested removing one of the principals from the scene. On March 10 C. O. "Doc" Erickson, the production manager for the film, was waiting outside Wanger's office as the producer concluded an emergency meeting with Eddie Fisher. Columnist Louella Parsons, Hedda Hopper's most hated rival, had just announced the collapse of the marriage. It was "no secret," Parsons wrote, "that Elizabeth has fallen madly in love with Richard Burton." (Not to be outdone, Hedda came out with essentially the same story a few days later.) It was a crestfallen Eddie who emerged from Wanger's office. Turning to Erickson, Wanger said, "I think I've convinced him to go back home to the States. There's nothing here for him but further embarrassment." Erickson was sympathetic to Eddie. Even people who had disliked him for the airs he'd assumed as Elizabeth's consort were suddenly sympathetic. "We all just felt so terribly sorry for Eddie," Erickson said.

Increasingly delusional, Fisher continued to insist that he and his wife remained "very much in love." But it wasn't just love that bound him to his bride. Like everyone else, he wanted a piece of the action. Eddie had dreams of becoming a great Hollywood producer. He'd been trying to package a deal for the two of them for some time, negotiating with Warners to make *The Gouffe Case,* in which Elizabeth would star with none other than Charlie Chaplin. Eddie was going to make $2,000 a week—a major sum in 1961—and there was talk of four more pictures in four years. Eddie—a kid from the tenements of South Philadelphia—would be set for life. But only if he remained Mr. Elizabeth Taylor.

Pacing around his Cinecitta office ashen-faced, Eddie was barely conscious of the phones ringing off their hooks. His bags were packed, but he was refusing to leave. He was getting desperate. Dorothy Kilgallen, whose inside sources resulted in scoops that left Walter Wanger flummoxed, wrote confidently in her column that "Eddie's friends think it won't be long before he resumes his singing career so long neglected while he danced attendance on Liz." Meanwhile Elizabeth was in a back room of the suite, refusing to see anyone and drinking Bloody Marys brought in on a tray by John Lee. Insisting to Eddie that the phones needed to be answered, Dick Hanley typed up a brief statement that read: "Mr. and Mrs. Fisher have no comment at this time." Handing the statement to Hank Moonjean, who had a desk in the same suite, Hanley instructed him to read the words to whomever called. Moonjean obeyed. And every time Elizabeth heard him read the statement from the other room, she screamed for another Bloody Mary. Finally John Lee, who was always a bit daft, approached Eddie and said, quite seriously, "You know, if this keeps up, you are going to have to get more *tomato juice!*"

Eddie left Rome a few days later, arriving in New York on March 21. The situation, he told friends, had become "unbearable." His wily agent, Milton Blackstone, arranged an appearance for him as the mystery guest on the television game show *What's My Line?*—"a neat stroke of public relations," Dorothy Kilgallen called it. Eddie predicted on air that the winner for the Best Actress of 1962 would be "Elizabeth Taylor Fisher" for *Cleopatra*, but as Kilgallen acidly remarked the next day, "Nobody who knows the scene at Via Appia Pignatelli in Rome is convinced that Liz will still be Mrs. Fisher when that Oscar-time rolls around." Richard Burton, she told her readers, was now the man at Elizabeth's side.

That same day Eddie swallowed a handful of Seconals with vodka (an echo of Elizabeth's own overdose and a foreshadowing of Kilgallen's own death three years later) and was admitted to Gracie Square Hospital on East Seventy-sixth Street. The press reported that he'd suffered a nervous breakdown and was being given shock treatments. In fact, he was beating his blues by becoming addicted to speed.

That explains the bizarre press conference that he called on March 30 at the Pierre. Before coming downstairs, Fisher was shot up with a full dose of what his doctor, Max Jacobson, called his "vitamin injections." Jacobson was known as "Dr. Feelgood" to a roster of celebrity patients that ranged from Tennessee Williams to President John F. Kennedy, and what he was really administering was amphetamines. The shot sent Eddie "through the roof," skyrocketing him to "the heights of elation." With a cocky swagger he faced the hundred or so newsmen gathered in the hotel's Sapphire Room.

Natty in his checkered sports jacket and gray slacks, Fisher sat on a sofa, coolly facing a battery of microphones while television lights flickered on overhead. "Elizabeth and I," he insisted, "have never been happier." As a special surprise, he phoned Rome and left word for his wife to call back and confirm everything that he was saying. Reporters cast doubtful glances at each other. For fifteen minutes Eddie—high and seemingly delusional—cracked jokes and denied any problems in his marriage. Then word came that Elizabeth was on the line. With a wink and a grin, Fisher told the reporters that he'd be right back. He took the call in an anteroom.

When he returned, he was pale and shaken. Elizabeth, he announced, would not be making a statement as he'd promised she would. "You can ask a woman to do something and she doesn't always do it," he said, all his bluster and swagger gone.

"Say, Eddie," lobbed one reporter, "did you know that an Italian newspaper has just published a photo of Burton and your wife kissing offscreen?"

"Really?" Eddie laughed, trying to feign disbelief. "I'd like to see it."

The next morning he got his wish. On the front page of the *New York Daily News,* under the banner headline FIRST PHOTOS LIZ AND BURTON, was a grainy telephoto shot of a man and a woman standing beside a car. They were kissing. And despite the poor quality, it was obvious they were Elizabeth Taylor and Richard Burton.

The enterprising Elio Sorci, who had taken those sensational shots of Ava Gardner, had once again scored a coup. Hiding all day under a car across the street from the Cinecitta studios, he had jumped out just at the right moment, that fleeting second when Richard's lips touched Elizabeth's to bid her good night. The photo had first appeared in *Lo Specchio* before making its way to New York; Elizabeth had certainly seen it. No wonder she told Eddie that she wanted nothing to do with his press conference. The truth could no longer be avoided; even Fisher, high or low, must have understood this as he slunk out of the Sapphire Room, cameras flashing, a beaten, pathetic figure.

"The 'kissing picture' of Elizabeth Taylor and Richard Burton," as Dorothy Kilgallen referred to it, "was merely their way of 'making it official' for Mrs. Burton and Eddie Fisher, in case they hadn't received the message already."

Finally, it seemed, Eddie had heard it loud and clear.

"Let's order fettuccine!" Elizabeth Taylor suddenly proclaimed, throwing her hands into the air during an impromptu party at her villa. "With gobs and gobs of cheese sauce!"

Roddy was there with John Valva. So was Dick Hanley with John Lee. And Tom Mankiewicz and Elizabeth's children. And Richard Burton—a regular fixture at Elizabeth's villa now that Sybil, in a strategic retreat, had taken their children and returned to London.

Elizabeth was feeling giddy. Eddie's departure had liberated her. Not that she didn't have compassion for him. "I was, I suppose, behaving wrongly because I broke the conventions," she said. "I felt terrible heartache because so many innocent people were involved. But I couldn't help loving Richard. I don't think that was without honor. I don't think that was dishonest. It was a fact I could not evade."

She also wasn't completely blasé about the possibility of another scandal. Many times she cried in Hank Moonjean's arms, "afraid of what the world was going to say." She had been through it all before when Eddie had left Debbie to be with her and the press had been brutal. "She knew she might have to go through it all over again, and it terrified her," Moonjean said. "But she couldn't help it. She was in love. That's all she knew."

Outside the paparazzi kept up their vigil. They camped out boldly in the street, setting up television cameras on tripods. Peering out a window, Elizabeth could see men perched in the trees. Or maybe she no longer saw them. "We eventually got used to all the photographers," said Tom Mankiewicz. "They just became a fact of life." When a car stopped out front and a man hurried up to the doorway, huge arc lamps switched on to illuminate the house. Might it be Eddie come to beg for a reconciliation? Or a lawyer from Sybil come to serve papers on Richard? But it was only the guy delivering the fettuccine.

Washing down her meal with endless glasses of red wine, Elizabeth was fascinated by tales of another Hollywood marriage in trouble. Roddy had just informed her that Tony Curtis and Janet Leigh were separating. "And here I thought they were so *happy* together," Elizabeth said, just as the doorbell rang again.

Blinding white light poured in once more through the windows of the villa from the television crews outside. Reporters once again chased after the man who approached the house. Elizabeth opened the door herself. It was her friend, the writer Meade Roberts. "Meade," Elizabeth said dramatically, her voice barely heard over the furious snapping of cameras and the shouted questions from reporters, "is it really true what I hear about Tony and Janet?"

No irony punctuated her question. She genuinely wanted to hear the latest. Yet as popular as they were, Tony Curtis and Janet Leigh never had to deal with the onslaught of attention that Elizabeth was attracting in Rome—attention she was now nearly oblivious to. Without appearing to notice the commotion she'd caused by showing her face, Elizabeth embraced Roberts and brought him inside. Once the door was closed, the lights went off, the paparazzi returned to their trees. This was the way Elizabeth Taylor lived.

All of the people around her—the newshounds, the publicists, Hedda and company, even friends like Dick and Roddy—all of these people lived for her, wrote about her, gossiped about her, chased after her, photographed her, served her, supported her, and waited on her. All of them fed off her stardom, sustained by their sliver of her reflected glory. If not for Elizabeth, where would they be? Who would they be? Their existence revolved around her—her needs, her whims, her illnesses, her romances, her mistakes. She was their sun. And each and every one of these devotees—like those far-flung fans reading movie magazines—believed that they knew her intimately.

It had always been this way, ever since she was a young girl on the MGM lot. "I don't remember ever not being famous," Elizabeth would say. This was a woman whose existence—fact, fiction, and reality, both heightened and harsh—had become conjoined, merging into something that few others, even other movie stars, would ever know the pleasures or costs of experiencing. That's really the key to understanding everything else about her. So famous, so constantly in the public eye, she was, as critic David Thomson has observed, "half asleep from being stared at." Of course, she wasn't really oblivious to the ubiquitous photographers. But she was never Marilyn, cowering in fear; she was never Jackie Kennedy, with whom she was so often compared in these years, pulling up her collar, wrapping a scarf around her face, and donning oversized sunglasses so that she wouldn't be recognized. For Elizabeth, recognition was a fact of her existence, "the air she breathed," said Mike Nichols. Sometimes it was fun. Sometimes it was a nuisance. Mostly it just was.

And then one night she grew tired of eating fettuccine from cardboard boxes and decided that she wanted to play on the Via Veneto. "They want pictures," she suddenly announced, her famous eyes blazing, "so let's *give* them pictures!" Donning her leopard-print fur coat and a matching hat, she took Burton by the arm and headed into the city. The paparazzi went berserk. Stepping out of her sleek black Cadillac, Elizabeth faced them head-on, smiling broadly. The crush of photographers grew so intense that the police had to call in reinforcements; within moments, a jeepload of Carabinieri—the Italian military police—came screeching to a stop beside the couple. Leaping onto the sidewalk, the gendarmes shouted to the crowd to back off, allowing Taylor and Burton to stroll arm in arm down the street.

This was always Elizabeth's way. "Nothing stood in her path when she decided she wanted to go out and have some fun," said Hank Moonjean. If Ava Gardner could do it, why couldn't she? Striding down the Via Veneto on Burton's arm with a pack of hungry photographers at her heels, Elizabeth was a woman liberated.

With the aromas of hot brioche and espresso wafting along the street, the stars held their heads high and didn't blink in the glare of the flashcubes. Passing cars slowed down to gawk at the famous pair. Unlike most of Rome's narrow, twisting roads, the Via Veneto is a wide boulevard; the author Ennio Flaiano described it like being at the beach, with the cars serving as gondolas and conversations at sidewalk cafes "baroque and jocular." This night, all talk ceased as everyone turned to stare at Liz and Dick.

Once more, their destination was Bricktop's. The hostess herself, cigar in hand and orange hair glowing like fire in the smoky club, welcomed them. Bricktop could be counted on for support. In the past, she'd tossed out tourists and darkened the lights so that the couple could "nuzzle over their vino." This night, when the photographer Umberto Spagna tried to enter, Bricktop confiscated his camera. But Spagna was still able to report back to his editors what he'd glimpsed inside: "Miss Taylor and Burton kissing each other many times." Gilberto Petrucci was, as usual, luckier than most, managing to slip into the joint with his trusty Rolleiflex under his coat. Approaching the stars' table, Petrucci asked Burton if he could take a picture. Perhaps eager to make amends for his assault on the young man, Richard looked over at Elizabeth, who just smiled enigmatically. "Yes," Burton told Petrucci. "You may take one picture."

They want pictures, so let's give them pictures.

Elizabeth Taylor knew how to be famous. By 1962 she was routinely called "America's queen," the sexy, glamorous counterpoint to that other Elizabeth across the Atlantic. Like authentic royalty, Taylor was expected to live in palatial homes amid riches and splendor that set her apart from common people—and she didn't disappoint. But like real kings and queens, she was also expected to show herself from time to time. Elizabeth understood this. At this particular moment the people needed to see her, and so out into the limelight she strode in her leopard-print fur coat. Yes, she'd give them pictures—but always in her way. When she'd had enough, she'd flip the photographers the finger, ruining their shots.

She knew how to end a publicity session. In 1962 there were still some pictures that would never be allowed in print.

She might not have jumped in the Trevi Fountain the way Anita Ekberg did in *La Dolce Vita*, but she might as well have. Elizabeth and Richard partied at Bricktop's until 3 A.M., causing another round of pandemonium as they left. The next day newspapers around the world splashed photos of the couple across their front pages. LIZ AND BURTON FROLIC IN ROME; KISS, DANCE, bannered the *Los Angeles Herald-Examiner*. "How did I know the woman was so fucking famous?" an astonished Burton asked. "She knocks Khrushchev off the front page!"

It was the kind of coverage publicists live for—yet Jack Brodsky was still unsure how the Taylor-Burton stroll along the Via Veneto would play with the public. As *Cleopatra*'s publicist, he'd been forewarned about their plans; he'd wired his assistant in New York the day before: "Burton, Taylor going out in public for first time. Get under the desk. Am terrified." So were the Fox higher-ups. But they seemed to agree that it was time to make a move, take a chance. But it was essential that Elizabeth and Richard not appear out of control. So Brodsky made sure every reporter got the memo that the two stars, despite their late hours, had arrived on time in the morning, ready to go to work.

That weekend brought more of the same. "Elizabeth Taylor and her three children piled into Richard Burton's black and white Lincoln today and they all went off to the beach," Reynolds Packard reported in the *New York Daily News*, "with photographers on motor scooters swarming around them like flies at a picnic." Burton was able to shake them off along the winding roads leading out of the city, but the happy family-to-be was caught later that day at Corsetti's restaurant at Torvaianica. Seated around a large table, Elizabeth, Richard, and the children were eating seafood cocktail and lobster. Afterward Elizabeth insisted on topping off the meal with a lavish dessert, a sweet concoction of ice cream, strawberries, pineapple, and Chartreuse, a liqueur made by Carthusian monks.

When she was finished, she patted her stomach and declared herself "quite satisfied all around."

That night Kurt Frings, the former pugilist who'd strongarmed Fox into agreeing to Elizabeth's groundbreaking salary, arrived in New York from Rome. He was carrying a "personal message" from Elizabeth to Eddie Fisher—as if all the publicity with Burton hadn't been message enough. Fisher was finally forced to face facts. On April 2, the day after Elizabeth and Richard's beach outing, Louis Nizer, the attorney for both Mr. and Mrs. Fisher, announced that the couple would be seeking a divorce in a release that one news report compared to "an official military or diplomatic conference communiqué."

No word from Sybil. Richard had not yet assured Elizabeth that he, too, would leave his spouse. But that didn't stop "Liz and Dick" from continuing to frolic—and sell lots of newspapers. They became the talk of two continents now more than ever, setting the stage for scandal. Hedda Hopper wasn't the only one sharpening her claws. Gossip columnist Suzy was the first to weigh in. "Elizabeth Taylor is going to have her cake and eat it, too," she wrote. "And if she wants *your* cake—watch out. Because she's going to get it. She got Debbie Reynolds' cake. Frosting and all. And she licked her ruby lips over every last crumb. Now she's after Sybil Burton's cake . . . Such a rich diet, no matter how strong a girl's stomach, can sometimes give her indigestion. I think Miss Taylor is going to get indigestion."

Elizabeth understood what she faced. Columnists like Suzy and Hopper were declaring that her career was over. A harried Dick Hanley was taking messages at all hours from studio executives worried that the publicity would tip against them. And though Elizabeth wouldn't learn of it for a few more weeks, her actions had even inspired passionate debate in the corridors of power—the Vatican and the United States Congress—over what to do about this moral "vagrant."

Some years later the poet Philip Larkin would famously opine that sexual intercourse was invented in 1963—a metaphorical observation of changing cultural mores—yet, in fact, Larkin seems to have been a year off. For it was in April 1962 that an adulterous couple first stared defiantly into the cameras and flaunted their "sin" without apology. It's hard to imagine today, with marriage being largely irrelevant among celebrity couples, how incendiary such behavior was once considered. But the last star who had so transgressed, Ingrid Bergman (who'd borne a child out of wedlock with the director Roberto Rossellini in 1950), had found herself persona non grata (at least in the United States) for nearly a decade. Elizabeth, by refusing to hide her affair with Burton, was confronting similar public standards. Yet she seemed to be betting that the world had evolved since Bergman's troubles. And if it hadn't, she was prepared to nudge it along.

Elizabeth Taylor knew what worked. She had been out there a long time and could sense the climate. Heading out with Richard once again along the Via Veneto, she wore her Egyptian eye makeup and hoop earrings from that day's shoot. Studio-generated press releases, run nearly verbatim in newspaper fashion sections, had been proclaiming for weeks that Cleopatra's "fantastic, exotic" beauty was the latest trend for women. The cover of *Look* featured Elizabeth's exotic face and asked, "Will her new Cleopatra look change your hairdo and makeup?" Society hairstylist Michel Kazan had developed a special Cleopatra hairstyle; Kurlash had launched a new line of false eyelashes called "Egyptian Eyes." Syndicated fashion columnist Tobe advised readers to copy Elizabeth's look if they wanted "to be first with the newest."

Elizabeth was fully conscious of her ability to set the vogue. Sitting beside Burton in the front seat of her Cadillac, her chin held high, her exotic Egyptian eyes undisturbed by the popping of flashcubes all around her, she looked every inch the queen.

And she knew very well that tomorrow morning millions of newspapers would be sold because she had decided to venture out onto the street. She was also just as confident about *Cleopatra;* hadn't every film in which she'd starred been a hit so far? Who could resist seeing Taylor and Burton together on the screen after all this?

Of course, she couldn't be certain about everything. She didn't know just how brutal the battle with Hedda and her cronies might become. She didn't know if the script Joe Mankiewicz was rewriting every night would turn out to be any good. She didn't know if Eddie would drag her name through the mud, or if he'd attempt to take Maria from her. And she certainly didn't know if Richard would ever divorce his wife.

But as she stepped out of the Cadillac and into the glare of the flashing cameras, she knew one thing and she knew it very well.

She knew how to be a movie star.

Two

Educating a Movie Star

Spring 1943–Fall 1945

SARA SOTHERN TAYLOR had just one thing on her mind that morning in the spring of 1943 as her driver steered her Chrysler down Washington Boulevard past the long stucco wall separating Lot One from the street: making her eleven-year-old daughter Elizabeth, seated demurely beside her, a star.

At the studio gates her driver rolled down his window to signal a turn as Sara and her daughter gazed up at the tall Corinthian columns guarding the entrance. It was here at Metro-Goldwyn-Mayer that Elizabeth Taylor learned her first lessons in how to be a movie star. As they drove onto the lot, Elizabeth kept her eyes on the white marble Thalberg Memorial Building with its central tower. Her mother had carefully explained that inside were the offices of Louis B. Mayer, the studio head who figured more prominently in Sara's cosmos than any deity.

Their driver let them out on the wide avenue that ran down the center of the main lot. Regular players affectionately called it "the alley." Elizabeth had been working at MGM for several months now, making $100 a week just to come in every morning even if she wasn't needed for a film. In fact, she'd made just two pictures in that time, one for the studio and one as a loan-out to Fox; both had been small parts that, while showy, had done little to promote the career of the dark-haired, blue-eyed girl. Sara was tired of it. Her daughter's future was her *job*, she believed. Wasn't MGM paying her an additional hundred a week for "coaching and chaperoning services"?

Not wasting a second, Sara spotted the director Clarence Brown, set to helm *National Velvet,* the story of a little English girl who masquerades as a boy and rides her horse to victory in the Grand National. Sara took hold of her daughter's hand, and Brown's quiet morning walk by himself was suddenly ended.

"Two diminutive but formidable females," as Brown described them, blocked his way down the alley where actors and extras in full-dress costume were making their way to the soundstages. Brown looked askance at mother and daughter, who spoke simultaneously.

"She's the right actress to portray Velvet Brown," Sara insisted.

"It's my favorite book," Elizabeth added.

Not wanting to give false encouragement, Brown—the director of Garbo and Norma Shearer—beat a hasty retreat down the alley, but his pursuers were not the kind to be shaken off easily. They pursued him all across the lot, "prattling on," hounding him past Stage Five, where production numbers for MGM's musicals were shot. Gene Kelly and Kathryn Grayson were there that day, tapping their way across the stage for *Thousands Cheer.* Judy Garland might have been there that day as well, shooting the final scenes of *Presenting Lily Mars,* the pinnacle of her teenage glamour period.

But nothing could distract mother and daughter from their chase. Shouting a breathless litany of reasons why Elizabeth would be perfect for the film, they stalked Brown past Stage Fifteen, the largest soundstage in the world, where MGM prop men were busy assembling a full-scale aircraft carrier for *Thirty Seconds Over Tokyo.* By the time Brown had reached Overland Avenue, the tenacious pair was still scurrying behind him, harrying him onto Lot Two, a surreal landscape of fantasy and illusion. The brownstone facades of New York overlapped with nineteenth-century London. Across the way was Tarzan's jungle and Esther Williams's shiny modern swimming pool. Mother and daughter pursued the director past mirage after mirage: the ruins of the Chinese temple from *The Good Earth*, the Main Line mansion of *The Philadelphia Story*, Andy Hardy's house. Opposite the train station last used in *Waterloo Bridge* stretched a replica of a New York pier, complete with a life-size ocean liner. Actually, one *eighth* of an ocean liner. That was all the camera needed. It was a landscape of bits and pieces.

No doubt Elizabeth paused to marvel, or at least tried to. "I was terrifically impressed," she'd recall after her first tour of the studio. "The lot was so huge—at that time they were doing maybe thirty films at once and it was teeming with life—people dressed up in Greek clothes, people dressed up as cowboys, people dressed up as apes, and real live movie stars. Of course, everybody, even the extras, looked like movie stars to me."

In 1943 MGM was a veritable city unto itself. "When I think of MGM," said actress Elinor Donahue, "I think of light and color and flowers and bigness. Everything was just *big*." Indeed, more than thirty soundstages on five different lots covered 176 acres. A private police force with nearly fifty officers kept the peace. There was a clinic, a dentist's office, a foundry, a commissary that fed employees at any time of the day. "It was a complete city," said actress Janet Leigh. "You could live there."

The commissary was surprisingly egalitarian, with extras rubbing elbows with stars, and everyone sipping Mr. Mayer's mother's chicken soup made with matzo balls. "The commissary seemed huge to me," Donahue said. "Years later, when I went back to MGM, it didn't seem quite so big, but for a young girl it was enormous. Lunches were called usually around the same time, so you'd have the whole lot in there. You'd look out and see Judy Garland and Spencer Tracy strolling in from their sets, still in costume. The place was filled with every star. I remember Xavier Cugat coming in carrying his miniature Chihuahua in his pocket."

The various players sat according to type. "I'm not sure if it was structured that way or if they just naturally gravitated together," Donahue said, "but the younger players sat together, and the western players. The comics were always together, horsing around, always very loud and cutting up. It seemed every day Red Skelton would stand up on top of the table and deliver some routine. Everyone would be laughing."

George Cukor observed, "I think people don't understand how a place like MGM needed to be fed, sustained, and organized every day." It wasn't just actors, directors, writers, cameramen, and editors who populated the lot, but also hairdressers, manicurists, tailors, musicians, architects, film loaders, electricians, prop men, script girls, sound technicians, bricklayers, painters, cooks, and dozens more. The wardrobe department went on for blocks. Studio press releases boasted that with just one day's notice MGM could costume one thousand extras. That's not even counting the regular background players, "the $75-a-week people with standard contracts," Donahue said, "who came to work every day and were told where to report, what film they'd be in that day. Crowds of people were always moving back and forth across the lot."

And by 1943 MGM lived up to its claim of being the most star-studded of all the studios. More than sixty top names—from Clark Gable and Katharine Hepburn to top character players like Edmund Gwenn and animal stars like Lassie—headed the Metro roster during the war years.

Now her mother was telling Elizabeth that she'd be a movie star herself. It all depended on Clarence Brown—and producer Mervyn LeRoy and, of course, Mr. Mayer—signing her for *National Velvet*. Brown, to his great relief, finally managed to shake off his pursuers that day, but the passion they'd displayed stayed with him. "What impressed me most," he said, "was [Elizabeth's] conviction that the picture . . . would provide a vehicle for her eventual stardom." Of course, it was her industrious mother whispering in her ear every morning who convinced the eleven-year-old that *National Velvet*—and stardom—were her fate.

In these years it was hard to discern where Sara ended and Elizabeth began. One movie-magazine writer immediately recognized the "spiritual affinity" between mother and daughter upon meeting them. They thought the same things; they used the same words to express them. And in the spring of 1943, even as war raged throughout Europe and the Pacific, one goal and one goal only existed for both of them—and it wasn't world peace.

Hustling Elizabeth back across the lot to the studio schoolhouse, Sara remained fired up about *National Velvet*. She knew the importance of breakout parts and how rarely they came along. She'd had a taste of fame herself once, playing the ingénue in Channing Pollock's play *The Fool*, which made her a sensation for a brief moment. After the London premiere in September 1924, Pollock remembered Sara being mobbed by fans, "clamoring for bits of her frock and locks of her hair."

A heady experience for the daughter of a laundryman from Arkansas City, Kansas. Sara was born "Sarah" Warmbrodt in August 1895. Her mother's family were Ohioans; her father's father had emigrated from Switzerland. Growing up in a neighborhood of railroad clerks, blacksmiths, and masons had made Sara quite the aesthete: She recited poetry at church socials with such eloquence that the locals declared her destined for the stage. In that booming industrial town with its busy intersection of rail lines that led to bigger cities like Wichita, Tulsa, and St. Louis, Sara's mother, who played the piano and the violin, encouraged her daughter to dream. After seeing Aline McDermott, the leading lady of a touring stock company, perform at Ark City's opera house, Sara went backstage and confessed her hopes of being an actress. McDermott did her best to dissuade her. "She was afraid . . . that I didn't know the world," Sara said. "So I thought the best way to know the world was to go out and be in it."

From then on, like Dorothy, she kept her eyes peeled for a way out of Kansas. Her own personal tornado came in the form of an itinerant moving-picture cameraman, who came through town looking for a leading lady. The local newspaper hosted a contest. Sara got a call in the middle of the night telling her that she'd won. "I was so excited," she said. "I dragged my poor dad out of bed and made him go downtown with me." In the little amateur thriller, the teenaged Sara played the damsel in distress "without any makeup." Her experience served her well. When a stock company from the Orpheum circuit came to town a short while later, Sara won a part—and not even a sprained ankle could keep her from it. Her brother teased her that she'd sprained it "romping down to the theater so fast to get a job." No matter the pain, she hobbled through her part for the week of the show's run. "I just felt as if my whole future depended on my sticking it out."

Her passion was so single-minded that she never had time for a serious beau. Channing Pollock thought Sara rather "plain," a "wallflower" even, delicate and petite. To Sara's way of thinking, the theater offered far more than any beau could: illusion, applause, and the opportunity to get out of Kansas on her own terms.

At an age when most girls were getting married and starting families, Sara, twenty-one, packed her bags for New York. Breaking away from the dusty back roads of Ark City and the steam of her father's laundry was an extraordinary sort of rebellion for 1917, when women didn't even have the right to vote. Few women of Sara's means ever thought of such independence. Certainly no one in her family had blazed a trail for her; as Sara boarded a train for New York, her brother remained safely behind in Kansas to run a small photography shop.

The first thing Sara did in the big city was change her name. Warmbrodt would never do; Sothern was the elegant substitute she had picked out. After Sara played a few bit parts on Broadway, the actors' strike in 1919 sent her into stock. A run with a Winnipeg company was followed in the fall of 1920 by a contract with the Thomas Wilkes troupe at the Majestic Theatre in Los Angeles. Sara played everything from ingénues to vamps.

In sunny California, Sara finally landed a beau at the age of twenty-six—unlikely as he was. Even back then Franklin Pangborn was known for his fluttery performances—the same kind he'd later bring to the Hollywood screen. Perhaps embarrassed by what was obviously a press agent's ploy to pair her off with such an obviously gay man, Sara told a reporter that she and "Pang" were just "pals" who went to the beach together on their days off. And Pang made sure she got home safely after every performance, for which Sara was "very grateful." An affinity for gay male friends was one more trait Sara would pass on to her daughter.

It's been assumed that Sara was merely a minor player during her stage career, her own frustration flowering into her ambition for her daughter's success. Yet between 1920 and 1922, Sara enjoyed quite a lively local fan base. Gossip columns noted the stir that she caused when she wore a "hectic" (read: sexy) bathing suit at Corona del Mar beach. While she might not have been known beyond the outskirts of the City of Angels, her name was mentioned in the same local columns as Lillian Gish's and Gloria Swanson's, and almost as frequently.

Then came *The Fool*. Playwright Channing Pollock, then riding high, intended to take the show to Broadway after its premiere at the Majestic. *The Fool* had "national dramatic importance," according to one critic—a real coup for the Majestic. Sara was thrilled to accept one of the play's most important roles, a lame girl cured by her own faith. Sara instinctively got what the part could do for her. If she scored in Los Angeles, there would be Broadway.

Pollock's choice was no mistake. When *The Fool* opened on July 13, 1922, in front of what the *Los Angeles Times* called a "brilliant first-night audience," Sara gave one of the evening's standout performances. Reviews for the show itself were mixed, but all of them singled her out. She was genuine, even moving, in a part that could easily have been sappy or cloying. The esteemed Russian actress Alla Nazimova told Pollock that he should keep Sara when he headed to New York. But it wasn't until mid-August that Sara got the word. By the time columnist Grace Kingsley reported the "shock" that local fans felt about losing "their fair Sara," she was packed and ready to go.

Beginning a practice that would reverberate throughout the lives of both mother and daughter, a bit of autobiography was layered onto Sara's public persona to capture the interest of the press. Sara had been such a hit in *The Fool*, Kingsley averred, because, as a real-life convert to Christian Science, her faith had cured her when she was "very ill" a few seasons earlier. "So she puts a real devotion into the role," Kingsley said. Clearly Sara's miraculous real-life "cure," true or not, was a publicity bonanza that Pollock could use to his advantage as the show headed to the Great White Way.

The Fool opened at the Times Square Theatre on October 23, 1922. Notices for the show ranged from outright pans to inclusion in critic Burns Mantle's ten finest productions of the year, but Sara was heaped with praise once again. *Theatre* magazine thought everyone "creditable but not startling," with the exception of "a little girl named Sara Sothern" who was "outstandingly fine."

The "little girl" was, of course, twenty-seven years old, but her diminutive size and delicate manner suggested a teenager. For a few heady months Sara lived her fantasy, hobnobbing with Clifton Webb and Elsie Janis and being caricatured in the theater pages of the *New York Times,* always a sign of an "arrival." *The Fool* ran for eight months and 272 performances before moving on to London, where for another five months it drew rapturous audiences to the Criterion Theatre. "A complete triumph," the *Times* declared of Sara's performance. One night after the show, Mary, the future Princess Royal and daughter of King George V, came backstage to bestow upon the little lame girl a diamond brooch "the size of a belt buckle." The brooch would remain among Sara's treasured possessions all her life, raising the question of whether an addiction to diamonds is genetic.

Two decades later Sara may well have thought back to that exciting time in London. It was her pinnacle. Her return to the United States in March 1925 was followed by a series of Broadway flops. Sara never managed the transition from ingénue to leading lady. And so there she was, seventeen years later, sitting in the waiting room outside the Little Red Schoolhouse with the mothers of Juanita Quigley and Butch Jenkins, listening to the click-click-click of their knitting needles. And she vowed yet again that she would make Elizabeth a star.

. . .

Across town, Hedda Hopper strode into her office seven floors above Hollywood Boulevard wearing one of her trademark picture hats, a silk daisy seemingly sprouting from the top of her head. "Hello, slaves," she called out cheerily to her assistants, passing through her austere reception area—likened by one reporter to the anteroom of a dentist's office—and into her "sanctum sanctorum," the headquarters from which she coordinated her various machinations and manipulations of the film capital.

Pausing in her typing, Hopper's secretary handed over several telephone messages as her boss passed her desk. At least one was from Sara Taylor. For weeks Hedda had been bombarded with Sara's pleas to help Elizabeth get *National Velvet*. The columnist had promised to do what she could—but the badgering was getting on Hedda's nerves. Glancing down at the shorthand hieroglyphics that only she and her secretary could read, Hedda considered inserting something into her next day's column—but then decided against it. Maybe another day.

Sara would be disappointed. "A few words from Hedda," *Time* magazine would observe, "can make or break a director or an actor, cool or clinch a deal. Hedda's chit-chat can materially affect the outcome of schemes involving millions of dollars."

From the windows of her office Hopper had an unobstructed view southwest over the plain of orange and palm trees toward the place where many of the studios were located. If she squinted and imagined hard enough, she could even make out Culver City, home of MGM, where Hedda herself had toiled for many years as a well-dressed supporting player. Stardom had once been a dream of Hedda's. But it was here, behind her plain desk adorned only with a big black typewriter and a leather-framed photo of the late actress Marie Dressler, that Hedda found her true calling.

She was fifty-eight years old, an age when most other women in Hollywood had retired or faded into walk-on parts. But Hopper was neither retiring nor fading. In 1936, just when she thought her career as an actress was over, she had landed a gossip show on a Hollywood radio station, sponsored by Max-O-Oil shampoo.

So popular did Hedda's "dispatches from Hollywood" become that the Esquire syndicate ordered up a daily newspaper column that was intended to rival Hearst's Louella Parsons, who'd been telling tales on Hollywood since before the talkies. The trouble was that Hedda, at least on paper, was too nice: no juice, no scandal. People who knew her well, like her manager, Dema Harshbarger, failed to recognize the ironic, sarcastic, private Hopper in her sanitized writerly persona. Harshbarger, a no-nonsense, heavyset lesbian who dressed in men's suits, told Hedda plainly that if she kept on being nice, she'd starve to death. "Wake up," Harshbarger advised. "Be yourself."

It worked. Hedda's newly aggressive style sold. Suddenly she was a personality, a household name. In 1940 she left Esquire for the Des Moines Register & Tribune syndicate, and in the following year scored her biggest coup: contracts with the *New York Daily News* and *Chicago Tribune*. "On that day," observed *Time*, "Lolly Parsons arched her back but moved over on the fence."

Now Hedda commanded nearly 23 million readers. Hollywood honchos courted her, flattered her, showered her with gifts—and took her name in vain behind her back. All for a few words in her column. On any given day Hopper's office would be filled with the fragrance of lilies from Joan Crawford or lilacs from Rita Hayworth, the cards attached usually saying something like "Just because." Staying on Hedda's good side was essential—because her venom was lethal. She'd gone after Orson Welles when *Citizen Kane* had offended her and was now leading the charge against Charlie Chaplin over the paternity case brought by starlet Joan Barry. Readers lapped up Hopper's vitriol. "Bitchery," she once said, when asked to explain her success. "Sheer bitchery."

Hedda was the kind of woman called "handsome" in her day—tall (5'8") when most women in the business were petite. As she got older, her features sharpened, her lips pursed noticeably. Born a Quaker, she had a schizophrenic attitude about sex. She loved hearing about the stars' sexual transgressions, and her closest friends were all gay or lesbian. But her friend Robert Shaw thought Hedda herself chaste, at least since her son's conception in 1914. After divorcing the actor DeWolf Hopper, she became Hollywood's gossipy maiden aunt—"a Quaker," said Dema Harshbarger, "from the neck down."

Sitting at her desk, kicking off her heels, and putting on more comfortable shoes, Hedda went to work. With long, slender fingers she began dialing, picking and choosing calls to return or ignore. The Chaplin case consumed most of her passion these days; Sara Taylor was just not a priority. Besides, Hedda had already done quite a bit for Sara's child. Back in 1939, when Elizabeth was just seven, Hedda had suggested that David O. Selznick cast her as Vivien Leigh's daughter in *Gone With the Wind*. It still rankled Hedda how disingenuous Sara could be about that whole experience, insisting that she'd never had any thought of putting her daughter in pictures. Sara claimed that it was only after "people on the street" had told her how much Elizabeth resembled Leigh that she had even given it a thought. Hedda scoffed at such baloney. At that point in time, no one had any idea what Vivien Leigh looked like! Of *course* the entire enterprise had been Sara's, right from the moment she'd showed up at Hedda's office with her daughter in tow, obsessed with the idea of getting her into the film.

And though Elizabeth didn't get the part, Hedda continued going to bat for her, suggesting that she might be a rival to singing child star Deanna Durbin (even though Elizabeth's singing had Hedda covering her ears; "one of the most painful ordeals," she called it). After Elizabeth's first movie, a trifle for Universal called *There's One Born Every Minute*, Hedda wrote that Elizabeth "walks off with a fat role" (even though it was barely a bit). In October 1942 she'd devoted the whole first half of her column to Elizabeth, proclaiming her "one of the most beautiful children I've ever seen." Most recently, she'd written that Elizabeth had been "so good" in her first MGM picture, *Lassie Come Home* (even though if you blinked, you missed her), that she'd been snatched up by Fox for *Jane Eyre*, starring Joan Fontaine. Hedda felt she'd done quite enough. Little Elizabeth Taylor had gotten more ink from her than many older actresses with bona fide résumés.

Hedda had first met the Taylors while they were living in England. After Sara's stage career was over, she'd married art dealer Francis Taylor (whom she called "Daddy," despite being two years older than he was) and moved with him to London, where he ran a gallery on Old Bond Street. The Taylors lived in a redbrick house opposite the vast green stretch of Hampstead Heath. It was here that Sara gave birth to a son, Howard, in 1929, and on February 27, 1932, to a daughter, Elizabeth Rosemond.

When Elizabeth was four, the family also acquired a country retreat near Cranbrook in Kent, where Hedda made their acquaintance. The house came courtesy of Francis Taylor's patron, Victor Cazalet, a Conservative member of Parliament who was a captain in the British Army. Hedda was friends with Cazalet's sister, Thelma Cazalet-Keir, also a Conservative MP. On weekends, the Taylors' driver motored them out of the city and into the rolling Kentish hills, where their cottage was located on Cazalet's estate. When Hedda was visiting once, Sara and little Elizabeth ambled up through the gardens to the main house for tea. The meeting wasn't apparently all that memorable: Sara would bring a letter of (re)introduction from Cazalet-Keir when she showed up at Hopper's office in Hollywood a few years later.

Hedda never cared much for Sara, seeing her as something of a climber. Of course, it took one to know one. Hedda was a butcher's daughter from Altoona, Pennsylvania, who'd run away from home as a teenager. She was bitter over being born poor and always having to fight her way; decades later she was still resentful of never having had a bicycle as a child. "When I was called the best-dressed woman on the screen, I had to laugh," she said, "remembering the days when I wore a pair of overalls, an old sweater, and an apron, and went into the cooler to cut off a quarter of beef and carry it out over my shoulder to the chopping block."

Hedda seemed to resent Sara's greater success in obtaining the finer things in life. Through Francis Taylor, Sara had acquired two homes, servants, and access to London society. Marriage to the respected stage actor DeWolf Hopper had given Hedda some cachet, but the divorce had left her high, dry, and a bit less than desirable. In Hollywood she tried to cultivate a sophisticated image, but there was still something garish and provincial about her. It wasn't just her hats. Her home in Beverly Hills had been filigreed to death by the former set designer Harold Grieve. On the walls of her office hung originals by Picasso and Renoir, "denoting Miss Hopper's appreciation of art," as one press release made sure to report—yet these were offset by bare radiators and scarred doors. Hedda's airs were often belied by the political tirades for which she was prone, right-wing rants about communists and socialists and "people who wanted to take away everything she had worked so hard to achieve," according to one friend.

Sitting at her typewriter, Hedda glanced over the dozens of press releases that had accumulated on her desk. Once more that name caught her eye: Elizabeth Taylor—cast in Metro's upcoming *The White Cliffs of Dover*. Relenting, she gave the girl another blurb, though she got her age wrong, writing that the eleven-year-old was nine. Fact-checking was never Hedda's strong suit. Gossip was. That's what made her so powerful. "Gossip," noted *Time*, "has become as indispensably bound up in the making of U.S. movies as cameras, kaolin smiles and surfboard-sized eyelashes. For Hollywood is a town doing a business based on vanity." Everyone involved understood that: Hedda, Sara, and even little Elizabeth herself, sitting at her school desk dreaming about fame.

Anne Francis, a pretty blonde teenager who'd arrived in Hollywood after appearing with Gertrude Lawrence in *Lady in the Dark* on Broadway, couldn't help but envy Elizabeth Taylor, the girl who sat next to her in the MGM schoolhouse. Elizabeth was making a big prestige picture starring Irene Dunne, and rumor had it that she was up for *National Velvet*, too. Anne, meanwhile, hadn't made a single movie since signing with the studio. Every day she simply reported to the schoolhouse and hoped her luck would change.

But Elizabeth's career had suddenly shifted into high gear. Although Elizabeth's part in *The White Cliffs of Dover* was small, her startling girlish beauty was already causing comment, just as it had in *Jane Eyre*. In her first scene in that picture for Fox, she descends a staircase in the background as Peggy Ann Garner, playing Jane, stands on a box in the foreground. Elizabeth is a tiny, unremarkable figure until a sudden luminous close-up takes our breath away. All of our attention immediately pulls away from Garner, the ostensible star. In that moment Elizabeth possesses what film historian Jeanine Basinger has called the "x factor" of potential stardom, "the infrared in the dark of the movie house."

Glancing over at her in the schoolhouse, Anne Francis had to agree with what people were saying about Elizabeth Taylor. "She was utterly gorgeous, even as a little girl," Francis said. "I was in awe of her. Hers wasn't the beauty of a child."

In her early pictures, Elizabeth indeed seems to be a miniature adult. Even at ten she stopped grown men in their tracks. Watching her shoot a scene in *Jane Eyre*, costar Orson Welles turned to a companion and whispered, "Remind me to be around when she grows up." Her first studio contract, with Universal, had been canceled when the casting director decided, "Her eyes are too old. She doesn't have the face of a kid."

But at Metro that face became her ticket to success—along with her accent. At the height of the war, Englishness was in vogue on the American screen, and Elizabeth was virtually the only young actress on the lot who could authentically play English. Sheridan Morley credited her "accurate memory for the vowel sounds of Hampstead and Kent." The accent would also help with *National Velvet;* the studio needed a girl with an accent who could ride horses. Even without Sara's campaign to draw attention to her daughter, it was only natural that the higher-ups would begin "casting glances" in Elizabeth's direction.

"Being in films then," she said, "was like the most magical extension of make-believe. It didn't occur to me that it was a career and that I was making money."

She'd always been an imaginative child. Playacting for the camera and dressing in costume was not so different from the game she'd been playing with herself all her life. "Walter Mittying," she called it—daydreaming, living out fantasies in her mind. She'd create whole scenarios for herself in which she traveled the world or explored some faraway land. Other times she relived moments from her past—riding her horse in Kent or steaming across the Atlantic on the gilt-plated ship that had brought her to America.

Looking over at her in the MGM schoolhouse, Anne Francis observed the way Elizabeth's lips moved when she was supposed to be studying, the way her extraordinary eyes, shaded by double rows of eyelashes, seemed to be looking at something that none of the rest of them could see. Elizabeth's fantasies of late were all about being a movie star; yet the little girl's ambition was not so much for herself. Not at this point. It sprang instead from a deep-seated desire to please her mother, still at her side nearly every waking moment. The director George Stevens considered the two of them "in a cocoon."

Her father, meanwhile, was mostly a background figure. In England it had been different, with Elizabeth very much the apple of Francis Taylor's eye. Back then she would sit in his lap as he read to her or she'd run across the grassy meadows of Kent into his arms. She physically resembled her father more than she did her mother, inheriting his dark hair and mesmerizing eyes. No question that, early on, Francis could be a stern disciplinarian, but back then he insisted on direct involvement in his children's lives—a practice that would steadily diminish after they came to America and Sara took the reins.

Like his wife, Francis Taylor hailed from the lower middle class; his father had been a dry goods salesman. Born in Springfield, Illinois, in December 1897, Francis moved with his family to Arkansas City as a young teenager, where he met the two-years-older Sara Warmbrodt. Yet any story that has them falling in love at this time is a publicist's invention. Elizabeth herself would tell stories of her father carrying her mother's schoolbooks, but if he did, it was a rare and probably inconsequential occurrence. Older and consumed by the theater, Sara moved in very different circles than Francis did. Besides, the future spouses overlapped in Ark City for only a few years. In 1915, at the age of seventeen, Francis was rescued from a life of drudgery by his affluent uncle, Howard Young, who ran an art gallery in St. Louis. Recognizing something artistic in his nephew—something that set him apart from other boys his age—Uncle Howard hired Francis as his assistant and brought him to St. Louis.

With no children of their own, the Youngs practically adopted their nephew. Possibly it was Howard's connections that enabled Francis to avoid registering for the draft during World War I. Instead of heading to the Western Front, Francis accompanied his uncle to New York, where the Howard Young Galleries opened at 620 Fifth Avenue.

It was in New York that Francis encountered Sara again and remembered her from Kansas. She was thirty-one years old, and when she accepted Francis's offer of marriage, she announced her "permanent retirement from the stage." (The *New York Times* theater critic wasn't so sure, adding that such was "her present intention at least.") Sara and Francis were married on October 23, 1926, at the Fifth Avenue Presbyterian Church. The newlyweds departed almost immediately for Europe, with Francis serving as Young's acquisitions agent, paying calls on private collectors in Paris, Vienna, and Budapest. The Taylors settled in London in 1929 when Young decided to open a gallery there.

Sara would later exaggerate their status in British society, writing about being invited to Downing Street by Mrs. Neville Chamberlain to view the Trooping of the Colors for the King's birthday—as if this were a personal little get-together with the prime minister's wife when, in fact, Sara was merely part of a larger group of ladies and was included only through the intercession of the family's benefactor, Victor Cazalet. She'd tell similar stories of being invited to Buckingham Palace. Even Elizabeth's ballet lessons took on an added sheen, with Sara insisting that among her daughter's fellow dance students were the young princesses, Elizabeth and Margaret Rose. They were students of the same school, true enough—but the instructors went to the royals, not the other way around. Elizabeth certainly never practiced her pliés and pirouettes with the little princesses.

Still, it was a privileged, upper-class life that Sara had secured for her children, far from the steam and smoke of the Warmbrodt laundry. Attending the Royal Ascot, Sara and her daughter wore matching blue silk dresses designed by Mainbocher. At home they employed maids, cooks, drivers, and nannies ("There is no one in the world like a good English Nannie," Sara believed). And not only did the Taylors have their country house in Kent, they also leased a beach house in Devonshire during the summer. Elizabeth and her brother grew up in the kind of comfort that Sara had only dreamed about.

The Taylors owed their lifestyle, of course, to the largesse of "Uncle" Victor Cazalet. They were living, after all, on his estate; invitations to social events and impromptu gifts of clothing and furniture all came courtesy of him. For Elizabeth's fifth birthday, Cazalet presented his self-appointed goddaughter with her own horse.

Cazalet's generosity to the Taylors raised a few eyebrows. Most people were aware that the marriage between Sara and Francis, while amiable, was never passionate. Like Sara's earlier "beau" Franklin Pangborn, Francis was discreetly homosexual, pursuing a clandestine affair with the art collector Kurt Stempler. (A letter in Hedda Hopper's files from a childhood friend of Francis's reported "all the girls thought him marvelous, but he seemed not to notice.") He may also have been involved with Cazalet himself, whose sexuality was whispered about in British government circles. Certainly Francis and the unmarried Uncle Victor were inseparable much of the time, attending concerts in Covent Garden and then spending the weekend in the city on their own. But Cazalet was on equally familiar terms with Sara. Some wondered if both Mr. *and* Mrs. Taylor might have been intimate with the good captain.

But when war with Germany seemed increasingly inevitable, the family bid good-bye to Cazalet and his country. On April 21,

1939, Sara sailed with her two children on board the SS *Manhattan;* Francis joined them in December. At first they tried living with Sara's father, who'd relocated to San Gabriel, California, where he ran a chicken farm. But that would never do. And Sara was horrified to discover that she had to learn to drive her own car.

Howard Young once again came to the rescue, arranging to open a gallery in Los Angeles, first at the Chateau Elysée and later on the first floor of the posh Beverly Hills Hotel. By 1941 Francis had saved enough money to buy a house on North Elm Drive in Beverly Hills. No doubt the down payment was augmented by Elizabeth's movie earnings, only half of which her parents were required by law to hold in trust for her. Elizabeth and Howard were enrolled in the nearby Hawthorne School.

"In that inbred little community," Elizabeth said, most of her parents' friends "had something to do with the film industry." At school, "every kid's father was a producer or a director or an actor." Elizabeth couldn't have escaped the movies if she'd tried. At her father's gallery, a range of Hollywood types from David O. Selznick to Greta Garbo regularly made their way through the doors. (It helped that the gallery was located just off the hotel's swimming pool.) Hedda Hopper frequently popped in and became particularly enthused by the work of the Welsh artist Augustus John, whom Francis represented exclusively. Hedda adored Francis Taylor, "a lovely, sweet, kind man," and considered his opinions on art as gospel. Any favors she'd grant Elizabeth in the coming years weren't done for Sara; they were done for Francis.

Hedda was in conspicuous attendance on the night of May 19, 1941, when the Taylors hosted a dinner in honor of Victor Cazalet, whom Hedda informed her readers was a "great-grandson of Queen Victoria" (actually, he was only her godson). Cazalet's lecture afterward at the Wilshire Ebell Theatre on "America and Defense" was attended by some of Hollywood's biggest names: Greer Garson, Basil Rathbone, Mary Pickford, Robert Montgomery, Sir Cedric Hardwicke. Cazalet's visit edged Francis and Sara up a few more notches in screenland social circles.

As the Taylors moved up, more and more people in the industry became acquainted with their precocious daughter. Surrealist painter Oscar de Mejo held his first show at Francis Taylor's gallery, where he'd remember the nine-year-old Elizabeth serving hors d'oeuvres. "[She] had absolutely the most exquisite features, the kind of face Botticelli might have created had he painted her. She emitted an air of ageless, inculpable eroticism, enhanced by the fact that she always called you by name, making you very aware of yourself. 'Won't you have another caviar on toast, Monsieur de Mejo?'"

As Elizabeth's screen career progressed, her appearances at her father's gallery inevitably declined, and, perhaps just as inevitably, a schism emerged in the Taylor home on North Elm Drive. One family friend confided to a reporter that photographs of Elizabeth—some alone and some with Sara—studded each room of the house, while not one picture of Howard was to be seen. "You'd never have known there was a Taylor male around," the friend said. In these years, if Sara spoke to Howard at all for any length of time, it was to encourage him to take a screen test at Metro, a suggestion the levelheaded teenager rejected outright. Howard had seen his sister's life become consumed by their mother's ambition, and he'd recoiled from Elizabeth's dreamy-eyed acquiescence. Howard wanted none of that. At dinner, as the Taylor females prattled on about *National Velvet*, Howard and his father often ate in silence.

Elizabeth's father, once the final authority in her life, ceded his place to the ironclad ambition of his wife. It would be Sara, not Francis, who signed Elizabeth's contract; it was Sara, not her husband, to whom payment would be made.

The education of Miss Elizabeth Taylor did actually involve some conventional schooling, though the more conventional it was, the less it held any interest for the girl. Teacher Mary Katherine McDonald was not fond of Elizabeth's constant daydreaming. One day she walked up beside her inattentive student and rapped a wooden ruler across her knuckles. Elizabeth let out a yelp.

That would keep her focused, Miss McDonald believed. Just

because her students were budding movie stars was no reason to coddle them. Forty-three years old and unmarried, McDonald had taught science at a private school before being hired to run the MGM schoolhouse in 1932. The children were terrified of her. As Elizabeth rubbed her knuckles, Anne Francis tensed in her seat. "It was like a year of incarceration," Francis said of her time at what was popularly known as "The Little Red Schoolhouse."

In fact, all of the big studios had schoolhouses known by the same appellation, and none of them were red. The name was a nostalgic reference to the one-room schoolhouses of the past, where children of all ages learned together. As the ranks of child contract players fluctuated from year to year, some studios, like Universal or Columbia, would occasionally find themselves with just one or two students reporting for the fall semester. MGM, however, with its bumper crop of child stars, usually had a full class of between six and twelve students. By the time Elizabeth arrived, Mickey Rooney, Judy Garland, and Roddy McDowall had already passed through the school.

Once upon a time the schoolhouse had been a private dining room for Irving Thalberg, the MGM powerhouse producer and boy wonder who had died in 1936. Seven years later a four-foot-tall picket fence surrounded the wooden structure, with red, white, and blue petunias planted along its side. Inside there were two rooms, a classroom with regulation desks and a blackboard, and an adjoining study room, with soft, stuffed chairs where older students frequently sat. Miss McDonald moved easily back and forth.

She was assisted by Dorothy Mullen, a mother of two, who worked individually with students, and by Caroline "Muzzie" McPhail, whose job was rounding the children up and counting heads before class. The children might fear Miss McDonald, but they adored Muzzie. When the day went badly, "Muzzie . . . was someone whose shoulder we could cry on," said Jean Porter, the teenaged costar of *Andy Hardy's Blonde Trouble* and another classmate of Elizabeth's. Muzzie understood child actors; her own son had been one and was now playing bit parts on the lot.

Although the curriculum was approved by the Los Angeles Board of Education, and standardized tests were given to ensure that the studio kids measured up to their civilian counterparts, the lessons in the Little Red Schoolhouse "weren't particularly tough," Anne Francis said. At the Professional Children's School in New York, she'd been "loaded with homework." Not so at MGM, where teachers rarely taught anything past simple mathematics and basic English composition. Sara, not surprisingly, sugarcoated Elizabeth's education, calling the MGM school "wonderful," but Elizabeth herself would later dismiss her years there as "my so-called education." Her classmate Dean Stockwell was more blunt. About Miss McDonald, he said, "She didn't teach me shit."

Part of the problem was the haphazard school day. If a film was shooting in the morning, the child went to school in the afternoon. If the shoot was later in the day, then the schedule was switched. Children often would be called out of class if they were needed for a scene; Dorothy Mullen would troop along beside them down the alley to Lot Two, textbook in hand. "Between camera takes," Elizabeth said, "you'd cram in ten minutes, twenty minutes of study, going out to act, then being led by the ear back to school and snapping your brain back into being a student." Often she found herself taking tests in full makeup and costume, hunched down under an arc lamp, one eye on her paper and the other on the set, alert for her next call. So long as students managed to get three hours a day of schooling—in class or on the set—they were meeting the requirements of the law. "We were doing in that time what normal kids did in six," Elizabeth said.

Such a routine must have had a peculiar effect on the young girl. The boundaries of "real life" blurred. What was more "real" to Elizabeth—the school or the scene, memorizing her times tables or her lines? How could ordinary life ever compare to what transpired behind the camera? And what of childhood? Was Elizabeth a kid or did she just know how to play one? And were those youngsters whom Elizabeth and her friends played on screen real—or was "real" a description that could only apply to the children she saw outside the studio gates?

In press releases and publicity, the MGM child stars were portrayed as just like children everywhere, learning their lessons, playing at recess, preferring dogs and games and climbing trees to making movies. Yet, in fact, the kids who made their way through the Little Red Schoolhouse were anything but innocent. As a teenager, Jackie Cooper was seduced by Joan Crawford; Judy Garland was already popping pills to control her weight. The all-American children they played on the screen were in direct contrast to the more worldly lives they led at the studio. Dean Stockwell said that he and his classmates were "kids . . . out of place in time and ties and culture."

At a time when other girls her age thought only about dresses and dolls, Elizabeth was already the breadwinner in her family. "I paid the bills," she admitted. "People weren't buying art. It was hard on my father." She might not have mastered fractions or compound sentence structure, but she learned other things, like how to make money and live among adults. Cameramen swore blue streaks around her; wardrobe ladies gossiped about affairs as they fitted her in costumes; agents hammered out tough deals in front of her. By her early teens, Elizabeth was already cursing like a sailor and haggling with her mother over the terms of her allowance.

Although Elizabeth insisted that she envied Howard's going to a "real" school, it's unlikely that she would have fit in there very well. Even in the studio classroom Elizabeth chafed against the rules and regimentation, as inconsistent as they were. "I was in constant rebellion," she said. She'd escape to the bathroom and hide out. Eventually Miss McDonald caught on, instructing her to write on the blackboard the exact times of her departures and returns. Once the little actress wrote, "E exits bathroom, 10:06, mission accomplished." She was reprimanded.

Dorothy Mullen would remember Elizabeth as a "fair" student. Mary McDonald added, "I wouldn't put her in the same intellectual category as Einstein, but she wasn't stupid." Elizabeth's problem was not a lack of intelligence but a lack of disciplined concentration. If the subject didn't interest her, she simply tuned it out. To pass tests she relied on the same photographic memory that she used to learn her lines in a single morning. "Just before an exam," she said, "I would memorize the points I thought they would ask me about. Of course, two weeks later it was gone, so I really didn't absorb anything . . . And I knew, even then, that I was cheating myself."

But some lessons were more important. After school let out at noon (or later, depending on shooting schedules), there were dancing and voice lessons. In a rehearsal studio off Stage Five, Sara tied Elizabeth's tap shoes and then watched from the sidelines as her short, chubby-legged daughter struggled to keep up with the likes of Kathryn Grayson and Donna Reed. Sometimes Elizabeth didn't have time to change out of her leotards before running across the alley to the Thalberg Building for voice lessons with Lucille Ryman, who doubled as an MGM talent scout. Ryman lined the girls up in front of her—Elizabeth, Donna Reed, Susan Peters, Margaret Kerry—and made them repeat certain phrases. "Park the car in the yard." "Boogie woogie bugle boy." Regional accents were obliterated. The goal, Kerry said, was for all of them "to come out sounding identical." Eventually, especially once British pictures became less popular, Elizabeth's accent was painstakingly transformed into what she called "Americanese": the unmistakable cadence of Hollywood speech, with its perfectly modulated pitch and tone, properly all-American. The girls also learned the "Metro walk": sucking in the stomach, squaring the shoulders, and stepping off on the right foot.

"What mattered to the studio was that a star could sing and dance and speak and act like a star," said Elliott Morgan, the longtime head of research at MGM. "They didn't care if they couldn't spell or add a list of figures. And really, did anybody? So long as the stars looked good and sounded good up there on the screen, nothing else mattered."

. . .

But the trick was getting Elizabeth up there on the screen. Despite all the glances being cast her way, there was still no final decision on Elizabeth's being cast in *National Velvet*. Sara decided that the time had come for the final push.

In June 1943 Pan Berman took over from Mervyn LeRoy as the *Velvet* producer. Berman had made it clear to Clarence Brown that he felt that Elizabeth was too small to play a teenaged girl who passes herself off as a young man. Sara refused to be deterred by such a trivial matter as her daughter's height. With school out for the summer, the Taylor females had plenty of time on their hands to strategize. Berman was Obstacle Number One. He was an efficient filmmaker who'd begun his career at RKO, where he'd paired Ginger Rogers with Fred Astaire and turned Katharine Hepburn into a star. Arriving at MGM, he'd quickly distinguished himself with *Ziegfeld Girl,* and in a bit of inspired casting, teamed Lana Turner with Clark Gable in *Honky Tonk.* This was a man who knew how to make successful movies. If Berman thought an actress was wrong for a part, she probably was.

But then there was Sara, always righter than anyone. In early July she arranged a meeting with Berman. Sitting across from his desk, she calmly and carefully made her case. None of the other girls could be as convincingly English as Elizabeth. None could ride horses as well. To prepare for the part, Sara informed the director, Elizabeth had been riding for an hour and a half every morning at the studio's stables. The little actress, in a red bow and blue dress, sat there nodding and smiling.

Berman was amused by Sara's superciliousness. But he wasn't swayed. Asking Elizabeth to stand, he measured her against the wall, drawing a little pencil mark over the top of her head. Moving his hand up several inches, he told mother and daughter that Velvet Brown needed to stand at least that tall. Unless Elizabeth suddenly sprouted over the summer, he insisted, she would not be in *National Velvet.*

At least that's the way Sara and Elizabeth told the story. And there's likely some truth to it, because in *The White Cliffs of Dover,*

Elizabeth does appear too small, too doll-like, to play the plucky Velvet Brown. Yet Berman was far too canny a producer to utterly dismiss out of hand the one girl on the lot who seemed to fit the bill on so many counts. And it's no doubt significant that no other actress's name was floated in the press for the part during the summer of 1943.

Still the Taylors took no chances. Elizabeth, almost certainly, really did embark on a campaign that summer to "grow" the required three inches or so. "There was this place Tip's," she remembered, "where they had a thing called a Farm Breakfast—two hamburger patties, two fried eggs, a great big mound of hashed brown potatoes and after that a whole bunch of dollar pancakes. I used to have *two* Farm Breakfasts every morning at one sitting." Of course, all those calories were more likely to make her grow three inches *wider* instead of taller, and certainly Sara was not going to be a party to that. If she encouraged Elizabeth's appetite, it was simply because she never denied her precious child any kind of instant gratification—and Elizabeth had always loved to eat. During a visit several years earlier to see Francis's parents in Kansas, the Taylors had made a swing down to New Orleans. "It was high time," Sara said, "to introduce the children to the gustatorial delights of Antoine's." Elizabeth was four. She sat in a high chair "dining on oysters Rockefeller and pompano baked in a paper bag." Rarely had Sara seen her daughter so happy.

Children often grow in spurts at Elizabeth's age, so maybe it's true that she really did grow those three inches that summer. More likely, Berman simply decided that clever costuming and lifts in Elizabeth's shoes were easier than teaching another girl to ride or put on truly English airs. There was also the fact that, after seeing a screen test of Elizabeth shot by director Fred Zinnemann, both he and Clarence Brown were convinced that "something quite magical happened between Elizabeth and the camera."

On a day in late September, Sara was summoned to Berman's office and informed that Elizabeth had gotten the part. She burst into tears. Elizabeth clasped her hands and in a loud voice—in-

spired no doubt by her mother's Christian Science—thanked God
for making it happen. "This is MGM," Berman informed the
young supplicant, "not Lourdes."

Hedda Hopper, alerted moments later by a jubilant Sara, was
one of the first to report the casting, but it was columnist Harold Heffernan who predicted that Elizabeth and her horse would
"rocket to stardom" together. Fred Stanley, in the *New York Times*,
echoed studio talking points by praising Elizabeth's equestrian
skills, which, he said, had landed her what MGM was calling "the
biggest kid part in years."

The star-making machine now kicked into high gear. Soon after being cast, Elizabeth was ordered to report to the studio photographer for publicity shots. Wearing a lacy dress, holding her
arms demurely, little Miss Taylor posed against a backdrop of flowers. Even in black and white, the glossy eight-by-ten photographs
expertly highlighted her most-discussed feature. An accompanying Metro press release informed editors that Elizabeth's eyes were
"the bluest of blue."

This was an era before most stars had personal press agents
or managers; the studio offered personalized yet factorylike service. Headed by Howard Strickling, an authoritarian taskmas-
ter, the MGM publicity department employed between sixty and
one hundred personnel in offices on both coasts and in satellites
throughout the country. There wasn't a lot of turnover; this was the
dream team. "Mr. Strickling didn't pay the highest salaries," said
publicist Emily Torchia, "but neither did he hire and fire. Many of
us were in the department for years." What Strickling did was instill a fierce loyalty in his employees toward the studio and its stars.
No one talked out of turn, ever. Even the stars were trained to respect one another's privacy. In interviews and photo spreads, they
were unfailingly positive about each other, not to mention the studio. "MGM publicists were like none other in promoting the studio brand," said publicist Alan Cahan.

The publicity office was located just off the lot on the corner of Washington Boulevard and Ince Way. Each publicist in-

side was assigned three or four stars and a handful of upcoming pictures. Some specialized in the big newspapers, others handled the smaller heartland papers. Still others took care of the national magazines like *Look* and *Life*. Everyone worked with the fan magazines, especially *Photoplay* and *Modern Screen*. The eight Los Angeles dailies received special attention, with one publicist making the rounds every day to deliver tips to the newsrooms. In Hollywood there was little distinction made between moving-picture news and reports from City Hall. While East Coast papers traditionally segregated stories about the movies in the entertainment or gossip sections, the Los Angeles papers often treated such items as front-page news.

The lifeblood of the publicity department was on the first floor, where amid piles of newspapers and constantly ringing telephones toiled the "planters"—industrious drones who spent their entire days typing up two- or three-line items on onionskin paper and sending them out via regular mail and teletype, hoping and praying that some editor somewhere would run them. Sitting down with Elizabeth and her mother, a phalanx of Metro planters scribbled into their reporters' notebooks as many tidbits about the girl as they could elicit. Thus commenced the construction of the public image of Elizabeth Taylor, a process that would roll on for the next twenty years, gathering more and more steam, or simply hot air.

"Young Elizabeth loves animals more than anything except her mother, father, and brother," one plant read. "She has three dogs, two cats, and a menagerie of rabbits." True enough: Elizabeth did have several pets, but surely the Metro planters recalled how phenomenally successful Twentieth Century-Fox had been when the studio based Shirley Temple's public image around her love of animals. With a template already in place on how to create child stars, MGM publicists used it. How excited they must have been to learn of Elizabeth's horse in England, presented to her when she was just five. And so we got the stories about Betty, the horse who could sometimes go "absolutely native," with only little Elizabeth able to calm her. How fortunate MGM was to have such a tale to promote *National Velvet*. In the script, of course, the young heroine does exactly the same thing.

Invisible to the public was the worldly little girl who occasionally shocked her classmates with a well-placed "hell" or "damn." As presented by the press, the young Elizabeth Taylor was as innocent as a fawn, though she could also be plucky and precocious. Indeed, when they weren't busy promoting her love of animals, the publicists were hyping Elizabeth's determination, which seemed at times almost otherworldly. Those three inches, true or not, were indelibly imprinted upon the Taylor myth. CHILD LITERALLY GROWS INTO ROLE headlined one item prepared by the publicity department and run verbatim in several newspapers, including the *Los Angeles Times*. In these accounts Elizabeth is depicted as "willing herself" into the part of Velvet Brown, with a belief in her destiny as strong as any saint's—an echo, again, of Sara's Christian Science. Fan magazine writer Herbert Howe picked up on this theme, writing that some around the lot claimed that Elizabeth could perform miracles. "The child puts a spell on birds and beasts and studio bigwigs," Howe wrote. "She waved the wand and shot up like Kansas corn three inches. Her doctor said it was not possible, but she said it was if you realized it was God's plan."

Or her mother's.

Dick Hanley's desk sat just past the door that led into the private suite of Louis B. Mayer, the omnipotent godhead of the studio. Only the most privileged ever made it past Hanley's desk. Few but the top stars and directors—and the money men from New York, of course—had ever seen the inside of Mayer's private sanctuary. But today's visitor was a little girl who'd just turned twelve years old—the latest protégé of the studio's starmakers, the newest addition to Mr. Mayer's family of beloved "daughters."

Dick was thirty-five years old, a native of Indianapolis, the son of an Irish immigrant railroad clerk. As the youngest child of four, he'd been pampered by his parents, who scrimped and saved in order to send him to college while his older brothers trudged off to jobs as tire salesmen and railroad operators. In his early twenties, Dick taught English at a private school, still living at home. But he hankered to get out of Indianapolis. Like so many young gay men, both then and now, Hanley harbored a deep wanderlust, a yen to discover a place where it might be possible to lead a more fulfilling, authentic life.

So he found Hollywood, arriving in the movie capital at a time when many other men, not so much younger than he, were marching off to war. But a deferment kept Hanley safely stateside. A friendship with Kate Corbaley, the studio's chief reader of scripts, led to an introduction to the formidable Ida Koverman, once campaign secretary to Herbert Hoover and now executive assistant to Louis B. Mayer. Koverman had a job in mind for Dick. Although her boss was notoriously uncomfortable around male homosexuals, Mayer's respect for Koverman overcame any misgivings that he might have had. He hired Hanley as his personal secretary.

For the next eleven years Dick served Mayer "devotedly [and] loyally," Elizabeth would say, "available twenty-four hours a day." Hanley would never forget the afternoon in late 1943 when the young starlet and her mother passed by his desk on their way into their meeting with the studio chief. Dick had brought a box of cinnamon buns into the office that day, and Elizabeth's nostrils suddenly flared at the aroma. Hanley noticed a gleam in the little girl's eye.

"Would you like one?" he asked.

Of course she would—but even as she stretched out her hand, Sara was urging her onward. It wouldn't do for Elizabeth to greet Mr. Mayer with sticky fingers.

It was a courtesy call, but still the stakes were high. Mayer needed to be thanked, flattered, and bowed down to for agreeing to cast Elizabeth in *National Velvet*. If he liked her well enough, and if the picture performed as well as they hoped, there was a long-term contract on the other side of all this. Nothing could have pleased Sara more.

But Elizabeth wasn't entirely sure. Entering Mayer's office, she was distinctly nervous. She knew that people on the lot called the Executive Building "the iron lung" because "the executives tell you just how to breathe." Even at twelve years old, she was aware that "stars were born and built and died more or less at the whim of L. B. Mayer." The round little man frightened her, and as she took a seat opposite his desk, she kept her eyes fixed on him. "He looked rather like a gross, thick penguin," she said. "He had huge glasses and a way of looking at you that made you feel completely squash-able. You felt his vitality, but you also felt his enormous arrogance, his ego, his overbearing, driving personality. To know him was to be terrified of him."

But that day Mr. Mayer couldn't have been more gracious. He recalled—or *said* that he recalled—an interview he'd had with mother and daughter several years earlier, before they'd signed with Universal. He lamented the fact that they hadn't become part of the MGM family back then. (Sara, in her telling of the story, would always insist that Mayer had wanted to hire Elizabeth at that time, but *she* had turned *him* down—a rather unlikely sce-nario.) Mayer enthused about his high hopes for *National Velvet*, and with a twinkle in his eye, assured them that he already had other projects in mind for Elizabeth.

When he wanted to be, Mayer could be very charming—and there was no question that Sara was dazzled. It wasn't long before the stars in her eyes were noticed by other people on the lot. Ava Gardner would always believe that Sara and Mayer had had an af-fair; Francis Taylor's brother was convinced that if the studio chief had ever snapped his fingers, Sara would have left her husband for him. It's not so far-fetched. Sara was used to relying on older benefactors like Victor Cazalet and Howard Young. And having only recently lost Cazalet in a plane crash, she may have been, even unconsciously, looking for someone to replace him, someone who could ensure her well-being in a way that her husband never could and who could play doting godfather to Elizabeth.

But Elizabeth never warmed to Mayer the way her mother did. She found the enforced adulation of the man utterly unnerving. His very public birthday parties, held on the enormous Stage Thirty, were particularly egregious. A year earlier, before she'd become a hot property, Elizabeth had stood on tiptoe near the back of the crowd to see "Big Daddy Mayer, the benevolent white father," as she called him, standing up on a dais and beaming as hundreds of his employees sang "Happy Birthday" to him. Afterward he gushed how he considered them all his children. At his side were his top stars, people like Robert Taylor, Van Johnson, Greer Garson, and five-year-old Margaret O'Brien, then MGM's most popular child actress. O'Brien was so successful that she could even opt out of the studio school, taking lessons from a tutor in the privacy of her dressing room.

Elizabeth had envied O'Brien at the time. But now she was knocking at the gates of stardom herself. As she and her mother stood to leave, Mayer leaned down and kissed her on the forehead. But finding far more favor with Elizabeth was Dick Hanley, who made sure to slip her a cinnamon bun on her way out.

On the set of *National Velvet,* Elizabeth was happier now that she was playacting and riding horses. Brown was solicitous of her, aware that Sara was always just out of camera range. But that didn't prevent him from removing the MISS TAYLOR sign from her dressing-room door, replacing it with the simpler ELIZABETH. The director wanted to make sure that stardom didn't go to his little star's head.

Brown was also insistent that Elizabeth cut her long, luxurious hair for the climactic scene in which she dons a jockey's cap and uniform, and triumphantly rides her horse to victory in the Grand National. Here Elizabeth balked. Playacting had just reached its limit. In tears, she rushed into the hairdressing department, lorded over by a strutting peacock by the name of Sydney Guilaroff, who took pity on her. For the next week, Guilaroff worked around the clock to weave thousands of individual strands of hair into a short wig and attached it to Elizabeth's jockey cap. According to Guilaroff, whose stories sometimes were more than a little fanciful, Clarence Brown was completely fooled, and Elizabeth threw her little arms around her hairdresser and cried, "Thank you, Sydney." Guilaroff would remain her confidante for the next two decades.

But her hair was not the only problem during the shoot. Brown and Pan Berman had at one point worried that Elizabeth would look too young; now they had the opposite concern. At twelve, Elizabeth was fast becoming a woman. Suddenly she was busting out all over. "Not an ounce of puberty on her," Anne Francis said, in awe. "She was full-blown by the time she was thirteen."

Publicist Jack Hirshberg, lunching with Walter Pidgeon and Hume Cronyn in the commissary one day, nearly spilled his chicken soup all over himself when Elizabeth walked past their table. "She was thirteen," Hirshberg said, "but, oh boy. You might say she was in the early spring of her physical development."

On the set of *National Velvet*, Hedda Hopper watched in wonder as the adolescent star cinched her belt, showing "her charms to perfection." Hopper wasn't the only one transfixed. Twenty-three-year-old Mickey Rooney was already making a beeline toward his young costar when Hedda lunged and grabbed him by the seat of his pants. "Lay a hand on her," she warned, "and you will have to answer to me."

Rooney laughed. "I believe you would beat me up."

"I sure would," the columnist replied.

As Elizabeth blossomed, studio execs became jittery. Her virginal image needed to be safeguarded at all costs. "The studio was concerned because she'd just go flouncing around the lot," said Anne Francis. "So they corralled her mother and said, 'You'd better be next to her at all times because we're afraid something might happen.'"

Of course, Sara had no intention of ever being too far from Elizabeth's side. For all her developing womanhood and occasionally salty language, Elizabeth remained childishly dependent on Sara for everything from how to dress to what to eat for lunch. She was still a dreamer, easily reduced to tears by sad songs and unhappy stories. Fellow child actress Darla Hood, longtime star of the Our Gang series, would regale Elizabeth with movie plots, real and imagined. When they didn't end happily, Elizabeth would always interrupt and insist, "Oh, don't end it that way. I want it to end *happily*."

In 1944 most movies *did* end happily, of course, especially those made by MGM. Elizabeth—coddled and protected by her mother—grew up believing that unhappiness need never touch her. And so her distress was very real when Clarence Brown replaced Mona Freeman with Angela Lansbury as Velvet's sister. When she encountered Freeman, aged seventeen, sitting outside the sound-stage in tears, Elizabeth began sobbing herself. "She never knew until that very moment that anyone could be replaced," said Margaret Kerry, who was on the lot at the time. "It frightened her."

Elizabeth Taylor's ambition, as formidable as it was, would never be coldhearted. Her tears for Mona Freeman demonstrate that. But the incident reveals more than just her compassion. From that moment on, Elizabeth understood that she needed to make herself irreplaceable.

Elizabeth had brought her chipmunk, Nibbles, to the Beverly Hills home of Hedda Hopper. Cupping the furry little creature in her hands, Elizabeth told the columnist to lean in for a better look. As she did so, the chipmunk leaped onto Hedda's arm and clawed its way up her flabby, mottled skin. Hedda screamed, she recalled, "like a banshee."

But nothing could make Hopper cross with Elizabeth Taylor at this point. "You couldn't have wished for a sweeter child," she said. There was no longer a need for Sara to pester the columnist. From the moment it was clear that *National Velvet* was going to be a gigantic hit, Hedda became a one-woman cheering squad for Elizabeth's career. She insisted that the young star drop the "Miss Hopper" business and start calling her "Aunt Hedda."

"I haven't yet seen *National Velvet*," Hopper wrote in October 1944, "but I'll lay a wager right now it will be voted Metro's best picture of the year." A month later Hedda told her readers, "Elizabeth gets a star rating and deserves it." She added that Elizabeth was "beating Shirley Temple in her love of animals." It was more of the studio's party line about Elizabeth's menagerie of pets, yet by simply writing the words "she is beating Shirley Temple," Hopper was giving a terrific boost to the new star's standing. If Elizabeth was beating all-time child-star champ Temple in *anything*, she was doing very well indeed.

By now "Aunt" Hedda was eagerly gobbling up credit for discovering Elizabeth Taylor. Just as *National Velvet* premiered, Hopper recapped the starlet's short career in a lengthy column, writing how she and Elizabeth's parents had put their "plan into action" and brought the girl to MGM's attention. Hedda's frequent annoyance at Sara's ambition apparently had been forgotten, at least for the moment.

Velvet opened to rave reviews in December 1944. Bosley Crowther in the *New York Times* proclaimed that Elizabeth's "face is alive with youthful spirit, her voice has the softness of sweet song and her whole manner in this picture is one of refreshing grace." The *New York Sun* deemed her "one of the screen's most lovable characters," and the *Post* declared her "as natural and excellent a little actress as you would ever hope to see."

Indeed, *National Velvet* stands the test of time, and so does Elizabeth. She proved to be a very different kind of child star: charming, never cloying. And she accomplishes the near-impossible task of consigning that inveterate scenery chewer, Mickey Rooney, to the background, despite his top billing. Filmed around Pebble Beach on the Monterey Peninsula, the Technicolor film is visually gorgeous, with the plunging cliffs and deep blue skies perfectly evoking the story's English setting. By the end of 1945, *Velvet* would place among the top ten most profitable pictures of the year.

Soon after the film's release, Metro announced *Hold High the Torch* for Elizabeth, in which she'd play the owner of a devoted collie named Bill. Immediately those indefatigable publicists launched an aggressive campaign to keep their young star and her four-legged friends in front of the public. A big to-do was made over Louis B. Mayer's presenting Elizabeth with King Charles, the black stallion she'd ridden in *Velvet*, but the headlines didn't stop there. When columnist Sheilah Graham arrived on the lot to interview the young star, she found her walking her chipmunk on a red wool leash. Like Hedda Hopper, Graham reported that Nibbles scrambled up her arm. "Now if you can love a child after her chipmunk frightens the daylights out of you, that child's got something," Graham told her readers. "Elizabeth sure has."

When filming was delayed on *Hold High the Torch*, it became imperative that Elizabeth's name and face be kept circulating in the press. Adorable shots of the thirteen-year-old actress posing with two puppies hanging in stockings were released to newspapers in September 1945. Then someone in the publicity department came up with the brilliant idea to publish a book written by Elizabeth—a book that would confirm everything the public believed about its little heroine—and release it to coincide with *Hold High the Torch*. And so, in the spring of 1946, came *Nibbles and Me*, in which Elizabeth's pluckiness, honesty, compassion, and all-American girlishness were on full display. The book, an early example of a merchandising tie-in, was the perfect complement to her new film—which had been retitled *Courage of Lassie*, capitalizing on MGM's earlier franchise although the collie is still called "Bill" in the film.

The genius of *Nibbles and Me* was its studied appearance of happenstance. Press releases informed us that Elizabeth had written an essay for school, and Miss McDonald had thought it so good that she showed it to the studio higher-ups. They, in turn, were so impressed that they showed it to the people over at the publishing house of Duell, Sloan & Pearce, who suddenly had a brainstorm on the spot that the little essay might make a fine book. Of course that was the way the studio described the book's genesis. Certainly the idea couldn't have come from that building full of publicists and planters adjacent to the MGM lot.

"That's what was so great about the studios," said Dick Clayton, the agent who helped discover and promote James Dean and

Tab Hunter. "They could make you believe anything. [*Nibbles and Me*] was a great example of public relations."

Promoting both book and film, Elizabeth escorted Nibbles to "interviews" with Maxine Arnold of *Photoplay* (which ran an excerpt) and Sara Salzer of *Screen Guide*. Hedda Hopper, of course, gave the story lots of ink, featuring the little creature and its mistress several times in her column.

This offered a far more useful education than anything Elizabeth was learning in class. Watching her mother negotiate her contracts, she learned the art of the deal. For *Nibbles*, she received a $1,000 advance and a share of the royalties, all spelled out in an addendum to her contract dated October 31, 1945, signed and initialed by both Elizabeth and Sara. For her performance in *Velvet*, there also had been an enormous increase in salary (from $100 a week to $750 a week) plus a $15,000 bonus. And in a coup de grâce, Sara had engineered above-the-title billing for Elizabeth in *Courage of Lassie*. It had taken Judy Garland five years of small parts and low-paying contracts to make it to the top; Elizabeth—and Sara—had accomplished the task in less than half that time.

Elizabeth was also now a star in school, which meant greater leverage. Strolling into the Little Red Schoolhouse, she took a seat in one of the large stuffed chairs off to the side. Miss McDonald eyed her and finally asked if she'd like to come join them at her desk so that the lessons might begin. "Oh, I'm quite comfortable here," replied the star of two of the studio's biggest pictures. "But thanks for asking."

Part of her understood, however, that her world was make-believe, that other girls her age did not live as she did. To accommodate the orthodontic braces Velvet wears in the film, the studio had pulled two of Elizabeth's baby teeth and installed temporary ones, just so that the braces would fit properly—and Velvet's smile would look the way the director wanted it to in the finished film. One publicist thought the mole on her cheek should be removed; another wanted to lighten her hair. Elizabeth was continually fretted over, pulled one way then another, and spoken of as a commodity for this or that film. Although the perks of stardom thrilled her, Elizabeth understood even then that by signing a long-term contract, she had become the studio's "chattel." With Elizabeth's father and brother fading into the background, MGM—and its executives and publicists and hairdressers and makeup artists and directors and contract players—became her family.

The trade-off was stardom. In August 1945, during a train layover in Chicago, Elizabeth and Sara learned that the Japanese had surrendered and World War II was over. Amid the hullabaloo at the station, with hats flying and soldiers kissing girls, Elizabeth didn't escape notice. "We were so surprised to find in all the excitement that crowds of people recognized me as Velvet and wanted my autograph," Elizabeth said. "It made me feel very happy." In the midst of a national celebration, it was the reality of her own stardom that had the biggest effect on Elizabeth.

Yet not very long after this, she and her mother were cornered by a crowd in Paris filled with people who poked at Elizabeth as if she were, in Sara's words, "a china doll." Mother watched daughter with mounting concern. "Elizabeth stood there, at bay, cornered, miserable." After they got away from the mob, the young star wondered, "[Do] people who come close to you like that have the same feelings you have?" And therein lay the crux of Elizabeth's life. Stardom was all she knew, with both its thrills and its trials. What else might exist out there—what ordinary people were like and how they felt—she could only wonder about.

There's a scene in *National Velvet* where Velvet muses: "I want it all quick. I don't want God to stop and think I'm getting more than my share." In real life, no matter how many lingering questions she might have had, Elizabeth Taylor was about to get Velvet's wish.

Three

The Most Exciting Girl

February 1949–August 1951

IN HIS OFFICE on the Paramount lot, George Stevens was restless, puffing on his cigar, thumbing through the latest issue of *Life* magazine, lost in his reveries. Since returning from the war, where he'd helped liberate Dachau, the director had been a different man, no longer the brash, gregarious fellow who'd made *Alice Adams, Swing Time, Gunga Din,* and *The More the Merrier.* Colleagues now found him silent and taciturn, unable to summon any passion for the kind of lighthearted films he'd once made. "The edge had gone off the humor," said Frank Capra. "He had seen too much . . . a nightmare of the stupidity of man."

In his only film since returning from the war, Stevens had transformed *I Remember Mama* from what might have been merely a contemplative longing for a simpler time into something more truthful, a work of art suggesting that nostalgia obscured the difficult realities of the past. The blood-soaked fields of Europe had left Stevens with a cynicism out of sync with his prewar films. Yet his loss of innocence was tempered by a lingering hope that somewhere, somehow, such things as love and honor might still survive.

And so Stevens found himself drawn to Theodore Dreiser's novel *An American Tragedy,* the story of a young man who commits murder out of love for a beautiful, idealized girl. "The kind of girl," Stevens told Paramount execs, "that a young man could see at first glance and find his eyes so fixed upon that his attention will not turn. Her beauty and poise must give the impression that she is unattainable."

Sitting at his desk, turning the pages of the February 21, 1949, issue of *Life*, Stevens paused when he saw a full-page color photograph of a young woman from whom he could not turn away. The magnetic eyes of the seventeen-year-old Elizabeth Taylor caught and held his attention. This was the girl he wanted for the film. No one else would do, Stevens was convinced.

"It might appear," he dictated to his secretary in a memorandum addressed to Paramount talent chief William Meiklejohn, "that Sondra, the girl in the story, has only the responsibility that any bright, interesting, and attractive girl would have in a love story, but in this case it is more—it is much more. It is the fundamental part of the machinery that goes to make this whole story work." In other words, Sondra must be so compelling that audiences understand (and remain sympathetic toward) the boy who commits murder to have her. "The only one of whom I am aware who could create this illusion," Stevens argued forcefully, "is Elizabeth Taylor."

Though Stevens was stating the obvious, no one gave in immediately. Elizabeth Taylor was, after all, the property of another studio. Stevens wasn't surprised by the resistance; nothing about this project had been easy. *An American Tragedy* had been filmed before in 1931, not very successfully, and the studio worried that the material was simply too downbeat for a public increasingly distracted by the escapist medium of television. The film industry was suffering from its own form of American tragedy. Average weekly movie attendance was in sharp decline; Hollywood would lose a full one-third of its wartime audience within a year. Even worse, with the court-ordered sale of the studios' lucrative theater chains, profits were in free fall. Between 1949 and 1950 Paramount's bottom line would drop from $20.8 million to $6.6 million.

An American Tragedy would be a tough sell to the suits. But Paramount was never MGM, where the front office routinely issued the last word on creative decisions. Since the days of the smart, sexy films of Ernst Lubitsch and Josef von Sternberg (who, in fact, had directed the first movie version of Dreiser's novel), Paramount had been Hollywood's studio of sophistication, a place where filmmakers took chances, where the Marx Brothers tweaked convention and Billy Wilder broke the rules with *Double Indemnity* and *The Lost Weekend*. Metro might have the gloss, but Paramount had its own special reputation.

Still, Stevens knew that he'd have to stay committed. Every few days the broad-shouldered, deep-voiced director (Katharine Hepburn called Stevens a "very male member of society") summoned his secretary to dictate another letter to the Paramount brass. When he was told that the studio wanted more comedies—not a film where the hero ends up on death row—Stevens actually prepared two lawsuits against his employers for "frivolously" withholding their approval. This was not a man who took no for an answer.

Eventually the studio came around, encouraged by the enthusiasm being shown for the film by Montgomery Clift, who was riding a wave of acclaim for his performance in *The Heiress*. Dropping out of Wilder's *Sunset Boulevard*, Clift signed with Stevens just days later (on March 23) for *An American Tragedy*. This was not only a serious, important picture, but now it was actually going to get made. But Stevens kept reminding all concerned that without the right Sondra, the weight of the film would be foisted solely onto the shoulders of its male star—a burden that might prove too much even for Clift's considerable strengths. So Stevens insisted they do everything possible to get MGM to loan them Elizabeth Taylor.

Such a fuss over a girl whose meatiest bit of acting so far had been as Amy in *Little Women*, then in current release. To Hollywood, Taylor was a pretty girl who wore pretty dresses and photographed well in color. Her films over the last few years had been mostly frothy confections churned out by Metro's expert moviemaking machine. But Stevens saw something unique in Taylor's loveliness. "She was this extraordinary child," he told reporter Ruth Waterbury years later. "She was a child of great beauty and sweet personality." He had decided to scrap Dreiser's title and call the film *The Prize*, because "a girl in a young man's eye, in our society, can be the prize. And Liz, at that time, was the capital prize. If she played this part, and would be in this picture . . . she would be staggering as far as [the boy's] equilibrium is concerned."

By June, however, there was still no definitive word on Elizabeth's availability. Stevens was getting anxious. What he didn't know was that Metro had turned down the request after mistakenly thinking that Stevens wanted Elizabeth for the less-glamorous part that eventually went to Shelley Winters. But by the end of the month, with everything cleared up and a price of $35,000 agreed upon, Stevens had his Sondra. Ten miles northeast of her home studio in Culver City, the director began laying the groundwork for the film that would change Elizabeth's life.

Elizabeth, meanwhile, had no inkling of what Stevens was up to, or what it all might mean for her. Being fitted for costumes as a last-minute replacement for June Allyson in the gimmicky comedy *The Big Hangover*, all she knew was that she'd be loaned to Paramount sometime later that year to star opposite the exciting new actor Monty Clift. Posing and preening in front of a full-length mirror and holding her arms out wide so that costume designer Helen Rose could measure from her shoulders to her waist, Elizabeth likely didn't give the Stevens project any more thought than that.

After all, there were plenty of activities to keep a young starlet busy. In the last twenty-two months there had been five gala premieres of pictures costarring Elizabeth Taylor, each one taking her another step farther along the road to adult stardom. Metro had invested too much in Elizabeth to let her go the way of most child stars. Already Deanna Durbin was a fading memory, and even Margaret O'Brien, once the studio's surefire hitmaker, had entered an awkward adolescence that would soon render her obsolete. But Elizabeth, graced with a more mature beauty, was being carefully groomed into a sultry leading lady. After playing sweet and innocent in *Cynthia* and *Life with Father* (both 1947), she was allowed to vamp it up in *A Date with Judy* (1948), playing best friend to star Jane Powell. "The big surprise," wrote Otis L. Guernsey, Jr., in the *New York Herald Tribune*, "is Elizabeth Taylor as the petulant, dark-eyed banker's daughter. The erstwhile star of *National Velvet* and other films has been touched by Metro's magic wand and turned into a real, 14-carat, 100-proof siren with a whole new career opening in front of her. Hedy Lamarr had better watch out." In rapid succession came Elizabeth's sophisticated turn in *Julia Misbehaves* (1948), where she steamed up the screen kissing Peter Lawford (she was fifteen, he was twenty-four), and finally her spirited interpretation of the conceited Amy in *Little Women*.

But it would take more than movie roles to turn Elizabeth Taylor into an adult star. "You have bosoms!" exclaimed the renowned Philippe Halsman, the photographer for the *Life* magazine shoot. "Stick them out!" So she did—and all around the world men fell like dominoes. Howard Hughes wanted to date her. This new, more mature Elizabeth was presented to the public by none other than her mother in an article for *Photoplay*, a gig surely arranged by Metro publicists. "No longer do her worries center upon her pets," Sara wrote. "Now . . . there are other things that interest her—things like clothes and cars and boys. For, as Elizabeth says herself, 'You can't love just animals all your life.'"

So it was good-bye, Nibbles, hello, Robert Taylor—Elizabeth's first bona fide grown-up leading man. (Sara even wrote a poignant death scene for Nibbles a few years later in her *Ladies' Home Journal* article, providing an artful segue from one chapter of Elizabeth's life to another.) The pairing with Robert Taylor came in a melodrama called *Conspirator*, filmed in England the previous autumn by Victor Saville. With the picture in the cutting room, the publicity department was whipping up interest by leaking stories that the young star had been too distracted to return to her lessons after spending the afternoon kissing Robert Taylor. Envious housewives across America swooned on cue. Suddenly Elizabeth was wearing the latest designs of Parisian couturiers like Pierre Balmain and Christian Dior. "I learned how to look sultry and pose provocatively," she said. "I developed sex appeal, even though I knew that, somewhere inside, the child had still not completely grown up."

Elizabeth was awestruck at what was happening to her. "Truly a most remarkable machine," she said of the studio that made her, then made her over. "L. B. Mayer and MGM created stars out of tinsel, cellophane and newspapers. Their tremendous publicity staff built the background, built the personality, built the character. Makeup and wardrobe built the façade, and the story department found something just right for that personality."

The great studios were run like the successful corporations that they were, with various departments reporting along a chain of command that led to the chief executive. "Big Daddy Mayer" rarely visited sets or watched a shoot, but he always had the final word. At regular meetings in his private suite, which he liked to call "the Lion's Den," he was kept apprised of all production decisions by his top lieutenants: Eddie Mannix, Lawrence Weingarten, Hunt Stromberg, Benny Thau, among others. Wags dubbed them "the college of cardinals." These execs shared the top floor of the Executive Building with Mayer, and it was they who fanned out across the lot to lord over directors and stars. Benny Thau was the most influential man in Elizabeth's life, more so even than her own father—for it was Thau who was in charge of her contracts, who eased her way and got her what she wanted on every film she made.

Hurrying across the lot from Wardrobe, Elizabeth's next appointment was with Hair and Makeup. If she was to play a real grown-up woman in *The Big Hangover*—one even worldlier than her role in *Conspirator*—then she needed to look the part. Heading into the salon, Elizabeth encountered a cross section of Metro's talent. "When you walked into the hairdressing department," said Elinor Donahue, "you'd see Katharine Hepburn and Ava Gardner and Lucille Ball and Lana Turner—whoever was working on the lot that day—all in a row, getting their hair done." Sydney Guilaroff, repeating the magic he'd worked on *National Velvet*, sat the young star down in an available chair and spun her around a few times. After a few minutes of experimenting, he came up with a short, sophisticated do that made her look older—but not too old.

Next she was hustled over to Makeup, where the sweet fragrances of Max Factor were always "drifting out through the walls," as actress Ann Rutherford remembered. Department chief Jack Dawn positioned Elizabeth in front of his lighted mirror and tied a cotton cloth around her shoulders. With a few deft strokes of lipstick, eye shadow, and rouge, he turned the teenager into a glamorous movie star, making sure to darken and emphasize the mole on her cheek—the same one some myopic idiot had once wanted to remove. Dawn knew the mole gave Elizabeth a certain exotic allure.

Transforming ordinary folks into stars was taken very seriously in Hair and Makeup. The temperamental Dawn insisted that his staff be treated as artists instead of technicians, and their wondrous results did, in fact, earn them such a distinction. Elizabeth mostly just sat back and let them do their work—but she wasn't complaisant. When they wanted to change the arch of her eyebrows, she said no. When they suggested that she paint her mouth "way over," she declined again. Given the beauty of the face in the mirror, there wasn't much argument. Barbara Stanwyck, on the lot to make *East Side, West Side,* stopped by one morning and saw Elizabeth being made up in the chair. "No woman," she quipped, "has the right to be that beautiful at five A.M. with her hair up."

Selling a new star to the public was never easy, but it wasn't nearly as difficult as selling a star who'd been around since childhood and whose brand was now being recalibrated. The attempt hadn't worked with Shirley Temple at Fox. Despite several high-profile films, the public had never really taken to Temple as a teenage star. Metro understood, as Fox did not, that the most important part of a transformation had to occur in public. And so, after being dolled up at the studio, Elizabeth's crucial next assignment was to go out on the town—with a full entourage of publicists, press agents, photographers, and reporters in tow. It was time for her audience to see Elizabeth *dating.*

For a girl who never made a change to her hairdo without input from the studio, whose education, social outings, vacations, and birthday parties had always been coordinated and hyped by publicists, it seemed natural that dating, too, would fall under the auspices of her employers. With her mother or some press agent almost always at her side, Elizabeth had no concept of how to meet boys, or talk to them, or pick one out for herself. It probably felt quite natural when she had been called into the publicity department the previous summer and informed that a perfect date had been found for her.

Someone, maybe Howard Strickling himself, had noticed a small story on the sports pages concerning Lieutenant Glenn Davis, a three-time All-America halfback from West Point, who would be coming to Los Angeles to play one game with the Rams in their exhibition battle against the Washington Redskins. Linking Elizabeth with a sports and military hero was a press agent's dream. It mattered little that Glenn was twenty-three and Elizabeth just sixteen at the time. It was romantic in the desired idealized fashion and could proceed rather rapidly to a tidy conclusion: Davis was set to begin a three-year stint with the infantry in Korea that autumn.

Everyone agreed to the ruse. Hedda Hopper gushed via typewriter that the meeting between the two was "spontaneous combustion." While she'd admit later that "the romance was largely a studio directive," Hedda at the time made much of Glenn's sending Elizabeth a tiny gold football that she wore on a chain. "It was so childish," Elizabeth said. "I remember reading the papers at the time and I thought, 'My God, they think it's a big hot romance!'" But the stories that appeared in the summer of 1948 were so successful that the studio decided to further parlay Elizabeth's romantic interests. And the press went along, eager to play their part.

The craftsmanship of these escapades is revealed in the files of Louella Parsons, who preserved the script of a live, supposedly authentic radio interview that she conducted with Elizabeth around this time. On the air, the young star told the columnist that she'd "talk about anything," so Parsons asked her about her first on-screen kiss in *Cynthia*. "Why," said Elizabeth, "I tell you if a boy kissed me like that in real life, I-I-I . . ." It all sounded so off-the-cuff, but the script reveals that "real life" had been penciled in to replace the original phrase "private life" and the stammer "I-I-I" had been written in over the original line "I think I'd slap him." (Had that seemed too shrill?) The whole "interview" was, in fact, a little radio play written ahead of time by Louella's producers and vetted by Metro's publicists. Before she went on the air, Elizabeth was handed a script, much as she would have been on the set of a film. She had little or no say in it. As such, it's hard not to hear studio talking points when she mouths lines like "I was going steady . . . Gee, it was awful. A girl misses so many dates that way."

The next suitor was found not by Howard Strickling but by Howard Young, Elizabeth's granduncle—although the young man certainly had to pass muster with the studio. William Pawley, Jr. was the son of the American ambassador to Brazil, heir to his wealthy family's aviation business. This time Elizabeth was actually somewhat smitten, much more so than she'd been with the stage-managed Davis. It didn't matter that everything she and Pawley did was choreographed and sold to the public. They had a date at the Ice Capades in April 1949 with a gang of photographers in tow. Hedda Hopper said the young couple "didn't need skates . . . they were floating."

Elizabeth Taylor, Metro's romantic dreamgirl, was a hot sell. "The luscious, long-lashed lass of love," one studio press release described her. Such purple prose soon turned literal: The Elizabethan orbs—Hedda Hopper had called them "deep-set pools of blue" just a year before—suddenly became "violet" in the spring of 1949. That particular shade was a buzzword in beauty columns at the time; violet eye shadow and lipstick were said to make women more alluring. In Ellen Gatti's popular serial then running in the *Los Angeles Times*, fictional girl-about-town Lily Thorndyke was known for her "famous violet eyes." Did some studio press agent get an inspiration from reading that? Not only was Elizabeth ascribed the color, but other new stars like Paula Morgan were as well.

But what did hyperbole matter to the young Miss Taylor? It was all a romantic lark. From all accounts, the inexperienced teenager was enjoying the romantic attentions of her new suitor. By the early summer, around the time that the loan-out to Stevens and Paramount was decided and preparations began for *The Big Hangover,* Elizabeth was anticipating flying to Florida to see her Bill, her first real "crush"—despite the fact that, at twenty-eight, he was eleven years older than she was. The studio, although happy to promote the pair, considered Pawley merely another prop for her public image. When the time came, they expected the serviceable young man to obediently fade away. Florida, ruled the studio, was an unnecessary expense. "They weren't counting on the young lady herself," said Dick Clayton, who saw behind the studio's façade. "They didn't know then that this creation of theirs was actually going to have a mind of her own."

Elizabeth sat in the Lion's Den, the anger boiling up inside of her. Mr. Mayer had launched into a tirade. What had set him off wasn't clear—but he was shouting and swearing at Sara, who had requested this private meeting. His curses bounced off the white leather walls in that cavernous office (Samuel Goldwyn once quipped that an automobile was required to reach Mayer's desk from his office door).

It wasn't as if Elizabeth had never heard such salty language. Some of those very same words had tumbled out of her own pretty little mouth on occasion. But Mayer's ire only intensified her distrust of her lord and master. She became increasingly repulsed by the studio chief "foaming at the mouth," as she described him.

At last she could take it no more. "Don't you dare speak to my mother like that!" Elizabeth shouted, standing up and leaning in over Mayer's high-gloss, custom-designed wraparound desk. "You and your studio can both go to hell!" With a dramatic flair, she spun on her heel and ran from the office straight into the arms of Dick Hanley, whose shoulder she cried on not for the last time.

Although Benny Thau insisted that she apologize to Mayer, Elizabeth refused. For the rest of her life, she would take pride in telling people how she never again stepped foot inside Mayer's office. Maybe it wasn't only her choice; surely Mayer didn't relish a sequel to such a scene. But neither did he penalize his fast-rising investment, whose pictures had all made money. No doubt Sara, always more willing to compromise than Elizabeth, made all the necessary apologies as her daughter sobbed in Hanley's arms.

The contretemps with Mayer had occurred some three years before Elizabeth's romance with Bill Pawley, so perhaps studio officials should have been a bit more prepared when the young star insisted that she be allowed to fly to Miami to spend time at the Pawley family's beach house. After all, it had been obvious for some time that Elizabeth Taylor wasn't as malleable as most. Unquestionably cooperative during costume fittings, photo shoots, and makeup sessions, she possessed an independent streak, too—one that allowed her to sidestep the ordeal of pills and pressure that Judy Garland endured within the studio system. Neither would Sara, whatever her ambition, have permitted such treatment of her daughter.

Even as a teenager, Elizabeth had learned a great deal about self-preservation. Years later when she was making a film called *Divorce His, Divorce Hers,* she was surprised when the little girl playing her daughter left the set early. The director, Waris Hussein, explained that the girl was only allowed to work so many hours because she was a child. "We didn't have that at MGM," Elizabeth said incredulously. "You had to learn to survive on your own. I managed to do it, but Judy never did."

Tom Mankiewicz, a friend of both actresses, thought that the difference between Elizabeth and Judy "was one of temperament." Elizabeth came into the business "already strong," he said, while "Judy was emotional, needing affirmation. She sang these songs and you could hear the need and the doubt in her voice. Elizabeth survived the demands of the studio because she was confident that she could get what she wanted on her own."

By her early teens, Elizabeth had developed a crucial, clear-eyed perspective. "I began to see myself as two separate people," she said. "Elizabeth Taylor the person and Elizabeth Taylor the commodity. I saw the difference between my image and my real self"—an ability sorely lacking in many (if not most) Hollywood stars. "Before I reached my teens I resolved to separate my feelings of self-worth from the public image of Elizabeth Taylor. It was a lesson I never forgot." It also allowed her to do the things necessary to sell the commodity to the public without getting lost in the illusion.

That's not to say her journey through the studio system was a cakewalk. "A little red schoolhouse across from Stage 20, to me, is an extraordinary kind of confinement for youthful exuberance," George Stevens would say. Indeed, Elizabeth's highly regimented days often left her anxious and fretful. "I would get up early [and] go out on the polo field," she said. "To get some of my steam off . . . I would take forty jumps before I would go into work." Many times over the years she would lament never having had a real childhood—"no football games to go to, no proms to attend, no growing-up things."

There were compensations, of course. Stepping out onto the lot one crisp February morning, Elinor Donahue was awed by the sight of Elizabeth's birthday present from Mr. Mayer: a pale blue Cadillac. "Everyone was talking about it," Donahue said. "'Did you see the car they're giving to Elizabeth Taylor?' We all raced onto the lot, and there was the car with a big red bow wrapped around it. Maybe there wasn't a bow, but that's how I remember it, because it was such a big production in giving it to her." Jane Powell's mother was "huffy" about the gift, Donahue recalled, because Jane had wanted a car, too; but Mrs. Powell had felt girls so young shouldn't be indulged with cars. Mrs. Taylor, on the other hand, "was very agreeable about Elizabeth getting one," Donahue said. Miss Taylor was given a special license to drive the Cadillac so that she didn't have to troop downtown to pass a test with the City of Los Angeles.

But even taking a driving test is part of one's coming of age. "Elizabeth felt a part of her childhood had been taken from her," said Mark Miller, secretary to Rock Hudson and a fond acquaintance of Taylor's in the 1950s. "She was shrewd enough to know she'd missed out in some important ways." Anne Francis said that a sense of detachment from the real world was common on the MGM lot: "We were aware of living a very different reality from the rest of the world, and that was sometimes hard to balance." Elinor Donahue, emotional about her experience even sixty years later, said it was both "unreal and wonderful." She said that they all "lived in a fairy tale, but fairy tales come to an end."

Yet a Cadillac would not have offered much consolation to Elizabeth on the day in 1946 when her father moved out of the house and into the Beverly Hills Hotel, taking seventeen-year-old Howard with him. Mother and daughter were on their own, which they virtually had been for several years, with the Taylor men and the Taylor women living separate lives within the same house. Extramarital affairs were whispered about on both sides. Years later Elizabeth would describe the moment when her "idyllic, happy little family"—the one profiled in *Good Housekeeping* and *Ladies' Home Journal*—"fell apart." Francis "erupted," she said, as Sara increasingly "lived her life vicariously" through their daughter. He also resented Elizabeth making more money than he did.

In some ways, when her soft-spoken father moved out, Elizabeth felt "no special loss." She hadn't been close to him for years. Benny Thau remained her surrogate father, she admitted, and it was to Thau she went "for help and advice." But her parents' separation had an impact on her nonetheless. "It didn't show up at the time," one friend told a reporter. "But . . . [the rupture in her parents' marriage] played a part in maturing her."

What the breakup demonstrated was the toll that movie stardom took on personal lives. Francis Taylor's brother John candidly observed that Elizabeth's career was a "point of contention" that aggravated the "basic incompatibility" of her parents. Indeed, Elizabeth had watched for the past six years as the bond between Francis and Sara steadily disintegrated. Never passionate, they had once been at least companionable, with Sara still calling her husband "Daddy." But as his wife became more single-minded in her devotion to Elizabeth's career, Francis built up resentments. According to John Taylor, there had been more than just one separation between husband and wife.

Metro had a hand in reconciling the Taylors just at the moment their daughter was venturing into the dating pool herself. "Elizabeth learned early," said Dick Clayton, "that image was the most important thing, that love and all of that . . . had to be juggled [along with career and stardom]. How could you grow up in Hollywood and not learn that?"

It was to keep up appearances that the studio finally agreed to allow Elizabeth to head to Florida to see her Bill. But now they had a new problem: how to make it seem as if she hadn't jilted poor Glenn Davis, who was off serving his country in Korea. Fan-magazine readers had bought into the Davis story with a vicarious passion, and now letters to the editor demanded to know "if Liz had penned a 'Dear John' letter to Glenn."

Hedda Hopper, happy as ever to help, went to bat for Pawley, assuring her readers that he, too, was a war hero, having been a pilot during the war. The columnist spun romantic tales of the heartsick Pawley yearning to fly a plane to be near his beloved. Eventually, since the basic narrative was the same, the fan magazines simply exchanged Davis for Pawley and seemed content with that—especially because they got a much more satisfying payoff this time. On June 6, 1949, Hedda broke the story of the happy couple's engagement. The news was personally phoned in to the columnist by Elizabeth herself. Making it official, Sara sent an engagement notice to the *New York Times*. Significantly, the engagement was announced by only the star's mother. Had Francis declined to get involved because he saw the whole thing for what it was?

Of course, none of this could have happened without MGM's

approval. Elizabeth might buck her handlers from time to time, but an actual engagement would need to be officially sanctioned. Apparently they'd decided to milk the Pawley story for a little more publicity, consenting to an engagement party. Sara, in her official spin, would say that Elizabeth had begged her "to announce the engagement so she could wear her lovely diamond ring in public." She'd claim that she tried to do so quietly, "but when you are in the limelight it is impossible to do anything quietly. You are suddenly surrounded by cameras and publicity." Cameras and publicity, of course, were what everyone, including the studio, wanted—and an announcement in the *New York Times* and a phone call to Hedda Hopper hardly qualifies as doing it "quietly."

Photos of the happy couple holding a plate of hors d'oeuvres were distributed to the press. Swept up by the romance of it all, Elizabeth seems to have genuinely wanted to marry Pawley, even if the studio was already trying to find a way to untangle the knot. An engagement party was one thing; an actual wedding was another. Every time Elizabeth mentioned a date, Metro threw up roadblocks. She had to finish *The Big Hangover* first, they insisted, and then the loan-out to George Stevens and Paramount loomed, and after that she was scheduled to start immediately on a picture called *Father of the Bride*. They might let her *play* a girl getting married, but that was as far as Metro was willing to go.

The bloom was off the rose in a matter of weeks anyway. "Elizabeth saw the pattern of her future life with Bill unfolding," Sara said. "The longer we stayed [in Miami], the more homesick she became for California, the studio, her work, the old life she knew and loved."

Sara was just as homesick, no doubt. That "old life" promised considerably more yield than had yet paid off. The Pawleys might be rich, but the privileges of a Miami socialite were nothing compared to what awaited a top-ranked MGM star. Elizabeth's bosses weren't about to let her break her contract either. Like the rest of the studios, Metro was hurting financially, posting a $6 million decline in profits between 1947 and 1948. The new head of production,

Dore Schary, had gambled on an ambitious schedule of sixty-seven pictures that year, compared to just twenty-four the year previous. When profits began ticking upward (by the end of 1949 MGM's income had recovered by more than 50 percent), Schary was hailed as a visionary who rivaled Mayer. Key to Schary's plan to climb out of the red were pictures starring surefire moneymakers like Elizabeth. No way was the studio's teenage princess going to be allowed to retire to Miami, not after so much had been invested in her. Metro wanted its dividends.

No one was all that surprised, therefore, when Pawley announced in September that the engagement was off. No one, that is, but the public—which had now been deprived of a happy ending twice. The fan magazines, with their three-month lead time, were left embarrassed: *Photoplay* didn't have time to stop the presses on their October issue, which featured Elizabeth gushing with love for Pawley.

The press retaliated with a series of unfavorable articles about the star. Columnists started calling her fickle. "She leaves a trail of broken hearts," one reporter chided. "Our Little Liz is turning into a real man-eater." The Metro publicists hadn't anticipated a hostile backlash. Tone deaf, they just kept throwing more boyfriends into the mix. They sent Elizabeth off to the Mocambo with Vic Damone, only to watch in dismay as the gambit misfired. In London the *Sunday Pictorial* called for "a series of resounding smacks behind the bustle of her latest Paris creation," an entreaty that sent Hedda Hopper charging to the rescue. "Besides taking billions of our [war-relief] money," Hedda huffed, "the English now want the pleasure of spanking one of our prettiest screen actresses . . . What Elizabeth does is none of their business. I suppose the British would rather have her marry and divorce twice."

Back at the studio, Elizabeth was hurt by this negative turn in her press. "If I were the kind of person they write me up to be, I'd hate myself," she said. But she had now participated quite willingly in two largely counterfeit romances. Even Pawley, whom she had imagined herself marrying, was just another pawn in the end. "We went well together under the palm trees," she'd say. "We had nothing in common in our lives."

Once again experience had demonstrated that the personal would always be public for her. "Elizabeth isn't just any little girl, she's a star," Hedda Hopper explained sternly to the Taylor family at one point. And being a star meant doing some things and forfeiting others all in the line of "duty." Yet as much as Elizabeth understood this, as much as she accepted the compromises and realities that came with her ambition, she remained a bit wistful about it all. A part of her really did want the "happily ever after" of her films—finding a devoted husband in *Little Women,* for example, or fading out with Van Johnson in the last reel of *The Big Hangover.* In real life, however, such rewards were rare for movie stars; and this was a bitter pill to swallow for a sensitive teenager. While her outward appearance was telling the world that she was an adult, she was still, in fact, "an emotional child inside a woman's body"—her own observation. Elizabeth Taylor was no innocent at seventeen. She understood everything that was happening to her. But as often as her life thrilled her, it could make her a little bit sad, too.

Such was her frame of mind when she set out for Lake Tahoe less than two weeks after the Pawley breakup to start work on the Stevens film, now called *A Place in the Sun.*

It was sunny but cold on Sunday, October 2, 1949, the day George Stevens's assistant drove out to Truckee, California, to meet the train that was bringing Elizabeth Taylor from Hollywood. A century earlier in these parts, members of the snowbound Donner party had been reduced to cannibalism to survive the Sierra Nevada winter. Elizabeth Taylor, looking out from the windows of her train, had never gone on location like this before.

Belching smoke, the train clattered to a stop along the old tracks. Done up in Dior, the teenaged star stepped out onto the platform followed by her mother and a woman the assistant called a "welfare worker." Because Elizabeth was only seventeen, the state had sent along a watchdog to make sure that she wasn't overworked or mistreated. To be safe, Stevens ordered his crew not to swear in front of their young actress—a directive quickly forgotten once Elizabeth's own spicy vocabulary livened up the set.

A car took them the twenty-two miles to Chambers Lodge, an old weather-beaten hunting and fishing resort. All along the way they skirted the giant Lake Tahoe, its shimmering azure surface stretching eastward for almost as far as the eye could see. For Dreiser's archetypal story of hope and tragedy—which hinges on what happens one day on a lake—no makeshift watering hole on the Paramount backlot would do. Instead, George Stevens chose this "noble sheet of blue water walled by snowclad peaks," as Mark Twain described Tahoe, "surely the fairest picture the whole earth affords." And so the whole company made the trek up to Tahoe, their heads dizzy from the altitude of 6,255 feet.

Settling into her pine-paneled rooms at the lodge and unpacking the long flannels that Hedda Hopper reported she took with her, Elizabeth quickly became aware that this was going to be a very different kind of filmmaking experience. She heard the sounds of speedboat jockeys enjoying one last romp on the lake before winter drifted in. But if she thought that she might have time to join them, she was wrong. This wasn't some lighthearted romp with Van Johnson on an MGM soundstage. This was a serious picture, and for the first time, Elizabeth was insecure on a movie set. She might be a pro at hitting floor marks and matching her costar in two-shots, but all that craft seemed feeble here. She felt "very much the inadequate teenage Hollywood sort of puppet that had just worn pretty clothes and hadn't really acted except with horses and dogs."

The emotion in the script was certainly heavy. Dreiser had based his novel on the true story of one Chester Gillette of New York, an ambitious young man who had drowned a factory girl pregnant with his child in 1906. The state contended that he had done so deliberately because she had complicated his plan to marry a rich girl. Found guilty, Gillette died in the electric chair in 1908. Two decades later Dreiser used Gillette's story as an indictment of the social and economic disparities in American society. Liberal in his politics, Stevens shared the author's sympathetic approach to the protagonist but differed in his conception of the wealthy young woman who inspires the killing. Stevens reimagined Sondra—now rechristened Angela Vickers because he liked the "ring" to it—as both emotionally and physically compelling. The audience couldn't be allowed to hate the hero who kills for her love; they had to understand his temptation. Angela had to be worth everything, even the electric chair.

But was the actress playing her up to the task? As Elizabeth went before the cameras in Lake Tahoe, the MGM star-making bandwagon continued to roll. After much finagling by Metro publicists, she'd recently made the cover of *Time* magazine. International society figure Elsa Maxwell was drafted to write a flattering piece for *Photoplay* describing Elizabeth as "The Most Exciting Girl in Hollywood." The magazine hit the stands just as the young star arrived at Lake Tahoe. Crew members recalled seeing copies strewn around the set.

It was precisely for such notoriety that Stevens had wanted Elizabeth. Production manager Doc Erickson watched her walk onto the set for the first time in her close-fitting Dior dress and was struck by her sheer presence as she shook hands with the crew. "There was a sense that she knew she was a star," he said. "Not in an arrogant way. She just knew what she was. She carried it with her."

For several days Elizabeth had little to do but walk around shaking hands. Principal photography began on Tuesday, October 4, but the 6:30 A.M. call was just for Clift and Shelley Winters. Stevens was shooting the scenes that took place at the pier, including the important one where Clift rents the boat to take Winters out on the lake. Elizabeth wandered by at one point, her hair tied up in a scarf. She sat cross-legged and watched her costars work. Clift and Winters "were very intense and concentrated," Erickson said, and no doubt Elizabeth noticed this. These were *actors,* after all—artists from the New York stage, serious about every second of their performances. Elizabeth hurried back to her room to run lines again with her mother.

Her first call was for 9:30 A.M. the next day for hair and makeup. Clift and Winters had already been up and working for three hours at that point. Elizabeth was right on time for her 10:30 call to the set, reporting to the grassy banks of Cascade Lake, a little less than a mile southwest of the much larger Lake Tahoe. Stevens was preparing to shoot her idyllic lakeside scene with Clift, and though the two stars barely knew each other, the chemistry between them crackled to life the instant Stevens began rehearsals. "She just seemed to come alive when Clift looked at her," Erickson said. With Clift's head resting in her lap, Elizabeth projected an image of mature confidence in her black bathing suit, even if she was still terrified inside.

She was also freezing. Between takes she ran over to Sara, who was waiting on the sidelines with a blanket. The day was sunny, but it was also about forty-five degrees. The next day, when her first call came an hour earlier, the temperature had dropped even lower. That night a couple of feet of snow fell on Tahoe. Looking out of her window on Friday morning, Elizabeth expected the day's shoot to be cancelled, but Stevens's assistant told her to be at the lake by noon. The director was having the snow hosed off the grass. No matter how chilly it was, Elizabeth would still be expected to run playfully into the lake in her bathing suit. Sara was furious, complaining that her daughter was menstruating and that such exposure to cold would leave her unable to bear children. Nobody paid her much mind, least of all Elizabeth. In any event, they only worked a couple of hours. Renewed snowfall ended the day's shoot at 2:15 P.M.

Looking at those first days' rushes, one thing was plainly evident to Stevens: He'd made the right choice in hiring Elizabeth Taylor. Cinematographer William Mellor, whose aesthetic eye Stevens trusted implicitly, had been instructed to shoot passively. "I use the camera to create a mood," Stevens said, but he didn't just mean capturing the play of light and shadow that so defines the visual look of the film. Rather, the director saw his camera as a "passive witness" to the intrinsic beauty of his actors. Stevens thought that Elizabeth's appeal was enhanced by her lack of self-consciousness, a refreshing attribute that shone through in the rushes. "She had this enormous beauty and she was not charmed by it," the director said, in awe. In fact, she "discouraged people being overimpressed by it." That humility was precisely what made the character of Angela Vickers appealing.

Elizabeth would insist that she wasn't so special; Ava Gardner was her idea of beautiful. When she looked in a mirror, she saw "too many freckles," she said, "all the things that were wrong." That didn't mean she wasn't keenly aware of her appearance or how important it was to her career. A reporter for *Photoplay* had caught a glimpse of how Elizabeth really thought about herself when she'd spied the star preening in front of a mirror. Elizabeth appeared quite proud of her small waist, but it was always a struggle to keep it. "I've just got to take off ten pounds," she told the reporter. At 110, the teenager was heavier than she'd ever been. The problem was that she liked "everything that's fattening. I can eat a whole pie."

The pies would continue, but her teenage metabolism and the hustle-bustle of filmmaking kept her svelte. No wonder Stevens insisted that she wear the bathing suit on that cold day at the lake. Her glamour and sex appeal would be a major selling point of the picture. Her costume budget of $6,600 was more than four times that for Winters or Clift, the latter of whom wore some of his own clothes in the film.

Stevens didn't stop with just her finery. He began to push her—and everyone else—hard. One visitor to the set, Phil Koury of the *New York Times*, thought that Stevens drove his actors and his crew "with a sort of benign tyranny and singleness of purpose," which had the effect of uniting the cast "in the same direction—no mean trick in Hollywood." Known for his autocratic nature, Stevens tolerated no dissent. Certainly he got none from his young leading lady, who admitted to a case of "hero worship."

Clift was less easy. He brooded around the set; his deep-set dark eyes seemed to burn holes in the back of Stevens's head every so often. Watching the director rehearse a scene with Shelley Winters,

Clift decided that everything was all wrong. "Downbeat, blubbery, irritating" was not how Clift saw Winters's character. He loathed the way she telegraphed her "tragedy from the minute you see her on screen." She should be stronger and more noble than that, he argued. But Stevens wasn't listening. "I know I'm right," Clift griped to Shepperd Strudwick, who played Elizabeth's father. "I'm right and I'll keep saying I'm right."

For the first time Elizabeth saw an actor on fire with his own artistic convictions and not docilely dependent on screenwriters and directors. Shivering under blankets with him as the crew readied a scene, Elizabeth became entranced by the charismatic Clift. At twenty-eight (he'd turn twenty-nine during the making of the film), Monty wasn't fond of Hollywood and was openly disdainful of the culture of stardom—like the kind of buildup that Elizabeth was getting at the moment. "I'm not called an actor out there," he'd complain to his New York theater friends. "I'm called a hot property. And a property is only good if it makes money."

Clift was moody, dark, and sultry, with the kind of smoldering good looks that made studio executives nervous. Since becoming a star overnight in *The Search* (1948), in which he played a sensitive American GI helping a little boy find his mother in war-torn Czechoslovakia, Clift had been a challenge for Hollywood press agents, who were forced to dispel perceptions that he was too pretty or not quite masculine enough. Campaigns for *Red River* and *The Big Lift* aggressively sold Clift's macho credentials to the fan magazines, but not everyone was buying. In her column Hedda Hopper called Monty a "pantywaist" compared to the real air force flyers used as extras in *The Big Lift*.

Hedda, of course, had the dirt. She knew that Clift was not only homosexual but relatively open and unapologetic about it. She got wind of an arrest in New Orleans on a possible morals charge even before Monty's agent learned of it. But it wasn't Clift's homosexuality per se that perturbed the columnist, but rather his insufferable New York superiority and his refusal to go along with the Hollywood game. She hated his blue jeans, his flip answers in interviews. Once she asked him what other profession he might enjoy. "Bartending," he said. This was unforgivable. Hedda, who never got irony, saw it simply as disrespect for the industry for which she lived and breathed.

But Elizabeth found Monty delightful. She loved his rebellion and hipness. Their chemistry built during the two weeks of filming at Tahoe. Hiding out in his dressing room, they snuck sips of brandy and made up silly names for everyone on the set. Sara would come by, knocking frantically on the door in search of her daughter. Hunkered down with Monty, Elizabeth just plugged her ears and pretended not to hear. She was suddenly eager to be all grown up, describing her mother as a "pain in the ass."

On October 17 they all packed up and returned to Hollywood, where, the next day, cast and crew were given an early-morning call to report to Paramount's Stage 9—all but Elizabeth, who was given a day off to regroup. But she found it difficult to get back into the swing. On the 20th, given a call for 9:00, she didn't appear until 2:30.

Perhaps she was getting ready for that evening's festivities, which may have seemed more exciting to her than that day's script. She was to be Monty's date to the premiere of his film *The Heiress* at the Carthay Circle Theater on San Vicente Boulevard. The decision to pair them off for the benefit of the newsreel cameras was made by agents and publicists, but given how fond they were of each other, Monty and Elizabeth were, no doubt, happy to oblige. Everyone knew that Clift hated these things, but paired with "Bessie Mae" (his term of endearment for his teenaged costar) he might be able to get through the experience. That fan magazines would depict them as a couple was a given.

Huddled in the backseat of a long black limousine, an anxious Monty nudged Elizabeth and suggested that they stop for a hamburger before the show. The girl let out a whoop and happily agreed. As they chowed down, careful not to drip too much grease on their formal attire, they were watched by Monty's stone-faced acting coach Mira Rostova and the press agent Harvey Zim, who could barely conceal his amusement. So buoyant and "foul-mouthed" was Elizabeth, Zim said, that she accomplished what he'd thought impossible: She got Clift to relax and enjoy himself.

A few blocks from the theater, Zim and Rostova were dropped off so that the two stars could arrive on their own for the photographers. Stepping out onto the red carpet, they set off an immediate explosion of flashcubes and cheers from the crowd. Inside, as Monty squirmed in his seat, critical of his performance, Elizabeth told him that he was nuts. She thought he was magnificent. When it was over, he grabbed her hand and they rushed out before the crowds could get to them. At a post-premiere party at the director William Wyler's home, the unlikely couple drew everyone's gaze like a pair of magnets. "The combination of their beauty was staggering," said the actress Diana Lynn. The next day the newspapers were filled with breathless reports of their love affair.

In his New York office, Russell Holman, Paramount's East Coast production manager, wired an emphatic memo to the studio's front office. Surrounded by tabloid photos of Monty and Elizabeth, Holman urged the higher-ups to drop the title *A Place in the Sun* and replace it with *The Lovers*, since the pair was "already being linked together press-wise." And not just in the tabloids either. Holman pointed to the current issue of *Time*, which also featured them as Hollywood's newest couple. "Confident George will make fine picture," Holman continued, "but there still will be problem of getting it reception commensurate with its merits from exhibitors and public unless we give it attractive title ... I plead on behalf of every executive here that we at once set title *The Lovers*. It would be a terrible showmanship shame not to use it." So terrible, Holman said, that it could mean the difference of $750,000 or more to the gross.

But back in Hollywood, Stevens folded his big arms across his barrel chest. He wasn't interested in showmanship. The title, thankfully, would not be changed.

The Lovers might have been an apt title for the Monty and Liz show that was raging in the press, however. Fan-magazine readers were giddy at the thought of such a beautiful star couple. After what columnist Ruth Waterbury called all "those boy boys," finally La Liz was pairing off with a consort worthy of her. Paramount was thrilled at the publicity, hoping to ride it through to the film's release, and no doubt Metro was pleased as well, for the stories bolstered its own efforts to turn Elizabeth into a full-fledged adult star. Stories of Monty and Liz sneaking out for hamburgers were cranked out on purple mimeograph machines. Carefully posed photographs of the couple were distributed widely. It wasn't long before Hedda got into the act, striding onto the set wearing a tall pink hat and peering from behind the camera as Stevens shot Clift and Taylor in a romantic clinch. "Liz did the old Garbo trick," she told her readers. "She took him. Not a carpenter, electrician, prop man or laborer left the set. Some even sat on ladders to get a better look. That Liz gets them all—from 15 to 50. What a dish!"

Except that Elizabeth didn't get Monty—no matter how much has seeped into Hollywood legend. So good was the publicity in 1949–50 that, even now, Elizabeth Taylor's love for Montgomery Clift is a "fact" that everyone knows. Romantics still push the story that Monty was her one great love and that despite his sexual orientation, he was unable to resist her charms. This belief persisted even after Elizabeth repeatedly told the truth. "He was my best friend," she said, describing "a loving and lasting friendship." Jack Larson, who was Monty's lover for many years and a witness to his friendship with Elizabeth, said the pair shared a tremendously affectionate yet always platonic friendship. Clift's close friend Kevin McCarthy agreed: "The romance was publicity, what people wanted to believe."

As young and inexperienced as she was, Elizabeth had no problem accepting the truth about Clift. Right from the start she had sensed something different about him. "I was a virgin . . . not a world expert on sexuality," she said. "But I loved Monty with all my heart and . . . knew that he was meant to be with a man and not a woman, and I discussed it with him." While she may have lacked a concrete understanding of sexuality, Elizabeth had always been an instinctive creature—and she had known plenty of homosexuals from her youngest days on. At the moment Roddy McDowall, her pal and costar from *Lassie Come Home* and *The White Cliffs of Dover*, was also coming to terms with his gay identity—a process that he shared with Elizabeth, who supported him unconditionally.

Of course, Elizabeth might have had some hope that Monty might "change" for her. George Stevens, who discounted any romance, nonetheless thought that Clift "might have suggested fancies" in the sensitive teenager's mind. The romantic dream of wedding bells with Bill Pawley, as unlikely as it may have been, was still fresh in her mind. Being held in Monty's arms every day on the set, being kissed by him, being fired up by his ambition and talent, Elizabeth easily could have become smitten. But she was never the type to bang her head against closed doors.

And as much as he adored her, Clift was very conscious of the fact that Elizabeth was just seventeen years old; it would be a while, said Jack Larson, before their friendship deepened emotionally, at least from Monty's perspective. For now, it remained a happy, sometimes childlike association, with giggling fits and dripping hamburgers. Monty's gayness fostered a deeper and safer intimacy than she would ever have with most men. When Elizabeth spent a weekend with Monty and Roddy McDowall at the Park Plaza in New York, there was no hanky-panky or sexual tension, just good-natured (if somewhat out-of-control) fun. They drank lots of martinis, pelted each other with chrysanthemums, turned the paintings on the walls upside-down, and stole bathroom fixtures. And no one seemed to worry too much about a teenaged girl developing such a fond taste for vodka.

As October rushed to a close, George Stevens was increasingly under pressure. Elizabeth had called in sick on the twenty-fifth and twenty-sixth, and time was an issue. Her contract stipulated that she be finished with all her scenes by November 26 in order to be back at MGM to start work on *Father of the Bride* the first week of December. Stevens began to push hard. Monty pushed back, openly disagreeing with much of what the director was telling them. According to Mira Rostova, he privately coached Elizabeth himself, rehearsing her in several scenes and taking "copious notes" to review later. Elizabeth was learning how to *act*—not just put on a costume and perform for the cameras.

Rehearsing a scene, Stevens played Franz Waxman's prerecorded score as inspiration. It was a pivotal juncture in the picture, the moment where a guilt-ridden Monty shares his heartbreak and Elizabeth comforts him. Standing in front of his actors, practically acting out the scene himself, Stevens instructed them to go through the motions without any dialogue, to just *feel* their characters. For once, Clift found the idea worthwhile, but Elizabeth was flummoxed. She'd never known filmmaking to be like this. Halfway through the rehearsal, she froze. Jumping in and taking her by the hand, Stevens prodded her along, assuring her that they'd "work at it, talk about it, do it over, change it, adjust it," until they got it right. To his great satisfaction, Elizabeth was game.

"I don't presume to be a great actress," she told him at one point, exhausted. "I presume to be an effective actress." But Stevens thought she could do more. Despite her inexperience, Elizabeth's performance was pleasing him, and not just because of the way she looked. What truly thrilled him was the wise, almost "earth mother" quality in her performance. "She had been associating with older people a good many years and there was a great maturity about her," Stevens said. He believed that she "had all of the emotional capabilities, the intelligence . . . Anything she wanted to do, she could do."

And finally, it seems, she started to believe it herself.

When the time came to actually shoot the scene, Stevens told Bill Mellor to pop a six-inch lens into his camera. It would all be done in one gigantic close-up. To Stevens's mind, there was no more important moment than this one. He'd been up till two A.M. that morning, still tinkering with the dialogue. His actors had only gotten the new script a short time before they were called to the set. Elizabeth took one glance at the page and reacted sharply.

"Forgive me," she said, "but what the hell is this?"

In the new script, Monty was to say, "If I only could tell you how much I love you ... if only I could tell you all." And Elizabeth was to respond, "Tell Mama all."

The words seemed absurd to the teenager. No longer the obedient rookie, Elizabeth had been emboldened to think for herself. But Stevens didn't bend to her "distemper." Not only did he insist that she say the words, he insisted that she *believe* them, that she take them into her head and her heart, and speak them as if she really *were* this woman, loving this man as powerfully as if she had borne him herself. Elizabeth hesitated, then said she would try. Stevens knew she could do it. And when he called "action" and Mellor turned on his camera, she proved him right.

"Brilliant!" the director shouted after calling "cut." Of course, whether anyone else would share his view remained to be seen. They went on shooting, way past their deadline. Metro finally insisted that Elizabeth come home to start *Father of the Bride* on December 8, though she was back at Paramount on the twenty-seventh and twenty-eighth for some last shots. Stevens finally finished principal photography on January 3, 1950, then retired to the cutting room with editor William Hornbeck and dozens of cans of celluloid. It would be more than a year before anyone other than the two of them saw the film.

On May 6, 1950, Dick Clayton arrived soon after dawn outside the Church of the Good Shepherd in Beverly Hills, around the corner from the posh boutiques on Rodeo Drive. The sunlight was filtering through the fronds of the palm trees as the first of the crowd began to gather. By noon, three thousand people would be jostling each other on the street outside the small white church with the tiled roof, standing on curbs, on walls, on cars, drinking coffee from paper cups, passing around boxes of doughnuts. Most had cameras dangling from their necks. Some carried portable telescopes and home-movie cameras. Not since the funeral of Rudolph Valentino twenty-four years earlier had this many people assembled around the church.

"It was quite the party scene," said Clayton, then a thirty-four-year-old bit actor starting over as an agent. "It wasn't every day that ordinary people like us could see Liz Taylor get married in person just like she did on the screen."

Elizabeth Taylor, now properly eighteen years old, was finally giving the fan magazines the payoff they'd been clamoring for—and, not coincidentally, just in time for the release of her picture, *Father of the Bride.*

After a year of jilting her Dear Johns, it was, perhaps, inevitable. So many suitors, so many unsatisfactory endings. It was time to get Elizabeth Taylor hitched. After all, she was now an adult, having graduated from the MGM school in January. To receive her diploma, she'd trooped over to a real high school to sit among teenagers she didn't know, strangers who lived a few blocks and a zillion psychic miles away from her. When the graduation speaker encouraged the students to persevere so they could make it in life, Elizabeth got the giggles. She was already making $2,000 a week.

And at that price she was a girl who couldn't say no—at least to the studio. When Monty Clift balked at continuing the publicity ruse, canny press agents kept the spotlight on Elizabeth through a series of romantic pairings that would climax with the wedding in Beverly Hills. To find the next beau, she was actually raffled off. Paramount staged a contest at UCLA to name the school's "Great Lover" with a particularly inventive crowning touch: The young lothario's prom date would be Elizabeth Taylor. The winner, a handsome blonde sophomore named Bob Precht, was fitted in white tie and tails, and loaned a Cadillac so he could pick up his date. In a lime green taffeta-and-tulle gown designed by Paramount's top costumer, Edith Head, Elizabeth looked stunning as she waltzed out of her front door. But along for the ride came twenty-five press agents and dozens of photographers, and Precht was barely able to say more than a few words to his date all night. Each time they got up to dance (the prom was held on the Paramount lot with Bob Hope as emcee) they were blinded by camera flares. Afterward, to Precht's regret, there was no goodnight kiss—although Sara did offer a snack of spaghetti and milk when they got back home, all duly recorded for the fan magazines.

"Taking her out isn't like dating a coed," Precht complained to a reporter. "She's from a different world." Elizabeth was quoted as saying that the prom had been "more fun than going to Mocambo"—certainly a disingenuous statement, if she said such a thing at all.

Then came Ralph Kiner, outfielder for the Pittsburgh Pirates and home-run king, the only National League player with two fifty-plus seasons. Elizabeth was photographed on his arm in December at a premiere, invoking memories of the last athlete passed off as her boyfriend, Glenn Davis. But Hedda called Kiner "a real guy."

But what the public wanted was something that would last. This became glaringly obvious to the Metro publicity department once filming of *Father of the Bride* got under way. In a film far less complex than her last one, directed by the far less demanding Vincente Minnelli, Elizabeth was playing a girl deeply in love and preparing to be married in a lavish ceremony. Elizabeth's fans—it didn't take Einstein to figure out—would adore seeing their heroine in a wedding dress. The problem was that some people still called her a flighty heartbreaker who jumped from beau to beau offscreen. And so the Metro press agents got to work.

"All that engagement press had been very good," said Dick Clayton, referring to the fan-magazine euphoria when Elizabeth announced that she'd marry Davis or Pawley. "Now the studio seemed to be saying, 'Let's give 'em a real marriage.'"

Here lies the origin of Elizabeth Taylor's long marital history and her iconography as a much-married star. MGM's lucrative positioning of her as a bride-to-be in 1950 ensured that romance and marriage would forever be essential components of her fame.

According to Dick Clayton, who drew on his longtime close association with many Hollywood agents and publicists, the studio had decided that "Liz should get married and it should be [coordinated] with the release of [*Father of the Bride*]." MGM publicist

Emily Torchia admitted, "There were always marriages made by the studio . . . [like] that first one of Elizabeth Taylor's." But before anyone could proceed, they needed to figure out who would be her husband. It was like casting a movie.

Enter Conrad Nicholson Hilton, Jr. The tall, handsome playboy son of the millionaire hotelier had met Elizabeth briefly at Mocambo a few months earlier. That introduction would be retroactively assigned by press agents as the start of the romance. For chroniclers of Elizabeth Taylor's life this would present some awkwardness, since this was also the point at which she was supposed to have been head over heels in love with Montgomery Clift. Trying to calculate it all, many concluded that the new guy must have been a rebound romance. But the wedding to Hilton was more like an extended photo opportunity for a picture that needed to be promoted. *Two* pictures, in fact, since by late January a sequel to *Father of the Bride* had already been ordered up even before the first film had been released. So a tremendous amount was riding on all of this. A real wedding alongside the cinematic one could mean another million dollars in profit.

What made Nicky the ideal candidate—aside from his own celebrity, something Pawley had lacked—was how cooperative he was regarding Elizabeth's career. It had been no coincidence that he'd been formally introduced to her by the son of Y. Frank Freeman, the head of Paramount; Hilton understood from the start that this would be a studio deal. Much would be made of Nicky's asking Francis Taylor for Elizabeth's hand—just as her fiancé in *Father of the Bride* asks Spencer Tracy—but no doubt another important meeting took place as well: between Nicky and the heads of MGM. "Of course they'd insist on [meeting him]," said Dick Clayton. "Elizabeth was one of their most valuable properties. They had to make sure they weren't taking too big a risk by marrying her off."

Hilton had his own reasons for wanting in on the deal. Five years older than his bride-to-be, he was not only his father's namesake but also his favorite. Yet Nicky's lack of ambition had often troubled the senior Hilton. Despite his education at the Ecole Hôtelière in Switzerland, the young man's chief claim to fame had been his idea to install pens too long to be easily stolen in all of his father's hotel rooms. Meanwhile, the more industrious younger son, Barron, had already married and sired two children, who would one day expect a sizeable slice of the family fortune. Nicky expected that a spectacular marriage to Elizabeth Taylor would nudge his brother out of the family limelight.

And so he was prepared to be extremely accommodating. "He won't be annoyed because of the things I have to do," Elizabeth told Louella Parsons soon after their engagement was announced in February of 1950. "Nick understands we'll be photographed most places we go and that there will be pictures made of even our honeymoon house. He understands that these things are part of my career and he does not resent them."

Wedding plans unfolded that spring, and it was uncanny how much they paralleled what Elizabeth and Spencer Tracy and Joan Bennett (playing her mother) were acting out on the Metro lot. Looking back now, calling it all a coincidence seems the height of naïveté. The press, no doubt, understood the arrangement. Louella Parsons said, "It tickled [Elizabeth] to be going through all those movie angles and problems in real life." Hedda, always keen to signal that she knew the score, wrote just before the engagement was announced, "With all this 'bride' talk, it will be a miracle if they don't push Liz into wifehood and motherhood in real life—as well as reel."

One day toward the end of the shoot, Hedda arrived on the set just as Elizabeth was taking off her wedding dress. "I wish you'd seen the wedding," the young star said dreamily. "The ceremony was so wonderful, I cried just as brides do." Perhaps illusion and reality were beginning to blur dangerously. Or maybe she was just acting, as she was learning to do.

The fact was that just as the onscreen Elizabeth was being fitted for a wedding dress, so too was the real-life Elizabeth flying off to New York with her mother to see the famed couturier Ceil Chapman, who had been tapped to design her trousseau. Just as Spencer Tracy blustered about onscreen as the harried father of the bride, so too was Francis Taylor portrayed in the fan magazines as forever fretting and bellowing. Asked whether he wanted to serve hot or cold hors d'oeuvres at the wedding reception, Francis supposedly huffed, "I won't have cold fish at *my* daughter's wedding"—which sounds nothing like the urbane Mr. Taylor but very much like Tracy's screen persona. When Elizabeth's character Kay was surprised by a diamond ring, Elizabeth herself suddenly sprouted a five-carat square diamond on her finger. All of this was planned so that when *Father of the Bride* was released, audiences would feel as if they were witnessing not movie fiction but the behind-the-scenes preparations for Elizabeth's real-life marriage.

That many of her wedding plans were publicity-driven didn't mean that Elizabeth, ever the romantic, didn't love playing the happy bride on either occasion. For her, it was just one more instance where fame and public image spilled over into real life, blurring—perhaps obliterating—the line between them. The studio's orchestration of her marriage was simply par for the course.

And she liked Nicky well enough. He was dashing and never boring. They ate hot dogs and chili beans and French apple pie on their dates. He bought her beautiful things. At a Beverly Hills jeweler, looking for "something nice" for his fiancée, Nicky was asked, "Blonde or brunette?" He replied, "Platinum and diamonds." The public loved it.

So did Elizabeth. She was getting used to major gems and the kind of life a wealthy fiancé could provide. "Every day I love him better," she gushed to Louella Parsons, clearly not sinking much effort into the script. After all, they would be married in a Catholic church; she wouldn't be going through with it, she insisted, if she didn't think that the marriage would last forever. Catholics didn't allow divorce, after all. Yet while she "studied" the religion, Elizabeth never actually converted. Someone was hedging their bets.

Someone was advising her not to take too many chances. The bride would admit to crossing her fingers behind her back as she took her vows.

But the question lingers: Why did the sometimes stubborn and often independent Elizabeth agree to this—the kind of celebrity fairy tale that her new hero, Montgomery Clift, openly despised and never would have tolerated? Well, it was fun, for starters. What young woman doesn't want to be the bride? Besides, she'd been trained not to think too far beyond her next part, and this one sure was a blast. She was feted all over town. The Metro wardrobe girls pitched in to make her bedroom slippers that were wrapped in a box of white satin studded with seed pearls. Hedda Hopper declared that there hadn't been so many lavish bridal showers in Hollywood since Vilma Bánky had married Rod La Rocque in 1927. As usual, Hedda was doing her part, calling the union "ideal," since the couple would live in Beverly Hills and there would be no disruption to Elizabeth's career.

And so, on the late afternoon of May 6, Elizabeth arrived outside the Church of the Good Shepherd in a limousine escorted by an honor guard of off-duty policemen on motorcycles, their sirens blaring. Although it was against regulations for policemen to use sirens while off-duty, Elizabeth had kissed the lead cop on the cheek and said in her sweetest, most seductive voice, "Let's hear it for the bride. Let them know I'm coming." Never underestimate the power of a great entrance. As the limousine and the shrieking motorcycles slowed to a stop in front of the church, the crowd, many of whom had been waiting all day, let out a roar of applause. Elizabeth stepped out of the limo just as regally as Princess Elizabeth had from her carriage a few years earlier. The comparisons were duly made, usually in the American Elizabeth's favor.

"Metro had stage-managed it down to the slightest detail," Dick Clayton said. On his toes to watch Elizabeth walk into the church, he was awestruck at the smoothness of the production. They'd even managed to get her there on time, he marveled. Elizabeth moved with the supremely confident air of someone accustomed to the eyes of a crowd. With a practiced wave, she turned once and smiled, then gathered her dress to proceed through the front door. "It was almost as if there was an invisible director telling her, 'Okay, now wave, now walk,'" Clayton said. "It was like a movie scene, so slick, so smooth. I couldn't get over it."

Certainly Elizabeth looked every inch the movie star. Her hair had been styled, naturally, by Sydney Guilaroff and her dress designed by Helen Rose. Liberated from the censor for once, Rose had designed the flowing white satin to emphasize Elizabeth's small waist and large bust. "It's about as plunging as anything could be," she gleefully admitted after a description of the dress was "leaked" in advance of the wedding by a "spy" in the MGM publicity department. ("That was standard," said Dick Clayton. "Get what you wanted out there, then smile and blame it on a spy.") Every last glittering detail of Elizabeth's wedding dress was gobbled up by an avid public, many of whom then copied the pattern for their own weddings, from the chiffon at the neckline to the embroidery of seed pearls to the "misty" veil worn over the face.

Inside the church, Metro organizers kept up the cinematic illusion. Studio florists arranged the flowers; studio photographers patrolled the aisles; a studio contract singer trilled "Ave Maria." Elizabeth's attendants, billed as her "girlfriends," were, in fact, fellow contract players like Jane Powell and other girls with studio affiliations (with the exception of Mara Regan, soon to be the wife of Elizabeth's brother, Howard). And the seating plan devised by the studio made sure to place Elizabeth's parents together—*all* of them. Donald Crisp and Anne Revere, who'd played Elizabeth's mother and father in *National Velvet*, sat with each other in one pew; not far away, Greer Garson sat with Walter Pidgeon, preserving the movie family of *Julia Misbehaves*. And, in a place almost as prominent as Sara and Francis, Spencer Tracy was paired with Joan Bennett, reliving the roles they'd just finished in *Father of the Bride*.

"It was as the soft rays of the setting sun streamed through the stained-glass windows that Monsignor Concannon pronounced the words that made Elizabeth and Nicky man and wife," Louella Parsons breathlessly reported. Outside the church, the newlyweds embraced passionately on cue for the adoring crowd. Police had to forcibly push back the throngs so the limousine could speed away with its celebrated passengers. Fans chased after the limo, throwing white roses. One woman fainted, overcome with joy. As Elizabeth and Nicky headed for a gala private reception at the Bel-Air Country Club, they left behind a raucous crowd, broken street-lamps, overturned signs, and half a ton of trash. "I'd prefer a gang war to another Hilton-Taylor wedding," groaned the Beverly Hills police chief at the end of the day.

Father of the Bride went into wide release all across the nation just as Elizabeth and Nicky sailed off on their European honeymoon. Living up to everyone's hopes, the picture was a runaway hit, raking in more than $4 million and ending up the sixth biggest film of the year. Already the machinery was in place to start the sequel as soon as Elizabeth returned to work. Despite the acting accolades for Bette Davis in *All About Eve* and Gloria Swanson in *Sunset Boulevard*, the sheer number of magazine covers and newspaper articles about Elizabeth made her the true star of the year. And, thanks in no small part to its violet-eyed princess, MGM saw its profits spike up for the second year in a row.

Meanwhile, behind closed doors at Paramount, George Stevens was doing his best not to pay attention to all the headlines. He had 400,000 feet of film to edit down into a two-hour picture. *Father of the Bride* had started shooting after *A Place in the Sun* had wrapped, and it was already showing in the nation's theaters. But Stevens and his editor remained hunched over their cans of celluloid in a darkened room. "I think this is the best thing I've ever done," the director told a reporter who came by asking what was taking so long. "The story is there—on film—when we can get the best of it together."

Elizabeth, in marrying Nicky Hilton, had brilliantly mastered one key aspect of movie stardom. George Stevens, his eyes bleary in a darkroom across town, was getting ready to offer something a little bit more.

In her office high above Hollywood Boulevard, Hedda Hopper was spitting mad. Her assistants knew to keep their distance. She banged around the office, slamming drawers, throwing newspapers (usually the *Examiner,* which carried Louella), and bouncing obscenities off the walls like tennis balls. On this day in the early winter of 1951, what had her in such a state was Elizabeth Taylor—the girl she'd spent the better part of the last ten years prodding, promoting, and praising. All that was about to change.

"Hedda felt Elizabeth let her down," said longtime Hopper legman Robert Shaw. It began, Shaw said, with the marriage to Nicky Hilton, which was supposed to be "a happily-ever-after kind of thing"—at least as Hollywood defined it, which meant a respectable few years anyway. Divorce was commonplace, even expected, in the movie capital. Hollywood realists—who included Hedda—knew that even as the happy newlyweds waved to the crowd, the marriage would last only so long. But Elizabeth had left Nicky less than *six months* after their glamorous wedding. There were stories of drinking on Nicky's part, and gambling, and other women (including his father's ex-wife, Zsa Zsa Gabor). But in Hedda's mind nothing could justify the way Elizabeth had so callously damaged her public image. Such childish behavior only made a mockery of all the hard work that so many people had done on her behalf—Hedda chief among them.

Capping Hedda's outrage were the stories coming off the set of Elizabeth's latest picture, *Love Is Better Than Ever.* Her spies reported that the young star was having an affair with the director, the married Stanley Donen. Barely nineteen and separated from her husband, Elizabeth had crossed a line—and Aunt Hedda was planning to tell her so. Calling for her driver to whisk her over to Elizabeth's new "bachelor girl" apartment on Wilshire Boulevard in Westwood, Hedda was "all set to give her a verbal slugging."

But Hedda didn't know the half of it. The Hilton marriage had crumbled for reasons even more disturbing than drinking, gambling, and other women. "Nick kind of got a kick out of beating the shit out of me," Elizabeth admitted years later. He was a spoiled rich kid, whose promises of respecting his wife's career were soon forgotten as he found himself resenting her greater fame and celebrity. When he drank, he thought nothing of hitting her. Once Elizabeth was hurt seriously enough to cause a miscarriage, she said. Beauty was no protection from Nick Hilton. Stardom was no shield. And Elizabeth was just eighteen years old.

The turmoil made for a very difficult filming of *Father's Little Dividend*, the sequel to *Father of the Bride*, in which Elizabeth played a happy newlywed expecting a baby. The synchronicity of Elizabeth's art and life had suddenly been sadly perverted.

Had any other outcome been possible? Only in the movies, perhaps. No one had seemed to worry about the wisdom of marrying off an inexperienced teenage girl—still a virgin—who had never been out of her mother's sight. The glamour of the wedding, the tie-in with the movie, and the fervor of the fans had carried them all through on what Elizabeth later called "a pink cloud"—a phrase she would often use to describe the unreality of public life in Hollywood. "I was naïve and knew nothing about sex," she said, though she claimed that "I was ready for love and ready for the experience of lovemaking." What she wasn't ready for was the reality of Nick Hilton's ego—or his fist. For the pampered darling of MGM, blows across the face and the pain of a miscarriage were her introduction to life beyond the studio gates. She grew up almost overnight. "It scarred me," she said of the marriage, "and left me with horrible memories."

And like many real-life princesses trapped in unhappy royal marriages, Elizabeth was expected by some to put up with the indignities and the abuse, to endure her struggles stoically for the sake of her public image. But she was far too strong, far too independent for that, no matter what it might do to the fairy tale.

So she walked out. "Divorcing Nick was the first grown-up decision I ever made absolutely alone," she said. In January of 1952, the marriage ended as it had begun, staged and orchestrated for maximum benefit. Appearing before a judge at the Santa Monica Courthouse, Elizabeth wept into her white-gloved hands. It was revealed that Nicky had preferred to gamble rather than spend time with her—*her!* The screen's great love goddess! After composing herself in the judge's chambers, Elizabeth emerged to face the swarm of photographers, wearing a brave smile—and a specially designed Ceil Chapman ensemble.

Yet no matter how bravely she smiled or how lovely she looked, Elizabeth was roundly booed. Without knowing the truth of her abuse, the public resented its illusions being shattered. "The fairy tale's over, and the princess of dreams has told it to a judge," fan-magazine writer Ida Zeitlin snarled in *Photoplay*. In an outrageously misogynistic article, Zeitlin placed the fault of the breakup solely on Elizabeth, calling Nicky "an earnest citizen, forging his hardworking way into his father's hotel kingdom." If Elizabeth had settled down and had babies, Zeitlin argued, the marriage would've lasted. Instead, Elizabeth was "willful, flighty and headstrong" and didn't know "the meaning of love." Worst of all was her brazen appearance at a Hollywood premiere on the arm of Stanley Donen, estranged but not yet divorced from his wife. "With the rift from Nicky so new," Zeitlin huffed, "she should have stayed at home, preferably weeping."

"Spoiled brat" now replaced "beaming bride" in Elizabeth's press, just at the moment her psyche was in need of tender care. As the judgments raged, Metro did its best to protect its property. Studio execs were suddenly very willing to besmirch the reputation of the man they'd lionized only months before. The breakup was due, Metro insisted, to Hilton's "gambling and playing around and ignoring her as a wife." The unusually candid official line was no doubt the studio's best shot to end the criticism being leveled at their star without revealing the more damning truths about their matchmaking.

For the moralists in the press—and in 1951 there were many—it was the affair with Donen that made things worse. Had Elizabeth taken Zeitlin's advice and stayed home weeping in her mother's arms, she might have been more quickly forgiven. But that was never Elizabeth's way—especially not now. Marriage to Hilton had been as eye-opening as it was difficult, and she had tasted life beyond Sara's control for the first time. Her mother was pushing for a reconciliation with Nicky, which infuriated Elizabeth, since surely Sara knew about the beatings. Feeling betrayed, Elizabeth resolved not to return to her parents' home despite what the busybodies might have preferred. Instead, the studio found her an apartment so that she could live like a real "modern girl." But because Elizabeth Taylor couldn't live alone (she'd admit to not even knowing how to boil water), they gave her a companion-secretary, Peggy Rutledge, who was billed as her "girlfriend."

With such media scrutiny came another disturbing reality. Elizabeth began receiving obscene threats by mail and by telephone, an increasingly common consequence of celebrity. At one point the police kept her on the line with the caller so that they could try to track him, but they were unsuccessful. Not long afterward, a man was apprehended climbing over the wall of her parents' house. Back at the intruder's motel, the police found charts of Elizabeth's daily movements tacked to the wall. A British citizen, the man was deported—but would surface to stalk Elizabeth again a year later when she was filming in England.

Sara, understandably, was not happy about all this. She wanted her daughter back home. Before moving into her own place, Elizabeth had lived briefly with her agent, Jules Goldstone, and his family; Goldstone's son-in-law, Henry Baron, recalled a "schism" between Elizabeth and her mother that would have been unimaginable just a few years before. Sara was particularly incensed over the relationship with Donen, who believed Sara's hostility was rooted in anti-Semitism, which may have been true. Yet the biggest resentment that Sara bore Donen was the way he'd usurped her place in her daughter's life. Donen, a genial twenty-six-year-old who had wowed the critics with his first two films, *On the Town* (codirected with Gene Kelly) and *Royal Wedding*, had been kind to Elizabeth when she needed it. At their first meeting, she had dissolved into tears. "Here was this gorgeous damsel in distress saying, 'Help me,'" Donen said. "Who could resist her? What fool would try?"

He gave her little gifts—a sure way to win Elizabeth's heart—and when she was hospitalized for nervous distress and ulcers, Donen took charge of ordering all her meals, making sure she ate only foods that would not aggravate her condition. Elinor Donahue, who had a small part in *Love Is Better Than Ever*, saw nothing overt between Elizabeth and the director, but everyone was aware of the affair. "They were both in bad moods for the whole film," Donahue said. "Elizabeth was sulky and Donen was very dour." Because of their mutual marital unhappiness, they found some brief solace with each other. The affair didn't last long. But it moved Elizabeth one step farther away from her mother.

Sara didn't take this desertion lying down. She called gossip columnist Sheilah Graham and told her that Donen was both a homosexual and a Communist and "should be run out of town." No doubt she called her old friend Hedda and said the same thing. But while Hedda shared Sara's disapproval of the match, she was starting to feel that maybe all of Elizabeth's troubles could be traced back to her "movie-minded mother." It was "high time," Hedda said in print, that the young star "break the umbilical cord." Of course, Hedda had never really liked Sara. Perhaps, if Mrs. Taylor were out of the way, the columnist could assume an even more influential role in Elizabeth's career.

That was the background to Hedda's decision to give the star a "verbal slugging." Climbing up the back staircase of the newly built apartment complex on Wilshire Boulevard, the old meddler was struck by the modern design—perhaps fitting for a girl as untraditional as Elizabeth had become. Inside, she demanded a tour, commenting on the sea green paint in the living room and the darker green wall-to-wall carpeting. The place had clearly been styled by Metro's designers, with glass end tables and pink armchairs. The heavy white and gold curtains were always kept drawn.

Cigarette boxes and candy dishes were found on every table, but the walls were devoid of any art that interested Hedda. "Dreadful," she sniffed. "And you the daughter and niece of international art dealers."

Dragging out a chartreuse chair that Hedda thought gave the stark modern room "something," she sat down and began peppering Elizabeth with questions. Her heart began to melt when the young star confided that while she might be happy, she wasn't "nineteen happy." Suddenly Hedda reversed course. Instead of a critical piece, her article painted Elizabeth as a misguided, confused teenager—far from the spoiled brat others were calling her. If only Elizabeth had married Bill Pawley, Hedda mused, she might have found true happiness—even though the columnist had been all too glad to see Elizabeth dump Pawley two years before. But the public had a short memory. "If Mamma hadn't interfered," Hedda wrote, "Liz might be a happy young matron today." Blaming Sara for Elizabeth's troubles had become the plan.

In another piece—Hedda got a lot of traction out of that one interview—she actually had the hubris to scold Elizabeth for behavior that she, Hedda, had helped engineer. "You're growing up fast, Elizabeth," Hedda quoted herself telling the star. "You should know that the public felt you were going off the beam when you jumped romantically from Glenn Davis to Bill Pawley to Nicky Hilton at a pace so fast it left us dizzy." Of course, Hedda knew very well that Davis had been a tool of the publicity department, that Elizabeth had had nothing to do with it; and that Hedda herself, along with others, had breathlessly promoted all of those young men. But Elizabeth was the star; it was she who needed to make her mea culpas to the public. And so she did, assuring Hedda that she was going to straighten out her life and her career by saying, "I'm going to learn to assume responsibility."

This was the spin used to restore Elizabeth's public image. And just in time, too. Word was out that George Stevens had crafted a masterpiece. An advance screening of *A Place in the Sun* was held in May at Paramount for magazine writers, and publicist Lindsay

Durand told Stevens that the response was the greatest he had ever seen during his eleven years at the studio. "The surprise of the evening," Durand reported, "was Elizabeth Taylor's sensitive portrayal which was definitely attributed to your direction."

As more Hollywood insiders got a look at the picture, Stevens was inundated with praise. "I sincerely believe that with 'medicine' like *A Place in the Sun*," wrote producer Irving Asher, "our ailing box office would recover in no time to fight ten more rounds with television or any other opponent."

But most people had to wait until the official premiere on August 14, held at the Fine Arts Theatre in Beverly Hills. Edwin Schallert of the *Los Angeles Times* was impressed by the invitation-only crowd—not only Paramount people, he observed, but stars and executives from other studios as well, not to mention a large number of East Coasters anxious to get a peek before the New York premiere two weeks later. *A Place in the Sun,* already being called the "film of the year," drew a remarkable cross section of who was who in Hollywood. As klieg lights swept across the purple sky, fans crowded around the theater to catch glimpses of their favorite celebrities arriving in limousines. Lucille Ball and Desi Arnaz sat in Row 14 with Irene Dunne; behind them sat Metro exec Joseph Schenck. Groucho Marx was down in Row 11, and Hedda Hopper was even farther up front in Row 8 alongside Bob Hope and Danny Thomas. Jerry Lewis brought a party of nine, including Mr. and Mrs. Dean Martin and Tony Curtis and Janet Leigh. In Row 10 sat Margaret O'Brien, who'd once been more important than Elizabeth at MGM. Debbie Reynolds, Donna Reed, and Zasu Pitts took their seats in Row 22; Roy Rogers and Dale Evans took theirs in Row 18; and Mrs. Theodore Dreiser was in Row 7. George Stevens's party filled two rows. But of the picture's top stars, only Shelley Winters was there, with Farley Granger in Row 14. Monty Clift didn't do premieres, of course, and Elizabeth had sailed for London, where she was scheduled to shoot *Ivanhoe.*

It didn't matter. They were there on the screen, more magnificently than ever before. When the words THE END appeared—after the powerful, tender, brilliantly understated final scene where Monty says good-bye to Elizabeth as he heads off to his execution—there was a collective gasp from the audience. Only after they recovered their wits did they burst into wild applause. Stevens was overcome.

The critics largely shared that audience's admiration, and much of their acclaim was for Elizabeth. Edwin Schallert thought that her portrayal had given "special illumination" to the picture. "Here is a heroine as beautifully created as any seen in recent days on the screen," he wrote. "What Miss Taylor brings to the picture as a young actress is sheer magic. There is no question, to my mind, but that she will be a top contender for Academy honors." A. H. Weller in the *New York Times* called Elizabeth's work "the top effort of her career." *Variety* thought her performance was "so far beyond anything she has done previously that Stevens's skilled hands on the reins must be credited with a minor miracle."

All one has to do is watch *A Place in the Sun* to understand why Elizabeth, despite her provenance as merely a screen beauty who made headlines, rose above it all to ultimately eclipse her contemporaries. In that unsparing and breathtaking close-up in what Stevens rightfully knew would be the pivotal scene of the film, Elizabeth Taylor cradles Montgomery Clift as he pours out his pain to her. In that moment she transcends all of the lighthearted roles she had ever played and all of the scandal and sensation associated with her. With that one radiant scene, she became one of the great movie stars.

Elizabeth Taylor learned a very important lesson with *A Place in the Sun*. To be a truly great star required more than just manufactured romances and haute couture and fan-magazine covers. No press agent could do this part for her. To become truly great, Elizabeth had to do it all by herself.

And she did it magnificently. "Tell Mama," she says in that unforgettable scene, fully real, fully believable. "Tell Mama all."

Four

Acting Out

June 1955–October 1956

TOM ANDRE WAS HEADING into a war zone. Rattling over the back roads of west Texas in an open-air Jeep on a swelteringly hot afternoon, he was all too aware of the strife that awaited him on the set of George Stevens's film *Giant*—the director's first reunion with Elizabeth Taylor since their triumph in *A Place in the Sun*. The previous week, production manager Ralph Black—highly regarded in Hollywood as an efficient location man—had walked off the job. According to the report Black had made to Warner Bros., the studio producing the film, he could "no longer take the embarrassment of being abused before the entire company by Mr. Stevens." Andre had been hired to take Black's place, charged by Jack Warner himself with bringing some peace to the set.

It wasn't just the problems with Black. One memo called the entire set "explosive." The team spirit that had characterized *A Place in the Sun* (Monty Clift's occasional outbursts notwithstanding) was nowhere in evidence on *Giant*. Little mutinies were taking place almost daily. Long known for his demanding style, Stevens had become increasingly dictatorial in the past five years. After the huge success he'd had with *A Place in the Sun* and again with *Shane* two years later, few had the temerity to talk back. Stevens firmly believed that every last detail on a picture fell within his jurisdiction—a view that splintered the collaborative enterprise of filmmaking.

Case in point: Against the advice of veteran makeup supervisor Gordon Bau, Stevens had hired rookie Bill Wood to serve as his personal makeup advisor. Wood's résumé consisted mostly of B pictures, yet he was routinely asked to critique the work of people whom Bau called "far more capable men." Writing to the studio, Bau complained, "This situation is creating great disharmony in the makeup crew to the point that several of the men are threatening to quit the production. Should this occur, the situation will be most critical because there are no replacements available."

No kidding. Marfa, Texas—the site of the location shooting—was a forlorn little ranching town of 3,600 inhabitants drowsing under a big orange sky. The *Giant* company had been there several weeks now, and some of them were going stir-crazy. Browbeaten from long days in the sun, they had to drive twenty-six miles to the town of Alpine to reach the nearest swimming pool. Occasionally some of the younger actors like Earl Holliman and Dennis Hopper would commandeer a Jeep to the Mexican border town of Ojinaga, sixty miles away, where they drank lots of tequila to forget, for a night anyway, the pressures of working for George Stevens.

Driving in from the tiny airport north of town, Tom Andre looked out along the hot, flat desert plains. Nothing for the eye to see but prickly pear cactus and dry, rugged earth stretching off toward the horizon in every direction. Marfa itself was just a main road with a couple of shops and an old movie theater. During the war, the army had set up an airfield in town, training several thousand pilots, but they had abandoned the site about ten years ago. "There was nothing to do in Marfa," said Jane Withers, the former child star who had a small part in the film. She would host Monopoly tournaments at her boarding house where she was allowed to serve nothing stronger than Coca-Cola. No wonder Holliman and Hopper were hightailing it to Mexico. The heat, strife, and boredom were wearing these worldly Hollywood types down. Their nerves were frayed. Tom Andre knew his work was cut out for him.

And the stars were just as combative as the crew, perhaps even more so. Of the three top-liners—Elizabeth, Rock Hudson, and James Dean—only Hudson, facing his first real test as an actor, got along with the director. "I followed him around like a puppy," Hudson said, glad to turn himself into "putty" and place himself squarely in the director's hands. But the mercurial, Method actor Dean wasn't nearly so pliable. He regularly infuriated Stevens by snarling in the middle of a scene, "Cut, I fucked up"—a decision that Stevens believed was his and his alone to make.

Elizabeth was having her own troubles with the director. No longer the pampered minor protected from Stevens's tirades by a state social worker, she had to face him like any other actress. Carroll Baker, playing Elizabeth's grown daughter in the film's later scenes, thought the star was still plagued by a lack of confidence in her craft. "She'd had the MGM training where nothing moves," Baker said, "where you're very beautiful but very stiff." As Stevens grew impatient with Elizabeth, he'd begin shouting that all she cared about was glamour and appearance and that she'd never become a real actress. And Elizabeth—twenty-three and no puppy like Hudson—shouted right back.

Tom Andre had been chosen carefully by the studio to mediate. Known as an efficient manager, the fifty-year-old Iowa native had been in Hollywood since 1930, serving first as a studio secretary and then as a production manager, most recently for William Wellman on *Blood Alley*, starring John Wayne. His wife was Eloise Jensson, chief costumer on television's biggest show, *I Love Lucy*. Andre had clout, connections, and tact. He'd been instructed to bring order to the town like a frontier sheriff.

What he found when he arrived in Marfa on Saturday, June 18, 1955, was a massive Hollywood enterprise laid out in west Texas. Enormous fans had been erected to whip up dust storms; a network of hoses had been installed to pump out molasses that looked like gushing oil. On the cracked desert floor, Stevens had built the towering façade of a Gothic ranch house, the film's legendary Reata, home of Bick Benedict, wealthy cattle rancher (Hudson) and his beautiful wife Leslie (Elizabeth). And on the surrounding prairie, prop men had created miniature oil derricks, symbols of the conflict between Benedict and his nemesis, Jett Rink, played by Dean.

Stevens may have been at odds with his crew, but he went out of his way to win over the townspeople, opening the set and allowing hundreds to congregate each day to watch the filming and eat the free lunch that he provided. The presence of so many onlookers made Elizabeth nervous and the crew anxious. Under the blazing sun, surrounded by so much volatility, it's easy to understand why tempers often boiled over.

The only two people who seemed to really like each other were Elizabeth and Rock. From day one they'd been the best of pals. Hudson, twenty-nine, was sympathetic to any worries that Elizabeth may have had about her craft. Like her, he was known more for gorgeous good looks than for his acting talent. Despite this, Stevens had chosen Rock over Clark Gable for the role of Bick, and the actor was feeling the pressure. Elizabeth offered him an escape. "They were both a couple of kids at heart," said Mark Miller, Hudson's close friend. "When they got together, they could act out and have fun."

As the sun sank past the horizon and stained the desert red, Tom Andre watched with a mixture of concern and amusement as Elizabeth hauled out the booze. With Stevens having called the last "cut" of the day, she and Rock were playing their daily game of "Prince of Wales," chanting at each other as they chugged down beer after beer. Their drinking had become legendary. When a freak thunderstorm hit Marfa and dropped hailstones all over town, Elizabeth and Rock ran around collecting them in buckets to use as ice in their Bloody Marys. Another night they devised a chocolate martini—vodka and Hershey's syrup—and proclaimed it perfection, at least until they woke up with monumental hangovers the next day. Though they were never late to the set, Stevens couldn't have been too pleased when his two stars kept running to the "honey wagons"—the portable toilets—to throw up between takes.

Some people thought that such behavior was extremely unbecoming, especially on the part of Elizabeth, who was by now respectably married to a respectable man and the mother of two children, the second one born just four months earlier. Of course, her close association with Rock also led to rumors that the two were having an affair, but certainly Andre had been around long enough to know that Hudson was gay. At one point Rock entertained a visitor from Hollywood, his agent's secretary, Phyllis Gates, whom he was thinking of marrying to deflect the stories that swirled around him.

Elizabeth's husband, the urbane British actor Michael Wilding, also visited the set, and it's likely that no chocolate martinis were mixed for the duration. Chroniclers have tended to portray Wilding as worried that Hudson was trying to steal his wife, but surely the man knew better. Still, he was committed to the marriage, and he saw what was happening. Out there in the heat of the desert, far away from Hollywood, Elizabeth was rebelling—not just against the tyranny of George Stevens but the tyranny of her life. For twelve years everything in her life had been determined by the needs of her career. That included her marriage to the staid, much-older Wilding, designed for the public as an antidote to Nicky Hilton. If Elizabeth had hoped that being liberated from her mother would give her more independence, she found that she was still duty-bound to the studio, to her public, and to her fame. She might be one of the most popular stars in the world, but she increasingly felt that the only way out, the only way to preserve some small part of herself, was to go over the top. To act out. To say *to hell* with the rules. It was the same spirit of independence that had saved her from being eaten alive by the studio the way poor Judy Garland had been. And everyone—her studio, her director, her husband—was wise to take heed.

· · ·

Sitting in the house that the studio had found for her, gigantic electric fans rattling in the windows, Elizabeth read over the latest updates to the script of *Giant*. As angry as she might have been at Stevens, she remained grateful to him for casting her, especially since she knew that he'd wanted Audrey Hepburn first, and when he couldn't get her, he had hoped for Grace Kelly. Elizabeth had been his third choice. "Dearest George," she'd cabled the previous May. "Thank you so much. I hope I will be everything you want Leslie to be."

For *A Place in the Sun*, Stevens had never wanted anyone other than Elizabeth. But *Giant*—the story of three generations of Texas cattle ranchers and oilmen that was based on Edna Ferber's epic novel—was as big and sprawling as *A Place in the Sun* had been small and intimate. The simpler style that had served Elizabeth so well on the earlier film was never going to work here. For *Giant*, she needed to act in big, broad gestures that could command the wide screen of CinemaScope, but she had to be careful never to come across as garish or theatrical.

It was a heady challenge. The role of Leslie Benedict was a big, meaty one, with heart and spunk and passion. In a key scene, this former delicate flower from the verdant hills of Virginia stands up to the rough-and-tumble Texas cattlemen and demands to be treated as their equal. Not since her last project with Stevens had she been called on to do this much real *acting*. Despite all the acclaim she'd received for *A Place in the Sun*, no Academy nomination had materialized; no great follow-up parts had come from Metro. Instead they kept putting her in lightweight trifles like *Callaway Went Thataway* (1951), *The Girl Who Had Everything* (1953), and *Rhapsody* (1954). In *Elephant Walk* (1954), filling in for Vivien Leigh at Paramount, all she had to do was scream effectively when the pachyderms attacked. *Beau Brummell* (1954) was simply an excuse to dress her up in exquisite period costumes. The *New York Herald Tribune* called her a "china doll."

Only in *The Last Time I Saw Paris*, released in November 1954, did Elizabeth actually have to act, to apply some of the lessons

Monty Clift had taught her. Based on a story by F. Scott Fitzgerald, the film reunited her with Van Johnson from *The Big Hangover*, but now Elizabeth was billed first. As the independent spirit whom Johnson tries to tame, Elizabeth was playing a character more multilayered than usual. For a change, she had to learn "more than just glib dialogue." Director Richard Brooks drove her hard, sometimes pushing her to tears. Despite the film's overlong script and a bland performance from her costar, Elizabeth proved quite creditable in the part. She was, in fact, playing a variation on her public image: a sweet, basically decent girl who loves jewelry and clothes maybe a little bit too much, and who craves attention so much that she jumps into fountains to get her name into print. At one point she turns to her aspiring-author husband and asks, "Will you still worship me when you're famous?"

In real life, everyone knew how much her husband worshiped Elizabeth. She'd married Wilding on February 21, 1952, a week before her twentieth birthday, in a ten-minute ceremony at the Caxton Hall registry office in London that was as simple as her first one had been extravagant. The only thing the two weddings had in common was the mobs gathered outside. Despite the fact that most Londoners were still in mourning for King George VI, who'd died just two weeks earlier, three thousand people waited outside the registry for the newlyweds. When they emerged, a roar of applause rattled the windows along the street. In the crush of fans, Elizabeth lost her hat; several people hopped onto the running boards of the car and held on as the couple sped off for their reception at Claridge's. Safe upstairs at the hotel, Elizabeth and Michael could hear the constant chanting of "Liz! Liz!" from below. The new Mrs. Wilding wanted to wave from the balcony, but Mr. Wilding balked. "We are not royalty," he said. But Elizabeth knew better. After she coaxed him outside, they basked in the cheers for nearly half an hour.

Michael refused her nothing. He wasn't wealthy like Hilton, and that would take some getting used to for Elizabeth. But her new husband did his best to give her everything she wanted. The image that emerged from fan magazines suggested absolute devotion. According to the official publicity surrounding their marriage, it was Elizabeth, nineteen, who proposed to Michael, thirty-nine, who found himself absolutely unable to refuse her teenage charms. Wilding's adoration offered an important contrast to Nicky Hilton's disinterest, which had threatened to devalue her stock as an alluring screen goddess. The publicity around her second husband was intended to rectify that situation.

If the choice of Hilton as husband had been career-driven, then the choice of Wilding was even more so, some believed. "Wilding fixed everything," Dick Clayton said. No longer was Elizabeth the fickle girl shedding a husband after just six months. Now she told the press, "I just want to be with Michael and be his wife. He enjoys sitting home, smoking his pipe, reading, painting. And that's what I intend doing—all except smoking a pipe." It was a picture of domestic bliss that was meant to stifle the carping of moralists like Ida Zeitlin. And it worked, too. The press loved the Wilding marriage, assuring readers that Elizabeth had finally "grown up." *Look* magazine pronounced Michael "everything a doctor could have ordered."

To understand the etiology of the Wilding marriage, it's necessary to consider the full context of Elizabeth's life at the time. In late 1951 she was nearing the end of her MGM contract. Her agent, Jules Goldstone, was encouraging her not to sign again, proposing instead an independent production company, where she'd be able to enjoy more control. As shrewd as Hollywood agents came, Goldstone was a trust-busting attorney who delighted in subverting the autocratic control of the studios. As a founder of the Goldstone-Tobias Agency, he had created one of the first boutique talent agencies in Hollywood. Setting Elizabeth up as an independent would have been a real coup for him. But Goldstone was also smart enough to know that Miss Taylor's reputation needed a bit of sprucing up after her sensational divorce. So it was with real interest that all eyes turned to Michael Wilding in those final months of 1951.

He was a tall, distinguished, even elegant man. Elizabeth had first met him while making *Conspirator* in London some three years before, when she was just sixteen. Zealous publicists would later insist that it was then and there that she'd first fixed her eye on him as a potential mate. (This was at the same time, of course, that she was supposed to have been in love with Glenn Davis and William Pawley, but, as always, the public's short memory served to everyone's advantage.) When Elizabeth again encountered Wilding during the making of *Ivanhoe* in October 1951, she was no longer a schoolgirl but rather a not-so-gay divorcée. Someone—maybe even Elizabeth herself—got the idea that the debonair actor might just be the solution to her public-relations problems. It was true that he was married, but he hadn't lived with his wife, the actress Kay Young, for years. Certainly Goldstone must have agreed to the idea, since he immediately began representing Wilding as well. Sara, too, gave the match her blessing, since it meant that Stanley Donen wouldn't be coming around anymore.

Wilding did indeed fix everything. The fact that Elizabeth's glamorous sapphire and diamond engagement ring was paid for not by him but by the bride suggests that this was an enterprise arranged by interested parties. The alacrity with which Kay Young filed for divorce in November, after years of an amiable separation, also tells the story. The suddenness and unlikeliness of the Wilding-Taylor union left some bewildered—perhaps even the groom himself. "They were married [with] Liz wearing a dove gray suit and Mike wearing an air of surprise," one scribe observed.

Yet like his predecessor, Wilding had his own reasons for agreeing to the marriage. Popular in Britain as the frequent co-star of Anna Neagle in a series of melodramas directed by Neagle's husband, Herbert Wilcox, he had his eye on the kind of big-time American success his friend, the bombastic, flamboyant Stewart Granger, had achieved. Granger lived in a gorgeous house in Beverly Hills and starred in Technicolor swashbucklers for Metro-Goldwyn-Mayer—including *Beau Brummell* opposite Elizabeth Taylor. But since Wilding was an unknown to most Americans, the independent production company that Goldstone envisioned was not nearly as desirable for him as a contract with MGM.

By November Elizabeth and Goldstone had reversed course. Contract talks were restarted with the studio. But it wasn't just Elizabeth under discussion anymore. When Wilding came to Hollywood in December to ostensibly promote Neagle's film *The Lady with the Lamp*, he was, in fact, meeting with Metro execs. Goldstone made the pitch: If the studio signed Michael, Elizabeth would agree to stay put. Desperate not to lose her, MGM agreed. Elizabeth's about-face would be explained by saying that she'd gotten "cornball sentimental about Benny Thau and all the other nice people at the studio"—so much malarkey when one recalls how intensely she'd always disliked the studio system. But the despised Louis B. Mayer had been toppled and replaced with Dore Schary. A new regime, Elizabeth assumed, could only be better.

Even if the studio wouldn't have placed Wilding under contract if Elizabeth hadn't insisted, it's apparent that MGM saw the benefit of the marriage. The stories that appeared in the press of Elizabeth and Michael taking a "fishing trip" in northern California with Stewart Granger and his wife, Jean Simmons, were clearly the result of well-timed studio "plants." Such stories allowed the romance to take its place in the headlines, even as the studio officially denied any marriage plans. Within days the newspapers were inundated with romantic stories of "Liz and Mike," and soon the fan magazines had taken up the refrain. As studio publicists cranked out their releases, the press eagerly did its part to obliterate any memory of Nicky Hilton and the embarrassments he'd caused.

That is, all except Hedda Hopper, who let it be known that she did *not* approve. Elizabeth had chosen Wilding without any input from her. Hedda was furious—especially because she believed that she knew something Elizabeth didn't.

"I don't think you know what you're getting into," Hedda lectured the couple, whom she'd summoned for an emergency meeting at her home in Beverly Hills. Elizabeth and Michael sat demurely on the long settee in her den. "In the first place," Hedda argued to her honorary niece, "he's too old for you." Then she delivered the bomb: "And the rumor around town is that Michael Wilding and Stewart Granger are very, very close!"

Hedda didn't make such allegations lightly. "She knew who was gay and who wasn't," said Robert Shaw. "She never made a charge unless she had reason to believe it was true." Plenty of circumstantial evidence backed her up: the long, childless, separate-but-cordial union with Kay Young; the close friendship with Granger; the companionship of Marlene Dietrich, who was known to prefer gay men as escorts; and the idolization of Judy Garland, who made Wilding so nervous the first time he met her that he had to have several drinks to steady himself. There also would have been, Shaw said, more direct evidence collected by Hopper from her network of spies. "She had the dirt on everybody," Shaw said. "She knew where the bodies were."

In Hedda's mind, Wilding's marriage to the nineteen-year-old Elizabeth was like Granger's marriage to the twenty-two-year-old Jean Simmons: a cover-up that took advantage of a young girl. "The Wilding marriage was arranged from the start," Shaw believed, and his impression came directly from Hedda. Others agreed. Elsa Maxwell, when told of the impending marriage, discounted it as a rumor, insisting that Wilding was too "sophisticated" to marry the pretty teenager. Perhaps, then, marriage to Elizabeth Taylor offered another kind of benefit to a man looking to become a big American star.

As she confronted the couple, Hedda turned her gaze to Wilding. "Are you denying it, Michael?" she asked. He just sat there, as Hedda described, "with eyes downcast."

The columnist seemed apoplectic. "Are you going to marry a man like that?" she bellowed at Elizabeth. "Do you know what kind of life you'll have?"

Hedda Hopper has been called homophobic, but that's an oversimplification. With so many gay cronies, she clearly didn't hate homosexuals. To be sure, she had her generation's usual prejudices and wasn't above gay-baiting when it served her purposes. But she held no particular moral objection to gay people. Cole Porter and George Cukor were just dandy in her book—because they didn't make a pretense of who they were. They never tried to *pass*. Of course, homosexuality in Hollywood was kept secret from the general public, and Hedda understood that—but she had no tolerance for phonies within the industry. "If you tried to pull the wool over her eyes," Robert Shaw said, "she resented it." That was why she always despised Cary Grant for marrying all those wives. "Whom does he think he's fooling?" she wrote to the publisher of *Look* magazine. "He started with the boys and now he's gone back to them."

According to Stewart Granger, who would deny having a sexual relationship with Wilding, the bride-to-be was unfazed after the meeting with Hedda. "Oh, Mikey, don't worry about it," she said, brushing off the entire episode. For a girl whose best friends were Monty Clift and Roddy McDowall, marrying a gay man might not have been the worst thing in the world—especially after the horrible Nicky Hilton. Elizabeth thought of Wilding as "an oasis," she said. "He restored all sanity [and] represented tranquility, security, maturity—all the things I needed."

And for all her spite, Hedda could be counted on to keep mum about her accusations, at least in print. It would be years, in fact, before she'd make public what transpired at her house that day in late 1951. Had she written up her charges in her column at the time, as some biographers claim, Wilding's career would have been ruined. The only comment she made in print came a few days after the wedding when she asked Kay Young if she was "as fond of Stewart Granger as Michael is." Wilding's ex-wife took the bait. "Not really," she said. "He has a very strong personality but he doesn't take me in."

Yet there's no question that Wilding was a devoted husband to Elizabeth and that he was determined to make the marriage work. And, at least in the beginning, his wife did her part as well. Knowing that Wilding suffered from occasional epileptic seizures, she was very solicitous of him and watchful for any warning sign. The connection was strong enough for a time that Elizabeth could indulge her romantic fantasies, which were never very far from the surface. With all the fervor she would have brought to a similar role onscreen, she played the part of a twenty-year-old woman in love and seemed to enjoy every bit of it. The journalist Doris Lilly spotted the couple at a New York restaurant, seated in a corner table, "holding hands and rubbing their legs together" while passing notes back and forth to each other. Elizabeth "had wildly romantic notions about life," Lilly believed, "which included her approach to love and her desire to do things differently."

The newlyweds spent money "like drunken sailors," Michael Wilding said of the giddy early days of their marriage. Driving up a twisting mountain road in Beverly Hills, the Wildings found their dream house. It wasn't large but it was certainly out of the ordinary, designed by George MacLean, the architect for billionaire shipping magnate Daniel K. Ludwig, who later developed Westlake Village. A hidden chimney and a wall made of bark covered with ivy and orchids gave the place a kind of "Walt Disney, *Snow White* setting" for Elizabeth. The swimming pool and enormous chrome bar suggested more adult pleasures. Best of all, there was sufficient closet space for all of Elizabeth's clothes and shoes. Stamping her foot, she told her husband that no other house would do. Wilding just shrugged and agreed. He had to ask the studio for help, but he bought the mountaintop retreat for his wife. "We got a great deal of pleasure from giving each other expensive presents which we could not afford," he said. "Life, we both thought, was all too short, so why not enjoy it?" But money would be a constant worry.

The Snow White house gave the fan magazines the storybook ending they'd been denied with Hilton. On January 6, 1953, Elizabeth gave birth to Michael Howard Wilding; two years later, on February 27, 1955, her own twenty-third birthday, she bore a second son, Christopher Edward Wilding. Various organizations would name her Mother of the Year during this time, and she would be frequently photographed bouncing her two beautiful boys on her knees. In some photos she even wore a checkered gingham dress. Elizabeth was giving her fans the perfect picture of an American family.

Meanwhile those parts of her public image that had proved troublesome in the past were cheerfully forgotten. "Elizabeth Taylor is an example of what a girl does when real love comes along," wrote one columnist, surely working from press agents' talking points. "When married to Nicky Hilton, she loved only her career. With Mike Wilding, she loves only Mike and the things around him, like their children, their home, and the hundred little things that go with a happy marriage."

All this mythmaking was given official sanction by Sara, whose piece for *Ladies' Home Journal,* published in the early spring of 1954, became a bible for writers who chronicled the life of her lustrous daughter from then on. In the final installment of the three-part article, Sara described Elizabeth rocking baby Michael in her arms, calling the star "a born mother [who] knows now why she was born."

Yet while her love for her children was never in doubt, Elizabeth Taylor was hardly the average hausfrau reading *Ladies' Home Journal* at the end of a hard day. From the moments of their births, Michael and Christopher had nannies to feed them, change them, and teach them to walk. Only at dinnertime would Elizabeth receive the boys, all dressed and cleaned up, their patent leather shoes shining. "She doted on the boys," said one close friend. "She loved them with all the passion she had. But she was emotionally still a kid herself. I'd hardly say she raised them."

There's a scene in *The Last Time I Saw Paris* that rings with some real-life truth. Elizabeth's free-spirited character stands cooing over her newborn baby. "The last nine months I've devoted to you," she says sweetly. "Now I'm going to have fun!" Laughing, she tosses the baby in the air while her husband looks on, horrified.

A thousand miles away from Beverly Hills in Marfa, Texas, Elizabeth was indeed having fun, kicking up her heels and knocking back shots of tequila with Rock Hudson. She missed her little ones, of course: Jane Withers recalled bonding with Elizabeth over their shared sadness at leaving children behind. But after three years of playing the lead role in that picture-perfect life, Elizabeth was tired of it and ready for some action.

At the little theater in downtown Marfa, ranchers in six-gallon hats rubbed shoulders with Mexican immigrants and movie stars. Singing cowboy Monte Hale, who was playing a small part in *Giant*, strummed his guitar in the lobby as folks arrived. George Stevens took a seat up front, and Elizabeth and Rock slid into the row behind him. Just as he did every night, Tom Andre had ensured that the film for the evening's show had arrived in time from Hollywood. But this wasn't the latest studio release. Stevens was projecting the rushes for everyone to watch. This was what passed for an evening's entertainment in Marfa. Sometimes the rushes only consisted of endless stretches of cattle and Elizabeth and Rock sitting on horses. But the show would still draw packed houses. With no film lab nearby, the day's raw footage had to be flown to Hollywood, developed overnight, and sent back. Tom Andre saw to it that the show always went on.

Jimmy Dean, if he came at all, would be slouched against a far wall, ready to split before the lights came up. Dean rarely socialized with his fellow actors, preferring to learn rope tricks from local cowboys and shoot rabbits with the crew. His mumblings around the set—his way of staying in character, a hallmark of Method acting—unnerved his costars; Jane Withers once asked him what all that limbering up of his shoulders and shaking of his fingers meant, and he looked at her as if she were mad.

Despite the stories that have come down to us about the great friendship between Elizabeth Taylor and James Dean, there was no love lost in the beginning between the glamorous Hollywood-trained actress and the surly New York thespian. Under the tent where everyone ate their meals, Dean would "make fun of Elizabeth and Rock because they didn't come from the Actors Studio," said Carroll Baker. Elizabeth represented all that Dean despised about Hollywood. Where Monty Clift had found her charming, Dean considered her ludicrous. She'd waltz into the "dingy" dining area wearing white chiffon, Baker said, and Dean would shake his head derisively. For her part, Elizabeth seethed every time Dean broke a scene saying he needed to rethink his motivations. Off to her trailer she'd go, swearing a blue streak.

Yet somehow Andre managed to get the production back on track, smoothing over differences and arranging reconciliations, even if temporary. The studio had been worried that the location shooting might stretch through the summer, but by the first week of July they were all packing to head back to Los Angeles. On July 9 a convoy of Warner Bros. trucks packed with costumes and props rattled down Marfa's main street. Elizabeth and her costars went on ahead by train.

Filming resumed at the Warners lot in Burbank. On the day Elizabeth first appeared wearing her old-age makeup, Hedda Hopper was invited onto the set to get a look. Possibly trying to insinuate herself back in the star's good graces, the columnist reported that given the makeup results, she could now "guarantee Liz Taylor will be as handsome [at fifty-five] as now." Yet all Stevens had done to age her was shake some powder in her hair and give her a few lines around the eyes. The middle-aged Leslie Benedict still had the hourglass figure of the twenty-three-year-old playing her.

Her figure had, in fact, been a concern at the start of the film, especially since she had just given birth to Christopher. As the pampered wife of Michael Wilding, Elizabeth had become well-known in Hollywood for her rather hedonistic relationship with food and drink. Tables at her parties sagged with gourmet delicacies. "My tastebuds get in an uproar," she admitted, "and I get a lusty, sensual thing out of eating." Before starting *Giant*, she had been at least fifteen pounds heavier than she should have been, mostly from eating ice cream drenched with fudge and peanut butter and mayonnaise sandwiches right before bed. But whenever she was faced with starting a picture, she simply starved herself, she said, explaining how she'd managed to fit into Leslie's tailored dresses for *Giant*. "I have coffee for breakfast, scrambled eggs for lunch and steak for dinner—with pink grapefruit juice coming out of my ears."

But the alcohol was putting the pounds back on. Every night during production, Rock invited people up to his house in the hills above Sunset Boulevard, and the drinking that ensued there was prodigious. "The pile of empty bottles in the trash the next day told the story," said Mark Miller. Most of the cast would show up, even James Dean, though he had an ulterior motive. His rivalry with Hudson, increasing every day as the film neared completion, had turned Elizabeth into a prize to be won. As one party wore on into the early morning hours, the other guests began asking where Jimmy and Elizabeth had disappeared to. They were discovered outside in the backyard talking together in hushed tones. All the strife in Marfa was forgotten. "He became very introspective," Elizabeth recalled, "and told me some things that just blew my mind." She chose never to reveal what he'd said. But Carroll Baker said Jimmy was saying, in effect, "Hey, Rock, I can take Elizabeth away from you."

But it was with Rock that the real friendship remained. Elizabeth and Michael hosted him one night for dinner. "It was a very liquid evening," Hudson admitted. The next morning they were shooting the wedding scene in which the estranged Bick and Leslie are so moved by the couple's vows that they reconcile on the spot. It was all to be done without dialogue, using only their eyes and expressions. As the scene was being filmed, many observers were moved to tears by how effective the two actors were, how romantic they seemed—when, according to Rock, they were really just "dreadfully hung over."

Like Clift, Hudson offered Elizabeth a friendship that could be intimate without being sexual. And she seemed drawn to the oversized "camp" nature of gay men like Hudson, who dressed in outrageous costumes for parties or bantered together in preposterous, phony accents. Mark Miller recalled a night soon after their return from Marfa when Rock and Elizabeth sat drinking with George

Nader, the sword-and-sandal movie actor who was Miller's lover. Well past midnight, they developed a yen for nachos and cheese. Rousing Rock's chauffeur, they toured several all-night Mexican eateries, sampling the nachos in the backseat of the car. And when they got home, Miller said, these three glamorous Hollywood stars "sat in a circle on the floor and held a belching and farting contest, laughing like crazy." Elizabeth, of course, won.

She'd never had a childhood. Now she was a wife and a mother, expected to parade her maturity and good sense before the world. No wonder she acted out. No wonder she looked for ways to escape the tedium, the schedules, and the commitments. George Stevens was still shouting at her on the set, accusing her of being late and holding up the entire company just so that she could get her makeup right. Elizabeth bellowed back that she'd never been called to the set. No wonder she began to call in sick.

On Friday, July 15, right around the time of the late-night nachos fiesta, Tom Andre received word from Elizabeth's doctor that the star had a throat infection that had spread to her bladder, "causing acute pain." Dr. John H. Davis diagnosed it as a slight case of pharyngitis and cystitis—strep throat and a urinary infection, both bacterial. Jack Warner, head of the studio, was informed that "she must have medication and at least forty-eight hours rest in bed, possibly seventy-two hours." Elizabeth would not be working that day or the next, and Davis would determine if she'd be able to report on Monday. In fact, she did *not* work that day, but managed to come in for a few hours for wardrobe talks.

Two weeks later she was complaining to Dr. Davis about a pain in her left leg. He diagnosed it as thrombophlebitis—vein inflammation—"caused by wearing very tight breeches." As Leslie, she was frequently dressed in riding gear that showed off her shapely legs. Once more she was unable to work and didn't return until August 8.

Only Elizabeth, it seemed, could get injured from wearing tight pants. Her delicate constitution was becoming legendary in Hollywood. "I catch cold even from weather forecasts," her character says in *The Last Time I Saw Paris,* yet another bit of autobiography in that film. Once, sitting with Michael by their pool, both of them were stung by a bee. Michael just pulled out the stinger, but Elizabeth's swelling lasted a week and a half. "If she opens a beer can, she cuts herself," said the director Richard Brooks. "If there is a chair in the middle of the set, she falls over it." On the *Elephant Walk* set an electric fan had blown a splinter of steel into Elizabeth's eye, which eventually turned into an ulcer. Press agents, sensing a good story, leaked word that "lovely Elizabeth Taylor might be facing blindness in one eye." In an inspired bit of publicity, Albert Teitelbaum, the furrier to the stars, sent over an ermine eye patch. "I couldn't wear it because of the danger of fur next to my eye," she told reporters, "but how I loved the idea!"

The illnesses and accidents weren't so much fabricated as they were exploited, and as a form of rebellion against the strictures of her life, they often served Elizabeth very well. Just a day after returning to work, Elizabeth collapsed after a scene where she had to jump on a bed. Although she had a congenital anomaly of the spine—a condition that would cause her considerable pain in the years ahead—this time the problem, her doctor insisted, was due to a ruptured intervertebral disc. After she was brought home, her back was strapped with adhesive tape. X-rays were taken the next day and Tom Andre was notified that the star was suffering from sciatica—an extremely painful and unpredictable ailment. Shot up with novocaine and hydrocortisone, Elizabeth was also given prescriptions for the painkillers Meticorten and Demerol. It was not clear when she would be returning to the set. If she needed to be put in traction, it could be several days.

George Stevens fumed. He was falling behind schedule. "Miss Elizabeth Taylor's illness from August 1 to August 8, inclusive, caused the *Giant* company to shoot around her as much as possible," Tom Andre reported to the studio. The second unit was brought in to do work originally scheduled for later, but eventually the company was unable to proceed without its leading lady and was "forced to lay off." Clearly the situation could not continue.

Metro was already hounding Stevens to get Elizabeth back to her home studio so that she could start work on *Raintree County,* another big epic picture slated to be shot on location. So Tom Andre was dispatched to find out what was really going on. Dr. Paul McMasters, the physician treating the sciatica, wouldn't say whether she was well enough to work. It was up to his patient, he explained. "If she felt well enough to come in," McMasters said, it was "all right" with him.

The next day Elizabeth was given a call for 8 A.M. makeup. She arrived only twenty minutes late, hobbling onto the set using crutches. Tom Andre asked if she'd prefer a wheelchair. She replied that she could manage better with the crutches. "Dr. McMasters recommended we keep Miss Taylor off her feet as much as possible," Andre reported to the studio chiefs, "which, naturally, we do."

Some people thought that she was playing for sympathy. At the end of the day, one member of the crew noticed her running after Rock yelling, "Hey, wait for me!" as if nothing were wrong. Although that's the nature of sciatica, it's also quite possible that she was having a better day because Stevens hadn't yelled at her quite so much. Certainly the director's view was that her illnesses were temperamental, or possibly just hangovers from too many chocolate martinis. On August 31, when she called in to say that she had a "very bad headache," Stevens bellowed that she'd better show up since "she was involved in everything [they] were doing." A studio memo suggested that she consider moving onto the lot until the picture was completed—a suggestion the star chose to ignore.

"You must understand that when Elizabeth got sick, she was in control," said one close friend, requesting anonymity. "It was her show, nobody else's. She always felt the pain, no question, but if she could drag it out a day or two longer, or insist she couldn't walk, she could live her days the way she wanted to, without any director or husband or publicist telling her when to sit, when to stand, when to smile, when to pose pretty for a picture." She could stay home, her friend said, like a kid playing hooky from school, watching television, playing records, and eating chili with ice cream. It was her little rebellion against those who ran the machinery of her fame.

On September 26 she was sniffling and sneezing with a bad cold. The company was in the midst of shooting the important fight scene in Sarge's Diner, where Rock, defending a family of Mexicans, gets drawn into a fistfight with a bigot. They had to stop filming at noon because Elizabeth looked so weak; first aid was brought in, and her temperature was found to be 99.6.

With such a low-grade fever, somebody else might have soldiered on, but a call to Elizabeth's doctor resulted in an order to send her home immediately. Stevens insisted that she at least stick around to shoot three close-ups before departing, and then her stand-in was used to resume filming the fight. Still trying to keep things running smoothly, Tom Andre called Elizabeth's doctor, who said that if his patient could "remain in bed" the entire next day he'd guarantee she'd be able to work the following. But if she were forced back to work too soon, the doctor said, all bets were off. A weary Stevens surrendered and gave her the day off.

But then James Dean was killed on September 30 while driving his Porsche 550 Spyder near Cholame, California. On the lot the next day, Elizabeth reacted dramatically to the news, snapping at Stevens for not appearing emotional enough and then "losing her breakfast in the makeup department." Those present attributed her vomiting to distress over Dean's death, but her doctors said that she might actually be suffering from appendicitis or an ovarian cyst. There was also the possibility, they said, that she'd sustained some serious damage from her caesarean section back in February.

On the night of October 2, Elizabeth was admitted to UCLA hospital. Dr. Robert Buckley grimly told Stevens that she was "more ill than she had ever been" in the twelve years he had been treating her. The *Giant* company was forced to suspend shooting once again on October 3, with MGM agreeing to release Warners from further payments for the use of their star until Elizabeth was able to return to work.

The film was far behind schedule by now. Once again, it was Andre who tried to fix things. He spent hours trying to get Elizabeth's doctors on the phone. When at last he reached them, he urged that they delay any "exploratory operations" and simply focus on getting their patient well enough "to finish the picture." Surprisingly, the doctors agreed to his request. Any major treatments could be put off until the end of shooting, they said. Andre was delighted. Only two interior scenes, including the final sequence with Hudson, were left to do, along with some loops with Elizabeth that he estimated would take about three hours. Dr. John Davis thought Elizabeth could handle that, and "following completion of the picture [she would be readmitted] to the hospital [to] correct all conditions which now exist with her."

Yet it's clear from private medical reports filed with Warners' insurance company that Elizabeth's doctors knew very well by this point that she wouldn't need to return to the hospital. The various fears of appendicitis, ovarian cysts, peritonitis, or caesarean complications had all turned out to be groundless. Dr. Davis finally concluded that Elizabeth was suffering from "extreme nervous tension" brought on by both the news of Dean's death and "the extreme mental duress she was put under by the director at this time." Although the primary diagnosis was volvulus, a twisting of the intestine possibly due to stress, Davis also listed bronchitis, suggesting that Elizabeth's cold from the previous week had simply gotten worse. (Viral bronchitis can also sometimes produce gastrointestinal symptoms.) On October 5 Tom Andre got the welcome news that Elizabeth's fever had broken and that the "obstruction in her intestine" had been relieved. On Saturday, October 8, Davis told Andre that "he saw no reason—unless something new came up—why she would not be able to [resume] work on Tuesday."

Something new frequently *did* come up, but they all hoped for the best. Studio chief Jack Warner had been kept apprised of "the Taylor situation" in regular memos. So it was with great relief, felt from top to bottom, that Elizabeth returned to the set on October 11. She was a bit hoarse but otherwise no worse for the wear. That shouldn't imply that she hadn't suffered through her ordeal. Dr. Davis stressed to Andre that "she had been a very sick girl all week." Though it would appear much ado had been made over a bad case of bronchitis, the star had suffered no less for the histrionics. When a doctor once told her that he could find no physical cause for an ailment, she shouted back, "Then why do I feel this terrible pain?" Elizabeth Taylor never faked an illness. She suffered through them all, even if someone else—someone who hadn't grown up with a constant flutter of attendants and caregivers around her—might have required less attention and less treatment for the same ailment.

She also demonstrated once again that she wasn't exactly powerless against the authoritarian system that governed her life. Stevens rode everyone hard, but it was Elizabeth who ultimately determined when she showed up for work and which days she got off. After the director had offended Elizabeth by refusing to call a halt to filming after Dean's death, he had no choice but to suspend production three days later when she checked herself into the hospital.

Of course, Elizabeth's absences from the set also meant that the studio's profits were undercut. Losses directly attributable to her illnesses totaled $44,309.40. It's not likely that Elizabeth lost much sleep over that. She might have considered it payback for the long, difficult shoot that she'd had to endure. She might be their chattel, but she was no mindless sheep to be herded along by the rigid studio machine.

At a party for Benny Thau at Romanoff's a few weeks later—with Dore Schary and Louis B. Mayer seated discreetly at separate tables—Elizabeth gaily made the rounds, Hedda Hopper reported, "and she's forgotten all about illness." When she'd been assessed back in May by the studio's insurer, the Fireman's Fund Insurance Company, Elizabeth had been rated as a "good" risk. No history of illness in the past six months had been reported, and when asked about any present complaints, she had replied, "None." She had told the insurer that in the past three years no accident or sickness had ever prevented her from working. *Giant*, however, changed all that. After what she went through on that film, Elizabeth learned one more lesson of stardom. To get what one wanted, every weapon in one's arsenal had to be used. All was fair in the game of fame.

But there was an additional reason for Elizabeth's distress over the past few months. Her marriage was disintegrating. And one scandal rag dared to suggest that her allure had paled against that of the burlesque queen who was rumored to be her rival.

Jennie Lee, whose forty-two-inch bust had made her the Bazoom Girl in the after-dark world of Los Angeles burlesque, peered out between the red velvet curtains. She knew right away that the gentlemen at the front table were upscale types. Jennie figured on doing her special trick for them: twirling the tassels attached to her breasts clockwise, then counterclockwise, and then in opposite directions at the same time in a stunning grand finale.

The twenty-six-year-old native of Kansas City, Missouri, headlined a show five nights a week at Strip City, a burlesque theater at Western Avenue and Pico Boulevard. Despite the clucking from some of the city's puritans, Strip City was no dive: Jazz lovers flocked from all over to hear the likes of Dizzy Gillespie, and comedians like Redd Foxx often performed between the striptease acts. Still, the place had a certain edge: Foxx's routines were laced with four-letter words, and anywhere whites and blacks mixed was considered outré in 1955. There were also drag queens and gay men. Anyone in search of something a little more dangerous than Mocambo was drawn to Strip City. One of those was Michael Wilding, who was sitting at the table up front with his pals.

Jennie Lee might not have known who he was right away, but she was a smart cookie. Since arriving in Los Angeles a few years earlier, she'd fought for the rights of "exotic dancers" (she disliked the term "stripper") by organizing her girls and affiliating with the American Guild of Variety Artists. She campaigned to raise the dancers' $85-a-week minimum wage, which she claimed was the lowest in the nation. With a shrewd eye for publicity,

Jennie threatened a "cover-up" strike. The girls appeared at a press conference in topcoats and refused to take them off until they got a raise. Jennie eventually won $100-a-week salaries for her hardworking team.

That summer—while Elizabeth was in Texas—Jennie had organized an exotic dancers' softball team and invited photographers to watch them play in Griffith Park. The girls' picture graced the front page of the *Los Angeles Times*. Michael Wilding—and the rest of the city—couldn't have missed it. Among the players showing off their gams and softball gloves was one Verena Dale, a voluptuous blonde like Jennie herself. It was Verena who recognized the upscale patrons at the front table. Among them were Michael Wilding, the husband of Elizabeth Taylor, and a well-known Hollywood writer.

After the show Jennie and Verena and two other girls stopped by Wilding's table. They often flirted with celebrities; Rock Hudson had been there on occasion, as had Dean Martin. Alcohol flowed fast and easy, and at the end of the night Wilding drove Verena to her home on North Hobart Boulevard, less than ten minutes away. According to one of Jennie's protégés, Elizabeth's husband and his friends returned frequently to Strip City over the next few weeks, and an unlikely friendship developed between these Hollywood uptowners and the freewheeling burlesquers. Wilding became especially fond of the high-spirited Verena Dale. Both had, at the very least, a love of liquor in common. The Associated Press reporter James Bacon, who was Wilding's good friend, recalled that the sophisticated actor was "fond of his Scotch—the drink, not the nationality."

After the last curtain fell on the night of Wednesday, June 22, Wilding and his writer friend decided to keep the party going a little longer and invited Verena, Jennie, and a male employee of Strip City back to the house in Beverly Hills. The fivesome piled into Wilding's white Cadillac along with the ladies' lacy costumes that they would need to shoot a "strip movie" the next day. Up they drove to Elizabeth's "Snow White" house where, presumably, the two Wilding sons were either fast asleep or away for the evening. There the girls swam in Elizabeth's pool and the men kept the liquid refreshment flowing. At one point Verena jumped up on a cocktail table in a red negligee and did a version of her striptease, minus the usual pasties.

Jennie left soon afterward, leaving Verena and the male employee at the Wilding house. But she had a whopper of a story to sell. The fact that the escapade ended up being splashed across the cover of *Confidential,* the most notorious scandal magazine of the era, meant that someone had squealed, and the most likely culprit—the only one with any motive—was Jennie. James Bacon, long rumored to be the friend who accompanied Wilding to Strip City, has never acknowledged whether he was there that night, but he did admit to knowing about the "encore party" at Wilding's house, and he was certain that *Confidential* had been tipped off by one of the strippers. The media-savvy Jennie had cultivated contacts well beyond the fellows at the *Los Angeles Times.* For a dancer struggling to make a living wage, the payola offered by the scandal magazines for dirt on the stars was extremely lucrative. Even as she slid into the backseat of Wilding's Cadillac, Jennie was probably already counting the cash she could make by letting *Confidential* know about the impromptu party at Elizabeth Taylor's house.

The magazine's publisher was Robert Harrison, a flamboyant playboy who drove white Cadillacs and wore white alpaca coats, and whose other publications included the girlie magazines *Titter, Wink,* and *Flirt.* In fact, many of the girls from Strip City, possibly even Jennie and Verena, had posed for Harrison. But it was *Confidential* that sent the publisher's fortunes skyrocketing. By 1955, midway through a decade that aggressively celebrated and promoted conventional values, the scandal rag was selling four million copies a month. For all the power wielded by Hedda and Louella, the columnists were, after all, dedicated to the advancement of the industry; they happily promoted its necessary fictions. In Burbank, even as Jennie was tattling to *Confidential,* Warner Bros. publicists were busy preparing a mock column for Dorothy Manners, Louella

Parsons's assistant and frequent Hearst substitute columnist. They made sure to include all of the talking points they wanted to pass on about Elizabeth and *Giant*. "The progressive coming of age of a violet-eyed, twenty-four-year-old mother of two named Elizabeth Taylor is a topic that has occupied Hollywood almost constantly," the studio wrote. "It will perhaps come as a surprise to many that in *Giant* ... Elizabeth emerges as an actress of great range and power." When Manners's column appeared in print, much of the Warners wording was left intact. Making a busy columnist's job easier was one of the studios' most effective tricks of the trade.

But *Confidential* and its copycats—*Top Secret, Whisper, Uncensored, Private Lives,* and others—heralded a new and very different kind of Hollywood press. Here the studios' much-vaunted publicity machine broke down. Their elaborate mythmaking—with their mimeographs and scripted interviews and ready-to-go columns—was challenged by the rise of the scandal magazines. "What *Confidential* proved," wrote *Time* correspondent Ezra Goodman, "was that there was too much pallid, punches-pulled reporting elsewhere and the average, untutored reader was probably wise to it and instinctively knew he was being hornswoggled. He undoubtedly realized that *Confidential,* in its own way, was giving him a glimmer of truth."

Harrison was based in New York, so he set up his niece, Marjorie Meade, as head of Hollywood Research, Inc., an information-gathering service that kept Los Angeles private detectives working overtime. These sleuths and spies were the doppelgängers of Hollywood's press agents, evil twins who undid all of their good brethren's hard work. Instead of building up the stars, *Confidential* was dedicated to tearing them down, "to flipping over the rock of the sleepytime Eisenhower '50s and showing the creepy stuff underneath," according to the son of its editor. In due course, Tab Hunter's lewd-conduct arrest with other "limp-wristed lads" was unearthed and exposed; the sexual adventures of Maureen O'Hara and Dorothy Dandridge were revealed; and the private companionship of Katharine Hepburn and Spencer Tracy, discreetly ignored by the mainstream press, was sensationalized. At the eleventh hour, a story exposing Rock Hudson as gay was killed in a quid pro quo deal with Hudson's powerful agents, exchanged for a story about Rory Calhoun's criminal past—and likely a considerable chunk of hush money as well.

Rats, stool pigeons, hookers, pimps, and strippers could earn ten grand or more by passing on dirt to *Confidential*'s spies, who were everywhere. It's not surprising that the magazine's editor, the alcoholic, goofball-popping Howard Rushmore, had gotten his start as an assistant to Senator Joseph McCarthy and had testified as a friendly witness before the House Committee on Un-American Activities. Rabidly anti-Communist, Rushmore actually thought that McCarthy wasn't tough enough on subversives; none of that kind of mollycoddling would be allowed in the pages of *Confidential*.

It was in the middle of September, just before Elizabeth came down with the bad cold that had turned into bronchitis, that the November issue of *Confidential* hit the stands with Wilding's little party headlined across the front cover: WHEN LIZ TAYLOR'S AWAY, MIKE WILL PLAY. "There are millions of red-blooded hubbies in this world who think they'd be as faithful as the rock of Gibraltar—if they had the right wife," the article read. "You're an exception to the rule if you never sat in a darkened theater watching the contours of Elizabeth Taylor and vowed you'd always be on time if you had *that* to come home to." But Wilding, the magazine implied, seemed to know something that the rest of the public didn't. "His high jinks program rolled into high gear within hours after Liz took a plane to Texas," the article continued, describing Wilding as unable to keep his hands off Verena Dale and mentioning his promise to her that she could be his girlfriend. Considering Hedda Hopper's allegations, these likely were exaggerations on the part of the informer, who, after all, wanted *Confidential* to feel that it was getting its money's worth. Wilding and Dale were probably more drinking buddies than anything else. Yet no matter how many details were true, the main thrust of the article was that not even Elizabeth Taylor was alluring enough to keep her man.

The "respectable" Hollywood press rarely acknowledged claims made by *Confidential*, but the industry was always abuzz with them. Copies of all the scandal rags were delivered hot off the press to the desks of every Hollywood producer, agent, and columnist. Hedda Hopper couldn't resist publishing a blind item. "A neighbor of Liz Taylor and Mike Wilding was so incensed over a recent story that appeared in a magazine that she's taking matters into her own hands," Hedda wrote. "If her method works, I'll tell you what she's done." Just what this neighbor had planned—a camera monitor?—is unclear, but Elizabeth couldn't have been pleased by the scuttlebutt. Her handlers at both MGM and Warners likewise must have been horrified by the implications of the *Confidential* story because it directly undercut their promotion of Elizabeth as a sexy star. If *she* couldn't keep her man happy, what woman could?

In private, Elizabeth's response to the article, all sources agree, was blasé. She "chalked it up to one of Michael's playful moods while under the influence," said James Bacon. Asked about it later by *Look* magazine, she commented, "Whether it's true or not, you can't let an article like that break up your marriage." But you *could* go to the hospital—which Elizabeth did about two weeks after the magazine hit the stands. The press made sure to note how Wilding was right at her side, attentive to her every need. Elizabeth's bronchitis seems to have come in handy for more than just leveling the playing field with George Stevens. It also distracted attention away from Verena Dale's red negligee.

But for all of her apparent open-mindedness about her marriage to Wilding, Elizabeth *was* distressed. The union had reached the end of its usefulness, and the tricky negotiations for extradition had begun. Elizabeth would admit that husband and wife had lived like "brother and sister" after the birth of Christopher. But that didn't imply a happy sibling relationship. Wilding recalled a "typical row." Relaxing after breakfast with the *Times* crossword, he was startled when his wife suddenly snatched the paper out of his hands, tore it in half, and lobbed it into the fireplace. "So much for you and your stupid games!" Elizabeth shrieked, trying to bait him into hitting her. "Go on, hit me, why don't you?" she shrilled. When he refused, she groaned, "If only you would. That would prove you are flesh and blood instead of a stuffed dummy!"

At twenty-three, Elizabeth was too young, too frankly carnal, to live like a sister to her husband. Hedda Hopper might have explained the lack of sexual passion one way, but later on Elizabeth blamed it on Wilding's epilepsy: "It does something to a man." No matter the reason, she was left frustrated by her sexless marriage. Her pals Rock Hudson and Monty Clift had tricks left and right, but she was expected to twiddle her thumbs while Michael worked out the crossword puzzle.

All that changed when she and Wilding headed off to Europe later that year. *Giant* was finally completed, and George Stevens was holed up in his darkroom with nearly 900,000 feet of film. Elizabeth was taking a much-needed holiday before starting *Raintree County*, and Wilding was playing a supporting part in the Arabic adventure *Zarak*, being filmed in India, Burma, and Morocco. The lead was the virile Victor Mature, the movies' broad-chested Samson, and Elizabeth seemed all too eager to play Delilah. She'd later tell Eddie Fisher, amid gales of laughter, how she and Mature carried on an affair right under Wilding's nose, sometimes in the very next room.

But Wilding may not have been entirely clueless. Even in far-off Morocco, *Confidential* had its spies, and the tale of WHEN MIKE WILDING CAUGHT LIZ TAYLOR AND VIC MATURE IN ROOM 106 was splashed across the magazine's July 1956 issue. "Remember that stripteaser you had in my house," the scandal rag quoted Elizabeth as saying when Wilding opened the door, "and how silly you looked at 6 A.M. dancing around with her G-string around your head? Well, snookums, you look just as silly now. So close the door before mama catches cold."

The dialogue, with its echo of Elizabeth's famous line in *A*

Place in the Sun, was likely pulled from the writer's imagination, providing *Confidential* with a terrific sequel to its original story. But the basic facts of the story are apparently true. One of *Confidential*'s strengths, as revealed in the legal trials it would eventually endure, was the magazine's requirement that two unrelated affidavits, signed and notarized, had to back up any actionable allegation. At least two sources with direct knowledge of the goings-on in Room 106 would have had to vouch for the story. The *Confidential* machine was, in fact, nearly as expansive and well-oiled as those run by the studios. Nothing was printed without first being vetted by detectives.

The question remains: Who leaked this one? Although it certainly wasn't positive publicity for Elizabeth, the piece did effectively refute any aspersions cast on her allure by the first article. Might a friendly hand have been involved in passing along the information to the scandal magazine? "It wasn't unheard of to work with *Confidential* if [studios or press agents] thought they could get what they wanted," said Mark Miller. He suggested that Mike Todd—Broadway impresario, wide-screen projection pioneer, and Elizabeth's eventual third husband—may have been behind the *Confidential* story. Dick Clayton, too, had heard the rumor: Whether true or not, "it seemed plausible."

Certainly the flamboyant, risk-taking Todd had a history with the scandal magazine. A few months earlier he'd planted a story with *Confidential* about actress Kim Novak that, while superficially unflattering, ultimately helped her in her fight against her home studio, Columbia Pictures. But if Todd's fingerprints might also be found on the story about Elizabeth and Victor Mature, it suggests that the producer was involved in the star's life months earlier than has ever been reported. This is supported by the memory of Hank Moonjean, who believed that Todd began playing an important part in Elizabeth's life as early as May 1956.

"The full story of how [Elizabeth and Todd] met has never really been understood," said Susan McCarthy Todd, daughter-in-law of Mike Todd. And it hasn't just been the timing that has been obscured. As McCarthy Todd revealed, Elizabeth did not meet Mike through mere chance, as most accounts have stated. Rather, the introduction came through his assistant, a gregarious Irishman by the name of Kevin McClory. In the late winter or early spring of 1956, Elizabeth met McClory on the MGM lot; they quickly formed a bond. At the time, Todd was renting space at Metro to develop his Todd-AO projection process, so during the whole *Confidential* brouhaha he would have been only a few doors away. (Elizabeth would acknowledge that her first encounter with Todd was in the MGM commissary.) Susan McCarthy Todd thought that it was possible that her father-in-law had taken an interest in Elizabeth's career even by that point, and not just as a favor to Mc-Clory. "He saw her potential," she said, "and I think he liked [playing the starmaker]." If he'd gone out on a limb for Kim Novak, he'd certainly do the same for Elizabeth.

The star herself was probably unaware of Todd's efforts on her behalf, at least on the particulars. No doubt she wouldn't have been too thrilled about a story that called her an adulteress. Yet despite the negatives, the *Confidential* piece provided Mrs. Wilding with some public vindication over her "cheating" husband. Even more important, it reassured readers that Elizabeth Taylor was just as desirable as ever. Todd and his publicity team understood that the best results required Machiavellian methods. "You had to be shrewd, very shrewd," said Shirley Herz, one of the press agents who worked for Todd. "You used everything you had." If there were any fears that Wilding might use the adultery with Mature against Elizabeth in a divorce suit, they would have been negligible, since Elizabeth—using *Confidential*'s first article as a basis—could have turned around and done the same thing to him.

This was the real significance of the scandal magazines. While four million people might read them monthly, *tens* of millions read Hedda, Louella, and their ilk in the daily newspapers and fan magazines. If the mainstream outlets could be convinced that even the muckrakers at *Confidential* now believed that Elizabeth had the upper hand against Wilding, that impression would play out in their coverage. Miller said that insinuations made by the scandal rags would "seep upward" to reach the bigger news outlets; any damage that Elizabeth's star reputation had sustained could now be canceled out.

Indeed, a month after the *Confidential* exposé of the Mature affair, Elizabeth was being called by one fan magazine "the beautiful wife that Mike Wilding is desperate to hold on to." *Look* magazine went so far as to describe a romantic all-night romp through Paris that "Mike" took "Liz" on during the filming of *Zarak*. All of this wasn't so different from the time Sammy Davis Jr.'s agent planted a story with *Confidential* that Sammy was having an affair with Ava Gardner. While Middle America might recoil from a mixed-race romance, Davis's standing within the industry instantly shot up—so much so that he sent Harrison a pair of gold cuff links as thanks. "The scandal magazines weren't always about hurting careers," the publicist Alan Cahan agreed. "Sometimes they could help."

What couldn't be helped, however, was the Wilding marriage. The strain was showing. At one magazine photo shoot, Michael suggested that Elizabeth move over to get the best light. "I know how to pose for a picture," she snapped at him. "When you have taken as many pictures as I have, *then* you can tell me how to pose. Meanwhile, just be quiet, Daddy"—a uncanny echo of Sara talking to Francis.

Four years earlier, Michael Wilding had been the perfect mate. But the job was done. Elizabeth had blossomed into a popular, even beloved star, heralded not only for her beauty and glamour but also for her motherhood and deep commitment to family. As the real woman rebelled—finding that living a charade was too frustrating—it became increasingly evident that Wilding's serviceability had run its course. "She needed someone bigger than Wilding," said Henry Baron. In Hollywood marriages lasted only so long as they were useful, said Dick Clayton, and "when Taylor needed a new image, her publicists would look around for something new on the romantic front." Something new—something to shake things up—but just what that would be depended on the kind of star that Elizabeth Taylor, now twenty-four, was going to become. And at the beginning of 1956, as the world awaited the release of *Giant,* that was still unclear.

Wilding had to have realized that he'd come up short in the deal. He was left with little—except, of course, for two sons, which surely counted for something. But the MGM contract had disintegrated after only three pictures, none of them major hits, and he was back working in British productions like *Zarak.* Wilding never fit in in Hollywood and, indeed, was never all that comfortable as an actor. "I feared it," he admitted. "I was not a born actor and the art of acting never came to me easily."

The marriage was over but for the technicalities. Wilding was weary of trying to keep up with his wife. He told his friend, the costume designer Noel Taylor, that "he went broke trying to satisfy Mrs. Wilding's whims and extravagant tastes." Another confidant of Wilding's told the reporter Aline Mosby that the actor was "restless to be back with his older, sophisticated crowd in London, where he would not be Mr. Elizabeth Taylor." Another friend suggested that the marriage had never stood a chance of longevity. "Mike Wilding was too subtle and sophisticated," this friend said. "He was a pixie who liked to drink and have fun. He wasn't exactly rich either."

And what was becoming apparent was that no matter what kind of star Elizabeth Taylor was set to become, a rich husband sure would help.

Even though she was new to Hollywood, Shirley MacLaine knew a few things about the glamorous residents of the movie capital that others did not. Letting herself into her Malibu beach house, she was followed by her husband, businessman Steve Parker, and her two friends, Kevin McClory and Elizabeth Taylor. And what the foursome found after their night out on the town was MacLaine's dog getting sick all over the floor. Without a moment's hesitation and ignoring the lovely dress and expensive shoes she wore, Elizabeth got down on her hands and knees, and helped Shirley clean up the mess.

It was more than just Elizabeth's refreshing lack of movie-star pretension that MacLaine understood. She was also aware that Elizabeth was having a serious affair with McClory and that they'd spoken of marriage once she could be divorced from Wilding. Indeed, it was on that night in the early spring of 1956, while he watched Elizabeth on the floor cleaning up after a sick dog, that he decided she was the woman for him, McClory admitted.

The young man had much to recommend him as a husband for Elizabeth. Born in Dublin, McClory had a passionate Irish temperament that contrasted powerfully with Wilding's passivity, and a quick wit that kept Elizabeth in stitches. His minor speech impediment, to her mind, was simply a touching flaw that endeared him all the more. And McClory was just six years older than she was, another striking comparison to her twenty-years-older current husband. He wasn't rich, unfortunately—but while Wilding was on his way out, McClory was on his way up. After serving as assistant to director John Huston, he'd been snapped up by Mike Todd, the Broadway bigwig whose wide-screen 70mm process had wowed Hollywood with *Oklahoma!* and who was now ready to release the first picture under his own banner, the colossal *Around the World in Eighty Days.* MacLaine had played the key part of the quirky Princess Aouda.

It was during this period, MacLaine said, that Elizabeth was poised between one chapter of her career and another. "They were planning to build her up to be the biggest star at MGM," she said. With advance word on *Giant* causing tremendous excitement, there was a sense that Elizabeth might finally ascend to the absolute top ranks. Although her popularity over the last decade had been prodigious, she had remained a glamorous costar always paired with a bigger male name. When Metro had tried to get her top solo billing for *Giant,* Warners had refused; she'd had to settle for second place after Rock Hudson, with both of them below the title. It was a fair call, since for all her profitability, Elizabeth had not yet broken through into the top ten at the box office. The only women to do so over the last few years were Marilyn Monroe, Susan Hayward, and Jane Wyman. By 1956 there was a growing belief that Elizabeth could join their ranks.

The nature of filmmaking was changing; television, of course, was the major catalyst. As the decade went on and the small screen increasingly siphoned off the movie audience, the studios responded by making films bigger. Gone were the simple seventy-minute programmers made cheaply on the backlot. Now movies got longer—two, three hours—and wider—along with Todd's process, there was CinemaScope, Cinerama, and VistaVision. Location shoots exploited film's potential for exotic verisimilitude that the stage-bound limitations of the small TV screen could never rival. Elizabeth's latest picture, *Raintree County*, which began shooting in April 1956 and reunited her with Montgomery Clift, was planned by its director, Edward Dmytryk, to rival *Gone With the Wind* as an epic Civil War romance. Shooting took place across Tennessee, Kentucky, and Mississippi. The final cut of the film would run about three hours.

And just as the films were getting bigger so, too, were the stars. With fewer and more costly pictures being made, there was no longer as much room for second-rank stars—the likes of Dennis Morgan or Ann Sheridan, for example—popular players "who kept the factory humming," in the words of historian Jeanine Basinger, churning out profitable pictures without ever really rising to the pantheon of greats.

Now, with the factories no longer humming quite as loudly (within a couple of years, more films would be imported from other countries than were produced at home by Hollywood) only a few rarefied actors remained reliable moneymakers for the studios. Usually these were the extravagant, larger-than-life, over-the-top headliners. This was the era of spectacle stars like Burt Lancaster, Charlton Heston, Yul Brynner, and John Wayne, of pop-culture phenomena like Frank Sinatra, Jerry Lewis, and Elvis Presley. The

biggest female stars of the period were usually femme fatales ooz-
ing the kind of sexuality banned from the sanctity of television
viewers' living rooms: Monroe, Kim Novak, Grace Kelly, Sophia
Loren, Brigitte Bardot. Despite notable exceptions like Audrey
Hepburn and Doris Day, it was the likes of Jayne Mansfield and
Mamie Van Doren who would define the va-va-voom 1950s. With
Elizabeth's curves and exquisite face, there was every reason to believe that—given the right film roles and the right kind of publicity
to go with them—she could surpass them all.

So back to the Metro machine. In the wake of television and
Confidential, it had gotten a bit creaky, but still it functioned, glam-
orizing starlets in Hair and Makeup, cranking out breathless press
releases, and placing strategic phone calls to Hedda, Louella, and
Sheilah Graham. When Shirley MacLaine first walked onto the
lot on loan-out from Paramount, she was a twenty-three-year-
old kid with big red curls and not a lot of experience. She looked
around in awe as she stepped into Sydney Guilaroff's hair salon.
There was Greer Garson, she recalled, "swathed in a turquoise blue
robe that set off her carrot-colored hair," and Deborah Kerr, "thin-
hipped and more bawdy than the world ever knew." In came Audrey Hepburn, "all Dresden," walking her small poodle and gliding
along "as if on satin roller skates." Then Debbie Reynolds bounded
through the doors, "the pride of Burbank, punching jokes and being cuddly." Sydney, tall and graceful in his finely woven, skintight
linen shirts, would pass up and down his row of ladies, "painting
and sculpting the beautiful hairstyles."

And finally, Elizabeth Taylor made her appearance, "chunky
and looking ten years younger with no makeup," said MacLaine,
who watched her with fascination. "She'd flop into any chair that
was vacant, eating a cheese Danish and plopping her feet up on
the table in front of her." MacLaine would tease her about her
big feet, saying that they looked like a weightlifter's, and Elizabeth would laugh in that high-pitched girlish cackle of hers. Then
Sydney would come around to light Elizabeth's cigarette, "and she

would draw the smoke long and deep into her lungs with the same low-down basic oral gratification she lavished on the cheese Danish." Another day at MGM had begun.

There was a "camaraderie of shared purpose" among the stars, MacLaine said. "Everyone seemed to understand that our purpose was to go on those screens and be loved by strangers." There was a recognition that it was especially important to gain and keep that love because the movies faced crises that threatened their very existence, that signaled an end might be in sight for their magical world of make-believe.

For Elizabeth, *Raintree County*, based on Ross Lockridge Jr.'s 1948 Civil War bestseller, was supposed to bring huge rewards to both herself and the industry that she had served so diligently, if not always so cheerfully, these last fifteen years. MGM hoped that the picture would even outclass *Giant*, still being painstakingly assembled by Stevens over at Warners. Elizabeth was playing the Scarlett O'Hara–inspired character of Susanna Drake, a tempestuous Southern belle who comes north and steals John Shawnessy (Monty Clift) away from his devoted childhood sweetheart (played by Eva Marie Saint). The film was big and brassy, with all of the heightened Technicolor melodrama so popular in the fifties. At one point the increasingly schizophrenic Susanna makes her way through enemy lines and ends up in a mental hospital down South. There's an implication of miscegenation, and she ends up drowning herself in a swamp. It was supposed to become a classic.

Although Edward Dmytryk was a capable filmmaker—*Crossfire* and *The Caine Mutiny* stand out on his résumé—he was not a master craftsman like George Stevens. More attention was paid to the film's bigness—it was shot in MGM Camera 65, a new process for capturing images in 65 millimeter—than to the overwrought, frequently dull script by Millard Kaufman. Due to the extensive location shooting, the cost of the film skyrocketed: An MGM memo estimated that the difference between filming on location and filming at the studio was $5,800 per day, not counting the cost of extras. Almost from the start Clift sensed that the picture could be a disaster, grumbling that MGM's five-million-dollar extravaganza was a "soap opera with elephantitis."

But worse was to come. On May 12, a particularly foggy night, Elizabeth and Michael, still keeping up the pretense of their marriage, hosted a dinner party at their house. The guest of honor was to be Father George Long, a man of the cloth so modern, Elizabeth gushed to Monty, that he actually said "fuck." (The English priest actually did more than that: He aided and abetted Elizabeth's extramarital affair with McClory by acting as "cover" when the lovebirds were seen around town.) Elizabeth was planning quite the gathering for the good father. In addition to Monty and his friend, the actor Kevin McCarthy, who was then making *Invasion of the Body Snatchers,* Elizabeth had invited Rock Hudson and his new wife, Phyllis Gates.

At first Monty declined. Lately he'd been feeling uncomfortable by the awkward middle ground he occupied in the Wildings' marriage. Undeniably fond of his beloved "Bessie Mae," he'd also grown close to Michael, who frequently showed up at Clift's house on his own for long heartfelt talks. But finally Monty agreed to attend the dinner and drove himself up the long winding road to the Wildings' house in Benedict Canyon in a leased sedan.

The party wasn't quite what any of them had expected. Father Long never showed. Wilding wasn't feeling well, so for most of the night he reclined on the sofa, aloof and not saying much. Elizabeth was nervous and chatty, her mind perhaps on the affair that she was carrying on at Shirley MacLaine's Malibu beach house. Soon after midnight Monty decided to head home. His lover, Jack Larson, who was not present, believed that he'd had a couple of glasses of wine with his meal, but that was it; Kevin McCarthy disagreed, saying they'd both made a decision not to have anything to drink at all that night. Either way, everyone involved insisted that Monty was not drunk. Standing in the driveway, he shared with McCarthy his dissatisfaction with the way Dmytryk was directing the picture, shooting nearly everything in giant close-up and chopping the actors' hands out of the frame. Then they bid each other good night, got into their respective cars, and drove off down the hill that Elizabeth called a "cork-twister." McCarthy was in the lead.

Within moments, he was back at Elizabeth's house, ringing her doorbell frantically. Wilding answered the door, and McCarthy blurted out that Monty had had a serious car accident. Elizabeth came up behind her husband and asked what was wrong; when Wilding tried to shield her from the news, she exploded. "Is it Monty? What's wrong with Monty?" McCarthy told her that Clift's car had struck a utility pole as he'd rounded one of the hairpin turns on the dark, foggy street. Elizabeth shrieked, demanding that McCarthy take her to the scene of the crash.

Monty's car was demolished, an "accordion-pleated mess," Elizabeth said. A 4,800-volt transformer, knocked off the pole by the impact, had narrowly missed hitting the car. McCarthy thought that his friend was dead. "The doors were so jammed that we couldn't get to him," he said. Without any hesitation, Elizabeth climbed in through a back window, heedless of the broken glass. "Adrenaline does something to you," she remembered. "Where I got the strength I don't know." Hauling herself over the bloody front seat, she steeled herself to the carnage. "All my revulsion about blood absolutely left me," she said. Monty's body had slipped down beneath the steering wheel, "literally under the dashboard," Elizabeth said. What was worse, she could barely make out his face. "It was like pulp," she remembered.

At first Clift didn't move, but after a few moments he began to react to the sound of Elizabeth's voice. He indicated that he was choking. Several of his teeth had been broken and were now lodged in the back of his throat. Reaching in with her fingers, Elizabeth pulled the teeth out, one by one. "I firmly believe, and the doctors agreed, that Elizabeth saved Monty's life that night," said Jack Larson. Otherwise, he said, Monty would have choked to death on his own blood and broken teeth.

The ambulance got lost and took nearly an hour to get there, so a handful of photographers had made their way to the scene by the time Monty was being lifted onto the stretcher. Kevin McCarthy remembered one from *Movieland* magazine. But Elizabeth knew how to deal with them. Both McCarthy and Larson confirmed the oft-repeated stories that Elizabeth positioned herself protectively between Monty and the photographers' cameras and told them that if they so much as took *one* picture of her wounded pal, she'd never allow them to take another picture of her. (Just imagine a world without photographs of Elizabeth Taylor.) "She was remarkable," said McCarthy.

In the days ahead, as Monty underwent painful reconstructive surgery on his face, Elizabeth was often at the hospital to cheer him up, jostling for position with the fifty-two-year-old Libby Holman, the torch singer and scandalous stage actress who was Monty's *other* best girlfriend. Holman had never liked Elizabeth, calling her a "heifer in heat." At least one mutual friend of Elizabeth and Monty's felt that Holman blamed Elizabeth for the accident. For her part, Elizabeth thought that Holman was a bad influence on Monty; at one point Elizabeth discovered Holman allowing Clift to sip a martini through a straw after he had returned home, bandaged and in traction. Although she bawled Holman out, Elizabeth wasn't averse to doing the same thing once Monty was able to sit up in a chair.

Holman's assignation of blame, however, may have had its desired effect on Elizabeth. "I'm not sure if she blamed herself," said Mark Miller, who heard accounts of the accident from Rock Hudson, "but I think she felt she had a responsibility to help Monty recover." Another friend of both Elizabeth and Monty's said, "After Montgomery Clift's car accident, Elizabeth kind of woke up and made some decisions about her own life. When something like that happens, you see how fleeting life can be. After all, it could have been her in that car."

The experience left Elizabeth with recurring nightmares. Monty's bloody face haunted her: "It would come up like a balloon in front of me at night." Certainly reaching into a friend's bloody mouth and withdrawing his broken teeth had been a pretty close encounter with real life—not a frequent experience in the pampered, protected, day-to-day existence of Elizabeth Taylor. With production of *Raintree County* forced into hiatus while Clift recovered, Elizabeth found herself at liberty to take stock, to consider the next steps in both her public and personal lives.

For one thing, she quickly realized that she needed a new agent. She'd once told Jules Goldstone that she'd be his client for as long as he practiced in Hollywood. But she'd also told him, "You'll never be really big in this town, Jules, because you're not a big enough shit." Goldstone was shrewd and efficient, but he was also essentially decent and aboveboard. To get ahead in Hollywood, to reach the very pinnacle of power, Elizabeth didn't need a nice guy; she needed a shark, a *bastard*. At least that was the counsel she was getting from Kevin McClory, advice that was backed up by his boss, Mike Todd.

Elizabeth had been spending more time with the flamboyant showman. At a post-premiere party for *Moby Dick* at Mocambo in July, reporters noted that while Michael Wilding table-hopped, his wife remained deep in conversation with McClory and Todd. In fact, Todd had begun cautioning McClory against being seen with Elizabeth in public, given that she was still married. Significantly, Metro issued a statement the day after the party that announced the Wildings had decided to separate, and Mike Todd, no coincidence, was at the studio in Benny Thau's office at the time.

Sailing with Todd on his yacht and bringing her children to barbecues at his home, Elizabeth witnessed the producer's incredible wealth up close and personal—and she found it mighty appealing. "For Elizabeth," one friend said, "wealth was the ultimate security. If she could be wealthy enough—something neither Michael Wilding nor her own career had yet been able to make her—she could make her own decisions and live the way she wanted and not be a slave to the studio." So money might be her way out. She admitted to Hedda Hopper that marriage to a rich man like Mike Todd would give her the luxury of not having to work. "I've never really been crazy about a career," she said. "I never wanted to be an actress."

That statement was true only as far as it went. Yes, it had been her mother who had thrust ambition upon her. But by 1956 Elizabeth knew life only as a movie star. She might wax poetic about the simple life, but every time she and Todd met—under the moonlight on his yacht or at a corner table at Romanoff's—he was telling her how much bigger she could be, how much more control she could have, how much more grandly she could live *if only* she had the right people around her. No surprise, Kevin McClory was soon replaced in Elizabeth's life by Todd himself.

One story encapsulates the reason. Don Tomlinson, Todd's editor on *Around the World in Eighty Days*, remembered the little gold locket that McClory planned to present to Elizabeth as an engagement gift. "It must have set him back twenty dollars," Tomlinson said. He told McClory that the locket wasn't going to be enough for the likes of Elizabeth Taylor. "What do you mean, that's not enough?" an offended McClory asked. Yet not long after this McClory found himself replaced at Elizabeth's side by his boss.

Mike Todd offered much more than a twenty-dollar locket. Once Todd entered the picture, Elizabeth Taylor's career went into overdrive. By the time *Raintree County* resumed filming that summer (Clift's face had healed, but was never quite the same), Todd was planning his next project, a spectacular film adaptation of *Don Quixote*, in which Elizabeth would star.

Giant finally premiered that October. Gala celebrations were held in New York and Los Angeles. At the Chinese Theater on Hollywood Boulevard, ten thousand spectators packed the street while enormous searchlights cut across the night sky. Once more, the Hollywood elite was out in force: Lucy and Desi, Bob Hope, Henry Fonda, Tab Hunter, Groucho Marx. A cheer went up from the crowd as a gray-haired Clark Gable stepped out of his limousine, smiling and gracious despite being passed over in favor of Rock Hudson for the role of Bick. America's Sweethearts, Debbie

Reynolds and crooner Eddie Fisher, arrived arm in arm, waving to their fans. Mr. and Mrs. Oscar Hammerstein came on the heels of Viscount and Viscountess Paul de Rosiere, representing Cartier jewelry, who were, notably, good friends of Mr. Mike Todd.

At the end of the picture, the applause was thunderous. Once again George Stevens had boiled down his gargantuan footage into a first-rate picture and provided Elizabeth with a personal triumph—no matter how rough he'd treated her during filming. For all of Dean's scenery chewing, it is Elizabeth who stands out best, utterly splendid in her portrayal of Leslie. When she takes on the cattle barons to demand her place at the table, she is incandescent: a powerful force of nature barely contained within her slim, girlish frame. In the second half of the film, she is the most believable of the three leads by far, transitioning seamlessly from young whippersnapper to wise old grandmother. "She got hold of that [transition] and did it," Stevens said, "and if she hadn't have done it, she would have sagged down into nothing."

Critics shared his appreciation for her work. The *Motion Picture Herald* said Elizabeth displayed "a new artistry." Bosley Crowther in the *New York Times* said that she convincingly turned her character into "a woman of spirit and sensitivity who acquires tolerance and grows old gracefully." *Variety* opined, "Miss Taylor, whose talent and emotional ranges have usually seemed limited, turns in a clever performance that registers up and down the line." Once more, predictions were made about an Academy Award.

Significantly, the ad campaign focused on Elizabeth and Rock rather than on the deceased Dean—though the cult that was already growing up around his memory surely contributed to the film's impressive grosses. Publicists, perhaps thinking it unseemly to hype a dead man (these were, after all, more discreet times), launched a campaign that promoted the love story between Leslie and Bick. Film posters bannered just three words in huge type: LIZ AND ROCK. Radio ads in sixty-, thirty-, and ten-second spots intoned a version of the same script:

Whad'ya got, whad'ya got? Liz and Rock, Liz and Rock! In the giant entertainment of them all! Giant! Giant! Giant! Giant! It's a big story of big feelings and big things! Liz and Rock, Liz and Rock, Liz and Rock, Giant!

And television, that great rival of the studios, proved that it could also be the newest, and perhaps most effective, medium for promoting movies. Against a sweeping shot of the Texas desert with the façade of Reata looming in the background, the TV announcer proclaimed,

Elizabeth Taylor and Rock Hudson. The giant entertainment of them all. George Stevens's production of Giant. *Elizabeth Taylor and Rock Hudson. The big stars. The big story. The big emotions. Elizabeth Taylor and Rock Hudson. The two big stars. The only picture big enough to bring them together.*

Giant proved to be a runaway hit, the biggest moneymaker until then in Warners' history. And with Mike Todd at her side for the New York premiere, Elizabeth was poised for success equally as impressive. Her alliances with men, dating as far back as Glenn Davis, had always been chosen, consciously and unconsciously, for what they could offer her. Nicky Hilton had given her romance and headlines. Michael Wilding had brought stability to her reputation. But Todd could give her much more than any of that. Mike Todd could give her the world.

Five

Over the Top

July 1957–March 1958

PRINCE ALY KHAN and his latest ladylove, the French model Bettina, were astride pink and purple horses on the carousel. Behind them, Sir Laurence and Lady Olivier (Vivien Leigh to the masses) waved enthusiastically to Baron Shawcross, former attorney general and the lead British prosecutor at the Nuremberg Trials, who was busy dancing a rumba with Debbie Reynolds. A light mist may have been dampening the partygoers' fine duds, but it did nothing to ruin their gaiety. Mike Todd, that master showman, had left nothing to chance, distributing plastic raincoats to every one of his seventeen hundred guests. He'd permitted himself only one moment of pique, stamping his foot and shaking his fist up at the clouds over London's Battersea Park, cursing God for daring to rain on his parade.

Watching from a perch on the raised wooden walkway known as the Tree-Walk, Dick Hanley breathed a long sigh of relief. The party, celebrating the London premiere of Todd's wide-screen epic *Around the World in Eighty Days,* was a smashing success. Hanley could relax and have a good time.

After being canned by Louis B. Mayer (some thanks for eleven years of devoted service), Dick had been hired as Todd's executive secretary, and it was his job to make sure that everything—from poker games at the Beverly Hills Hotel to extravagant galas like this one—went off without a hitch. Never far from Todd's side as the producer flew around the world making his big, extravagant picture, Dick jetted from Hollywood to New York, New York to London, London to New York, New York to Paris, Paris to New York, and New York to Hollywood—all in less than a month. But he was glad to do it. When the history of cinema was written, Hanley told friends, Mike Todd would be an even bigger name than Mr. Mayer. Though some people in Hollywood still considered Todd a carpetbagger, he was also being hailed as "the hottest man in show business" by the press. After all, no one could argue with success—especially not the big, unqualified success that Todd was enjoying—so rare in an industry still hemorrhaging audiences and profits every year.

Around the World in Eighty Days proved that the movies could still make big money. Since its New York premiere in October 1956, the film had smashed previous box-office records one by one: first *Giant,* then Cecil B. DeMille's *The Greatest Show on Earth,* and finally *The Robe,* a CinemaScope spectacle starring a Welsh actor named Richard Burton. Now Todd's picture—once dismissed as an overblown gimmick—was going head-to-head with DeMille's *The Ten Commandments* in an effort to overtake the biggest box-office champ of all time, *Gone With the Wind.*

Dick Hanley was smiling. He knew that his boss despised false modesty. That was Todd's whole reason for this party—to rub his success in the noses of all those in Hollywood who had doubted him. Here was Mike Todd, on the banks of the Thames, hobnobbing not with nouveau riche movie folk but with authentic aristocracy. He'd bussed them in by the hundreds on red double-deckers, their tiaras and jewelry bouncing along on the ride to Battersea. Helping the Duchess of Argyll alight, Todd cracked, "Imagine, a duchess on a bus." The quip went around the globe in an instant, and Mike Todd, the son of a poor rabbi from Minneapolis, was suddenly king of the world.

And at his side was his twenty-five-year-old queen, the radiantly beautiful and visibly pregnant Elizabeth Taylor. Todd, twice her age, helped her onto one of the boats that ferried guests across the Thames. A Spanish singer serenaded her with a flamenco guitar as she placed her hand to her heart and blew her husband a kiss. From the front came the bells and gongs of Oriental music; from behind, the soulful call of Hindustani strings. Seven different bands played music from the seven different countries visited by Phileas Fogg in the movie, turning the normally quiet waterway into a cacophony of music, laughter, and applause.

On shore it was more of the same. Seven chefs whipped up seven different national cuisines to satisfy every taste. Fish and chips were served in baskets lined with specially printed editions of the *Times*, dated 1873. Giant prawns were brought in from Hong Kong; curry dishes from India; sweet potatoes from Virginia. At the sideshows, partygoers dug their hands into buckets of copper pennies to use for playing the roulette wheel. The coins came courtesy of Todd in order that his guests would not have to pay for a single thing—not even the penny prizes. From caviar to stuffed bears, the entire night was on him. No wonder the champagne was still flowing well past dawn the next day.

Of course, Todd's generosity was matched only by his self-promotion. "An openhanded sort," *Time* magazine called him, "who would pass out salted nuts at his own hanging if he owned the beer concession." Todd did, in fact, own the concession; after *Around the World* he could do anything he wanted. Hollywood was his. Every studio was ready to open its gates—and its coffers.

At one point, however, his mood darkened. A drunken guest staggered a bit too close to Elizabeth, and Mike suddenly seized him by the collar and nearly shoved him into the river. "My wife is pregnant," he growled. "Will you please be a gentleman?" Raised eyebrows were exchanged between Lord Dalkeith and the Countess of Dartmouth. So *that* was the famous temper of the American showman. Elizabeth joked that she might have the baby right then and there, and if so, she hoped that it was a girl. "I don't know whether the world is ready for another Mike Todd," she said, eliciting a round of laughter.

They'd been married for five months; she was probably seven

months pregnant. They'd just come from Cannes, where Europeans had gotten their first glimpse of Todd's film, and where, just for the fun of it, the producer had invited a thousand people to a casino on the Boulevard de la Croisette and imported a circus from Paris. Lions and tigers paced in their cages as guests dined on smoked sturgeon. When Mike brought his wife around to the gambling tables, Elizabeth dropped her hand into his jacket pocket and withdrew a stack of notes. "There must be $10,000 here," she gushed, wide-eyed.

"Pocket money," he told her. "Put it back. And don't count it. It's vulgar to count money."

That much cash in the pocket of Mike Todd could be a dangerous thing, especially in a casino. At the age of fifty, he had already made and lost a million dollars in Chicago's construction industry, gambled away a second fortune, and declared bankruptcy twice. "He was a man who didn't look back," said Susan McCarthy Todd. "There was always something better ahead that he was planning to make happen."

And all he had to do was snap his fingers. Two days after his Battersea Park bash, Todd packed up his wife and entourage and planned to sail back home. His baby, he insisted, would be born on American soil. But at a farewell party in their hotel suite, attended by friends and a scattering of reporters, Elizabeth suddenly appeared in the doorway and announced that she'd lost their passports. Mike exploded.

"Call the American Embassy!" he shouted. It was left to Dick Hanley, as usual, to calmly remind him that it was the Fourth of July, and the embassy was closed. "Then call the American Consul in Southampton!" Hanley wasn't sure that there was time for new passports to be issued, since they were sailing in a matter of hours. But Todd was confident. "They'll fix us up somehow," he said. After all, he was Mike Todd.

Indeed, they all sailed later that day on board the SS *Liberté*, temporary passports in hand. The consul had opened its doors as a special favor to Mr. Todd. After that, their voyage was uneventful. Given Elizabeth's condition, Todd said that he had put in a special request for calm seas. There were some who took him at his word.

Sailing across the Atlantic, Mike Todd kept the telegraph operator busy, sending out regular dispatches to his publicist, Bill Doll, in New York. The American tabloids were eager for items about Todd and his fabulous London bash and all of the glittery guests who'd been in attendance. They wanted news of his wife and the baby she was expecting even more. Todd complied, sending ship-to-shore messages detailing Elizabeth's daily schedule of lounging on a chaise and eating sliced pears and chocolate peanuts. He wanted the public to be assured that he was treating her like a queen.

How different Elizabeth's life was from just a year before. When she met Todd, she'd been an unhappy wife pining for attention from a distant husband. Mike supplied that in spades, but he gave her even more. In those last few years with Wilding, what Elizabeth had really longed for was liberation from her masters at Metro—a seemingly impossible dream, since it would have meant sacrificing the money and the fame that enabled her to live in the style to which she'd grown accustomed. Enter Mike Todd, whose goals neatly complemented Elizabeth's. Looking to make himself a major Hollywood player, Todd recognized the benefits of being married to Elizabeth Taylor. "She was like the jewel in the crown," said Miles White, Todd's friend and costume designer on *Around the World in Eighty Days*. "He liked having her on his arm because she was a living, breathing, gorgeous symbol that he had made it to the top of the Hollywood pack."

The union of Taylor and Todd occurred because of what each could do for the other. Mike had the wealth that would free Elizabeth from dependence on Metro; she had the fame on which he could trade to make it in the film industry. In many ways their romance wasn't unlike the passionate pairing of another prominent couple nearly twenty years earlier. In 1938 Katharine Hepburn was a star in trouble, branded as "box-office poison" and desperate to climb back on top. Howard Hughes was an aviator with dreams of glory, who had captured the world's attention with a daring and ostentatious around-the-world flight. With this union Hepburn maneuvered herself back on the covers of the fan magazines even as her films were flopping, and Hughes solidified his shy lothario image by having won America's most aristocratic star. "He was sort of the top of the available men—and I of the women," Hepburn wrote. "It seemed logical for us to be together . . . We each had a wild desire to be famous."

While Elizabeth did not share Hepburn's "wild desire" for fame, she did have a very strong predilection for a certain way of life—which she had come to expect as her due after being a star for more than a decade. Making movies may never have been a passion for her—but living like a movie star certainly was. Mike Todd was the answer on both counts. Elizabeth knew from the start that the flamboyant showman could be her escape from MGM. She hadn't been in front of the movie camera since finishing *Raintree County* almost a year earlier, and the lack of film work had been absolute heaven. For Elizabeth, Todd held out the promise of a golden future—*not* the future Metro publicists tried so hard to sell to the public, the one that portrayed her as longing for a simple domestic life as a wife and mother—but rather something far more glorious than that: travel and adventure, fabulous parties and even more fabulous diamonds, palatial homes and easy living. Scrimping and saving and sitting home the way she had with Michael Wilding was definitely *not* going to be Elizabeth Taylor's fate.

But she did make the requisite noise about retiring from pictures in favor of home, hearth, and babies. "Mike and I hope to have many children," Elizabeth was quoted as saying in one Metro press release. "I think it's much more important for a woman to be a mother than an actress." She stated it even more plainly elsewhere: "I've been an actress for fifteen years. Now I want to be a woman!"

But even if Todd allowed her to think that way for a time, his wife's retirement from the screen was certainly not part of his game plan. He'd shrewdly placed her on the board of Todd Pictures, Inc., and was already using her name to drum up interest and money for his planned production of *Don Quixote*. Despite the fact that she could barely sing a note, there was also talk of Elizabeth's starring in the next Todd-AO project, the film adaptation of the Rodgers and Hammerstein musical *South Pacific*. Elizabeth's stardom was, in fact, her dowry, the currency with which her husband planned to do business in Hollywood.

And surely she understood that. Stepping out of their limousine one day soon after their marriage, the Todds had bantered with reporters, something that they seemed to enjoy. Asked if he looked forward to making pictures with his wife, Todd joked that he'd have it written into her contract that she wouldn't have to report to the set any earlier than four in the afternoon. Suddenly Elizabeth's emerald-studded purse clobbered him over the head. Yet for all her mock offense, no doubt the idea was appealing. Making movies as Mrs. Mike Todd would be very different from slaving away as one of Metro's "chattel." Production would be on *her* terms—or at least her husband's—and not those of the money-grubbers in the front office.

That doesn't mean that Elizabeth and Mike weren't crazy in love. In Hollywood the recognition of the mutual benefits of a relationship can be the greatest aphrodisiac of all. Hepburn and Hughes may have contrived their initial meeting for their own purposes, but eventually they developed very strong feelings for each other. The same was true for Taylor and Todd. "I love him madly, passionately," Elizabeth told the press. "Why do I love him so much? Because the first time he made love to me, I think my heart stopped beating."

And why wouldn't it? Making love to Elizabeth meant giving her gifts, extraordinary gifts. Even before the divorce with Wilding was official, Todd presented her with a diamond "friendship ring" that left her eyes bulging. And the gifts kept coming. Shortly before their marriage Todd had imported an expensive, British-made car that boasted its own bar and stove. "There's no such thing as a happy actress," Todd joked with the press. "But I think I know a girl who's going to be a happy housewife." Asked if he thought that Elizabeth would be happy cooking on an automobile stove, Todd replied, "Well, not exactly. I've bought a yacht, too."

To mark their official engagement, Mike had presented his bride-to-be with a twenty-nine carat, emerald-cut diamond ring. ("Thirty carats would have been vulgar," he told his son.) There were other rings, too: pearls, garnets, and another diamond (valued at $92,000) that was so big that Elizabeth couldn't get her glove over it when Mike gave it to her at Libby Holman's house. So the glove was left behind; Holman later had it framed.

The love story of Elizabeth Taylor and Mike Todd would be spun by the press as the spontaneous combustion of two people who meet and discover they are soul mates. Kevin McClory, who had proven so accommodating to his boss's objectives, was never mentioned. Instead, Todd was the knight in shining armor who had rescued Elizabeth from long, lonely nights "pacing through the rooms of her house trying to forget her memories." Just what those memories might be—broken romances, failed marriages, her children losing a father—was better left unsaid, at least in official accounts.

Yet it's surprising how, in the age of scandal magazines, these official accounts predominated when it came to Elizabeth and Mike. This most likely was something else that his wife could thank him for: Todd's glad-handing of the press meant that she was off-limits, for now anyway. At Sardi's in New York, Mike often power-lunched with Robert Harrison of *Confidential* and Harrison's crony, columnist and broadcaster Walter Winchell. Todd was one of the most important sources of news and scuttle-butt for both men—which explains the rather astonishing fact that Elizabeth was, for the moment anyway, not a subject of the scandal rags.

Given the kind of salacious stories that were printed every month about Lana Turner or Ava Gardner, the fact that Elizabeth, under Mike Todd's protection, was spared the scandal-magazine treatment is quite extraordinary because the longstanding rules of the Hollywood press were breaking down by the mid-1950s. The careful balance between studio, star, and public had been thrown off-kilter by the scandal rags, and it never fully recovered, not even after the industry marshaled its forces and brought lawsuits against *Confidential,* effectively ending its reign. Harrison had made the public aware of the game being played. "Hollywood is in the business of lying," he wrote in one editorial. "Falsehood is a stock in trade. They use vast press-agent organizations . . . to build up their stars. They glamorize and distribute detailed—and often deliberately false—information about private lives. They have the cooperation of large segments of the daily press, many magazines, columnists, radio and TV . . . practically every medium except *Confidential.* They can't influence us. So they want to get us."

Except one man *did* influence *Confidential:* Mike Todd. And so the "official version" of his love story with Elizabeth Taylor became virtually the *only* version in the months leading up to their marriage. Just as Harrison had described in his editorial, *Modern Screen* ran a piece that was probably lifted verbatim from one of the press releases put out by Bill Doll. According to this article, Elizabeth met Mike at a party thrown by Shirley MacLaine at the Bit of Sweden café (which gave away a bit of the truth, since MacLaine had helped facilitate the affair with McClory). "For the first time in weeks," the article read, "[Elizabeth's] laughter rang out—no longer forced and meaningless, but gay and spontaneous. And Mike, of course, was dazzled by the girl who has been called the most beautiful woman in the world. But it wasn't only her beauty that attracted him. There was something else—something that he wasn't really prepared for. To those who get to know the real Liz comes an amazing discovery—that this girl is not the flibberti-gibbet you'd expect such a beauty to be. She cares deeply about people, and is completely responsive to their needs."

There it was: the image of Elizabeth and her latest husband that their publicists wanted the world to embrace. But once again, such malarkey does the real Elizabeth a disservice. Columnist Bill Slocum, who traveled with Todd during much of his courtship of

Elizabeth, thought what they had was "a marriage of equals." Todd liked to bluster chauvinistically, saying that actresses were like burglar alarms ("They go off for no goddamn reason [and] need a good thumping to stop"). But in the next breath he'd admit that Elizabeth was no "little woman" meekly obeying his every command. "Glamour dames I don't particularly like," he said, "but Elizabeth has a warmth, a schmaltzy quality that's wonderful." For her part, Elizabeth said plainly, "It's nice to be married to someone who thinks I have a brain. That also contributes to making me feel like a woman."

That Mike Todd was bluff and bombastic, a real man's man, made him even more exceptional to his bride. "I loved it when he would lose his temper and dominate me," Elizabeth said. "I would start to purr because he had won." After Michael Wilding, Todd was a revelation. The important men in Elizabeth's life—from her father to her agent to her husbands to her best friends—had always been gentle, cultivated, sensitive people. The abusive Nicky Hilton might at first glance seem to be an exception, yet he was a pampered weakling, a poser. With Mike Todd, Elizabeth had encountered for the first time a big strong man who didn't simply want to use and overpower her, the way George Stevens—or worse, Louis B. Mayer—had done. Here was a tough-talking, masculine guy who wasn't a selfish brute.

Todd had another point in his favor where his wife was concerned: He bore no antipathy toward her gay friends. Coming from the tolerant world of the New York theater, Mike knew lots of homosexuals. He'd stood up to his brothers when they'd criticized him for keeping the overtly gay Dick Hanley around him. Mike was a regular at Greenwich Village drag shows, and in *Around the World in Eighty Days* he strove consciously for the camp sensibility that he had found there. After each actress had tested for the part of Princess Aouda, he'd inquire of Miles White, his gay costumer, "Are they camp?" White would sadly shake his head no. But then Shirley MacLaine came in, and Todd asked if *she* was camp. "Most *definitely*," White said. MacLaine got the part.

Never before had Elizabeth encountered such a man. She found the combination of Todd's tolerant worldliness and roguish masculinity irresistible. "I don't profess to know what makes ladies fall for guys," said Bill Slocum, "but if it's virility, unpredictability, generosity, an utterly magnificent sense of humor, and the gall of a successful second-story man, then Miss Taylor had found herself an ideal man."

They'd been married in Puerto Marquez, Mexico, on February 2, 1957, less than forty-eight hours after Elizabeth's divorce from Michael Wilding was final. Given the bride's condition, there was no time to waste. Best man duties were shared between Cantinflas, the Mexican star of *Around the World*, and Eddie Fisher, whom Todd had taken under his wing. Fisher's wife, Debbie Reynolds, was Elizabeth's sole attendant, chosen because Mike had wanted her, not because of any fondness Elizabeth had for her. In fact, Elizabeth regarded Debbie—she of the chipmunk-cheeked smile—as overly ambitious and a little too hungry for fame. She knew that the Fisher marriage, regularly hyped in all of the fan magazines, was as phony as the MGM backlot.

But even the presence of the Fishers couldn't keep Elizabeth from enjoying her Mexican honeymoon. Guarded at every turn by Mexican soldiers, the newlyweds were saluted by fireworks at the estate of former Mexican president Miguel Alemán. Since Elizabeth was still recovering from a spinal fusion to treat a herniated disc, Todd carried her up to the balcony so that she could watch the pyrotechnics exploding in the night sky. She was glittering in diamonds from her head to her hands. Mike had given her a matching bracelet-earring-ring set as a wedding gift, reported to have cost $80,000.

This was the picture of the Todd marriage that everyone tried hard to project over the next six months: Elizabeth a fragile, bejeweled doll carried along in her powerful husband's arms. But occasionally the public got a glimpse of something else—"the part of real life that press agents are paid good money to keep hidden," Mark Miller said. It was inevitable that the publicity would crack from time to time—especially when the subjects in question were as volatile and independent as Mike Todd and Elizabeth Taylor.

In the middle of Heathrow Airport, Mrs. Todd was having a meltdown.

"It's all your fault!" she shouted at her husband in full view of cameramen and reporters. "*Now* what shall we do?"

It was four months after their marriage and a month before the gala celebration in Battersea Park. The Todds had been living abroad, leasing homes in London and on Cap Ferrat in southeastern France. The press breathlessly chronicled their lives as glamorous international jet-setters. "Life in Europe is too exciting" for Elizabeth, Hedda Hopper reported, "and she insists on going out every night." Mike was "scattering Yankee dollars as if he had a private mint," one fan magazine reported, and swathing Elizabeth "in luxury such as even she had never imagined."

But that day at the London airport, the fairy tale suddenly exploded. As reporters watched, mouths agape, the Todds tore into each other once they realized that they'd missed their flight to Nice.

"For a change it was *my* fault that we were late," Mike snarled.

"I'm getting *fed up* with that line," Elizabeth spit. "I am always getting blamed for the delays. I could *hate* you for saying that."

Todd turned to his assistant, Midori Tsuji, and asked her to charter them a plane to Paris. Elizabeth, in a snit, plopped down in a chair, her bag on her lap. "I don't *want* to go to Paris," she said, sulking. "Paris bores me."

At that, her husband spun on her, giving her an Italian hand gesture universally understood to mean "up yours." One lucky photographer for the *Daily Mail* captured the moment for posterity. Todd's chin juts out at his wife, his fingers point up in the air, and Elizabeth's lips curl in a sarcastic comeback. That one picture, splashed all across the world, seemed to reveal much more about the Todd marriage than all of Bill Doll's carefully prepared press releases. "There's no doubt about what we were saying to each other," Elizabeth admitted later, calling it "the only talking still picture in the world." To the Todds' great chagrin, the photo often ran under the headline LIZ SAYS "PARIS BORES ME." The image of the spoiled brat was now enshrined.

So was the belief, in some quarters, that the Todd marriage was a big sham—or at least a public front for a private deal. But contracts always have consequences in Hollywood. "Sure Mike and I fight," Elizabeth said, trying to put the best possible spin on the row. "But some people just can't tell a fight from a family frolic."

Was that what Debbie Reynolds witnessed at the Todds' house in Beverly Hills one night? "[Mike] really hit her," Reynolds said. "Elizabeth screamed [and] walloped him right back ... He dragged her by her hair—while she was kicking and screaming at him." Trying to force Todd to release his wife, Reynolds leaped onto his back like a tigress. But she needn't have bothered. "The next thing I knew," Debbie said, "they were wrestling on the floor, kissing and making up."

This was the flip side of Mike Todd's sophisticated tolerance: his legendary temper. The row at Heathrow dominated every article about the Todds for weeks. Trying to put the scandal to rest, Midori Tsuji, who also worked with Bill Doll in publicity, was dispatched to tell reporters that Elizabeth and Mike were "just horsing around," and that there was no need to "make up" afterward "because nobody was ever really mad." Elizabeth, less disingenuous, admitted, "We scream at each other all the time, using those Latin gestures. Actually neither of us is inhibited, so we speak frankly to each other." And then she offered a bit of what was likely the real truth: "We have more fun fighting than most people do just making love."

It was inevitable that the Todds would fight. Elizabeth was still a whippersnapper, just twenty-five years old, fully half her husband's age. Mike was a bossy Broadway impresario, used to bulldozing his opposition. But his wife proved to be just as stubborn as he was, just as used to getting her own way. James Bacon would never forget his shock sitting in the Todds' limousine and watching "Elizabeth's beautiful mouth" yelling "Fuck you!" at her husband over and over again. "It shattered a dream," Bacon said.

Yet given the temperaments of Todd and Taylor, their butting heads was preordained. How different this new husband was from Michael Wilding, who just couldn't hold his own as a sparring partner. Mike Todd, in contrast, would shove his wife across the room when she yelled at him, whereupon she'd pick herself up, dust off her dress, and shove him right back. It was, after all, a marriage of equals.

He teased her in public, sometimes unkindly, something else the chivalrous Wilding never would have done. To reporters Todd referred to his wife as "Lizzie Schwartzkopf" and chided her for being too chunky in the derriere. Compliments were few and far between. Instead he said things like "She told me I was wonderful. What more brains and discrimination can you ask for than that?"

He'd never been a very romantic suitor, even with all those diamonds. "No deep-breathing declarations of adoration, no sentimental gush," said Bill Slocum. But Elizabeth preferred it that way. When she was younger, the romance of the movies had influenced her views of love and marriage. But now she found flying around the world with Mike, bopping and brawling, fighting and frolicking, to be a heck of a lot more fun than those simple, homespun, sugar-coated MGM love stories—especially since the deal with Todd included a new fur coat or piece of jewelry practically every week.

On one anniversary—whether the fourth month or the sixth, Elizabeth couldn't remember—Mike asked Teitelbaum the furrier to come around with two coats, a black diamond mink and a Diadem mink, so that his wife could have her pick. After considering them both carefully, she announced, "My choice is both of them"—and, indeed, she got two mink coats that day. After seeing the "chandelier-sized" diamond earrings that the Duchess of Kent had worn in London, Elizabeth hinted she'd like a pair herself. "Another Saturday night present," Mike said, sighing to reporters.

"It's the little things that count," Elizabeth cooed. Mike laughed. "Little diamonds, little rubies, little emeralds," he quipped.

The Todds' glittery life was followed by an avid public who waited on tenterhooks for every new chapter. It offered a panacea for an industry whose allure had faded. By 1957 old Hollywood—and its way of doing business and seeing the world—was dying off bit by little bit. For many oldtimers, the film colony had become nearly unrecognizable. "Talk about dull days!" Hedda Hopper wrote to the Todds soon after their marriage while they were staying at Cap Ferrat. "We have never had them duller with fifty-two pictures being made outside the country. You can imagine what we use for news." Trying to ingratiate herself, Hedda reminded the newlyweds that they'd invited her to visit; she hoped to make the trip right after she filmed the "first hour-long TV show for Lucy and Desi." It was television, not the movie studios, that now ruled Hollywood.

But if the old Hollywood was on its way out, Mike Todd, with Elizabeth Taylor at his side, did not intend to exit with the crowd. He was a new kind of producer, one who understood that the rules were changing; in point of fact, he was one of those changing them. To survive in a world where stars emerged more frequently from television and rock and roll than they did from the silver screen, Todd knew that the machinery of fame needed to be more enterprising and more pervasive. It wasn't enough anymore for a new movie star to pose for a spread in *Photoplay;* now Tab Hunter sang, however awkwardly, on *American Bandstand,* and Debbie Reynolds appeared on *I've Got a Secret.*

Mike Todd glimpsed the multimedia of the future better than most. Although he rented office space on the MGM lot, he had no intention of joining up with the studio. His dream, in fact, was to make the studios obsolete by creating a production empire that would encompass Broadway, film, music, and television—and every one of his projects would be big, bold, and better than anything that came before. "He was going to remake the entire field of entertainment," said Miles White. "A lofty goal, but that was Todd."

His movies were going to change the way the public went to the cinema: The screens would get even wider, the sound louder and deeper. He'd even begun talks about perfecting 3-D and other special effects.

"Dad felt that the films he was making were *shows* rather than movies," his son said. He wanted a return to big theaters with grand premieres. He conceived of the idea of "cameo" appearances, cramming as many stars into his picture as possible. His exhibitors were contractually forbidden to sell popcorn—a loss of revenue that they accepted from him, but no one else. "Mike thought food was distracting from the film," said his assistant, Glenda Jensen, "as well as the fact that he hated the smell of the butter sauce."

And he wanted television cameras in attendance at all times. The new medium would be put to work for him. By early 1957 he was already planning a major spectacle celebrating the one-year anniversary of *Around the World* that would be broadcast live on CBS. "By the time most movies are a year old," said Mike Todd Jr., "they have practically completed their theatrical distribution, but we were just starting." The film made money for a solid eighteen months.

Todd had the instincts of an entrepreneur even as a kid. Born Avrom Hirsch Goldbogen in Minneapolis in 1907, he was one of nine children of Jewish Polish immigrants. His father, a rabbi, took odd jobs to support his family, but some weeks young Avrom made more money than his father by selling discarded umbrellas and hats on the street. Later the Goldbogens moved to Chicago, where Avrom—called "Toat" by his siblings, hence the eventual "Todd"—was expelled from the sixth grade for running a game of craps. Eventually he gave up on school altogether. He took jobs selling shoes and laying bricks, which led to construction work, which led to a fortune before he was nineteen. But the following year, after gambling and bad investments, he'd lost it all.

While still a teenager, he'd married Bertha Freshman, and had a son to support. So he headed to Hollywood after landing a lucrative deal soundproofing stages for early "talkie" films. Encouraged by his success, Todd hung out his shingle as a general contractor.

But the deepening Depression meant that jobs were scarce, and it wasn't long before he returned to Chicago, penniless once more.

At the Chicago World's Fair in 1933, the year Elizabeth Taylor turned one, Todd found his true calling. "Mike was born to be a showman," said Miles White. "He could have done anything he set his mind to, but it was show business where he flourished." That was for sure. At the World's Fair, barkers announced Mike Todd's flame dancer, a pretty girl in a gauzy costume that got burned off nightly, leaving her naked. Or at least she *appeared* to be naked, since the flesh-colored asbestos bodysuit wasn't visible to the audience. The act, no surprise, was a huge hit. "I burned up four girls before I got it right," Todd told reporters. Right from the start he gave good copy.

New York was the next logical step, and no city has ever fit a man so well as this one fit Mike Todd. "He was big like New York was big," Miles White said. "He was over the top the way New York can be over the top." His first two shows tanked, but he came back with *The Hot Mikado* in 1939, a jazz version of Gilbert and Sullivan's *The Mikado* with an African-American cast. Over the next twelve years Todd produced thirty shows, including *Hamlet* with Maurice Evans and *Catherine Was Great* with Mae West.

His success was due less to the productions (some were excruciatingly bad) and more to the outlandish marketing of publicity wizard Bill Doll, who would serve as press agent for nearly all of Todd's shows. A hard-drinking go-getter from West Virginia, Doll "could charm a gorilla," one colleague said. Or at least a bear: To draw attention to the visiting Moscow Circus, Doll checked one of their grizzlies into a Manhattan hotel.

It wasn't just Todd that Doll promoted. He also hyped Silly Putty and Louis Armstrong and the New York World's Fair. But it was Mike Todd's shows that really let the publicity man shine—literally. It was Doll who came up with one of Times Square's first animated signs, a thirty-second repeating lightbulb display of Bill "Bojangles" Robinson, star of *The Hot Mikado*, in his famous staircase tap dance. Doll kept Todd's name in the papers with a very simple scheme. He convinced the *New York Times* that he was a legitimate entertainment reporter, thereby securing several articles about Todd under his own byline.

Mike learned a great deal from Bill Doll. Rather than let negative advance press for his show *The Naked Genius* wreck the box office, Todd used it to his advantage, printing posters that proclaimed GUARANTEED *NOT* TO WIN THE PULITZER PRIZE. Telling stories on himself enhanced rather than hurt his reputation. He loved informing reporters that his second show, *Call Me Ziggy*, had been such a flop that it was the only production on record to close during the second act of its first performance. That the story wasn't true—*Ziggy* actually ran for three full performances—didn't matter; what counted was the way Todd told it. For him, a play wasn't just a play, it was a show, and he wasn't just a producer, he was a showman. When he staged an extravagant production of the Strauss operetta *A Night in Venice*, Todd brought floating gondolas to the newly constructed Jones Beach Marine Theater on Long Island. *That* was how you put on a show.

For all his bottom-line business pizzazz, however, Todd wasn't heartless. When he had to close his underperforming show *January Thaw* in 1946, he penned a heartfelt note to his cast and crew. They had all been excellent, he wrote, "so it must be the producer at fault. I honestly hope I haven't let you down too much."

"He cared about his people and his productions," said Miles White. "He just overshot the mark a few times." Like when he bought the Del Mar Turf Club in 1946. A year later he had to sell the horseracing track near San Diego when his gambling losses necessitated a declaration of bankruptcy. "I lost a whole racetrack," he'd quip to the press with typical insouciance.

Federal investigators weren't so nonchalant—not with Todd's liabilities of more than one million dollars and the 116 creditors left with nothing. In December 1950 the FBI opened an investigation into whether Todd had concealed assets of $200,000 in loans and gambling wins. Stymied by "the fact that few books and records are available reflecting the true financial condition of Michael Todd," they amassed only circumstantial evidence, such as Damon Runyon's observation that Todd was the "greatest natural gambler he ever knew" and anecdotes of Todd winning and losing as much as $100,000 in a single day. None of that could be taken to court. Accordingly, David Carton, assistant United States Attorney for the Southern District of New York, declined any prosecution of Mike Todd nine months later. "No specific assets or bank deposits were shown to have been concealed by the bankrupt," he wrote to FBI chief J. Edgar Hoover, "nor is there any evidence to indicate that he has retained any of the proceeds of any loans."

Todd, meanwhile, had moved on to other things. His wife had died, and he'd married (and divorced) the actress Joan Blondell. He was restless. He'd conquered Broadway; now he looked westward to Hollywood. With the broadcaster Lowell Thomas and the inventor Fred Waller, he founded the Cinerama company, where they developed a process by which three film projectors cast a giant composite image on a curved screen. The three toiled in secret for over a year; Todd would later boast that it was the first time in his life "he'd kept his mouth shut." *This Is Cinerama,* a two-hour travelogue narrated by Thomas, was released in 1952. Despite only playing seventeen specially equipped theaters worldwide, it became the third-largest-grossing film of its time. In Hollywood the filming of the roller coaster scene had been a grand event. Even Lillian and Dorothy Gish showed up to watch. Todd figured that since they had been present for the dawn of one cinematic revolution, why not invite them to witness the birth of another?

But to really capitalize on the new technology, Todd needed a format that could play in every theater in America, not just a specialized few. He left Cinerama to develop a wide-screen process with the American Optical Company, called, appropriately enough, Todd-AO. Rights to the first film using the process, *Oklahoma!,* were given over to Rodgers and Hammerstein. But Todd wanted his own gigantic spectacle. And so: *Around the World in*

Eighty Days. It may have been officially directed by John Farrow and (after Todd fired Farrow) Michael Anderson, but Todd was always there, looking over his director's shoulder. Remarkably, the film cost just $6 million to produce. It earned back nearly quadruple that amount.

Established Hollywood both loved and hated Mike Todd. The twin emotions of gratitude and envy were consuming an industry in decline. Buddy Adler, head of Fox, hailed Todd for bringing back "showmanship and excitement to the movie business," but Hedda Hopper recognized the resentment that many filmmakers had for this newcomer, who enjoyed grosses of the kind they hadn't seen in years. Writing to congratulate Todd on his "standing room only" business, Hopper added, "You must know that most people in Hollywood are so jealous of you they could cut your throat."

Todd just laughed. Let them try. He felt invulnerable. Finally, after years of living on credit, he was rolling in some cold hard cash, though he often spent it as soon as it came in. Jensen remembered the telegrams that arrived daily from the theaters showing *Around the World.* They'd be in code, so the press couldn't read them before Todd did. The telegrams revealed the previous day's grosses, which Todd kept track of on huge charts, obsessively comparing them to *Gone With the Wind.* He was determined that he, Avrom Goldbogen, would be the biggest box-office champ of all time.

For the moment, however, he had to settle for Best Picture of the Year. On March 27, 1957, *Around the World in Eighty Days* was named the winner at the annual Academy Awards ceremony, beating out, among others, DeMille's *Ten Commandments* and a certain film by George Stevens called *Giant.* When his name was called, Todd leaped out of his seat and was halfway up the aisle before he doubled back to kiss his wife.

It was an unintentional oversight. Elizabeth had given him Hollywood bona fides in a way that Joan Blondell, a faded star from the 1930s, never could. It makes sense that, after getting a good look at her on the MGM lot, Todd nudged Kevin McClory aside and took Elizabeth for himself. For the Hollywood em-

pire he dreamed of building, there could be no more fitting consort—providing that they could keep any more episodes like the
one at Heathrow from leaking to the public.

At the Forty-eighth Street pier in New York, newspapermen
tripped over themselves as they scrambled up the gangplank, jug-
gling cameras and notebooks. At the top, Mike Todd waited, his
beady eyes watching them like a hawk. Bill Doll had cabled that
Mr. and Mrs. Todd would be willing to pose for some pictures on
their return to America.

Clapping the reporters on their backs and remembering all of
their names, Mike led them to his cabin, calling inside to see if
Elizabeth was ready. He'd instructed her not to keep them waiting, and she didn't. Wearing a light-colored maternity dress and a
plumed hat, the beautiful star stepped forward and cameras immediately began snapping. The reporters noted that Todd kept his
gaze fondly locked on his wife. Instantly, all rumors of tension in
their marriage were dispelled. Kissing his wife's hand grandly, the
showman told the newshounds, "This is for us, not for you." He
insisted that he and Elizabeth were deliriously happy—and "not
Hollywood happy either."

Mrs. Todd added a few words of her own about being happy,
but mostly it was Mike who orchestrated the press conference,
boasting about his wonderful wife and his soon-to-be-born baby
and his upcoming production of *Don Quixote,* for which he was
planning on "renting Spain." Reporters scribbled into their notebooks in a vain attempt to follow Todd's rapid staccato speech.
Even the best shorthand had a hard time keeping up with Mike
Todd.

Friends said that listening to Todd was like being assaulted by
machine-gun fire. He talked fast, he walked fast, his hands were
constantly in motion. It was impossible for him to walk by a telephone without picking it up to call someone. Before meeting Elizabeth, he'd smoked fifteen big cigars a day. Conference rooms were
quickly filled with thick blue smoke after Mike Todd walked in.

But when a doctor told him that he'd developed a precancerous condition inside his mouth called leukoplakia, Todd wrapped up all his high-priced cigars and gave them away. He never smoked again.

He wasn't tall but he was thickset, with a strong jaw and small, flashing, deep-set eyes—sexy in his self-confidence if not in his appearance. A study of incongruities, he drank expensive champagne with his corned beef sandwiches at Sardi's. When he'd inspect his custom-made shirts from London, he'd often hack off their tails with a pair of desk scissors because they were "too damn long." Mike Todd liked things his way, and no one was going to tell him otherwise.

"Dad's attitude was you don't ask a policeman if you can spit in a subway train," said Mike Todd Jr. "If you gotta spit, you spit, but you don't ask if you're allowed to."

Mike Todd never played by the rules. When he was filming *Around the World* in Paris, he plastered NO PARKING signs over an entire block so that he could empty the street without the messiness of involving the authorities. For decades he never had a driver's license and instructed his wives and employees that if they were ever pulled over by a policeman, they were to take the rap for him for "forgetting" to pack his license. Given the way Todd drove, they were pulled over quite often. And never once did he get a ticket.

By 1957 everyone from cops to columnists was eating out of Mike Todd's hand. Part of that was due to the state-of-the-art team behind him, one that made the Metro publicity department seem very old-fashioned. Telephones rang simultaneously in Todd's offices at the United Artists Building at Forty-ninth Street and Seventh Avenue and at his homes in Manhattan, Connecticut, and Beverly Hills, making Todd, even when he was away, "very much a part of the office operation," according to Glenda Jensen. Elizabeth loved to visit the office and marvel at her husband's routine. "He'd have ten different ideas going on at once," she said. "He'd have two telephones in his hands, a different conversation going on over each phone, plus a Dictaphone going." The staff was similarly linked by home-office phones. "There was a lot of coming and going by the employees and very few had desks," Jensen said. "They just checked in regularly"—a 1950s version of telecommuting.

Among Todd's staff were lawyers and accountants and technicians. Everything was covered. If a theater owner had any projection troubles, William Boettcher was on hand to fix things. Rivington Bisland, a former baseball player and boxing promoter, plotted box-office strategy. Ned Mann devised special effects for parties and premieres. Morris Lefko and Vincent Liccardi ran top-notch sales and advertising divisions; later they'd take their expertise to MGM and Paramount, respectively. The very faces of the Todd operation were unusually modern in their diversity: In addition to the overtly gay Dick Hanley and the Japanese-American Midori Tsuji, there were also Puerto Ricans and African-Americans on staff, and not in minor positions either.

Yet by far the most impressive element of the Todd operation was Bill Doll's press and public relations machine. These were hard-boiled New York press agents, the kind featured in the film *Sweet Smell of Success*—clever, cunning, ruthless when they needed to be, but amazingly effective in getting their clients coverage. "Those guys were nuts," said Shirley Herz, one of Doll's deputies. "They were crazy. They were creative. And press agentry was an art." Doll proved just how artful when he printed up a mock front page of *Daily Variety* announcing that production of *Around the World* had wrapped. 'THE WORLD' COMES TO AN END, blared the headline. BILLIONS OF PEOPLE AWAIT 'THE SECOND COMING'—OF NEW SHOW IN TODD-AO. The whole page was filled with items hyping Todd and his picture, and was inserted into real issues of *Daily Variety*. Many readers took it to be a legitimate part of the trade paper. Press agentry at its best.

What's significant is that by 1957—just as old Hollywood was winding down—Mike Todd had in place a structure and a system that could pick up where the studios' vaunted publicity machines had left off. His buddy Robert Harrison over at *Confidential* might rail about the studios' duplicitous press operations, but in fact Todd's PR team did pretty much the same thing. And despite being based in New York, the canny showman had every intention (and every ability) to expand his operations westward. If there were concerns that by liberating Elizabeth from MGM she'd lose the machinery that had long sustained her fame, the Todd press department was proving every day that it was equal to, if not better at, the task.

Certainly Todd's operation was considerably more farsighted than its West Coast counterparts. As the number of newspapers decreased and the number of television stations grew (almost all of them centered in New York), Todd directed his agents to adapt. "We had to learn to think visually," said Shirley Herz. It was no longer enough to send out eight-by-ten glossies. Now the stars themselves needed to be trooped out to sit under the harsh television lights for some face-to-face time with Edward R. Murrow or to sing and dance with Todd's buddy Eddie Fisher on his top-rated NBC variety show.

Elizabeth had already performed her own dog-and-pony show for the small screen, promoting *Giant* with Rock Hudson on *Toast of the Town*. No doubt Todd saw more of that in her future. He wasn't concerned, as some were, that television would diminish a star's appeal. In fact, television could significantly *enhance* it, he believed, by connecting the star more intimately to the public. No longer distant deities on the silver screen, stars now appeared right there in Americans' living rooms. That's why so many big names—from Charles Boyer to William Holden to Tallulah Bankhead—were clamoring to appear on *I Love Lucy* and other top-rated TV shows. "Mike Todd had enormous vision," said Susan McCarthy Todd. "He was an incredibly modern man." One trade paper declared he had "become his own brand." By the middle of 1957, with just one film under his belt, Todd had convinced the public that what he had for sale was exactly what they wanted to buy. It was a lesson learned well by his wife.

But his great wealth was an illusion. His productions were all about show—no surprise, so was his life. Much of Todd's world was as artificial as what he created on the stage and screen. His ostentatious style and standard of living far exceeded the reality of his true financial worth. Revenues piling up from *Around the World* were blown through with a delicious disregard. Money burned holes in Mike's pocket. So he took Elizabeth around the world, rented a mansion in Connecticut, and leased a private eleven-passenger Lockheed Lodestar plane that he named the *Liz*—a "needless extravagance," according to his son. It was the only plane in the world with a double bed, Mike boasted. He and Elizabeth "roughed it," he joked, by dispensing with a steward. His wife was a "rugged type" who "can pour her own champagne and carve her own pheasant."

By living so conspicuously, Todd created an image for himself that sustained the illusion he wanted people to believe. The publicity he generated with his lavish parties and premieres served as collateral when he went to sign his name at the bottom of a note. Despite the 116 fall guys from 1946 who might have argued otherwise, each and every one of Todd's creditors believed that they would eventually get paid. "I've often been broke," the showman famously quipped, "but I've never been poor." For him, being rich was simply a state of mind. Money in the bank wasn't needed to back it up.

It was a child's-eye view of the world in many ways, and that, perhaps, was the biggest bond between husband and wife. Mr. and Mrs. Todd were two excitable children grabbing what the world had to offer. The critic Brooks Atkinson mused that despite Todd's "brashness and cunning," it was his "basic immaturity" that defined him. "There is a certain innocence about the typical Broadway showman," Atkinson wrote. "Since he is primarily concerned with externals, he is interested only in the externals of his own life and never learns much about the nature of the world and its people." Todd's great success, *Around the World in Eighty Days,* was "enchanting [and] childlike" in Atkinson's opinion, and watching it today, that is still the impression one gets of the man who made it. He seems as if he's still a young boy standing on a street corner selling used umbrellas, dreaming about what the rest of the world might look like and how someday he might get out there and see it. No, not just see it. *Own* it.

And as Mike Todd and Elizabeth Taylor walked down that gangplank from the SS *Liberté* that day in July 1957, there was every reason to believe that they *could* own the world, that all of their dreams would come true.

Two weeks later Mike found himself huffing along out of breath at Elizabeth's side as medics frantically wheeled her into the Harkness Pavilion at Columbia-Presbyterian Medical Center in New York. With each spasm of pain that wracked her body, Elizabeth squeezed her husband's hand. "Premature labor," Todd told the assembled reporters. It would have to be: They had only been married five months.

"I'm spending all my time by her bedside," Todd announced after getting Elizabeth settled into a room. "She's in terrible pain, but unless it's a sheer, outstanding emergency they don't want to have to take the baby for two and a half weeks." The baby was due, he told reporters, on October 15—three months away.

Of course, that still put the date of conception several weeks before their marriage on February 2. In 1957 these things mattered—especially in public life and especially when the woman in question was a thrice-married Hollywood movie star. People were still talking about Rita Hayworth's baby born seven months after her marriage to Aly Khan; many had laughed off Aly's feeble explanation that premature babies were common in his family. And only in the last year had Ingrid Bergman received any kind of forgiveness from the public for having a baby with Roberto Rossellini while she was still the wife of another man. So it was critical that the public not think that Elizabeth had been unfaithful with Todd while she was still legally married to Michael Wilding.

But any cynic could do the math, and some did, writing letters of outrage to Hedda Hopper. It's likely that the baby was conceived in November 1956, just a few weeks after Elizabeth had filed for divorce from Wilding and some three months before the divorce was final. Even if the child *was* premature, it seems unlikely that it came a full *three months* early; babies born that young usually face major physical difficulties growing up, and the child who was born to Elizabeth on August 6, 1957—a girl she named Elizabeth Frances and called Liza—was a beautiful baby who grew up healthy and strong.

Thanks to Todd's rapport with the press, however, very little comment was made about the child's birth date. Hedda Hopper, eager to kiss up to the biggest man in showbiz, provided cover for the Todds, writing in her column how very much they had been hoping that the pregnancy "would go the full nine months." And so Elizabeth Taylor escaped the scarlet letter of Rita Hayworth and Ingrid Bergman.

She had her husband to thank for this. But, of course, there were so many things to be grateful to Todd for. Stretched out on a chaise near the pool at their Westport, Connecticut, home, Elizabeth flexed her toes as one assistant pampered her with a pedicure and another massaged her hands. A third was applying some of Marian Bialac's celebrated Yatrolin cream to her cheeks. She could hear Mike on the telephone inside the house, shouting at some studio official. She knew he was trying to free her from the despised Metro-Goldwyn-Mayer, which, unnerved by all the talk about her starring in her husband's pictures, had started protesting that she was still under contract to them. Now that the baby was born, the studio wanted her back to star in the film adaptation of Tennessee Williams's play *Cat on a Hot Tin Roof,* promising her an exciting, up-and-coming costar—either Ben Gazzara or Paul Newman.

But even a project as enticing as *Cat* held little appeal if it meant giving up this life of leisure. Lifting a cold cucumber slice from her eye, Elizabeth begged her husband not to make her go back to work. He surprised her by telling her that she *should* make the film—though he promised it would be the last one she would ever have to make for MGM. Ringing back just then, the studio countered that they were owed *two* pictures. And so the battle began.

Enter Kurt Frings, Todd's personal choice for Elizabeth's new representation. Gentlemen agents like Jules Goldstone and Leland Hayward were fading away. In this more desperate Hollywood, Elizabeth needed someone who used cunning, pressure, and threats to make things happen. Frings, one of Todd's regular poker buddies, was precisely the shark she needed, a harbinger of the high-powered agents who'd soon dominate in Hollywood and become almost as famous as the clients they represented.

A former lightweight boxing champ from Cologne, Germany, Frings was a small, compact man with jet black hair, flashing green eyes, and a temper that was all too easily triggered. "A notorious international character" was the way the United States government described him in 1940, when he was a war refugee in Tijuana waiting for asylum in this country. Although Congress recommended that Frings be admitted, President Roosevelt had vetoed the bill, citing allegations of moral turpitude. Particularly egregious from the government's point of view was Paramount's plan to make a film of the play *Hold Back the Dawn*, written by Frings's wife, Ketti, which portrayed the former pugilist as a heroic refugee, not the con artist the government considered him to be. "Imagination played a greater part than fact" in the play, the U.S. narcotics commissioner insisted. But the point was moot: *Hold Back the Dawn* was filmed in 1941 with Olivia de Havilland and Charles Boyer, and garnered a slew of Oscar nominations.

Once Frings finally managed to get into the country, he had an odd way of repaying his wife's advocacy. Their fights frequently brought out the police. But Frings's well-connected network of friends and clients (by 1958 his roster included Marlon Brando, Audrey Hepburn, Lucille Ball, Dorothy McGuire, Hume Cronyn, Jessica Tandy, and José Ferrer) ensured that the brawls were kept out of the press. That didn't mean Frings's clients always liked him: George Cukor would eventually terminate his representation when he felt that Frings demanded commissions he wasn't entitled to, and Cronyn was peeved that his own agent couldn't seem to remember his name.

Elizabeth, on the other hand, adored him. Like Mike, Frings

was bold and brash, and she'd laugh uproariously as the two men drank their whiskies and told off-color jokes about the studio heads. Even more important, Elizabeth's new agent was finally gaining her the upper hand in dealing with Metro. Frings had informed the front office that Elizabeth didn't need the studio now that she was Mrs. Mike Todd; if she wasn't accommodated, she'd walk out on her contract. If Metro wanted to sue, then they should go ahead. With such bravado, Frings managed to get Elizabeth's old contract rewritten with better terms. She'd be paid a weekly rate of $4,850 prior to the making of *Cat* and then a flat fee of $125,000 (plus per diems and overages) once principal photography began. If she did a second film for them (and that remained an "if" as far as Frings was concerned) then she expected the same deal, as well as the right to appear in *Don Quixote* or any other Todd production before any second film for Metro. And her mother was to continue being paid $300 a week—for doing nothing, unless babysitting grandchildren was part of the deal.

The balance of power had shifted. It was no longer Metro who told Elizabeth what to do; it was now Mike Todd who bossed the studio around. When *Cat* director Richard Brooks objected to Metro's decision to make the film in black-and-white, he knew whom to complain to. Referencing his two stars—Paul Newman had won the part opposite Elizabeth—Brooks told Todd, "For Christ's sake, when you get a chance to shoot the violet eyes of Elizabeth Taylor and the blue eyes of Paul Newman, do you use black-and-white?" Todd just nodded and said, "I see." The next day "three black crows," as Brooks called them, appeared from the front office and ordered him to switch to color. Brooks credited the change to Todd's influence.

Mike was eager for Elizabeth to star in *Cat*, despite the statements of some Taylor biographers to the contrary. His reasoning was simple: Now that profits from *Around the World* were finally leveling off, Elizabeth stood to be the bigger moneymaker in the household, and Todd was counting on cash from *Cat* to seed *Don Quixote*. He also may have been bracing for another looming financial crisis: The government was again investigating him, this time suspecting fraud in his recent tax returns. The results of the investigation would be inconclusive, but several people who knew him said that they wouldn't be surprised if Mike had routinely underreported his income.

As plans for *Cat* continued apace, Elizabeth became more excited about the film; she knew what it could do for her. Maggie the Cat—the sexually frustrated wife of a sexually confused scion of a Southern cotton family, as restless and as jumpy as a cat on a hot tin roof—was part spoiled sexpot, part compassionate earth mother, a role ready-made for Elizabeth. Paul Newman's part (as the tormented Brick) was actually the center of the piece, but Maggie—one of the greatest of Tennessee Williams's gallery of female characters—was a stunning and sexy opportunity for Elizabeth to cavort around a hot plantation bedroom in a white slip and draw upon the same sensitive attributes that had made her work in *A Place in the Sun* so memorable. Newman was a rising name but not yet the icon that he would become. For the first time Elizabeth Taylor was unquestionably the star of the picture, not playing second fiddle to a Clift or a Hudson.

Brooks had come to the film only after George Cukor, faced with objections from producer Pandro Berman, had bowed out. Cukor's idea had been to cast Joan Blondell as Big Mama, Maggie's mother-in-law, which would have brought the two wives of Mike Todd together on the screen. Instead, Brooks cast Judith Anderson and brought Burl Ives in to re-create his Broadway incarnation of Big Daddy. *Cat on a Hot Tin Roof* was shaping up to be one of the major films of the year. Everyone wondered how Metro would finesse the central conflict of the play—Brick's unresolved love for another man. The death of his childhood friend Skipper seems to have stilled his very existence. On stage there had been freedom of expression; in a Hollywood still fearful of the heavy-handed fist of the Production Code, such matters would need extreme delicacy. Cukor seemed glad to be free of the responsibility: "I couldn't do an emasculated version," he told Louella Parsons, "and I don't see how the movie itself could be properly presented." The controversy made the project even more interesting to anticipate. "This is one film that everyone expects to go sky high," Parsons said.

Elizabeth wasn't the only one in the family planning big things. As *Around the World in Eighty Days* finally reached smaller theaters across the country, Todd came up with the inspired idea to turn their premieres into fundraisers for charity. Bill Doll's press agents poured into small cities to coordinate things in the weeks prior to the opening nights. Flying in on the *Liz* for the film's premiere at the Strand Theatre in Hartford, Connecticut, Todd himself effusively thanked the audience who had paid the exorbitant price of $5.00 per ticket and raised thousands for two local children's charities. For his largesse, Todd received a thunderous ovation. Back in Los Angeles, in his continuing campaign for respect and recognition, he posed at the County Museum beside a weary-looking Elizabeth as he donated several paintings from his collection, including a Renoir, a Pissarro, and a Monet. Obviously exhausted from Liza's difficult birth, Mrs. Todd could still grasp the effectiveness of her husband's methods of self-advancement. Giving back cemented fame. Celebrity was a two-way street, and those who benefited from the public's attention and affection must never forget their part in the exchange.

Eighteen thousand people were jamming into Madison Square Garden on the night of October 17, 1957, for a "Private Little Party"—as the two thousand lights on the giant marquee spelled it out—being thrown by "Mike and Liz." Most of the men wore rented tuxedos and the women stumbled around in high heels. Many a mink stole was stepped on as the crowd pushed and shoved their way inside. Dick Hanley, hovering by the entrance, was so anxious that he started to sweat. His boss had thrown many a successful social gathering before, but never for this many people from so many walks of life. Ordinary Joes and Janes, who had been randomly selected to attend, knocked shoulders with movie stars and socialites. Hanley just held his breath and hoped for the best.

The Garden was decorated by British production designer Vincent Korda (*The Private Life of Henry VIII, The Thief of Bagdad*) in various hues of blue and pink. At one end a forty-foot tall Oscar made of gold chrysanthemums towered over everything. In the center sat an enormous cake, thirty feet wide and fourteen feet tall, made with two thousand eggs and fifteen thousand dollars' worth of cake batter. Workers had to carry the cake into the hall in pieces and assemble it right there on the floor. The famed Symphony of the Air, conducted by Arthur Fiedler, tuned up as people filed in to their seats. It was all to celebrate the one-year anniversary of *Around the World in Eighty Days*, which by now had grossed nearly sixteen and a half million dollars. A replica of the balloon used in the movie by David Niven and Cantinflas hovered over revelers' heads. The party, with its elephants, kangaroos, performing horses, Philadelphia Mummers, and Scottish bagpipers—all coordinated by Ringling Brothers–Barnum and Bailey—would be Todd's biggest public relations feat yet.

If, as Hanley prayed, nothing went wrong.

"Because it was the beautiful public who made *Around the World in Eighty Days* the great success it is," Todd had announced in advertisements in all the New York papers, "I would like to invite 1,000 wonderful people from the New York area to attend our little birthday party in Madison Square Garden on Thursday, October 17, as my guests." At the Rivoli Theatre on Broadway and Forty-ninth Street, tens of thousands came by to drop their names into a box. One thousand lucky winners were called the day before the event with the exciting news that they could hobnob with Mike and Liz and their famous friends for a night. Similar drawings were held at various theaters around the country, with two winners chosen from each theater to be flown to New York, put up at a swanky hotel, and then escorted to the party. It made for a large number of hoi polloi mixing in with the elite of Broadway and Hollywood. "Hope to see you at the party," Mike had ended his ad.

He sure did. "Everyone in town wanted to get into the Garden that night," said Miles White. "Not just ordinary people, but big shots, too. If they hadn't been invited they were begging for tickets. There was a crush of people at the gates trying to get in."

Having sent more than ten thousand invitations, Mike had made sure that "everybody who was anybody" got invited. Spotted entering the Garden were Tony Curtis, Ginger Rogers, Shelley Winters, Beatrice Lillie, Elsa Maxwell, Walter Winchell, and, of course, Hedda Hopper. If someone wasn't on the list, it was a deliberate omission. Glenda Jensen recalled a "major British actor" who was incensed that he hadn't been invited, and Mike, for whatever reason, remained adamant about not letting him in. Nonetheless, the actor finagled a ticket from somewhere and made sure to be there. To miss the biggest social gala in ages was unimaginable to those who counted themselves as "somebody."

The invitations, which had arrived in mailboxes about two weeks earlier, were designed to look informal and low-budget. Printed in a cursive typewriter font, they included a perforated RSVP postcard—the latest in smart, efficient party-throwing. "It seems the party grew from a few chums to an international exposition," Mike cheekily informed his guests. "Therefore we now have logistics, statistics, and other departments functioning and they want to know, 'Are you coming?'" He promised "no blood tests, fingerprints, or other information required. Just make an X." Then he added, "Sorry, Liz says black tie, so all the boys should look pretty."

There was also a postscript from "Liz" herself: "Girls, if you want to sit and look pretty, wear everything. But if you want to mix and mingle, don't wear a big flouncy ball gown. I did at one of Mike's parties and it was a mistake. Wear short evening dresses."

The entire Todd operation stayed at the nearby Taft Hotel, where they changed out of their work clothes into their fancy duds. Some of them were just as starstruck as the guests being flown in from the sticks. "What an evening it was," Glenda Jensen said. "I was overwhelmed with the glitter and glamour of the people and events going on." She could scarcely believe that she, the daughter of a coal miner from Nottingham, England, was "mingling with the greats and not-so-greats of Hollywood and Broadway."

Making it all even more exciting was that the whole world was watching. Todd, always keenly aware of the value of television cameras, had arranged with CBS to broadcast the party live. It meant preempting their highest-rated dramatic series, *Playhouse 90*, and paying Todd $175,000 for the privilege. A young journalist by the name of Walter Cronkite was assigned to narrate. For guests, this wasn't just a chance to attend a fabulous party—it was an opportunity to be on national TV.

Drinks, Mike promised, would be on the house. The champagne toast that kicked off the evening came courtesy of Renault Champagne. "Product placement," as it's called today, was everywhere. The food caravan that prominently made the rounds of the Garden offered cheeses from Kraft, shrimp from the Atlantic Trading Company, cream sandwich cookies from Burry Biscuit Company, crackers from Sunshine, frankfurters from Nathan's, beer from Pabst Blue Ribbon, and coffee from Chase and Sanborn. Everything was, of course, donated—fifteen thousand doughnuts, ten thousand egg rolls, a ton of Boston baked beans, two hundred gallons of vichyssoise—which meant that not only did Mike escape any costs for the extravaganza, he may actually have come out ahead. And then there were the free gifts being promised to "each and every guest" from such sponsors as Bristol-Myers, Cessna Aircraft, Decca Records, Fiat Motor Company, Guinness of Dublin, Hermes-Paris, Heublein, Olivetti Typewriters, and Vespa Motor Scooters. Raffles would be held throughout the night; the luckiest guests would walk off with an airplane or a new car.

Mike and Elizabeth arrived from their townhouse on Seventh Avenue just before the show started, and right away the eagle-eyed host saw that things weren't going quite as he'd hoped. Already guests were griping because unscrupulous waiters were charging them five bucks for bottles of wine that were supposed to be free. As Mike hustled emcee George Jessel up onto the rostrum, Elizabeth took her seat—but promptly had her hem torn when Mike Jr. stepped around her and hooked his shoe on her dress. As Dick Hanley had feared, it was all downhill from there.

The entertainment started with the popular Emmett Kelly, the famous circus clown, trying to sweep up the spotlight on the stage. But the acts that followed were more likely to be hokey than hot: Dieter Tasso, the "world's greatest juggler"; various bands from New York, including one from the city's sanitation department; the San Francisco fire brigade; folk dancers from Hungary; the Monarch Elks of Harlem. The crowd got restless, many preferring to chase after the beer wagon instead of watching the acts. By the time Buck Steele's troupe of ten dogs astride matching palomino horses came out, Todd had left his seat and gone down to the floor, yelling at the organizers to speed things up and to get all those ya-hoos milling around back into their seats.

"Dad [became] the unexpected star of the show," Mike Todd Jr. said. "The TV director [Byron Paul] kept zooming in on him, shouting and jumping up and down, waving his fists trying to keep the show going." Millions of television viewers got an up-close glimpse of the angry, cursing Mike Todd they'd previously only read about.

On the stage Sir Cedric Hardwicke was falling off Tonga the elephant, hanging on for dear life from the howdah on the animal's back. "Disaster struck and struck again," said Shirley Herz. Off to the side of the hall, there was suddenly a buzz of commotion. Herz found one of her colleagues threatening a guest with a wine bottle. The guest, disappointed by his raffle win of cheese samples from Kraft, was attempting to push a dishwasher out of the Garden. "He had been promised a gift and he wanted his gift and he was going to take it," Herz said. "He found this dishwasher . . ."

Meanwhile Elizabeth was getting pretty antsy herself. During rehearsals she'd told Hubert Humphrey, the senator from Todd's home state of Minnesota, that the speech he was scheduled to give was "corny" and that no one would buy it. Humphrey sat beside her now, frantically scribbling notes in a last-minute attempt to punch it up. All Elizabeth wanted to do was cut the cake—her only scheduled part in the show—and get the hell out of there. This was not the fun night that she had been promised. She wasn't happy that Mike left her alone most of the night, her only company being a politician she considered dull as dishwater. "Nobody told me who he was," she said.

Todd sure knew who Humphrey was; according to the columnist Earl Wilson, he'd tapped the senator's chest and told him he'd "make him president" someday. It was just the sort of grandiose statement that Todd was known for, and when he'd walked into the Garden earlier that night he was full of such swagger. But by ten o'clock he was running around raving like a madman, with dutiful Dick Hanley following behind, shrilly repeating his boss's orders just in case someone had missed them. That wasn't likely. Todd was loud and forceful, even if some chose to ignore him. When the Mummers decided to take a second loop around the Garden with their banjos and ostrich feathers, Mike blew his top. "Off! Off!" he shouted. "Get those Mummers off!" The head Mummer just lifted an eyebrow and said, "Screw you, sweetie, we dragged our asses all the way in from Philadelphia and we're going around twice."

The crowd was beginning to revolt. As the French comedian Fernandel performed his comic "glimpse of the future" onstage, fistfights were breaking out in the aisles. People were upset that many big prizes had been "openly and boldly hijacked Chicago-style." Candy vendors, angered by the unruly crowd, began pelting guests with bonbons; hot dog vendors did the same, staining expensive gowns with relish and mustard. People were slipping on melted ice cream while outraged women gathered their mink stoles and huffily stalked out of the Garden.

Elizabeth was horrified. "My God, the sight of chic, lacquered women fighting with little kids to get a hamburger," she said. At last she was escorted from her box and up the red-carpeted stairs to the giant cake to slice off the first piece. She scooped up a handful of icing and brought it to her mouth. Her husband stood behind her, anxious to get out of there.

"All hell's breaking loose," recalled Lenny Gaines, an assistant to Eddie Fisher who'd been roped into helping organize the Garden party, "and [Mike] turns and throws some keys up to me and says, 'Here, kid, lock up.' I am standing there with these keys, watching him disappear into the crowd, and I shout, 'Lock *what* up?'" By now the fighting had reached the very edge of the stage, where Duke Ellington and his orchestra had started to play, ostensibly so people could dance. Gaines told him to just play "The Star Spangled Banner" and be done with it. "It looked like all these guys wearing tuxedos were gonna rip the Garden apart," Gaines said. "They almost did."

The next day Todd hoped that a chartered boat ride around Manhattan for members of the press and a complimentary bottle of champagne would insure positive reports of the party. This time, however, his storied luck with the fourth estate ran out. "[Mike Todd] gave the public bread crumbs and a circus," lamented the *New York Daily News*. The *Herald Tribune* fretted that propagandists in the Soviet Union would use images of the party to denigrate America—"New York fiddling while the country burns." While many people would insist that they'd enjoyed themselves at the Garden, the fact that Todd's "little party" had been a massive debacle soon became the conventional wisdom—in part because thirty-five million people had watched it live. The slugfests and skirmishes had been kept off the television broadcast, of course, but the sense of distasteful ostentation was still readily apparent. "It looked on the whole like a bad circus parade," said television critic John Crosby, "combining both vulgarity and dullness to a stupefying degree."

Early on there had been some thought given to throwing another bash in Los Angeles for all those who'd been unable to make it to New York. Following the fiasco at the Garden, however, Mike decided to send a "do-it-yourself party kit" to his friends on the

West Coast. "It was just to poke a little fun at himself," said his son, "and it was a clever way of keeping the thing going." Or putting the best spin on it. In fact, the best thing the Todds could do at that point was to get out of the country for a while, which they did. Before Elizabeth started on *Cat on a Hot Tin Roof*, there would be one more fabulous trip around the world. Surely better headlines would come of that.

In Moscow Elizabeth was stuffing herself with chicken Kiev and black caviar, making a mess of her pearl-ornamented white gloves. All eyes at the banquet were on her. The occasion on January 27, 1958, was the Indian embassy's celebration of their republic's ten-year anniversary, but the reason for the party was immaterial to Elizabeth; she was just glad to be having fun and eating decent food. Laughing and sipping Russian vodka, she charmed everyone—even Nikita Khrushchev, who glanced her way several times, though he didn't address her directly. But his wife was certainly curious about the woman with the dazzling eyes in the black cocktail dress, trimmed in fur and sparkling with sequins. "Who is the pretty young lady?" Mrs. Khrushchev inquired.

Well might she ask, for Elizabeth's fame extended only as far as the western edge of the Iron Curtain. Maybe that's why Mike was so fond of Russia—"the only place in the world," reporters quipped, "where Mike Todd is not Mr. Elizabeth Taylor." In Red Square a girl approached Elizabeth and asked for an autograph, thanking "Miss Monroe" for her time. "People were staring at me," Elizabeth said, "but it was because of my mink coat and my knee-high, fur-lined red leather boots. When people came over to our interpreter, they asked if I was a ballerina—the height of Russian glamour. They stared at my hairdo, and my jewels, but otherwise I was ignored."

But this night Elizabeth's identity was well-known to the ambassadors of Britain, France, Italy, Canada, and Norway, all of whom were in attendance with their staffs. A wry *New York Times* reporter observed, "For some persons, the film star was an object of more curiosity than were the Kremlin leaders." Elizabeth just laughed and called for a second helping of chicken Kiev.

They almost hadn't made it to Moscow. First there had been the premiere of *Raintree County,* which critics, as expected, largely panned, even if the pairing of Clift and Taylor still provided excellent box office. Then it was off to Hawaii before heading to Sydney, where the distractions really set in. Criticized by the *Sunday Telegraph* for kissing his wife while seated next to the premier of New South Wales, Joseph Cahill, Todd instructed Bill Doll to blanket U.S. press outlets with his furious response: "I would be a phony if, when the urge came, I did not kiss my wife." It was a salvo fired less at the Australians than at the gossipmongers back in America who, in the wake of the Madison Square Garden fiasco, had hinted once again of troubles in the Todd marriage.

From Sydney it was on to Hong Kong and then to Tokyo, where Elizabeth suffered an attack of appendicitis. Todd announced that they were "canceling the rest of their world tour," and arranged for them to fly home in late November so that Elizabeth could have surgery in Los Angeles. Met by the usual crush of newshounds at the airport, they indulged in some more theatrics, just in case any doubts still lingered about how happy they were. When reporters banged on the windows of their black Cadillac limousine, Mike said cheerfully, "Come on, Liz, get out. The boys want some pictures."

Sliding out of the car in a tight black silk Chinese dress slit halfway up the thigh, Elizabeth trilled, "Hi there!"—not her usual response when besieged.

Cameras flashed. "Look at that dress!" Mike exclaimed. "She's gonna start a whole new epidemic! It's liable to bring sex back."

"Give her a kiss, Mike," a reporter urged.

Todd put up his hands. "In Sydney I gave her a little peck and you would have thought the whole economy was gonna collapse. Kissing's trouble."

"That's trouble?" Elizabeth asked, crawling back into the car.

"See, that's the way she talks. She says, 'Come on, flannel-mouth, get in here.'"

A reporter leaned in to see her diamond ring—"as big as a railroad conductor's timepiece"—so Elizabeth hopped out of the car again to show it off. Meanwhile Mike was being asked if he planned to throw any more parties. "No more parties with more than eight people," he quipped.

"Party!" Elizabeth said. "That's a dirty word." And she slipped back into the car.

"Come on, honey," Mike said. "They want some pictures."

Out came Elizabeth for a third time, revealing a "great expanse of satiny leg." She smirked. "I'm getting old just getting in and out of this car."

Mike was griping about being charged for excess baggage on their flight. "It was Mr. Todd's coats," Elizabeth teased as she posed next to him.

"It was nothing of the kind," her husband said, giving her a mock stern look. Then they turned and smiled widely into the cameras. Photos were taken all around.

At least one reporter—Jack Smith of the *Los Angeles Times*—was wise to their little show. "Mike Todd and Elizabeth Taylor, well-known man-and-wife comedy team, put on a dizzy domestic farce in one act for the press," he wrote. And it worked, too. Smith's story was featured prominently in the *Times* with a big photo of the smiling couple. In fact, the airport give-and-take, though clearly staged, offers as clear a window on the private relationship between Mike and Elizabeth as one can find—madcap, showy, querulous, calculated, but always deeply affectionate.

When Elizabeth underwent her appendectomy a few weeks later, Mike was at her side to comfort her and to tell reporters, "This will be her last time to the hospital." Good thing he was no longer a gambling man.

He also said that he hoped to resume their world tour once Elizabeth was better, stressing it would be "purely a vacation—no business." He was obfuscating again. In fact, what no one but his closest intimates (and the U.S. State Department) knew was that Mike Todd was determined to get to Russia. Nearly two years earlier, he'd harbored grand plans of making a film in collaboration with Russian filmmakers, and not just any film either. He'd wanted to make a gargantuan version of *War and Peace*—no matter that Paramount recently had beaten him to it with an adaptation of Tolstoy's classic starring Henry Fonda and Audrey Hepburn. That picture, Todd said, was boring and flat, and, besides, was shot in Italy. His would be colossal. And it would be filmed nowhere but in the Union of Soviet Socialist Republics.

Mike Todd Jr. would insist that his father's desire to film in Russia was altruistic, growing out of a belief that a cooperative cinematic effort between East and West could help "bring the people of the world together." But for this flamboyant venture capitalist and son of a poor Polish-born rabbi, there was more to it than that. The Soviet Union represented a vast frontier of untapped opportunity and challenge. If he could make it in Communist Russia, there would be no stopping Mike Todd.

At the height of the Cold War, however, doing business with the Soviets was regarded warily by the United States government. When Todd had first contacted the State Department about traveling to Russia back in April 1956—around the time that he was becoming friendly with Elizabeth—J. Edgar Hoover sent a personal memo to State Department agents in Los Angeles warning them against granting permission for the trip. His files, Hoover insisted, indicated "association by Michael Todd with pro-communist individuals and gamblers." Furthermore, there were Todd's "questionable business operations during his 1951 bankruptcy investigation." Yet nothing in Todd's FBI file backs up Hoover's charges. In fact, the Bureau had failed to prove any illegality on Todd's part during his bankruptcy, and one memo directly contradicts the chief's allegation of association with "pro-communist individuals" by reporting "no subversive info" whatsoever was found in Todd's files.

But Todd was a Democrat, and any Democrat who courted the Soviet Union was immediately considered suspect. Surely Mike knew this, and he was shrewd as always: He "expressed great admiration for Director Hoover and confidence in all Bureau operations." That message was relayed to Hoover in code via teletype. After that, there was no further opposition from the FBI chief to Todd's Russian sojourn.

To get what he wanted, Mike knew that he'd need to charm and manipulate the government in the same way he did the press and the public. Sponsoring a pair of Russian filmmakers on a visit to the United States, Todd kept the State Department apprised of their movements, offering to show the department the films the Russians had brought with them. Warned that the Soviets would try to use him for propaganda if they agreed to coproduce a film, Todd made assurances that he wouldn't tolerate any outside "artistic control." When asked to keep in touch with the State Department at all times, Todd replied that he "wouldn't operate any other way."

He was equally as charming to the Russians. His informal, jovial humor struck a responsive chord among the Soviets, and they came close to signing a deal with him. When they finally turned him down, Todd headed into Yugoslavia to try to secure a deal there. Once again he was unsuccessful. Although plans for *War and Peace* were eventually dropped, Todd did not give up his dream of a Russian production and hankered for the next two years to get back to the Soviet Union.

And so it was that in February 1958, Mike and Elizabeth celebrated their first anniversary clinking champagne glasses in Moscow. To both his wife and son, Todd hinted that he was on a "secret mission" for the U.S. State Department; his FBI records, however, reveal nothing of the sort. He was in Russia to sell Mike Todd, not democracy; he wanted distribution for *Around the World* and to jump-start talks for a U.S.-Soviet film production. Once again he got on famously with the Soviets, likening Khrushchev to a Hollywood movie magnate and admitting to being "fascinated" by him. Lest he be charged as being too friendly to the Communists, Todd made sure to tell reporters that he'd brought along America's "best secret weapon"—his wife. Let Elizabeth Taylor loose in Russia, Mike said, and it could "undermine their whole structure." Not quite—but the glamorous impression Elizabeth made touring Red Square wasn't lost on Soviet officials. Khrushchev decided to capitalize on the publicity of the Todds' visit by publicly renewing his call for a summit meeting between East and West.

Back in California in the middle part of that February, Elizabeth had little time to unwind because rehearsals for *Cat on a Hot Tin Roof* began on February 24. Since the birth of Liza, life had been a whirlwind, with the Madison Square Garden party, the jaunt to Asia, the appendectomy in Los Angeles. For New Year's, the Todds, with Eddie Fisher and Debbie Reynolds along for the ride, had planned to see Judy Garland and Harry Belafonte perform in Las Vegas. Elizabeth was still not all that keen on Debbie, but she'd come around to liking Eddie okay; he made her laugh, and there was something about the way his eyes lit up every time he saw her that she just couldn't help but find amusing. As they hustled on board the *Liz* with the champagne already flowing, no one thought to tell the pilot their destination, so it was taken for granted that they were headed to their home in Palm Springs. Not until they'd touched down and recognized the San Jacinto Mountains did the group let out a collective shout of surprise, and soon the plane was zooming back up into the air. The foursome welcomed midnight with a burst of bubbly somewhere over the Nevada desert.

A few weeks later the Todds were on their way to Russia, and after that, there was a flying trip to Paris, where Elizabeth "only had to utter an enraptured 'oooh'" to acquire new gowns at the salons of Dior and Balenciaga. "Liz bought and bought," as *Photoplay* commented on her jaunt down the Rue de la Paix to find some new shiny rocks for her rapidly growing collection. "The only French phrase Liz knows is 'Van Cleef and Arpels.'" Apparently Paris didn't bore her so much this time.

This was the lifestyle that Elizabeth Taylor was born for. There was no chance to get bored. At a time when air travel was still new to most Americans, Elizabeth was jetting around at will, often in her husband's private plane. So she was a little petulant when she was forced to put all of that on hold and return to work for the first time in more than a year. Yes, the film would be good for her career, and, yes, she thought that she could do a good job in the part. But that didn't change the fact that she preferred flying around the world to emoting on a soundstage. But as Mike spent his days still trying to secure Russian distribution of *Around the World*, Elizabeth turned her full attention to Maggie the Cat.

Rehearsals did not go well. Some people on the set thought that the star was behaving like a spoiled brat. Judith Anderson said that Elizabeth "dogged it" during rehearsals—meaning that she held back and refused to get into the part. Paul Newman was so frustrated that he complained to director Richard Brooks; Elizabeth, he said, was giving him nothing to work with. But Brooks, who'd been through all this before on *The Last Time I Saw Paris*, didn't share his actors' concerns. He told Newman not to worry. "Once the camera begins to roll," Brooks said, "she comes alive." The director understood his leading lady very well. "First, she's a beauty. Then, she's a combination of child and bitch. Third, she wants to love passionately and to be loved."

After a year of marriage, it was Elizabeth's desire for grand romance and passion that defined her. She adored being Mrs. Mike Todd. "Liz is blissfully happy," *Photoplay* reported. "Queen Elizabeth of the British Empire should have it so good as Mike's 'Queen Liz.'" It was the way she'd always wanted to live—life in all its wide-screen glory.

And so she was more than happy to participate in Bill Doll's latest public relations gambit, launched just as filming of *Cat* got under way. I'M SAYING GOOD-BY TO THE MOVIES blared the headline in the *Los Angeles Times* on March 16 over a piece written by "Mrs. Michael Todd." A Madonna-and-child photo of Elizabeth and baby Liza graced the page. "I won't really be leaving show business," Mrs. Todd wrote. "I'm just thinking of retiring the commodity known as Elizabeth Taylor. When that happens, the spotlight will be on Mike, which is the way it should be." Despite what some people were saying, she didn't feel that she "owed" her public a lifetime in the movies. "I owe the public exactly what they see on screen and nothing more," she said, "and I think my fans will be glad to have me do whatever makes me happiest." She insisted that she would make just three more movies: *Cat*, *Don Quixote*, and another picture for her husband sometime in the future. And then she'd call it a day.

There were at least a couple of motivations behind the story, including putting an end, once and for all, to those recurring rumors about troubles in the Todd marriage. "When we're separated," Elizabeth wrote truthfully, "we absolutely die." But the real point of the article was to ratchet up pressure on Metro, which still insisted that Elizabeth had one more film on her contract. The star, however, was determined never to do it. The more time she spent away from the studio, the more she loathed the idea of going back. After filming wrapped on *Cat*, she intended to walk off the Metro lot and never return.

Principal photography commenced on March 3 with the scene outside the plantation house where the bratty child throws ice cream at Elizabeth. As Brooks had promised, the star's performance noticeably improved once the cameras were on her. But as had become her custom, she called in sick a few weeks later, pleading a cold. (She'd later claim that it was pneumonia.) A reported 102-degree fever kept her from flying with Mike on March 22 to New York, where the Friars Club was planning to roast the showman at the Waldorf-Astoria. Instead of his wife, Mike took along the writer Art Cohn, then penning the authorized Todd biography and working on a script for *Don Quixote*.

Dick Hanley drove them to the Burbank airport, where the *Liz* took off at 10:41 P.M., helmed by pilot Bill Verner, a forty-five-year-old major in the air force reserves, and copilot Tom Barclay, thirty-four, a last-minute replacement for Verner's regular copilot. Settling into their seats, Todd and Cohn smoked cigars and sipped brandy as the plane rose into the clouds over Southern California. They'd use the trip to go over drafts of *Don Quixote*.

A little more than two hours later, at 1:55 A.M. Mountain Time, as turbulence over Arizona began to jostle the small plane, Verner called down to air traffic control in Winslow for permission to climb from 11,000 to 13,000 feet. He reported "moderate" icing conditions. Permission was granted, and the *Liz* began its ascent. If he hadn't done so already, Barclay probably told the two passengers to make sure their seatbelts were fastened. But the higher altitude did nothing to decrease the turbulence. The *Liz* was heading straight into a storm front, and ice was now forming rapidly on the wings. Shortly after two in the morning, Verner radioed air control in Zumi, New Mexico, that the icing conditions were getting worse. What he didn't know was that the right master engine rod as well as the right propeller were about to fail.

Far below, John Johnson was working the graveyard shift in the control tower at the tiny airport in Grants, New Mexico. Grants was a quiet mill town, the carrot-growing capital of the United States, nestled to the northeast of the snow-covered Zuni Mountains, the locus of many Indian legends. Johnson had had little to report all night. But around 2:30 A.M. he saw an intense, brief flash of what he thought was lightning in the purple winter sky. Shortly afterward he received a call from the pilot of an Air Force B-36 flying overhead, who reported seeing a plane go down over the mountains. Johnson noted the time as 2:40 A.M. and phoned Dick Lane, the airport operator. Lane could do nothing until daybreak, since the darkness would make any search of the snowy mountain terrain impossible.

There was, of course, a suspicion that this was Mike Todd's plane. No communication had been received from Verner since he'd radioed Zumi saying that the icing was getting worse. A search team was organized, including stringers from the Associated Press, which set out at first light into the mountains. "We had trouble seeing very much of the terrain because the ground was partly obscured by fog," Lane said. It was pilot Bill Hopwood who, after about thirty minutes of searching, first spied a column of dark smoke rising through the fog from the edge of a small arroyo. The searchers were stunned by the devastation. The burned wreckage of the *Liz* was scattered over a quarter of an acre, evidence of a massive explosion on impact. Glenn Hughes, an investigator for the Civil Aeronautics Administration, took one look at the scene and knew instantly that the plane had rammed nose-first into the ground.

The investigation would disclose that the plane had lifted off carrying 20,757 pounds—a ton more than the maximum allowable weight for a Lockheed of that size. Mike Todd never traveled lightly. Just four months earlier he'd been charged for excess baggage on a commercial flight. Had his excess finally been his undoing?

Dick Lane reported that all that was left of the *Liz* were "the outer portions of the wings and a small portion of the tail." And one other thing: a red cloth napkin with the words THE LIZ embroidered in gold.

The snow in the arroyo was melting, blackened by fuel and cinders, and stained a deep red in several places. The remains of three bodies were found far away from the site of impact. But the report from the Burbank airport had said that *four* people were on board. Searchers wondered if the report was wrong. But then an Associated Press freelance photographer named George Hight moved a piece of wreckage and discovered the gruesome, blackened remains of Mike Todd. Only his dental records—and his wedding ring—would identify him.

The bodies of the four victims were taken to Albuquerque, seventy-eight miles east of Grants. Just three days earlier Todd had been to Albuquerque, making a special appearance for a showing of *Around the World in Eighty Days*. The *Liz* had landed at the Albuquerque airport and was met by local officials who gave the gregarious showman a rousing welcome. But their idea to escort him into town with siren-blaring police cars was declined. "Sirens, in an instance like this," Todd told them, "are very undemocratic. They divide Americans into two classes and have a way of saying: 'Get out of my way, you peasants, here comes a big shot.'"

But Mike Todd *was* a big shot, as big as they came. And now, in the blink of an eye, with so many plans left unfinished, the big shot was gone. Dick Lane called the Burbank airport and told them that Todd's plane had been found. The Civil Aeronautics investigators called in their reports. The stringers called in their stories. One of them also called James Bacon, who called Dick Hanley and told him that Mike Todd was dead. It was left to Dick—devoted Dick—to break the news to Todd's wife.

Six

Protecting Interests

September 1958–May 1959

As Hedda Hopper barged into her office, her secretaries sat bolt upright at their desks. They knew when the "old harpy" (as some of them called her behind her back) was on the warpath, and this was clearly one of those times. Tossing her flowered hat onto the ratty sofa, the columnist barked out an order to get Kurt Frings on the phone. The gleam in her eyes told her secretaries that Hedda was on to a scoop.

Everyone in town was looking for Elizabeth Taylor, who'd just returned from New York. A posse of reporters had been left stymied after chasing the star to the Beverly Hills Hotel, only to lose her when she escaped through the Polo Lounge and was whisked away by a waiting car. But Hedda had a hunch "she would be hiding out in the house of Kurt Frings"—a man she despised with every breath of her aging body, blaming him for "squeezing producers dry and making the stars [the] rulers of Hollywood." At seventy-three, Hedda was getting a little old to play the game in this new world order created by Frings and others like him, but she wasn't going down without a fight. And that meant finding and nailing Frings's prize client, the Widow Todd, who, after all, was only a star because Hedda had made her so. Or so Hedda believed.

It had been exactly five months and eighteen days since Mike Todd had died in that fiery plane crash. Elizabeth's grief had been broadcast from every newspaper, magazine, radio, and television.

Fan magazines quickly pasted stock shots of Elizabeth and Mike onto their covers with headlines like FAREWELL MY DARLING, FAREWELL MY LOVE and saw their newsstand sales spike. A comment supposedly once made by Todd—that when he was separated from his wife, he felt like one half of a pair of scissors—was kept in heavy rotation in nearly every article written about his death. Photos of Elizabeth at Mike's funeral in a black veil, being held up on either side by her brother Howard and her doctor Rex Kennamer, her mouth open in a wail of anguish, became iconic, anticipating the photos of Jackie Kennedy a few years later, though Jackie would never be as dramatic in her grief.

To the young widow, the press bowed low. Louella Parsons temporarily dropped "Good News" as the title of her column in *Modern Screen,* explaining she couldn't use it because of the "sorrow of Liz Taylor's great tragedy." All those notorious fights between the Todds were forgotten as columnists rewrote history. Louella recalled the night at Romanoff's after the Academy Awards a year earlier when Mike won the big prize and tenderly held his wife's hand and asked, "How can one man know such happiness?"

And now, if the fan magazines and newspaper columns were to be believed, Elizabeth had remained inert for the past five months, sitting alone in her bedroom—"a small figure with hands lying listlessly in her lap, face white as chalk, eyes swollen with weeping, staring vacantly, seeing nothing." She sat caressing Mike's wedding ring that had been pulled from the wreckage of his plane or the statue they had bought together in Hong Kong. "The goddess Todd had built went to pieces when Mike's plane crashed," *Motion Picture* magazine wrote, summing up the image the public seemed to want and expect from its heroine. Prophetic words that Todd was supposed to have uttered ("I'm flying so high maybe I have to come down!" or some version thereof) were mixed into the narrative in an attempt to fashion a truly Shakespearean tragedy.

Yet for all the theatrics, Elizabeth's grief was real. For three days she vomited everything she tried to eat. "She had never experienced any kind of real loss before," said one person close to her who asked for anonymity. "That such a thing could happen to her was unthinkable, and she grieved for Todd with as much passion as she had loved him." Bolting out onto the lawn screaming in her nightgown, Elizabeth was forcibly brought back inside the house by Dick Hanley and Dr. Kennamer. After discovering she'd consumed several bottles of vodka on her own, Sydney Guilaroff made a beeline to Elizabeth's room and cleared away all of her pill bottles. Guilaroff would maintain a vigil on the floor beside her bed for several nights, reaching up to take her hand whenever she called out Mike's name.

Her life with Todd had been over the top; why shouldn't her grief be the same? Fainting into her brother's arms at the funeral wasn't any less genuine for all the histrionic effect it had on the public. Melodrama was the stuff of Elizabeth's life. When she finally steeled herself to return to work a few weeks later on *Cat on a Hot Tin Roof*, she was greeted with flowers from director Richard Brooks. On her thank-you note she took a pen and extravagantly crossed out the embossed "Mrs. Michael Todd."

Elizabeth would insist for the rest of her life that if only Mike had lived, their marriage would have lasted forever. But Mike Todd Jr. wasn't so sure. "He said the marriage might have lasted only if Dad never had a financial downturn," Susan McCarthy Todd revealed. What if *Don Quixote* had been a flop? What if Todd's creditors had finally started demanding payment? After all, Todd-AO, so profitable in mid-decade, would eventually go the way of other fads of the fifties. Would Elizabeth have been content to remain Mrs. Mike Todd if Mr. Todd was no longer king of Hollywood?

But for the moment, she still took refuge in the Todd organization, on which she had come to rely, especially as she eyed life beyond the gates of MGM. Midori Tsuji became her assistant and traveling companion, Bill Doll her de facto personal publicist. It had been the Todd office that had coordinated the publicity around her return to filming *Cat* and made her latest New York travel arrangements. And it had been Todd protégé Eddie Fisher who had met her when she stepped off the plane.

Oh, how Hedda steamed when she read that. Not long ago she'd extolled Elizabeth as "a lost lamb . . . staring at a door that Mike would never again walk through, a little widow who has the sympathy of the world." But all that sympathy was about to evaporate, Hedda suspected, if the reports she was getting out of New York were true. Her spies insisted that they were. Elizabeth Taylor, the sainted Widow Todd, had taken up with her late husband's friend who, with his wife, Debbie Reynolds, made up America's Sweetheart Couple. Hedda was nearly apoplectic.

Making the situation even worse was that Elizabeth had lied to her aunt Hedda, telling her that she was only stopping over in New York on her way to Europe. Just days before Hedda had waxed lyrical over Elizabeth's "beauty, talent and youth" in her column. So it was with considerable indignation that she read Earl Wilson's column in the *New York Post* on August 29, 1958: "Elizabeth Taylor and Eddie Fisher were dancing it up at the Harwyn [nightclub] this morning, Eddie having been Mike Todd's close friend and now sort of an escort service for Liz." Wilson reported that they'd also seen the play *Two for the Seesaw* with Henry Fonda and Anne Bancroft the night before at the Booth Theatre. That was enough to send reporters on a hunting expedition to discover if a romance was indeed blooming between Taylor and Fisher. It seemed that there might be.

"Hedda was outraged by Liz Taylor's affair with Eddie Fisher," said Robert Shaw. "When I got confirmation of it, she hit the roof. She kept yelling into the phone, 'That bitch! That slut!' She was very good at passing moral judgments."

In the last few days, despite the Soviets' launch of Sputnik, the vote for Alaskan statehood, and the arrest of Dr. Martin Luther King in Alabama, the top headlines in many newspapers were the rumors of "Liz and Eddie." Could they be true? Liz—so soon after Mike's death? Eddie—so soon after Debbie had given birth to his son?

For MGM, the stories were tumbling out at the worst possible time, since *Cat on a Hot Tin Roof* was set to open in New York in less than two weeks and would go into general release soon thereafter. The limited Los Angeles opening on August 29 had been wildly successful, with critics agreeing that Elizabeth's performance surpassed anything she had ever done before. So enormous hopes were riding on the picture. The trade publication *Boxoffice* predicted: "The ready-made market should result from the provocative nature of the original and more importantly because this is the picture that top-lining Elizabeth Taylor was making when her husband, the late Mike Todd, met his tragic death. That event and her return to work were so widely and sympathetically publicized that most theater patrons are eager to witness the results."

Yet promoting a film was the farthest thing from Elizabeth's mind. Alone in her room at the Plaza, her months of loneliness and grief melted when Eddie smiled kindly at her. Asking Midori to leave the suite, Elizabeth let Eddie put his arms around her. Then she began unbuttoning his shirt. That night they made love for the first time and "couldn't get enough of each other," Eddie recalled. The next day they strolled around the city in a daze, kissing in public on Fifth Avenue, delighting in the kind of anonymity that only New York can offer.

But they couldn't go unnoticed forever. Reporters perked up when the pair showed up over Labor Day weekend at Grossinger's, the Catskills resort where Eddie had gotten his start and where he'd married Debbie. Walter Winchell hinted heavily at a romance in his column, and soon the whole press corps was after the story. Photographers caught them hurrying into a car outside a nightclub, with actress Eva Marie Saint doing her best to block Elizabeth's face. One gossip columnist sniffed, "Eddie Fisher says Debbie's home with the children. He means while he was out dancing with Liz Taylor. So that sums Eddie up briefly."

Elizabeth was stung by the coverage. She'd meant no offense to anyone. Eddie had comforted her, and she'd enjoyed it more than she'd expected. And she saw no moral quandary with that. Like much of the press who chattered with such vexation, she knew that

Eddie's marriage to Debbie was in name only. Still, she denied the affair on her return to Los Angeles, considering that to be prudent, at least for the moment. Eddie arrived in the middle of the night to avoid the newsmen who were waiting for him. But it didn't matter. On September 8, 1958, the *Los Angeles Herald Express* emblazoned EDDIE FISHER IS DATING LIZ TAYLOR in bold red letters across the top of its front page—*above* a headline about Khrushchev's threat to retaliate if the United States attacked Red China. The secret was out.

On September 10 the *Herald* ran an "exclusive" interview with Eddie and Debbie landed by Louella Parsons, in which the couple insisted that all they'd had was a "misunderstanding." But the story remained so hot that every newspaper, including Hedda's flagship *Los Angeles Times*, was rushing to be the first to uncover the truth. No doubt Hedda was peeved that Louella had scooped her on getting to Eddie and Debbie. And likely she was frustrated that it was night city editor Ted Sell, and not she, who'd landed the front page of the *Times* with a story on the scandal. Hedda fumed. No one, she determined, was going to crack this story but her.

Finally getting Frings on the line, she told him not to deny that Elizabeth was staying there and insisted on speaking to her immediately. Frings told her he'd call her back. When the phone rang a short time later, it was Elizabeth. Hedda waved frantically at one of her secretaries to pick up the extension and start taking notes in shorthand. "Level with me," the columnist admonished the star, "because I shall find out anyhow. What's this Eddie Fisher business all about?"

Elizabeth, no doubt with Frings's approval, had decided to come clean. According to Eddie's recollections, he had promised to find a way to marry her by this point, and so apparently everyone figured that further denials would only look pathetic in retrospect. Besides, as Eddie said, "Elizabeth lived by her own rule: She wants what she wants when she wants it." And at the moment she wanted Eddie Fisher.

"I don't go about breaking up marriages," Elizabeth replied defiantly to Hedda. "You can't break up a happy marriage. Debbie's and Eddie's never has been."

Hedda could hardly believe what she was hearing. Was it true, she pressed, that they'd gone to Grossinger's, where Eddie and Debbie had been married?

"Sure," said Elizabeth proudly, "and we had a divine time, too!"

Hedda was aghast. She asked if Elizabeth loved Eddie.

"I like him very much," she said, an interesting choice of words. "I've felt happier and more like a human being for the past two weeks than I have since Mike's death."

Hedda pressed the point. "What do you suppose Mike would say to this?"

Elizabeth's answer has become legendary. "Well, Mike is dead and I'm alive."

Did she really say that? It sounds so much like her plaintive cry in *Cat on a Hot Tin Roof*: "Skipper is dead and I'm alive! Maggie the Cat is alive!" Surely Hedda had seen the picture at its Los Angeles premiere. And even if most moviegoers had yet to see the film, the line would soon be familiar enough. Was there, perhaps, a deliberate echo of Maggie in the interview? Was Elizabeth still caught up in the character—like herself, a lonely, sexually frustrated young woman? Or was Hedda so furious with the star that she manipulated her response to sound like the sexy siren she played on the screen?

But if so, there was more fury to come. After bantering for several more minutes, Elizabeth said something that sent the columnist's "anger soaring like a rocket." In the resulting story, Hedda described the star's comment as "unprintable." But it was more than that. To such a staunch guardian of Hollywood morality, Elizabeth's words were unforgivable and were certainly the reason Hedda wrote the piece with such striking venom. "What do you expect me to do?" Elizabeth had asked her. "*Sleep alone?*"

Never in her two decades of reporting had Hedda been so offended or felt so personally betrayed. "I've known Elizabeth Taylor since she was nine years old," she began her story. "Always liked her. Always defended her. She never wanted to be an actress. That was her mother's project. I've seen her through her marriages to Nicky Hilton, Michael Wilding, and Mike Todd. She had the sympathy of the world after Mike Todd's death. But I can't take this present episode with Eddie Fisher."

And so she "snapped out" the story "in five minutes flat" and sent it out on the wires around the world. Even without Elizabeth's "unprintable" comment, the story revealed the star's seemingly cavalier attitude toward breaking up America's Sweethearts. It ran on the front page of the September 11 *Los Angeles Times* under a photo of Debbie in pigtails at the wheel of her car, smiling bravely as her button-eyed daughter Carrie, just twenty-three months old, stared forlornly into the camera from over her shoulder. It was those sad eyes that did the trick.

All hell was about to break loose.

Elizabeth had no idea of the tumult that she had caused. Not even after the scene a few days earlier at Los Angeles International Airport when photographers rushed her plane as she descended the steps. She'd kept her chin lowered, her eyes diverted. The afternoon sun glinted off the diamond in her blue turban and the diamond-studded collar of the Yorkshire terrier that she cradled so carefully in her left arm. Dick Hanley was beside her, a protective hand on her shoulder, and Kurt Frings, "nervous in an off-white silk suit," waited at the bottom of the steps to ease her through the mob shouting her name.

A TWA station wagon whisked them across the tarmac. The photographers sprinted after them in pursuit, cameras bouncing around their necks. A hundred feet away Elizabeth and her entourage slipped into Frings's Cadillac sedan. Only then did she roll down the window and raise her beautiful eyes to the battalion of cameras. The questions bombarded her like machine-gun fire. "Do you know if Eddie and Debbie are breaking up?" "Do you expect to see them?" "Why did you come back to the coast?" And, when she remained silent: "Miss Taylor, won't you please say something?"

"Hello," she said coolly and rolled up the window. The Cadillac sped away.

The chase was on. Reporters hopped into their cars, screeching out of the airport onto La Cienega Boulevard, desperate to keep the Cadillac in sight. Running red lights and passing wildly, they followed Frings to his office in Beverly Hills. But their quarry wasn't caught yet. Frings honked and shouted something to a man waiting at a third-floor window, then swung his car back around onto the street and headed north on Beverly Drive. Another madcap chase in and out of traffic ensued until the Cadillac roared into the curving drive of the Beverly Hills Hotel. There Elizabeth and Frings jumped out and dashed into the lobby, leaving their car doors wide open. When reporters followed them inside, they found Frings alone, mopping his brow, his silk suit soaking wet, refusing to say where his star client had gone. Meanwhile, as heated words were exchanged in the lobby, Elizabeth was slipping out the back way into another car. Reporters learned that her baggage "had been delivered to a private home."

So far only Hedda had found her. Elizabeth felt safe for the moment, ensconced in Frings's marble-and-glass hillside house on Summitridge Drive in Beverly Hills. Frings's wife, Ketti, a recent Pulitzer winner for her adaptation of *Look Homeward, Angel*, listened wide-eyed to the star's grand tales of passion and adventure. Elizabeth was ecstatic. After so many lonely months sitting around the house, her high-flying lifestyle cut so suddenly and horribly short after Mike's death, she was once again having fun.

Not even the phone call from Hedda had upset her. Despite the columnist's rants, Elizabeth had always been able to count on Hedda to do right by her. Surely she knew that there would be some carping in the press—there always was when stars got divorced—and some clucking by busybodies who felt that she hadn't spent enough time mourning Mike. But nothing was going to stop her from marrying Eddie. Ever since she was eighteen, Elizabeth

had done whatever she pleased, and hadn't the public always followed along eagerly? There was no reason to think it would be any
different this time.

And Frings—her new risk-taking, fast-talking agent—was all
for the match. A decade earlier it might have seemed a little too
much at once: Mike's death, Elizabeth's romance, Eddie's impending divorce. But now, in this rapidly changing, poststudio, scandal
magazine–dominated Hollywood, Frings was actually encouraging his client in her romantic exploits. Old notions of how stars
were "supposed to" behave in public were being replaced by a radical new idea: that press coverage—*any* press coverage—was better
than none at all.

Chroniclers have usually described Elizabeth's romance with
Eddie Fisher as simply a case of love on the rebound: the heartache of a passionate widow who turned to her beloved husband's
"best friend" for comfort and solace. That's the way the fan magazines would eventually rationalize it, and so that became the standard line adopted by successive biographers. But Fisher was far
from being Todd's best friend; he was a sidekick and protégé, an
important part of the massive Todd entourage but never really in
the big man's league. Still, Eddie remained connected enough to
the Todd operation to provide continuity when Elizabeth needed
it most. After all, she had staked her whole future on her husband's promises; she couldn't go crawling back to MGM now. On
her own, she'd lose her bargaining clout; only if she remained part
of the Todd organization could she possibly keep her power. So
it was with great delicacy that she solicited Mike Todd Jr.'s support for her match with Eddie. They'd always been friendly, and he
liked Eddie, too. "She asked for his blessing," said Susan McCarthy
Todd. With great magnanimity Elizabeth's stepson bestowed it.
Mike might be gone, but Elizabeth wanted to be treated as if he
were still alive.

Staying attached to the Todd operation was also, of course, an
emotional thing. It's understandable that a widow might cling to a
familiar framework, to the comforting network of associates of her

late husband. Hanley and Tsuji were just two of the Todd minions who moved over to her employ. Yet such continuity was also crucial if Elizabeth were to realize the kind of future she'd envisioned for herself: free of studio control, starring in the occasional independent picture in order to keep the diamonds on her ears. Mike's estate, with all his debts, had been worth just $1 million, and only a quarter of that was cash in the bank. It was also split equally between Elizabeth and Mike Jr., and distributed in installments. In other words, it was not nearly enough to sustain the kind of high-flying lifestyle she'd become accustomed to, thanks in part to the generosity of her husband's creditors. Revenues from *Cat on a Hot Tin Roof* would only go so far; this was before actors started taking a percentage of the gross. So it's no surprise that Elizabeth sued the owners of the *Liz* for $5 million, charging gross negligence in allowing the plane to take off with excess weight.

Lawsuits, of course, could take years to pay off, so Mike Jr. gamely tried to fill his father's shoes. He announced that he would produce another roadshow extravaganza, *Busman's Holiday*, in which Elizabeth would star. And Eddie Fisher, stepping forward with even more temerity, insisted that he could manage her career with all the aplomb of her late husband. Everything, they assured her, would continue as if Mike were still alive.

But there was another reason for the romance with Eddie. Elizabeth hated to be bored. As much as she truly did mourn her husband, playing the grieving widow had gotten tiresome very quickly. After all, she'd gone from jetting around Europe on a moment's whim and clinking champagne glasses with Russian diplomats to moping around the house in her pajamas all by herself in just a matter of weeks.

And in certain rather delicate areas, Eddie even managed to eclipse the great Mike Todd. "Simply put, Eddie was great in bed," said one friend of Elizabeth's, pleading for anonymity when discussing such an irreverent topic. "I don't think the sex with Todd was ever all that fantastic, since he was much older, and then suddenly, wow! Eddie comes along, and she can't get enough."

Elizabeth Taylor, movie star.
© CinemaPhoto/Corbis

Sara Warmbrodt in 1916, just before starting her stage career, which would take her to Broadway and inspire her dreams for her daughter. *Collection of Allan Trivette*

'INT
JOCKEY
ROOM
SHORTER
CROP

From Elizabeth Taylor's 1944 screen test for *National Velvet*. MGM had been concerned that Taylor was too short to play the little jockey, but her relentless mother promised to make her grow. *MGM Studios*

Francis Taylor with his three-year-old daughter in 1936 in Brighton, where the English went to bathe. The two were never particularly close. *Collection of Allan Trivette*

Sara Taylor with Elizabeth and her rarely mentioned brother, Howard, at the time of the family's return to the United States.
Collection of Allan Trivette

Elizabeth Taylor's first
publicity portrait, taken
in 1941, at age nine,
when she was under
contract to Universal.
Universal Studios

An MGM publicity shot,
mid-1950s. By then the
world knew that Elizabeth's
eyes were violet, and they
really were—sort of.
Collection of Allan Trivette

The photo might be staged, but the friendship was real. Elizabeth and Roddy McDowall grilling on the beach. They would be lifelong confidants.
Collection of Gary Shaw

This poster promises a more joyful storybook union than the
Taylor-Hilton marriage turned out to be. *MGM Studios*

A marriage made by Mr. Mayer. Elizabeth and Nicky Hilton leave for their honeymoon after an elaborate marriage ceremony artfully crafted by studio personnel. Six months later, battered and bruised, the bride had had enough. © *Bettmann/Corbis*

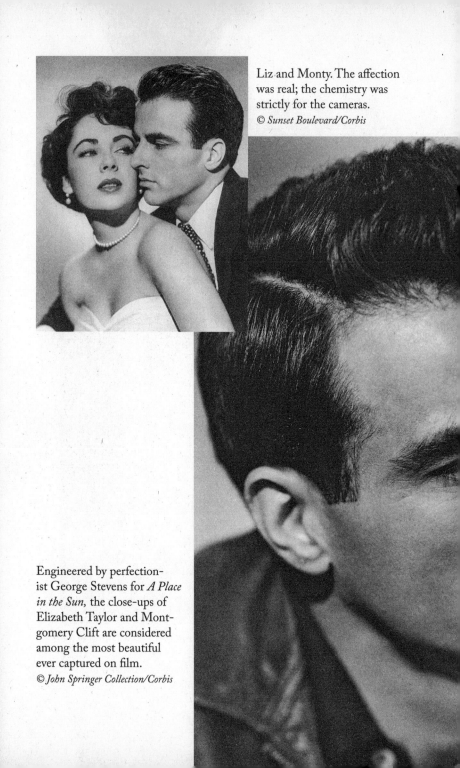

Liz and Monty. The affection was real; the chemistry was strictly for the cameras.
© Sunset Boulevard/Corbis

Engineered by perfectionist George Stevens for *A Place in the Sun*, the close-ups of Elizabeth Taylor and Montgomery Clift are considered among the most beautiful ever captured on film.
© John Springer Collection/Corbis

Elizabeth Taylor and her second husband, Michael Wilding, looking the picture of domestic bliss. It was, in essence, another marriage played out for the public, but Taylor found safety and serenity with Wilding.
© *Bettmann/Corbis*

She always took credit for making Taylor a star, but Hedda Hopper, the archetypal Hollywood gossip columnist, did her best to destroy Taylor's reputation on more than one occasion. © *Allan Grant/Time Life Pictures/Getty Images*

Taylor arrives at the 1956 New York premiere of *Around the World in Eighty Days*, the box-office smash produced by husband number three, Mike Todd (left). At right is Todd's protégé, singer Eddie Fisher. *© United Artists/The Kobal Collection*

When Todd died in an airplane crash, America reached out with sympathy for his grieving widow. *© Francis Miller/Time Life Pictures/Getty Images*

Elizabeth, longtime pal Rock Hudson, and James Dean on the set of her second movie for George Stevens, the legendary *Giant*.
© *Michael Ochs Archives/ Getty Images*

A disgruntled Debbie Reynolds and her then husband, Eddie Fisher, with Mike Todd and Elizabeth Taylor. Was this snapshot a preview of what was to come? © *Ampas/The Kobal Collection*

This was what was to come: Taylor with her man of the moment, Eddie
Fisher, who left Debbie Reynolds to marry Elizabeth. © *1978 Bernie Abramson/*
mptvimages.com

The next marriage "interrupted" by Miss Taylor was that of her *Cleopatra* co-star, Richard Burton, and his wife, Sybil Burton. Here the much-discussed couple relaxes in Rome. © *Stan Meagher/Getty Images*

New York, 1961. Mobs rushed to the hospital to greet Elizabeth on the day she was released after her "miraculous" recovery from pneumonia, an affliction that would become one of her best publicity opportunities.

© *Edward Miller/Keystone/Getty Images*

▲ London, 1962. A rare shot from the costume test for the scrapped version of *Cleopatra*, which was to have been directed by Rouben Mamoulian. This version of the Egyptian queen would never be seen on film. *Collection of Allan Trivette*

➤ Cleopatra—the final, more sedate version—adds some finishing touches. *Collection of Allan Trivette*

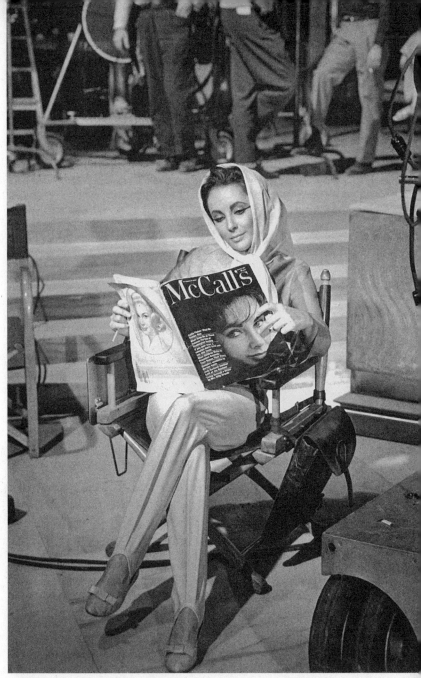

On the set of *Cleopatra*, Elizabeth Taylor reads about all the fuss she's making on the set of *Cleopatra*. *Collection of Allan Trivette*

Mr. and Mrs. Burton, all done up.
Their tempestuous, off-and-on,
always transporting love affair
and marriage kept a generation
enthralled and titillated.
© *Associated Press*

On the set of Burton's film *Night of the Iguana*, Taylor, simple and sweet,
reminded the world that she was just plain beautiful, even without the
diamonds. © *Gjon Mili/Time Life Pictures/Getty Images*

Madame in Europe, dressed to kill.

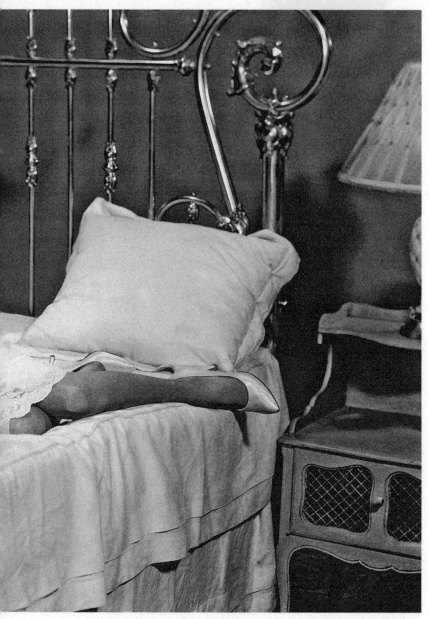

Maggie the cat is alive: Taylor on the set of *Cat on a Hot Tin Roof.* Her portrayal of Tennessee Williams's extraordinary heroine reminded the world once again that she was an actress as well as a star. © *Bettmann/Corbis*

Mike Nichols prepares his star for another grueling scene in *Who's Afraid of Virginia Woolf?*, the film that earned Taylor her second Academy Award.
Collection of Allan Trivette

Taylor, with Burton, anticipates Cher at the premiere of *Boom!* in 1968.

© *Associated Press*

On a night out in Los Angeles in the late 1960s, she was every inch the Elizabeth Taylor the world had come to expect. © *Frank Edwards/Fotos International/Getty Images*

Staying hip: in 1969, Taylor looks more like the girlfriend of her son, Michael Wilding, Jr., than his mother. © *Leonard Burt/Central Press/Getty Images*

At last the movie star hits the Broadway stage in *The Little Foxes*. Taylor stands beside Lillian Hellman, the creator of Taylor's character, Regina Giddens. © *Bettmann/Corbis*

Farewell for now.

For all the Todds' passion, more than two decades had separated them in age, and at twenty-six, Elizabeth was long overdue for a regular, fulfilling sexual relationship with a man as lusty as she was. None of her husbands had fully satisfied her in that regard, but the liaisons with Donen and Mature (and possibly others) had given her lessons in how good sex could be. Elizabeth would become increasingly open about her love of sex. "All I can say is I dig sex," she'd say, "and fortunately I never had to go to a teacher!" Her sensuality, she boasted, was something innate: "I guess it's in my genes."

Eddie concurred. "She was a woman who loved men as much as they loved her and was not shy about it." She described sex as "absolutely gorgeous" and told Eddie that she "loved being sexual." Fisher would joke to friends that Elizabeth had "the face of an angel and the morals of a truck driver." In the breathless, often self-serving prose that defines his memoir—which nonetheless seems largely on the mark—Eddie revealed, "We'd make love three, four, five times a day. We'd make love in the swimming pool, on Mexican beaches, under waterfalls, in the back seat of a limousine on the way home from a party. There is nothing more erotic than a moonlit beach and Elizabeth Taylor. We fit together as perfect sexually as we did mentally."

That last statement, some say, could be taken literally. "Eddie was hung like a horse," said the same skittish and anonymous friend. The actor Dennis Christopher recalled that when he starred with Elizabeth on stage years later in *The Little Foxes*, he once asked her if she wanted to see his Eddie Fisher impersonation. When she said yes, he turned around to reveal an "enormous, ridiculously large cucumber" stuck down his tight pants. Elizabeth screeched with laughter. "How did you *know?*" she asked. Christopher replied that he'd always heard the rumors but had never known for sure—"until now."

For Carrie Fisher, after she grew up and came to understand the whole situation, the story of her father comforting Elizabeth in her grief had a decidedly humorous twist. "My father consoled

Elizabeth with his penis," Carrie quipped. "You can say it with flowers or you can . . ." Her voice trailed off, her point made.

As for Elizabeth, after a week of quite possibly the best sex she'd ever had, it's no surprise that she would return to Los Angeles with her hormones still raging and prepare to do whatever it took to make Eddie her next husband. In that brief, heady moment, Eddie Fisher held everything she wanted: continuity with the Todd organization, prodigious sex appeal, and a celebrity that, if not quite a match for hers, would certainly prevent him from being dwarfed by her own fame. There was no fear that he'd be relegated to being "Mr. Elizabeth Taylor" like Hilton and Wilding. Instead Eddie could hold his own like Mike Todd. He was a huge recording star, boasting more consecutive top hits than even Elvis Presley would achieve. His television show, named *Coke Time* for its sponsor, aired twice weekly on Wednesday and Friday nights, and pulled in some of NBC's biggest audiences. The show was also broadcast over the radio on sixty-eight different stations.

Eddie's popularity was a bit of an anomaly, for his throwback style had more in common with Al Jolson and Tin Pan Alley than current favorites like Frank Sinatra or Perry Como. And while the arrival of rock and roll—championed by Presley, Chuck Berry, and Bill Haley and his Comets—threatened to make his sound permanently passé, there was an undeniable magic to Eddie's voice. "I sang to the ladies I fell for," he recalled. "I used to be friendly with a lot of men, macho men, and they wanted to hang around me to find out my secret. There was no secret. I just showed up with a clean shirt and a sweet song." And all around the world, ladies swooned. Including the fairest of them all.

Born in South Philadelphia in 1928, just three and half years earlier than Elizabeth, Eddie was a working-class Jewish kid whose father, well educated in Russia, resented how he had ended up laboring in leather factories in the land of opportunity. His frustration was taken out on his wife and kids. One of Eddie's earliest memories was running around the house shutting all the windows so the neighbors wouldn't hear his father shouting. The Fishers, always short on cash, sold produce on the street to make ends meet and were forced to move twenty times in ten years. It was a hardscrabble childhood, so different from Elizabeth's. From a very young age, Eddie longed for security and acceptance and power and money—and the kind of appreciation that he found when his mother pushed him forward to sing at synagogue. The accolades of the rabbi and all the nice ladies convinced Eddie that he had what it took to break out of his miserable life: a golden voice.

And so he made his way to local radio contests, and then to the hotels and resorts of Pennsylvania and New York, crooning for newlyweds on their honeymoons. One day at Grossinger's, the most famous resort in the Borscht Belt, he was heard by Eddie Cantor, who hired him for his national radio show. In 1952 Fisher recorded his first number one hit, "Wish You Were Here." After a stint in Korea, he landed his television show, which was an instant smash. Around the same time, he was embraced by Mike Todd; with the showman's support, Eddie's career was made. Mike would always be Eddie's hero, so much so that when his son was born, Eddie named him Todd.

Though he regularly drew thousands of screaming bobbysoxers at every public appearance, Eddie remained insecure and distrustful of his success. "Somewhere deep inside," said Debbie Reynolds, "I think he always felt South Philly, the little boy who sold vegetables, who sang on the radio on Saturday mornings." For almost two years he'd watched Mike and Elizabeth in awe, dumbstruck by her beauty and envious of the passionate relationship that the two of them shared. Despite what America thought, Eddie had never been in love with his wife. Debbie might be bubbly and lovable in public, but in private she was taciturn and controlling.

And so when Elizabeth began flashing those gorgeous violet eyes at him after Mike's death, Eddie couldn't believe it. Sure, he was good-looking, and sure, he had legions of teenage girls screaming his name—but *Elizabeth Taylor?* "Believe me," he said, "I was probably more surprised that Elizabeth was this crazy about me than the rest of the country would be when they found out about

us. I'd always felt she was beyond me, definitely out of my league."
But there was the Widow Todd, sitting on one side of him at a
Hollywood restaurant, putting his hand under her tight black silk
dress while Debbie sat on his other side. At a party on another
night, she surreptitiously took his hand and placed it on her breast.
It was, Eddie said, his "greatest fantasy" coming true.

Lonely, bored, frightened about her future, and sexually starved,
Elizabeth was making it clear what she wanted. And there was one
other thing Eddie could do for her. She was unable to sleep as she
tossed and turned and relived the night of Mike's crash. "I had the
answer for that," Eddie said. One night at the Tropicana lounge, he
introduced Elizabeth to Dr. Max Jacobson—"Dr. Feelgood" to celebrity clients like Anthony Quinn, Tennessee Williams, Frank Sinatra, and Truman Capote. Jacobson's "vitamin injections" were, in
fact, at least thirty milligrams of amphetamines—otherwise known
as speed—combined with steroids, hormones, placenta, and bone
marrow. For Eddie, Jacobson's injections had provided limitless energy as he bounded across the stage to shake the hands of hundreds
of shrieking girls. But the German-born doctor with the quirky accent could offer the opposite, too: barbiturates that induced sleep
or a dreamy euphoric wakefulness, and it was just such an injec-
tion that he gave to Elizabeth that night at the Tropicana. She was
thrilled and grateful to Eddie for the introduction.

Both Elizabeth and Eddie thought that their marriage would
be treated as par for the course. They expected some moralizing in
the press. But divorces happened all the time in Hollywood. The
public would quickly move on as it always did, eager to follow the
next chapter in their favorite stars' lives. Elizabeth wasn't overly
concerned. After all, she'd survived some pretty nasty press when
she'd split with Nicky Hilton. Surely nothing could be worse than
that.

Then Dick Hanley showed her Hedda's story on the front page
of the September 11 *Los Angeles Times*.

• • •

"You betrayed me!" Elizabeth shrieked. "I didn't think you'd print it."

Holding the phone to her ear, Hedda exuded all the smugness of the morally self-righteous. "You didn't say it was off the record," she purred. "And it *had* to be printed."

It was her *duty* to print it, Hedda believed. This wasn't just the story of one actress or one marriage being broken. This was about Hollywood, about the values it needed to promulgate if it hoped to survive. She didn't like the loosening of morals that she saw all around her. At a recent Hollywood party that she had attended with Debbie Reynolds, no less, Hedda had been aghast at all the young starlets wearing those tight new Capri pants: "Whoever invented Capri pants had his mind on rape," Hedda sermonized.

This wasn't the Hollywood that Hedda knew and venerated. "Filthy" pictures like *The Moon Is Blue* and *The Man with the Golden Arm* were destroying the industry, she believed, even if she conveniently turned a blind eye to their box-office successes. So she was taking a stand, fully cognizant that, in her front-page story about Elizabeth, she was depicting the girl she'd once petted and fawned over "as being as cruel and heartless as a black widow spider." But to Hedda's mind, Elizabeth deserved it. "This will hurt you much more than it ever will Debbie Reynolds," she quoted herself in the article as telling Elizabeth. "People love her very much because she's an honest and wonderful girl." The implication, of course, was that Elizabeth was not.

"You'll probably hate me for the rest of your life for this," Hedda went on scolding in print, "but I can't help it. I'm afraid you've lost all control over reason. Remember the nights you used to call me at two and three in the morning when you were having nightmares and had to talk to somebody and I let you talk your heart out? What you've just said to me bears not the slightest resemblance to that girl. Where, oh where has she gone?"

On some level, Hedda had to have known that that girl had never existed. She had been a creation of studio publicists and their handmaidens in the press, prime among them Miss Hopper herself. Whether or not Elizabeth had ever called Hedda in the middle of the night is immaterial; what the old woman lamented was her own loss of clout and control. But with every newspaper in the country—even her hated Hearst rivals—picking up her story, Hedda had reclaimed a bit of her waning power for a moment. She had scooped Louella and Sheilah Graham and every other columnist. It was a flashback to her glory days, when she had broken news of Carole Lombard's death and Bette Davis's pregnancy.

Elizabeth was too smart to think that Hedda wouldn't run a scoop when she landed one; what surprised her, no doubt, was the columnist's combative tone and that Hedda was no longer carrying water for her the way she'd done in the past. Like the MGM executives who contended that Elizabeth was still their property, Hedda and her diatribe symbolized the stubborn refusal of old Hollywood to simply roll over and make way for the new. "I must say I had no regret," Hopper said. "If she'd been my own daughter, I'd have done it. Without a sense of integrity you can't sleep nights."

All during that warmer-than-average late-summer week, people around the country (and then the globe) picked up their newspapers to read about "Liz, Eddie, and Debbie." The scandal trumped all other news: the financial improprieties of Eisenhower aide Sherman Adams, the massive commuter train crash in Newark that killed forty-eight people, even the Supreme Court's landmark decision ordering Little Rock High School to integrate. Elizabeth was stunned by the massive interest. From behind the curtains of Frings's well-guarded house, she watched in disbelief as the furor grew.

But Debbie Reynolds—like Elizabeth a graduate of Metro's last class of studio-trained stars—was definitely not in hiding. Debbie, a former Miss Burbank, had skyrocketed to stardom with her brisk turn opposite Gene Kelly in *Singin' in the Rain* (1952) and then worked her way up the old-fashioned way, gamely playing the perky girl next door in a succession of routine studio vehicles. At twenty-six (just a month younger than Elizabeth), the blond

El Paso native was a five-foot-two dynamo—and "one very smart girl who knew how to work any situation," said her friend, the producer Hank Moonjean.

Indeed. As soon as rumors began reaching her of Eddie and Elizabeth's cavorting in New York, Debbie did two things. First she telephoned her husband (or he telephoned her; their stories differ) and learned the truth. Eddie admitted that he was in love with Elizabeth and wanted a divorce. He also said that he wouldn't be returning on the day he'd originally planned, the Tuesday after Labor Day, but would stay in New York a couple of days longer. Then Debbie called the studio. "And they told her what to do," said Dick Clayton, who knew exactly how the Hollywood studios operated. "At times like these, the star went to the studio and they figured out how to [proceed]."

On the day that Eddie was originally supposed to arrive back in Los Angeles, Debbie showed up at the airport bright and early, devoid of makeup, her hair pulled back in a girlish ponytail. Reporters took note as she watched and waited, waited and watched, then seemed to give up. Her chin set bravely, she marched past the reporters and returned home. Eddie steamed. "The fact that I'd just told her I was in love with another woman didn't keep her from going to the airport like the loving wife," he said.

She was met with more cameras at home. Ever since the rumors had begun, reporters were assembling on the well-manicured front lawn of the Fisher house on Conway Avenue in West Los Angeles, their numbers growing as each day passed. Whenever movement was spotted in one of the windows of the house, a volley of questions was shouted. When a friend of Debbie's, the dancer Camille Williams, showed up for support, she was hounded up the driveway and nearly reduced to tears.

Then Eddie came home. Debbie made sure she was cooking lima bean soup—his favorite. When he walked through the door, the aroma drifted out onto the front lawn. But home-cooked meal or not, there was an argument—overheard by the crowd outside—in which Debbie's chief complaint wasn't so much her husband's infidelity but the damage that it did to their reputations as America's Sweethearts: "It doesn't look good to have stories like this in the papers! You never see stories like this about me!"

With the studio's backing, Debbie was fighting back. She and the studio believed that this thing could be fixed, that the Sweethearts could be saved. Editors at *Motion Picture* magazine told of a personal call from Debbie that day, pleading with them not to blame Eddie, insisting that he was "a great guy." She (and the studio) believed that the marriage could be saved, at least for a while—at least until it no longer looked as if Elizabeth Taylor had broken it.

That was important. To lose her husband to another woman was going to be humiliating; to lose her husband to Elizabeth Taylor when Debbie was a movie star herself was a public ignominy with far-reaching career implications. An actor's stock in Hollywood was a valuable commodity, and Debbie's had just taken a critical hit. Already wags around town were poking fun. "Eddie left Debbie for Elizabeth?" Oscar Levant reportedly quipped. "How high can you stoop?"

So it was no surprise that the reporters jostling one another for position on Debbie's front lawn would witness a parade of Metro "flacks" going in and out of the house. Although Debbie and Elizabeth were both MGM stars, it was clear who the studio was backing in this situation—even if the big New York premiere of *Cat on a Hot Tin Roof* was just days away. After all, Elizabeth had severed all practical ties with the studio once the filming of *Cat* had finished, and she was never going to sign another contract with them. Debbie, on the other hand, had just starred in the phenomenally popular *Tammy and the Bachelor* and was about to begin another important picture, *The Mating Game,* costarring Tony Randall. Debbie loved the studio as much as Elizabeth loathed it, and as always, Metro took care of its own.

No doubt it was the studio that arranged for the Fishers to visit a marriage counselor—rather late in the game, but it was good for appearances. To get there, they had to slip out the back way and climb over a wall to reach Camille Williams's waiting car. Eddie, sighing and shrugging, went along partly because Elizabeth was incommunicado and partly because he never could say no to Debbie. As he hiked his wife over the wall in her capri pants (what would Hedda say?), one of those Metro "flacks" was stepping out onto the front lawn to read a statement. "We have never been happier than we have in this past year," he quoted Debbie as saying. "There was no trouble between us until he got to New York." And then the kicker: "I still love the guy."

But Hedda's explosive front-page interview with Elizabeth changed the arc of the story dramatically the next day. Now headlines blared: DEBBIE: I LOVE EDDIE; MISS TAYLOR: HE DOESN'T. For all Hedda's supposed advocacy of "poor little Debbie," she had placed her so-called friend in an extremely awkward situation. Columnist Irv Kupcinet saw this immediately, deploring the "untenable positions" that both Debbie and Eddie now occupied because of the way Hedda's story (and those that resulted from it) "blew the case wide open." Now *hundreds* instead of dozens of reporters took up camp on the Fishers' front lawn. Police had to cordon off the street.

Of course, the marriage counselor did no good, and Eddie moved out a day later. The press was in an uproar, but Debbie seemed unfazed. When she emerged from the house now, she was cheery. Dressed in dungarees, her hair knotted in a long pigtail, she'd clipped a couple of diaper pins to her blouse. She explained to reporters that she'd just put baby Todd down for his nap. Then she called in to little Carrie, who came stumbling out the door perfectly on cue and ran directly into her mother's arms. As she settled her daughter into the family car, Debbie was asked if it was true that she and Eddie were separating. There was a pause as Debbie slid into the car. Then she turned to face the photographers. Her eyes were moist, but she didn't cry. "He isn't coming home," she said plainly. The tabloids had their picture—and their headline—for the next day.

"That was Debbie Reynolds's greatest performance," said Mark

Miller, who had some key insight into the proceedings from Rock Hudson. Others agreed. Debbie "wasn't quite the 'little darling' she appeared to be," said columnist Earl Wilson. "To put it bluntly, Debbie has more balls than any five guys I've ever known. She pretends to be sweet and demure, but at heart she's hard as nails."

Debbie would insist that she had acted with complete authenticity. Those diaper pins were stuck in her blouse simply so she wouldn't "forget them"—though she did admit to "obliging" photographers with a picture that came to symbolize the "Rejected Woman" in the next day's newspapers. So obliging was she, in fact, that when one reporter called out that he hadn't gotten a shot, Debbie stopped the car as she was backing out of the driveway and posed again. Eddie griped that she was "playing the martyr thing."

"But what other choice did she have?" Dick Clayton asked rhetorically. After all, she had to "protect her own interests," said MGM publicist Rick Ingersoll. Alan Cahan, who was just then starting a long career as a publicist, thought that Debbie's behavior was a classic example of how a star can use the media for her own advantage. "Debbie Reynolds considered her options and made a choice," he said. "Either be typed as the undesirable woman, which would've been pretty pathetic, or go for the sympathy vote. It wasn't going to make her as glamorous as Elizabeth Taylor, but who could compete with that? So she went the other way and decided to be the Good Girl to Liz's Bad Girl."

Plan A—preserving the marriage to keep her reputation intact—hadn't worked, so it was time for Plan B, which turned out be far more achievable. The press, uncomfortable with nuance and easily susceptible to archetypes, loved the Good Girl–Bad Girl dichotomy—a narrative as old as time and still trotted out today. The words used to describe Debbie were significant. She was always "brave" or "plucky" or "unassuming." When she spoke, she always "managed a smile" or "held back tears." For the next several months hundreds of photographs of Debbie and her children would be taken—but, in direct contrast to the usual practice, it was usually only those in which Carrie and Todd looked sad and distraught that made it into print.

One other bit of manipulation seems to have been attempted as well. On the very day that most other newspapers were reporting that the Fishers had separated, some provincial papers were printing a piece supposedly written by Eddie in which he claimed to be "still very much in love with my wife." It forced a quick denial from Eddie's lawyers, who insisted that he hadn't penned the article. Of course he hadn't. It was likely written by the Metro publicity department before Hedda's bombshell interview with Elizabeth had changed the storyline, and only those far outside the Hollywood loop—like the *Times* of Chester, Pennsylvania—still considered the press release relevant.

Meanwhile Elizabeth kept mum, refusing to get out of bed at Frings's house, eating carton after carton of beef-and-pinto-bean chili from Chasen's restaurant, and speaking to no one. But Eddie ventured forward in an attempt to prevent the bad press from sticking to his ladylove. "I'm the heavy," he said. "Don't blame Elizabeth." But he offered no such solicitude for Debbie. Though he accepted "full responsibility" for their problems, Eddie stated, "My marriage would have come to an end even if I had never known Elizabeth Taylor." This, though the truth, directly contradicted what Debbie had said, and led to her announcement the next day that she'd sue for divorce.

Once more, Debbie was forced out front to "protect her interests." To reporters, she issued a mawkish statement about "how blind love can be." She knew what she was doing. Faced with this humiliation from her husband, she knew exactly which cards to play. "I will endeavor to use all my strength to survive and understand, for the benefit of my two children," she said. Of course the press ran her statement under pictures of her holding Carrie and Todd.

The archetypes—Good Girl, Bad Girl, Errant Husband—were hardening into place, no matter the more nuanced picture that a few tried valiantly to describe. Veteran Hollywood journalist Vernon Scott was one of those who attempted to tell the truth to his readers. "Insiders know the Fisher family has had serious problems from the very beginning." But the public wasn't listening. All they knew was "poor little Debbie," as Hedda had described her, had been abandoned with two small children. "It seems unbelievable," Debbie told the press, "to say that you can live happily with a man and not know he doesn't love you. But that—as God is my witness—is the truth."

Debbie didn't just invoke God in that statement. She conjured up the greatest fear of many housewives—that a more beautiful, more desirable woman lurked around the corner, waiting to sneak in and destroy their marriages and ways of life. Hands down, the public-relations battle was won. In just two days' time—from September 11 to September 13—the world turned sharply against Elizabeth Taylor. No longer the beloved young widow, she was now that blackest of fifties stereotypes: the home wrecker.

The first delivery of letters—maybe a couple dozen—arrived at Hedda's office on September 12, the day after her front-page exclusive. On the 13th, one of her secretaries lugged in a heavy burlap sack that had just been dropped off by messenger from the *Times* building downtown. As Hedda sat back wide-eyed and slack-jawed in her chair, the secretary proceeded to empty the sack onto her desk. Hundreds of letters spilled out, growing into an enormous pile, several slipping off and falling to the floor. Many were addressed simply to "Miss Hopper, Hollywood." The post office knew how to find her.

Hedda dug in gleefully. "For many years, I have been a fan of Elizabeth Taylor," read one of the first letters, from a woman in Lompoc, California. "I haven't missed a single movie that she has appeared in. I was definitely looking forward to *Cat on a Hot Tin Roof.* But now I wouldn't go to see her movies if someone paid my way. She has made herself sickening and disgusting . . . I surely hope that [Eddie Fisher] will see the light of day before it is to [*sic*] late and return to his sweet wife and family."

Nearly every letter contained more of the same. On the 14th, two sacks were delivered to Hedda's office, and secretaries began sorting the cards, letters, and telegrams into piles on the floor. As Hedda's story was syndicated across the nation and the saga of Liz, Eddie, and Debbie dominated the news, the flood of mail increased. Missives arrived from every state in the union and as far away as Norway and Australia.

The scandal had clearly touched a nerve. Letter writers described themselves as "heavy-hearted" and "broken," unable to stop thinking about Debbie's pain. Several prefaced their comments with the admission that they'd never before written to a newspaper about a celebrity. Many wrote long and personal accounts that reflected the relationship the public still had with movie stars in 1958. "I consider the show people to be my family," one housewife wrote. "I love them all and have made excuses for their marital troubles, flirtations, etc." But Elizabeth's behavior, she said, was "too much to take." Some writers were surprised by the depth of their emotion: "I am so disgusted with myself because I have let the Fisher-Taylor scandal upset me [but] one hears about it everywhere." Another stated: "There is *so* much feeling about this wherever we go."

Elizabeth's fans were turning on her. Hedda preserved in her files the torn-up glossy photos of Elizabeth that were sent to her, some with the word *hussy* scrawled over them. A young mother from Natchez, Mississippi, penned a four-page letter pouring out her feelings of betrayal: "As far back as I can possibly remember I've held a driving fascination for Elizabeth Taylor. The only movie magazines I ever read had to have a story or some write-up about her. I have defended her like a best friend." But no more. Now she asked, "Is Miss Taylor such a money item to the Hollywood industry that she can't be criticized truthfully—look at all the bull about her poor premature daughter—there's no such thing as a 6-month baby." Others homed in on the same point: "I had little respect for

Liz after her mix-up with Todd while married to Mr. Wilding. Most of us can do a little adding in arithmetic!"

All of Elizabeth's carefully constructed press was unraveling. Her fans were now calling her a "detestable little tramp," "just garbage," "nasty little alley cat," and "the meanest snake on earth." One woman from Affton, Missouri, thought Elizabeth belonged "not to the acting profession but rather to the oldest profession in the world." Another letter writer included a piece of cheese wrapped in aluminum foil—a treat for "Maggie the Cat" to feed to the "rat she trapped." Hedda would keep the foil, cheese and all, in her files for years.

But the rat wasn't getting as much heat as the cat. Eddie was usually called "misguided," while Elizabeth was "piggish." Eddie might be a "heel," one woman from Omaha wrote, but "Liz" was more to blame: "I always feel it's up to the woman to keep a man in his place." A housewife from Glastonbury, Connecticut, observed that, in these situations, "the blame should be placed on the other woman." When comedian George Jessel, appearing on *The Steve Allen Show* on September 16, defended his old pal Eddie by saying it would be hard for any man "to resist Elizabeth Taylor," he was summing up the opinion of many. Elizabeth was the villain here, the black widow luring away a defenseless man. Columnist (and famed Illinois restaurateur) Fanny Lazzar went so far as to scold the star for usurping male prerogatives. "Imagine a woman who proposes to a man," Lazzar wrote, referencing the publicity around Elizabeth's pursuit of Michael Wilding. Hedda kept a copy of Lazzar's column, marked with arrows, in her files.

The prevailing sexism of the era meant that few observers would recognize, let alone criticize, this view. Instead, Hedda was applauded for standing up for what was "right." Among those writing in to congratulate the columnist were several prominent people, including Pat Scott, the wife of actor Randolph Scott. "Randy and I were very much elated over your article this morning," she wrote. "We have always admired you and now all the more so." An executive of *Town and Country* magazine complimented Hedda's "beautiful job of reporting," and silent film star Corinne Griffith called it "one of the finest jobs done for American decency in a long, long time." Even rival columnist Florabel Muir hailed the "gutsy and slashing piece that ripped the phony pretense from one shriveled soul . . . Hopper at her very tops." Film director (and former journalist) Samuel Fuller sent Hedda a wire, praising the interview as "one of the best pieces of first-person reporting since H.L. Mencken took over the Baltimore literary mantle." Hedda, quite understandably, was in the clouds.

What was so remarkable about the piece—what Fuller and the others were reacting to—was its direct confrontation with, even repudiation of, Elizabeth's public image. That was hardly the traditional role of the Hollywood reporter. But with the times changing so quickly, traditional Hollywood was resorting to untraditional measures. Hedda knew that she could still rally a sizable and vocal minority to put pressure on the industry—the same bloc that had demanded the reforms (and threatened the boycotts) that led to the establishment of the Production Code almost thirty years earlier. This was the aggregate of the cultural transformation that the Liz-Eddie-Debbie scandal was measuring. With the Code collapsing under the weight of its own intransigence, with more and more pictures pushing the bounds of what was acceptable onscreen (and more and more stars acting with an impunity unimaginable under the ironclad rule of Louis B. Mayer and the other moguls), conservatives latched onto the scandal as a cause célèbre. And for many of them, Hedda was both crusading heroine and mother confessor.

"Please do something about this monstrous thing," one writer begged the columnist. For many, this was a sacred Christian mission: "Keep the Catholic teaching against adultery and fornication your real fight," one Chicago woman urged Hedda, "so that young folks won't become loose in the morals because of the applause and approval of the Fisher rottenness." Several letter writers insisted that if Elizabeth were to come to their neighborhoods, she would face the Biblical punishment of stoning. A correspondent from Hickory, North Carolina, compared the star's behavior to Esau selling his birthright for a "mess of pottage." A doctor from Inglewood, California, lamented Hollywood's "multiple marriages that flaunt [*sic*] the sanctity and permanence of the marriage sacrament." To these people, Elizabeth was "the devil's daughter," and Hedda was their deliverer. "God bless you, Hedda!" one writer exulted. "These women who wantonly wreck marriages and deprive children of their fathers should be held up to public scorn, and nobody can do it as well as you can." Hedda took the remark as a point of pride.

Perhaps not surprisingly, many of these writers also gave vent to a deeply ingrained anti-Semitism. "The die was cast," one man wrote, when Elizabeth married Mike Todd, because "a gentile woman becomes crude and common with close association with a Jew." From Coronado, California, came the opinion that Eddie was "just another beak-nosed Jew," and "dear little Debbie" should find a good Christian husband. It was all rather an uncanny echo of Elizabeth's part in the film *Ivanhoe*, six years earlier, where, as the Jewish girl Rebecca, she was tried publicly as a witch and a seductress.

"Gone are the days when Hollywood policed itself and transgressors were punished," one Alabama newspaper lamented, a clear reference to Ingrid Bergman's European exile. Now a riot of scandals had torn through screenland in the last few years and their perpetrators had largely escaped any repercussions: the discovery of nude photographs of Marilyn Monroe; the tempestuous marriage (and brazen extramarital affairs) of Frank Sinatra and Ava Gardner; the "grunt and groin" music of Elvis Presley; and, just five months before the Liz-Eddie-Debbie headlines, the stabbing death of Lana Turner's gangster boyfriend, Johnny Stompanato, by her fourteen-year-old daughter Cheryl Crane. Some believed that Turner herself was the real killer and had gotten off scot-free.

It was enough to turn a segment of the public off Hollywood forever. "I was so thoroughly disgusted when the Ingrid Bergman–Roberto Rossellini scandal came out that I have not attended one movie since," one Wisconsin woman wrote to Hedda. "And [I'm] disgusted over Frank Sinatra's flings. I point out to my niece ... to refrain from buying Frank Sinatra and Elvis Presley records."

But Elizabeth's theft of Debbie Reynolds's husband was the last straw. "Taylor is even worse than Bergman," one writer opined to Hedda. The letters continued flowing to newspaper editorial boards across the country. "You play by the rules in life," one writer declared. "Does Elizabeth Taylor know there are rules?"

When Chesterfield cigarettes announced that it intended to continue its sponsorship of Eddie's television show, set for its season debut on September 30, there was a call for boycotts. "So the Eddie Fisher sponsor has taken the attitude of the 'public be damned,'" one furious letter writer from Chicago vented to Hedda. Chesterfield, the writer said, was spending its money on "heels" and "strumpets" and "in fact anything that violates decency." Where was the demand for "decency in performers and entertainers"? And why didn't Chesterfield "observe such a code"?

Because, in fact, the code was gone—and it wasn't just the Production Code that was breaking down. The codes—the very standards of living—that many had grown up with were being rewritten. For those appalled by such a turn of events, there was little to do but huff and puff—and write letters. MGM received its share of them, and given the imminent wide release of *Cat on a Hot Tin Roof,* no doubt there were some worries that the scandal might affect business. Various petitions were received from people who vowed "never to see Miss Taylor again in a picture or stage production."

But of even greater concern were the letters being delivered to the NBC offices and the headquarters of Liggett & Myers, the parent company of Chesterfield cigarettes. Being a TV star and dependent on the vagaries of public taste from week to week, Eddie was far more vulnerable than Elizabeth. The letters pouring in to his sponsor raised real alarm. "I am more than a little shocked to find you would allow a man of such moral turpitude as Fisher to represent a supposedly reliable product as Chesterfield," one woman wrote. "Or are we to assume that the perfidious character of the entertainer who represents you is indicative of the basically insidious nature of your product, as claimed by the medical fraternity who point to cigarettes as a causative factor in lung cancer?"

Even if not every letter was so potently worded, such sentiment didn't go unheeded by the corporate giant. According to Fisher, he and his sponsor were at one point getting "7,000 nasty letters a week"—not to mention the occasional voodoo doll stuck with pins. Hedda, meanwhile, kept turning the screws, writing that if Eddie and his sponsor could read the letters she was getting, both would be "shaking in [their] boots."

But for all of that, the season debut of Eddie's show (now retitled *The Eddie Fisher Show*) won the highest ratings for its time period, vindicating, at least for the moment, Frings's tenet that any press was good press. Eddie beat out his competitors, *Sugarfoot* and *Wyatt Earp*, popular Westerns both, by several points; the Associated Press credited the show's success to the "value of front-page publicity." The appearance of guest stars Dean Martin, Jerry Lewis, Ernie Kovacs, and Bing Crosby certainly helped, but many viewers had clearly tuned in to see if Eddie might betray any hint of his romantic entanglements. He didn't. He sang "Moonlight Becomes You" and joined Kovacs in a rousing rendition of "That's Entertainment." It was all sweetness and light, jokes and happy smiles.

For Eddie's critics, this was only cause for further outrage. Letters continued flowing in to Hedda, to MGM, to NBC, to Chesterfield. Now it wasn't just the principals being targeted, but "those appearing with Fisher" as well, for their blatant disregard of "the public feeling." Jane Powell—an old comrade of both Elizabeth and Debbie's from MGM—had felt it prudent not to appear on Eddie's show and was applauded for her "loyalty and good sense." But anybody else was fair game. Letters to Hedda indicated that a boycott of Eddie's program might be expanded to include George Gobel, whose show had the unfortunate position of alternating with Fisher's. When Steve Allen announced at the end of one of his shows that Eddie would be his guest the following week, the audience booed. Shaken by this, everyone agreed that it would be better if Eddie didn't appear.

The concern was growing at the network. "Some cautious ad men," observed one trade paper, "fear any long, bitter divorce battle might react unfavorably for [Fisher's] sponsors." Movie stars, these ad men argued, had demonstrated that they could sustain careers in similar situations. But this was "the first serious test for a television star"—who depended on provincial, often conservative viewers to invite him into their living rooms every week.

It was a test Eddie ultimately failed. After that first show, his ratings began to slip and continued in freefall over the next several months. *Variety* called the response to the scandal the "war whoop of the bluenoses." Indeed, it was a textbook example of media spin whipping up base public sentiment to conceal more nuanced facts on the ground. And yet it also demonstrated a very real truth about Hollywood: In the end, the public decides. One Chicago man, seeming to feel personally betrayed by Eddie and Elizabeth, wrote quite astutely to Hedda: "In their profession they are public property—they belong to us. We the public made them what they are and they should not forget it."

They would not. The scandal was not going to blow over any time soon despite Kurt Frings's fervent hopes.

Elizabeth remained in hiding. Eddie moved in with her at Frings's house. "We spent most of our time in a small room up several flights of stairs," he recalled. They slept on a sofa bed, calling the place their "womb with a view." Eventually reporters figured out where Elizabeth was and lined the street outside Frings's house. On the rare occasions when they ventured out, Eddie and Elizabeth would lie on the floor of Roddy McDowall's car covered with blankets. It was the only way to sneak past the press.

Across town, however, Debbie Reynolds was still making sure that reporters got a good look at her. According to MGM publicist Rick Ingersoll, Debbie came to feel that Metro, possibly because of growing concern over *Cat on a Hot Tin Roof,* was now "siding with Elizabeth." So she hired her own public relations firm. While it's clearly not true that the studio was favoring Elizabeth, there *was* a limit to how far they'd go in attacking the star of one of their biggest pictures of the year. But Debbie wanted a much more aggressive campaign on her behalf, and she got it. From the fall of 1958 through early 1960, it was virtually impossible to pick up a fan magazine or entertainment section of a local newspaper and not see the face of Debbie Reynolds.

The Liz-Eddie-Debbie triangle was the first major scandal of the poststudio era. In the old days, the studios' mass production of star publicity—all those purple mimeographed press releases, glossy eight-by-tens, and scripted "interviews"—had fed the ever-hungry maw of the press, and the public's curiosity about its heroes and heroines had been sated, if often deceived. When a scandal like Rita Hayworth's "premature" baby or Robert Mitchum's marijuana bust erupted, the disclosure of the star's "transgression" was, as film scholar Adrienne McLean has described it, "oriented toward short-term profit and gain." That is, after a suitable period in which the newspapers and fan magazines were allowed to reap the financial rewards of sensational headlines, the studio pulled back, gave the word that it was over, and received the full understanding and cooperation of its collaborators in the press. In the studio era, most scandals flared up and died very quickly. Aggressive reporters who tried to keep the story going would be barred from further access. No one benefited if the scandal went on too long.

But that was then. As studio control declined and independent press agents—like Bill Doll and the public-relations firm that Debbie hired to represent her—came to predominate, the single narrative that had determined press coverage in the past was split into two or three competing versions. It's not difficult to page through issues of *Photoplay* or *Motion Picture* and distinguish between which stories were planted by Doll and which ones by Debbie's publicists. In this poststudio arrangement, the back-and-forth story lines ensured that the press continued to make money from the scandal for many months afterward. Indeed, *Time* magazine reporter Ezra Goodman called the Liz-Eddie-Debbie coverage "the greatest binge of marathon mush" that he had ever seen. The triangle narrative stretched on for more than a year. And for most of that time, it was Debbie's advocates who led the spin, who won the battle for the most pages, covers, and sympathetic treatment.

That success can be attributed as much to the lady herself as to her agents. "Debbie was going to win the war, not just the battle," said publicist Alan Cahan. In many ways, Debbie Reynolds was very much like the character played by Shirley MacLaine in the film *Postcards from the Edge,* based on her daughter Carrie Fisher's semiautobiographical novel: the iron-willed survivor whose red sequined gowns and perky charm belie the warrior within. Debbie was everything Elizabeth was not: a compulsive entertainer, a Hollywood booster, a spotlight chaser. She could go from girl next door to high-kicking chanteuse in an instant.

As a girl, Carrie was riveted by that process. She called her mother's closet "the Church of Latter-Day Debbie" because it was the place she entered as an ordinary mom and "emerged as Debbie Reynolds." Carrie and her brother Todd would watch the transformation in awe. "She'd twirl her hair up into pincurls that she'd use to pull her face tighter, then she'd put on her make-up base with a sponge." Next came the false lashes, lipstick, rouge, and powder—"great puffs of glittering clouds of powder, followed by hair, which was a big deal, getting the wig on right." Finally she'd clip on earrings, slip a sequined dress over her head, and step into her tiny shoes. "When she was finished," Carrie said, "her Debbie Reynolds movie-star accent got stronger, her posture got better and she looked incredibly beautiful." Later Carrie would observe the process in reverse. The makeup came off with a facecloth, followed by a bubble bath. "Debbie Reynolds would slowly return to being our mother," Carrie wrote. "The coach was once more a pumpkin, the footmen went back to being mice."

Debbie was the classic showbiz pro. Robert Shaw, Hedda's legman, was unabashed in his admiration of Reynolds: "She took what could have been a disaster for her and turned it into a triumph." Alan Cahan was even more succinct: "Debbie knew what sold."

Indeed, the Liz-Eddie-Debbie scandal was ready-made for the housewives who read the fan magazines. In contrast to the glamorous Elizabeth, Debbie had always been someone with whom they could identify, the slightly less pretty, slightly less successful member of the Todd-Fisher quartet. In October 1957 *Photoplay* had published a photo of Debbie looking wistful as she'd "oh'd and ah'd" over the splendor of the Todds' lifestyle—exactly the way any housewife would've acted if she'd been asked along on one of Mike's private-jet trips to Las Vegas or New York. And when Mike died, those housewives recalled, it had been Debbie who'd been there for "Liz." "Dear Debbie," *Photoplay* had written. "She asked the same question Liz asked: 'What about the children?' And took them all into her own home." No wonder one fan wrote to Hedda tarring Elizabeth as "Judas Iscariot."

To the public, Debbie was the Good Mother. Elizabeth was anything but. "A no-good mother," one fan declared. "Why doesn't she stay home and take care of her children?" Another was tired of the "excuses for her neglect of her children"—who, after all, were left in the care of nannies while their mother hid out at her agent's house. "Does she not even have a mother's love?" asked a Mississippi woman.

And if this developing narrative revealed that Elizabeth didn't love her children, then she mustn't have loved her husband either. "It makes me furious all these lies about how broken up over Mike Todd's death she is," a Texas housewife griped to Hedda. The *New York Daily News* ran a letter from a reader saying Elizabeth should win an Academy Award "for her recent role as the grief-stricken widow."

It was absurd, of course; everyone who knew Elizabeth attested to how much she mourned Mike. But without the studio's controlling hand, whichever side spoke the loudest won the round. And it was Debbie's voice—or the voices of her publicists—that drowned out most everything else, ensuring that what the public got was, in fact, the exact inverse of reality.

Case in point: If conventional wisdom held that Elizabeth hadn't really loved Mike, Debbie's love for Eddie was treated as certain beyond any and all doubt. "Debbie loved Eddie with a fervor and intensity that surpassed any emotion she had ever known," one fulsome scribe wrote. "To her marriage she had given every joy and every hope she had tucked away in her heart. When Eddie Fisher left her home for the arms of Liz Taylor, he took it all with him. [Debbie] drew the curtains of silence and sadness around her life and in the sudden and terrible loneliness that overwhelmed her, she grieved."

It didn't matter that Debbie had actually thrown the curtains open wide and practically invited the press into her living room. The paradigm was put in place. *Motion Picture* magazine summed it all up in a single image: When Eddie announced that he was leaving, "Debbie Reynolds—her hair in a single ponytail and her tired face completely devoid of makeup—heard her baby son cry and reached automatically for the diaper pin pinned to her blouse." That was all millions of housewives needed to hear.

The fan magazines that had once deified Elizabeth now went on the attack. "[She] has spent most of her life in a sheltered, unreal world all her own—a soft, comfortable, pretty world, with her beautiful self at the center," wrote *Photoplay* in December 1958. Fan-magazine readers all knew girls like her—girls who had it easy, who didn't need to struggle the way they did. Now their envy and resentment were aimed at Elizabeth. Another magazine opined, "Elizabeth Taylor may discover—for the first time—that her outrageous beauty is not sufficient justification for her attitude throughout this crisis."

Debbie, by contrast, was a paragon of virtue. "No sweeter girl has ever lived in Tinseltown," declared one report. Hedda's mail was filled with similar accolades for the folksy blond star. "Debbie is a thousand times better than Liz," a Sherman Oaks, California, resident wrote. Another correspondent thought Debbie had "an intelligence far above her years," and another, from Sydney, Australia, was moved to defend Miss Reynolds because, after all, "*Tammy* gave enjoyment to so many." One particularly riled fan insisted, "Debbie has more beauty in her little finger than that jezebel."

This became the prevailing image of the scandal because, bottom line, Debbie wanted it to be. The truth, of course, was very different. Even at the time, there were those who recognized a myth in the making. Ezra Goodman had no patience at all when he heard writers describe the Fishers' marriage as "ideal": "In Hollywood, all marriages are considered 'ideal' until they are suddenly splattered all over the front pages." When "friends" were quoted wondering if "poor little Debbie" could survive this terrible blow, one writer for *Motion Picture* had the guts to write: "You know who those friends were? Publicists and press agents. They knew the line to feed to the fan magazines, and the editors knew what would sell to the housewives who made up their readership."

In cold hard truth, the marriage of Eddie and Debbie had been a masquerade from the start. Even their daughter Carrie would admit, "[Their] whole relationship was basically a press release." Their courtship had been arranged by MGM, concocted by a publicity department that saw magic between the two "All-Americans." Both Eddie and Debbie knew the game they played. "That's how [stars] would meet," Debbie explained years later. "They would have premieres, and each studio would have . . . their new young stars meet the other new stars, and that's how we'd go out on dates. That's how Janet Leigh met Tony Curtis. Like [how] Jeff Hunter married Barbara Rush." Such candor wasn't found in her memoir, however, where she tried to maintain, some thirty years after the whole ordeal, the spin that her relationship with Eddie had been authentic and heartfelt. But MGM had arranged matches for her in much the same way that she had described for those others, first with Robert Wagner, then Tab Hunter, and finally Eddie.

Fisher, for his part, simply did what he was told. "I had no control over my own life," he said. "I went where Milton [Blackstone, his agent] told me to go, I sang the songs RCA wanted me to sing, I married Debbie Reynolds because ... To this day I still don't know why." The reason, quite simply, was because the public wanted it. The fan magazines had built them into the most-watched couple in America, with photographers chasing them everywhere shouting, "Give her a kiss, Eddie!" There was so much interest in the couple that even the queen, after a show Eddie gave in London, inquired whether they were going to marry.

Eddie had tried to back out at the last minute. According to one friend, Eddie had grown increasingly concerned about Debbie's "strong personality and was worried about being dominated by it." But marry they did, in September 1955, with the honeymoon to New York "more or less a business trip, specifically requested by Fisher's then-TV sponsor." To the public, Debbie and Eddie seemed a real-life version of Betty White and Del Moore of *Life with Elizabeth,* or Joan Caulfield and Barry Nelson of *My Favorite Husband,* or any of the other perfect young couples then dominating television. But like those sitcom twosomes, the Fishers' lives were entirely scripted. Their first costarring film, *Bundle of Joy,* was timed to coincide with the birth of their daughter Carrie. Or maybe it was the other way around.

Their domestic bliss was a well-orchestrated fiction. Tension between husband and wife increased in the summer of 1957, when Debbie's recording of "Tammy" spent five weeks at number one and then stayed an unprecedented thirty-one weeks on the charts. Eddie, despite his hot TV show, hadn't had a hit in over a year. There was jealousy. There was fighting. A number of times they separated, only to reconcile for the good of their squeaky-clean image. Privately, Eddie agreed that Debbie was indeed the girl next door—"but only if you lived next door to a self-centered, totally driven, insecure, untruthful phony."

For a man who had been used to bedding as many girls as his schedule would permit, the marriage to Debbie was like being exiled to a vast, arid desert. Sex between them, Eddie said, was "non-existent" except to "make babies." Debbie admitted that she was "frigid and sexually unresponsive" until she was much older.

Eddie even thought that his wife might be a lesbian: "The idea crossed my mind," he said. Rumors about Debbie's sexuality had been floating around Hollywood for years, and Eddie wondered if they might be true. "My father's story is basically that my parents' relationship had gone south because my mother was gay," Carrie Fisher said, though she made sure to express her opinion that Eddie's tale of leaving Debbie "in the house with her lover" was "insane" since, after all, "the press [was] living in the yard."

Still, many wondered about this Camille Williams "on whose slender shoulder Debbie Reynolds wept through the resounding smashup" of her marriage. Those reporters out front noted that when Debbie and Camille returned home from the movies, the lights in the house went dark—"all except the light in Debbie's bedroom upstairs." Like Debbie, Camille had been Miss Burbank, and had made something of a career of beauty contests, being named Miss Magnolia Park in 1956 and coming in third in the Miss San Fernando Valley pageant. She'd also competed for the unwieldy title of Queen of the 162nd Tactical Control Group of the California Air National Guard. Debbie would describe Camille as a "voluptuous" brunette forever being chased by men. Sounds a little like Elizabeth. But at twenty-seven years old, Camille had so far managed to elude all offers of marriage and was currently dancing in Dan Dailey's Vegas act—a comeback attempt by the former movie star who'd been outed as a cross-dresser by *Confidential*.

There was one other "very close friend" of Debbie's, as Eddie called her. This was Jeanette Johnson, another old pal from Burbank who had served as Debbie's maid of honor and frequent traveling companion, and "who had become the gym teacher Debbie once dreamed of being."

Whatever the truth of Debbie's sexuality—and it's likely far more nuanced than any one label could describe—the fact of her artificial, largely sexless marriage to Eddie radically alters the narrative that seemed so sure, so true, in the fall of 1958. One thing is certain: Elizabeth was no home wrecker. When she told Hedda Hopper, "I'm not taking anything away from Debbie Reynolds because she never really had it," it definitely upset a lot of people. But it was 100 percent true. And Elizabeth's candid violation of the set of fictions that she herself had sometimes exploited must have been very threatening to Hedda, one of the chief perpetrators of Hollywood untruths.

"Although Liz and I have been cast in the villains' roles, with Debbie as the heroine, there are just a few things wrong with all the reports that have come out about us and the picture created in the public's mind," Eddie complained to the press. Art Buchwald was one of the few journalists who provided a platform to explain what those "few things" might be. Eddie said: "The legend that [Debbie and I] were the ideal couple was to blame more than anything else for what happened when Elizabeth and I announced that we were going to get married. I'm just a guy whose marriage was at an end. I knew it. Debbie knew it. Our friends knew it. The public didn't know it. Debbie's studio wouldn't admit it. So I was happily married, as far as the public was concerned, long after I was unhappily married."

The problem was, no one cared to hear the truth. The fiction sold so much better.

In the midst of all this, *Cat on a Hot Tin Roof* opened in New York at Radio City Music Hall. Unlike *Giant,* there was no gala East Coast premiere; Elizabeth remained sequestered in Beverly Hills. But that didn't stop the crowds from showing up. If MGM had worried that the scandal would deter people from seeing the movie, their fears were relieved by the lines that snaked around the corner from the theater all the way down Seventh Avenue. Fans started gathering at daybreak, jamming into the lobby and spilling out onto the street. The first show was scheduled for 10:30 in the morning, and all six thousand seats sold out. Ushers in their crisp white jackets and bow ties did their best to find seating for everyone who showed up, but even then there was an overflow. Anxious patrons waited in the street for one of the next shows—1:22, 4:17, 7:17, and 10:11. Every seat was filled at every screening. In between shows the famous Rockettes kicked up their legs—but who cared about them when Liz Taylor was up there on the screen, her larger-than-life image filling up that enormous, darkened theater, her heaving breasts and hourglass hips barely contained in a clingy white slip for most of the film's 108 minutes?

"Ferocious and fascinating," wrote the *New York Times'* Bosley Crowther after seeing the picture—and Elizabeth, who "quite obviously has the proclivities of that cat on the roof," was "terrific as a panting, impatient wife wanting the love of her husband as sincerely as she wants an inheritance." *Variety* praised her "well-accented, perceptive interpretation," and *Time* was impressed by her "surprising sureness."

There had been doubts from the beginning that director Brooks could pull off this adaptation of Williams's play. Despite the steady erosion of the Production Code over the last few years, the homosexuality of Brick could still not be mentioned or even clearly alluded to. That left many moviegoers wondering why a stud like him didn't want to pounce all over a woman as sexually irresistible as Elizabeth's Maggie. The "logical conflict" of the play, as Crowther said, was missing, yet in its place was a tour de force of "visual and verbal displays of vulgar and violent emotions." In other words, one stopped asking *why* and was instead just carried along by the power of the performances: Elizabeth, longing and libidinous; Newman, bitter and boiling; and Burl Ives, duplicitous and dispirited as the dying Big Daddy.

It's remarkable how well Elizabeth holds her own alongside such acting heavyweights. She does more than that, actually. She carries the picture. She is the cat, after all; she is the star. All those early doubts about her acting now seemed like so much needless anxiety. "People sometimes forget that Elizabeth Taylor wasn't just a great movie star, but occasionally a very fine actress as well," said the writer Gavin Lambert.

And never finer than here. As Maggie, she is both scheming and sincere, predatory and pitiful. Even at her most aggressive, spitting curses at her husband or at the "no-necked," monstrous children around her, she never loses our fascination or sympathy. She would be rightly praised for her big, hot-blooded scenes—the shrill "Maggie the Cat is alive!" for example—but even more affecting are the smaller moments, as when Newman asks her what victory might mean for a cat on a hot tin roof. "Just stayin' on it, I guess," she says in a small but confident voice. "As long as she can." Whether she was drawing on the emotion of Mike's death to inspire her, as she would claim, or simply reaching down deep to discover her own gifts, as she had in *A Place in the Sun,* she is superb.

The film was a massive box-office success. Going into widespread release in mid-October, it had grossed several million dollars by the end of the year, and by the time it finished its long tour in the spring of 1959, it had racked up an impressive total of $6.1 million. That was enough to land the film in the top ten moneymakers of the year. Although it was half of what *Giant* had made, it was about equal to *Raintree County.* And since *Raintree* had made most of its money in the first months of the same calendar year, the annual Quigley poll of exhibitors named Elizabeth Taylor—no matter what the fan magazines were saying about her—as the most bankable female star of 1958. Soon ads for *Cat* were carrying the tagline: "Year's most popular actress!"

Surely Hedda and her true believers weren't pleased. But their demonization of Elizabeth had played a part in the extraordinary success of *Cat.* Like Eddie's season debut, many people bought tickets to the film just to see how seductive this Miss Taylor really could be. And on that score, she delivered the goods. Her Maggie is a determined sexual aggressor, literally stripping off her clothes for all those thousands of spectators hunched down in their seats looking up at her in the darkened theaters. She is supremely confident of her allure—every bit the slinky, sultry feline her detractors were describing in their outraged letters to newspapers, networks, and corporate sponsors. And when Brick finally succumbs to the charms of his ravishing wife, the two of them falling onto the bed for the final fadeout, the reputation of Elizabeth Taylor, siren, was secure. There were no doubts that she would always get her man.

And while that fact infuriated some, it delighted many others. If the "value of front-page publicity" had helped *Cat*'s initial screenings, it was the film's inherent quality—and Elizabeth's undeniable appeal—that kept audiences coming back, ensuring that the picture would still be in theaters nine months down the road. For all his popularity, Eddie Fisher had no such enduring star appeal; he could do nothing but watch in dismay as his ratings dropped a little lower every week. But Elizabeth was the object of the world's fascination more than ever, and her drawing power was not lost on Hollywood's moneymen. Just a few days after *Cat*'s premiere, Seven Arts signed her for her first independent picture, an adaptation of another Broadway hit, *Two for the Seesaw*, for the unprecedented sum of half a million dollars.

In the fall of 1958 the public was dramatically polarized on the subject of Elizabeth Taylor. Some wanted her films banned; others bought tickets to sit enraptured by her image. It's become conventional wisdom that the Liz-Eddie-Debbie affair turned public opinion against Elizabeth, and certainly she was being attacked from many quarters. But for all those hundreds of angry people who took pen to paper to denounce Elizabeth, there were thousands more who did not. We cannot gauge their feelings in the same way we can those of their letter-writing counterparts; if Hedda received any missives defending the star, she did not keep them. But the pro-Elizabeth base seems to have left a record of its own: the box-office receipts of *Cat on a Hot Tin Roof*. Even if some of those in the audience remained judgmental of Elizabeth's off-screen behavior, and even if others simply didn't give a hoot about star scandals at all, the rest, perhaps the majority, were sending Elizabeth a message of support—not with letters, but with their pocketbooks. It was this support that she came to understand, appreciate, and, increasingly, rely on.

By October it was clear to Hollywood insiders that they ostracized Elizabeth at their own risk. Gradually she emerged from her cocoon at Frings's house and returned to the Hollywood social swirl. There were luncheons and parties and discussions of her next picture. "People keep stopping me to ask if Elizabeth Taylor is being snubbed," Hedda Hopper wrote. "My answer is no, because no one in our town snubs success." No matter how much it surely pained her to admit it, Hedda understood the wisdom of being seen hugging the star at a party for restaurateur Mike Romanoff in November. There is no record of what either lady might have said to each other through their clenched-teeth smiles.

In December, again at Romanoff's, Elizabeth took the next step: She appeared in public with Eddie for the first time. At their side, to blunt any criticism, was Mike Todd Jr. But even if Hollywood stood in awe of Elizabeth's box-office clout, it remained in many ways a small town that liked to gossip, and the latest was that the Widow Todd was pregnant with Eddie's baby. No longer protected from the scandal magazines by her late husband, Elizabeth found herself targeted by *Inside Story*, which suggested Eddie's divorce wasn't "the only event he and Liz were looking forward to." Reporters noticed that she had gained some weight—especially glaring since her svelte image from *Cat* was still plastered everywhere. One person who saw her at a gathering at Chasen's restaurant told the scandal rag: "It was really a coming-out party. Liz was coming out all over." Although the pregnancy rumors were never stated up front, the innuendo was strong: "The race to get Eddie Fisher divorced, and married to Liz Taylor, is going neck and neck," one item read. "Odds are they won't make it." There were also rumors that Elizabeth hadn't been hiding out at Frings's house at all, but instead had suffered a nervous breakdown and checked herself into the Menninger Foundation.

What Elizabeth faced as 1958 turned into 1959 was not a crisis of career, but of public relations. She may not have been snubbed, but she *was* the target of scorn and rumors. Her record as the biggest female moneymaker in town didn't protect her. Even as the studios fell, image still mattered. And image was still shaped largely through the fan magazines. Since becoming an adult star, Elizabeth had always been depicted as sensual and passionate, but also as sweet and kind; now she was vulgar and coarse, a perception only reinforced by her concupiscent portrayal of Maggie. The Elizabeth Taylor of the fan magazines—a distinct creature from her real self—had gone from saint to sinner in the space of two issues. And sinners could not go unpunished in the world of the fan magazines. "If Taylor was not to be smote in some way," explained the writer Lee Israel, "the world made no sense at all; the lives of the righteous were wasted."

To counter this, Bill Doll tried to fan some sympathy Elizabeth's way. One entire issue of *Photoplay*, on the stands in February and March, was secured for this purpose. The cover article —WHAT'S HAPPENING TO LIZ NOW?—presented the star as contemplative and regretful for having caused so much unhappiness. Readers were told that she was just "a shadow of the dynamic person" she once had been. And in a detail sure to stir every mother's heart, Elizabeth was described as heartsick that her boys had to overhear salacious gossip about their mother.

But was it enough? Or was more smiting still in order?

The answer came in April. Nearly three thousand fans lined Hollywood Boulevard outside the RKO Pantages Theatre for the annual Academy Awards ceremony. As the stars emerged from their limousines, resplendent in tuxedos and sequined gowns, the crowd let out rousing cheers. Magnanimity was in the air. Ingrid Bergman, returning for the first time since the scandal that had exiled her from Hollywood, beamed as the crowd began to chant: "We want Ingrid!" For Elizabeth, there was more of the same. When she arrived in a filmy, low-cut black dress, clinging fiercely to Eddie's arm, a huge cheer went up—more evidence that the whole world had not turned on her. With a "fixed smile," Elizabeth made her way inside the theater.

The question on everyone's lips was whether she would win the coveted statuette. Of course she'd been nominated; how could she not have been? There was widespread belief that she had given the best performance that year; her competition was weak, with her only real rival Susan Hayward in *I Want to Live!* But Academy voters have always been a conservative lot; for all of Hollywood's liberal politics and cosmopolitan live-and-let-live attitudes, a cautious core has defined the town from its very beginning, when Jewish immigrant moguls sought above all else the approval and acceptance of America's middle-class heartland. And right now, despite the cheers on Hollywood Boulevard, that heartland was not happy with Elizabeth Taylor. When the award for Best Actress was announced, Hayward's name was inside the envelope.

Some felt that the passionate, redheaded star had earned it, having been bypassed once too often after powerhouse performances. Others felt that the award rightly belonged to Elizabeth for a picture far weightier and more complex than Hayward's prison drama. Yet no matter how much money Elizabeth might be bringing in for them, the industry was not going to reward a home wrecker rumored to be pregnant by another woman's husband. "Liz lost the Oscar at Grossinger's," Sidney Skolsky astutely observed.

But for Elizabeth, the time for hiding, bowing, and scraping was over. On May 12, once the divorce with Debbie was final, she married Eddie Fisher at a Las Vegas synagogue. "There's nothing blue about this wedding," she jubilantly told reporters, explaining that while she might be wearing something old and something new, there wasn't a stitch of blue. "I broke with tradition." She certainly had—and in more ways than just her choice of apparel. A few weeks earlier, she'd announced her conversion to Eddie's (and Mike Todd's) Jewish faith.

So much for the darling little English girl who'd once been held up as the ideal—the "prize," as George Stevens had called her—desired by every American man. If the bluenoses were scandalized before, now they were enflamed. "A traitor to Jesus Christ," one woman called Elizabeth in a letter to Hedda Hopper. A poster for *Cat on a Hot Tin Roof* in Arlington, Virginia, was spray-painted with the word "Jewess."

It was a period of intense anti-Semitism in America; throughout 1959 and 1960, vandalism struck Jewish targets in what one historian has described as a "swastika epidemic." Much of this was the leftover prejudice of McCarthyism, but part of it may also have been a response to the many celebrities who had very publicly converted to Judaism in the last few years: Marilyn Monroe, Carroll Baker, Sammy Davis Jr., and others. Now Elizabeth had joined their ranks—even if, according to Eddie, she never attended any formal service at a temple again.

Her conversion was her decision, and hers alone. Neither Mike nor Eddie had ever asked her to do so. In many ways, it was an act of defiance against her mother, who'd once railed against Stanley Donen (but who nonetheless smiled wide for photographers at the wedding in Vegas) and against her uncle Howard Young, who reportedly had snarled, "What the hell does she see in all these Jewish guys?" But even more, it was a deliberate flouting of the sacred canon of all the scolds who'd taken her to task—not only Hedda and Louella and the fan-magazine writers, but the busybodies in the public who'd written such vile letters condemning her. It was Elizabeth's "fuck you" (a favorite phrase) to her critics. This shouldn't imply that her conversion wasn't sincere; Elizabeth was always too heartfelt, too childlike in her enthusiasm, to ever be insincere for very long. But her Judaism does seem to have had a more social than spiritual application.

If she had wanted to stir the pot, she succeeded. Outside her Vegas hotel, protestors carried signs reading LIZ LEAVE TOWN! She ignored them, turning up everywhere in white chiffon and diamonds. The protestors were doing her a favor by ensuring that her name stayed in the papers even when she had no picture to promote. Frings's theory that no publicity was bad publicity might be true after all. At Eddie's nightclub shows, she sat front-row center, her head held high, her neck and ears sparkling in diamonds. Audiences came to see her as much as they did Eddie. "It's a double act," Skolsky said. "She's part of it."

Eddie, no doubt, was grateful. His television show had been canceled just weeks earlier. Now his fame depended less on any Vegas act than on the lovely, glittering bride who dazzled from the front row. Not without reason had the judge who'd handed them their marriage license suggested that Eddie sign first. "It will be the last time you will be first for a long time to come."

Seven

A Second Chance on Life

May 1959–April 1961

ABOARD THE *OLNICO*, a two-hundred-ton chartered white yacht, Elizabeth Taylor and Eddie Fisher sailed up the northeast coast of Spain on a very public honeymoon. Their cabin was decorated to look like Christopher Columbus's berth on the *Santa Maria*, and a chef prepared a daily smorgasbord of meats, fish, cakes, and pies. Dropping anchor off the coast of Saint-Tropez on the French Riviera, Elizabeth left the yacht to sashay into the resort town and buy armloads of new clothes. The newlyweds gambled at the casino in Cannes until the early hours of the morning, drinking champagne and winning enough to pay for their suite at the exclusive Carlton Hotel. "I'm so happy, so happy," Elizabeth gushed to reporters. Far away from the sniping and backstabbing of the American fan magazines, it was almost as if she were rubbing her marriage in the faces of her critics.

By the end of the month, with Elizabeth's three children now in tow, the Fishers had settled in England, renting a house at Englefield Green in Surrey, about twenty miles outside London. Reporters waiting at the gate counted forty-four pieces of luggage and made sure to comment on Elizabeth's ermine-lined purple coat and low-cut dress. It wasn't their first brush with a movie star. Marilyn Monroe and Arthur Miller had spent several months at Englefield Green following their own honeymoon. Stopping to chat, Eddie told the reporters he was weighing some British television offers. But that was blarney. The real reason they were in England was so that Elizabeth could make *Suddenly, Last Summer* for producer Sam Spiegel, her first independent picture.

With both *Busman's Holiday* and *Two for the Seesaw* falling through, Elizabeth had agreed to yet another Tennessee Williams adaptation about the ways in which repressed homosexuality can destroy a family; the first one had done pretty well by her, after all. Kurt Frings had accepted Spiegel's offer on Elizabeth's behalf, provided that she was paid as much as Seven Arts had been promising. Spiegel agreed: half a million. The money was needed to maintain the yachts and the clothes and the chef. For Elizabeth, however, the icing on the project was the chance to play opposite Monty Clift again.

"There was a joy and a freedom in being able to choose your own projects," said Shirley MacLaine, who, like Elizabeth, was also breaking away from studio control at the time. "The old moguls were essentially hard-fisted authoritarians who had created a system of linked dictatorships to control the creative people. We were supposed to be the children; mad, tempestuous, brilliant, talented, not terribly smart children. We were to be led, guided, manipulated, bought, sold, packaged, coddled, and tolerated. But we were not to be allowed to master our own destinies."

But Elizabeth was now in charge, at least for the moment, and she dove into the project with gusto. It was wild stuff, way over the top. Her character, driven mad by the cannibal murder of her cousin, screams and cries and pulls at her hair. At Shepperton Studios in London, Elizabeth emoted her way through a painstaking re-creation of a New Orleans garden, complete with Venus flytraps. She was solicitous of Clift, who was drinking heavily and a far cry from his once-handsome self, and worshipful of Katharine Hepburn, who played her overbearing aunt. She liked the crew, too, sharing their bawdy humor. "Come here, you asshole!" became her own personal term of endearment.

But it was with director Joseph Mankiewicz (*A Letter to Three Wives, All About Eve, Guys and Dolls*) that she forged her closest attachment. "Are you planning to lose any weight?" the director had asked upon meeting her, shaking the flab on her arm and likening it to "a bag of dead mice." All those extravagant meals and bottles of wine onboard her yacht had left the twenty-seven-year-old star a little fleshy, and Mankiewicz suggested that she tone up. Elizabeth didn't take offense. In fact, she was enchanted. And she allowed him to push her in her performance, too, which required her to go from shrinking to shrieking.

A big, strong-willed man with a sharp wit and an intense focus on his craft, Mankiewicz had recently been through the painful suicide of his wife. Elizabeth found his combination of strength and vulnerability irresistible. She also appreciated his consideration of Monty—which directly refutes Hepburn's famous contention that the director had run roughshod over Clift during the shoot. "Elizabeth wouldn't have tolerated any mistreatment of Monty," said Mankiewicz's son Tom. If the director had abused her good friend, she certainly would never have begun an affair with him—which is exactly what some people believe she did in the summer of 1959.

"Beyond a shadow of a doubt, I believe they had an affair," Tom Mankiewicz said. "You wouldn't know it from looking at Michael Wilding or Eddie Fisher, but the Elizabeth I knew really, really loved strong men. Mike Todd probably spoiled her forever in terms of strong men. Dad was a strong man—bombastic, smart, confident. She wanted that in a man." The actor Martin Landau, who'd later make *Cleopatra* with Elizabeth and Mankiewicz, also heard stories of an affair between the two. When asked by a friend on the Roman set of that later film if he was having an affair with his glamorous star, Mankiewicz quipped, "Hell, no! That was during our *last* picture!"

Not three months after her marriage to Eddie—a marriage that had rocked her public—Elizabeth was very possibly in the arms of another man. And maybe *two* men: Another off-and-on romance reportedly began during this period with the much-older political columnist Max Lerner, who'd written a piece defending Elizabeth during the Liz-Eddie-Debbie debacle. By Lerner's own admission, Elizabeth would slip out after shooting and meet him in some darkened, anonymous corner in a London pub.

It was unusual behavior for a newlywed who'd just bucked the world to get the husband that she wanted. But Elizabeth was restless. "I think very soon after her marriage to Eddie, she started asking, 'What have I done?'" said one friend. In public, they remained the picture of happiness—no brawls like the ones with Mike Todd—though Eddie often came across as defensive. "Her name is *Mrs. Fisher*," he angrily corrected newsmen who persisted in calling Elizabeth "Miss Taylor." Elizabeth would respond with her high, girlish laugh. Some friends thought that she was laughing *at*—not *with*—her husband.

Their private life was very different from their public one. Eddie, as his memoirs would reveal, remained hopelessly in love, but Elizabeth seems to have lost respect for her husband very quickly. His career had tanked, and he didn't seem to care. This made for a stark contrast with Mike Todd, which Elizabeth found deplorable. Eddie would admit that he lost his way during these years. He'd regret that, unlike Sinatra or Como, he never built a legacy of "songs that meant something." Instead, he had banked everything on his marriage to Elizabeth, counting on her career to ensure his future as a producer and actor. She was to be his ticket to success and a certain way of life. It wasn't all that different from the way Elizabeth had once counted on Todd.

But as steward of his wife's career, Eddie was a failure. He set up the Fisher Corporation to produce films for himself and his wife, but none of his projects ever got off the ground. Still, he tried his best to act like Mike, showering Elizabeth with emerald earrings and diamond-studded evening bags—but they were paid for from their joint account, which these days was being filled more by Elizabeth's earnings than by his own. It's not surprising then that when Eddie gave her gifts, Elizabeth didn't gush quite the way she had done with Mike. After receiving one diamond necklace, she turned it over in her hands and asked how much it had cost. "Fifty thousand dollars," Eddie boasted. Giving her husband a withering look, Elizabeth said, "There's not a decent stone here. You've been taken." So much for filling Todd's shoes. Eddie didn't even know how to buy good diamonds.

As Eddie's mentorship of her career faltered, the Todd organization was also coming apart. Mike Todd Jr.'s attempts at filmmaking—a gimmick called Smell-O-Vision—went nowhere. The once-formidable support team of publicists and lawyers and accountants all went their separate ways. It was Kurt Frings who ran Elizabeth's career now, largely on his own. Though great shows were made of Eddie's reviewing his wife's contracts, it was simply a way for him to save face. Eddie had become irrelevant only a few months into their marriage.

Kurt Frings, however, was rewriting all the rules of Hollywood, and Elizabeth was the beneficiary. No longer content with the record-breaking sum of $500,000, Frings told producer Walter Wanger, who'd inquired about Elizabeth's appearing in his production of *Cleopatra* for Fox, that her asking price was now $1 million. Although much has been made of Elizabeth being the first star to make a million dollars a picture, in fact William Holden had beat her to that sum for *The Bridge on the River Kwai* in 1957. But Elizabeth *was* the first woman to ask for such a salary, and Wanger's initial reaction was to balk. "An unheard-of price for an actress," he wrote in his diary.

Such sexism didn't discourage Frings. He was masterful in positioning Elizabeth as being in the driver's seat in these negotiations; Wanger's diary reveals that it was the star, not her agent, who made the million-dollar demand in a phone call on September 1, 1959. While Mike Todd had certainly toughened her up in the ways of business, no doubt Frings (who, after all, came to her through Todd) had prepped her on what to say. "Kurt worked behind the scenes," said Dick Clayton, who as a fellow agent was privy to the kind of wheeling and dealing that went on. "As a good agent, he'd tell her what he thought was the highest they could get." So he instructed Elizabeth to ask for what Bill Holden had gotten for a similar big-budget movie. It was only fair.

No doubt Frings was aware that Fox's 1960–61 production schedule was budgeted at $60 million; surely they could afford to pay Elizabeth one-sixtieth of that if they really wanted her. The economic walls of the industry were due for stretching, Frings believed. Actors had been left stranded for too long outside those walls even though their drawing power was what brought in the profits. Until now, that money had been collected and controlled by the studios in an effort to sustain their massive operations. But times were changing. When Wanger came back with the news that Spyros Skouras, president of Fox, had refused the million-dollar demand, Elizabeth (with a few tears thrown in for effect) countered that she'd accept $750,000 against 10 percent of the gross.

This counterdemand was clearly a strategy of Frings's, who was well aware of the similar deal given to Holden and John Wayne the year before for *The Horse Soldiers*. He also knew, being a friend of Wanger's, that the producer had never wanted anyone else but Elizabeth to play Cleopatra and was ready to move mountains to get her. So by October 10, according to Wanger's diary, the $1 million asking price was back on the table. And through a bit of sleight of hand on Wanger's part, Elizabeth got it, and possibly more. Fox would pay her $125,000 for sixteen weeks of work, plus $50,000 a week for every week of overtime, plus $3,000 a week in expenses, plus (and this was the revolutionary part) 10 percent of the gross. In the end, if *Cleopatra* had the kind of grosses that everyone was expecting (*Bridge on the River Kwai* had made $18 million), Elizabeth would make much more than $1 million.

The million-dollar deal transformed the financial future of the industry. "You're worth what you can get," Tony Curtis quipped to one reporter, summing up in six simple words the new thinking in Hollywood. Like Elizabeth, Curtis was no longer content with a set salary but rather opted for a percentage of the gross. He was hoping to make nearly a million from *The Vikings*, then finishing up its successful run on the nation's screens. Studios, meanwhile, were being forced to settle for a steadily decreasing percentage of the profits—an arrangement that could only lead to a fundamental shift in the way movies got made.

That's precisely why so many of the old guard—like Hedda Hopper—shuddered. "It is . . . basically a fight between the older generation and the younger generation," actor Rod Steiger observed, likening the struggle to Ibsen's *The Master Builder,* in which an older architect fears being made obsolete by younger men with new and different ideas. The handwriting was on the wall. The studios were on their way out—dealt a potentially fatal blow by a star who had hated them ever since that day in Mr. Mayer's office when he'd made her mother cry.

Sam Spiegel was worried, and he was not a man who worried needlessly. One of the shrewdest of the new breed of independent Hollywood producers, the Austrian-born Spiegel had an Old World charm and a New World sensibility. He knew how to make films and he knew how to sell them. His productions tended to be edgy—and successful. He'd won an Academy Award for Best Picture for *On the Waterfront* in 1954 and produced the biggest box-office hit of the year, *The Bridge on the River Kwai,* in 1957. But now he was worried. And with good reason.

The initial reviews of *Suddenly, Last Summer* were not good. Much of the film is, after all, a talkathon with long, tedious stretches of monologue for each of the three principals. Moreover, the unsavory aspects of the script, like the famous death by cannibalism, proved too much for some critics. *Time* compared the experience of watching the film to being crushed in the "clammy coils" of a giant snake; *Variety* termed the picture "possibly the most bizarre film ever made by a major American company." Bosley Crowther in the *New York Times,* who'd waxed lyrical over Elizabeth in *Cat on a Hot Tin Roof,* thought that she was "rightly roiled" here, "but her wallow of agony at the climax is sheer histrionic showing off."

Even Hepburn hated the film, disappointed in how literally

Mankiewicz had directed Gore Vidal's script, which she felt was all about metaphor. Spiegel was worried that he had a disaster on his hands. Hedda Hopper agreed. In her column, noting the reluctance of the three stars (all of whom she disliked) to participate in publicity, she wondered how "Sam Spiegel expects to sell that one." Spiegel wondered himself.

But he had an idea. Working with the publicity department at Columbia, which was distributing the film, Spiegel laid out a daring marketing campaign. "The idea was to sell Elizabeth Taylor," said Tom Mankiewicz, and downplay the lurid subject material. And so, once again, the movie poster that dominated Hollywood for a season featured Elizabeth Taylor dressed in flimsy white, her breasts seeming to throw themselves at the spectator. This time, instead of the slip she'd worn in *Cat,* she was photographed in a low-cut bathing suit—in a pose not seen in the film, but designed merely to sell the picture. The copy line read: SUDDENLY LAST SUMMER CATHY KNEW SHE WAS BEING USED FOR EVIL! The ploy worked. The film, which went into general release in January 1960, defied its critics and became the fourth-highest grossing film of the year, making $5.5 million in the United States alone.

"Elizabeth was a sex symbol, the most desirable woman in the world," Mankiewicz said. "So they used that to their advantage."

The same thought was on the minds of Metro executives, who had finally settled on the picture that they wanted her to make for them. Instead of running from Elizabeth's Bad Girl persona, MGM wanted to embrace it. Even though the fan magazines were still calling her a home wrecker, Elizabeth's risqué image had proven its box-office value. So the script for *Butterfield 8,* based on the novel by John O'Hara, made sure to play up all that smut and scandal—even if this seemed to confirm the opinions of those fans who'd written to Hedda calling Elizabeth a "harlot" and a member of the "oldest profession in the world." The protagonist, Gloria Wandrous, is a party girl who jumps from man to man, accepting gifts and free rent in exchange for sex. The film charts her rise and fall in sexy, salacious detail.

Elizabeth was horrified when she read the script. "Little more than a prostitute," she said about Gloria. She knew that the studio was trying to exploit her offscreen publicity for their own advantage. It's no surprise that she would always hate the picture. Deeply offended, she flat-out refused to do it.

Her protests were met with smug smiles at Metro. They reminded her that as long as she still owed them one last picture, they had the power to preempt any deals that she might make with other producers. If she wanted to make *Cleopatra*—and all that *money*—she'd have to make *Butterfield 8* first. Elizabeth sulked. It wasn't supposed to be this way. Mike had promised her that she'd never have to go back there, but now Eddie—and even Kurt Frings—were powerless to prevent it. Finally she agreed—so long as they could shoot the picture in New York. Hollywood—the industry *and* the town—had become anathema to her.

Just how much Gloria was modeled on Elizabeth's public image can be discerned by reading the description of the character that director Daniel Mann scribbled on the shooting script. "Finds men the source of her regeneration," Mann wrote. "She needs to call the tune. A will to find and lose herself. She has a great sense of humor. Changes come fast. Emotion flows—flips—flops. She's up, she's down. Big-hearted." It's hard not to think that he was describing Elizabeth.

And there's more. The film, which began shooting in February 1960, unfolds almost as a dramatization of the last two years of Elizabeth's life. Making that point clear, Eddie Fisher was cast as the man so besotted with her that he is ready to leave his sweet blond girlfriend (played by Susan Oliver, clearly chosen for her resemblance to Debbie Reynolds). "What are we going to do," Oliver asks, "you, me, her—the three mixed-up musketeers?" Later, when Eddie kisses her, Oliver complains: "You can't kiss me thinking I'm Gloria anymore." All of this would have seemed very familiar stuff to those who'd followed the scandal in the fan magazines.

"I get it," says Gloria's lover, played by Laurence Harvey. "*You* pick the man. He doesn't pick you. You also drop the man when you want." Gloria replies coolly, as many people thought Elizabeth might reply in real life: "Yes. And without a parachute." But Gloria is forced to admit later, in the film's most famous melodramatic moment: "Face it, Mama! I was the slut of all time!" It was a line that could've been lifted directly from many of the letters to Hedda.

The script of *Butterfield 8* went even further than simply dramatizing Elizabeth's life. It also made her pay for her "sins" of the last year and a half. Screenwriter John Michael Hayes, a pro at adapting material to suit both censors and audiences (he'd scripted *Peyton Place* and would later work on *The Children's Hour*), clearly understood that Gloria couldn't get off scot-free the way her real-life counterpart had. One minute Gloria is having a grand old time kicking up her heels, the next she's mouthing platitudes about the "utterly conventional" being the truly beautiful. Girls who "kick up their heels," she is explicitly warned, are doomed. And so, of course, Gloria is killed in a car accident. The studio seemed to be hoping that audiences on both sides of the Liz-Eddie-Debbie scandal would flock to see the picture: one side to delight in Elizabeth's free love and high living, the other to take satisfaction in her punishment.

There was no satisfaction, however, in Eddie's performance. Producer Pan Berman wrote to Hayes asking him to rewrite Eddie's scenes to make them easier to play. Scenes that would "normally be clear in the hands of most actors [seem] dubious when played by Eddie Fisher," Berman said. But Elizabeth had insisted on her husband being cast. During filming, she displayed a "fetish" (Berman's word) for Eddie's character to be consistently portrayed as treating her solicitously. She knew the public was going to be reading a lot of autobiography into the film, and that much she wanted to control.

It's understandable that she wouldn't be happy making the film. "A walking time bomb," first assistant director Hank Moonjean described her. She started to doubt her decision to film in New York instead of Hollywood. If they were back on the Metro lot, they wouldn't have to stomp on the soundstages to scare away the rats the way they did at the Gold Medal Studio in the Bronx. And scenes outside Gloria's apartment, shot in Greenwich Village at Sixth Avenue and West Tenth Street, brought the inmates of the adjacent House of Detention for Women to their windows, where Moonjean said they yelled "all sorts of epithets" at Elizabeth, swathed in her fur coat with emeralds dangling from her ears. "Ah, fuck you!" the glamorous star shouted right back at the hecklers, which, of course, simply set off a whole new round of hoots and whistles.

It was a new world making movies in the poststudio era. It would take some getting used to. Depressed, Elizabeth just didn't show up on the set some mornings, and Moonjean would be sent to fetch her. "Her servants knew me," he said, "so I'd just go up to her room and wake her up. I must say that never have I seen anyone as beautiful first thing in the morning as Elizabeth Taylor. No makeup, no hair fixed. She'd say, 'Why don't you put coffee on?' and we'd sit there and talk, and pretty soon the studio would send a car looking for *me* too!

"But here's the thing," Moonjean added. "She might have hated the movie from the very first day but she didn't sabotage it. Once she got to the set, she worked very hard, gave it her best. On the set, she was a model of cooperation." About a month into the shoot, the Screen Actors Guild called a strike against the studios that was scheduled to begin Monday, March 7. Director Mann rushed to get as much filmed as he could. "Elizabeth worked right up until 11:59 on Sunday night when they pulled the plug," Moonjean said. "She didn't need to do that."

The high regard in which she was held by the crews on her pictures did not cross over into the press. Even after a year and a half, she was still the most popular villain in the newspapers and fan magazines. This despite Kurt Frings's well-known ability to contain scandal. At the same time as his client's troubles, he was dealing with some sensational headlines of his own. Actress Mary Murphy, best known for her part in *The Wild One*, had filed a complaint with police that Frings had kicked her in the abdomen and bitten her thumb when she refused his advances. But before police got around to arresting the agent, Murphy had a change of heart and dropped all charges. "Kurt sweet-talked her," said a friend of Elizabeth's. "He knew how to escape unscathed."

Yet he didn't manage quite the same success for his client. Editorials deplored Elizabeth's exorbitant salary, calling a million dollars unmerited for any actor, but especially for her: "A lot of citizens are old fashioned enough to think that somehow it flies in the face of public morality." And just as filming on *Butterfield 8* began, *Motion Picture* ran a cover feature "exposing" how cold Elizabeth was in person, even to her children. The magazine told of her struggle to be a "lady," instead of the hard-drinking, foulmouthed nymphomaniac the fan magazines regularly made her out to be.

Elizabeth's press only got worse. Soon came a cover of *Photoplay* featuring Debbie and two of the saddest-looking children ever captured by the camera, Carrie and Todd Fisher, with their bottom lips protruding so far as to nearly reach the collars of their shirts. Inside, Debbie promised to reveal WHAT I TELL MY CHILDREN ABOUT LIZ AND EDDIE. Then came another sensational headline in *Motion Picture*—EXCLUSIVE! DEBBIE THREATENED!—with a photo of an angry Elizabeth cropped next to a photo of a demure Debbie, giving the clear implication of *who* was doing the threatening, even if the article inside revealed nothing of the sort. (The threat wasn't from Elizabeth, but from "hangers-on" who were apparently keeping Debbie from getting back into the swim of life.)

Yet it's a fact that most fan-magazine stories contained a glimmer of truth, some thread that led, however tenuously, back to real life. Elizabeth *was* hard-drinking and foulmouthed, and her practice of motherhood was definitely of the laissez-faire kind—though no one who knew her would ever call her "cold," especially not toward her children, who were petted and fussed over when she saw them. But the fact that she wasn't out being photographed with them constantly in her arms—the way Debbie was with Carrie and Todd—allowed housewives across the country to make their own judgments. It was clear that Elizabeth Taylor was not the kind of involved, children-first mother they believed themselves (and Debbie) to be. And in some ways, they were right.

A similar strain of truth was spied in another series of fan-magazine pieces that started appearing around this time. Word was seeping out that things weren't all that rosy in the Fisher marriage. HOW MUCH CAN EDDIE TAKE FROM LIZ? blared one headline. Elizabeth was depicted as being embarrassed that her fame outweighed his and was pushing him to become a bigger star. "Must Eddie now take from Liz what he reportedly would not take from Debbie?" the article asked. While the piece may have gotten the specifics wrong, it does capture an underlying reality. Elizabeth was waking up to the fact that Eddie Fisher could never replace Mike Todd—and this couldn't be disguised for long in the fishbowl of Hollywood.

When they could snare an article or two, Frings and Bill Doll fought back on Elizabeth's behalf. *Photoplay* was the outlet most likely to be sympathetic. One piece in the autumn of 1960 was clearly a response to the depiction of Elizabeth as being cold. She's showcased as a doting mother who hopes to retire soon from pictures (that old chestnut again) and devote herself entirely to her family. But the images on the screen and in so much of the press didn't match the saccharine sentiment in articles like these. Elizabeth seemed cognizant of this fact of her public image. "I've never been America's sweetheart," she told Art Buchwald, so she could never hope to compete with Debbie on that level. It was best that she didn't try.

And yet, even with all the negative press, she truly expected to win an Oscar for *Suddenly, Last Summer*. "My ambition," she told Sidney Skolsky, "is to win an Oscar before I retire." This was her year, many insiders told her, especially after her snub the year before. Reporter James Bacon, long known as Hollywood's shrewdest handicapper of the Oscar race, gave Elizabeth the best odds to win. Joe Mankiewicz was certain as well, urging his star and former lover to attend the awards ceremony on April 4.

Fortified with this confidence, she once again stepped out of her limo on Hollywood Boulevard to the delight of the fans thronging the red carpet. Her dress had been chosen with the kind of care and strategy that would later become de rigueur for actresses on Oscar night. If she was going to walk up onto the stage and be photographed clutching that gold statuette, she wanted to knock 'em dead around the world. Her original plan to wear a yellow chiffon gown was scrapped at the last minute, no doubt because she wanted to set off the bronze skin she'd earned from lying around her Beverly Hills pool during the strike-induced hiatus from *Butterfield 8*. Her plan worked. "The crowd ooh'd and aah'd at the striking contrast between Miss Taylor's deep tan and her white gown, which featured a daringly low V-neck," the Associated Press reported.

But the other part of her plan—winning the award—wasn't achieved quite as easily. When the name of the relatively unknown French actress Simone Signoret was announced as the winner—for a British film, *Room at the Top*, no less—Elizabeth was crushed. It seemed that her peers had no intention of ever honoring her. No matter how much money she made for them, she would forever be known as the scarlet woman of the fan magazines, unworthy of their accolades or affection.

Yet if Elizabeth had learned anything from the scandal, it was how to play the game. Once again leaving the Pantages Theatre empty-handed, she resolved to do what a movie star must always do. She decided to rewrite the rules of the game.

S. Rexford Kennamer, MD, Elizabeth Taylor's personal physician, stepped off the plane from New York at the London airport and was greeted by a somber-faced Eddie Fisher. It was late on the night of November 14, 1960. Less than a week earlier, John F. Kennedy had triumphed over Richard Nixon in the U.S. presidential election. Kennamer had flown clear across the country, and then across the Atlantic, because his star patient, in London to make *Cleopatra*, had just been rushed to the hospital with a mystery illness. The queen's own physicians were tending her, but Elizabeth wanted Kennamer, whom she considered her personal friend as well as her doctor. After all, Rex had been by her side through the agonies of Mike's death and funeral.

Forty years old, a native of Montgomery, Alabama, and the son of a federal judge, Kennamer was widely respected in his field of cardiology for his insightful articles in peer-reviewed journals and discerning lectures at universities and medical societies. With his office in Beverly Hills, he was also more commonly known as the "doctor to the stars." In addition to Elizabeth, he treated Joan Crawford, David Janssen, Montgomery Clift, and many others. Elizabeth trusted him completely—even if she did disregard his warnings to stay away from Max Jacobson and his "feel-good" injections. Riding with Eddie to the London Clinic on Harley Street in Marylebone, Rex admitted to being stumped over what could possibly be ailing Elizabeth. Her symptoms seemed to defy diagnosis.

She had been in a bad mood ever since she, Eddie, and the children had arrived in London on August 31, after a tour of the Mediterranean. Still haggling over the terms of her contract, she also churlishly refused to pose for any press photographs, explaining that she remained in high dudgeon over what she considered the "harsh" treatment by British reporters during *Suddenly, Last Summer.* When the press hinted that they might boycott her and *Cleopatra,* she just shrugged. Walter Wanger didn't seem to be worried. "I must say she has a lot of courage," he wrote in his diary. "There are very few actresses with nerve enough to stand up to the British press."

Wanger was a thoughtful man, one of the rare intellectuals in the Hollywood studios. His films tended to say something, to rise above mere entertainment. Among his early projects were Rudolph Valentino's *The Sheik* in 1921 and the controversial political drama *Gabriel Over the White House* in 1933. His recent *Invasion of the Body Snatchers* was a science fiction metaphor about McCarthyist paranoia. He'd also produced Susan Hayward's *I Want to Live!*—the film that had deprived Elizabeth Taylor of the Oscar that she believed she deserved. But Wanger was perhaps best known for firing a gun at the agent Jennings Lang when he thought that Lang was having an affair with his wife, the actress Joan Bennett. For the crime, Wanger served a four-month sentence.

Throughout the whole long ordeal of *Cleopatra*, Wanger displayed tremendous affection for—and patience with—Elizabeth. Even when she was petulant and cross, as she was now. She insisted that Sydney Guilaroff, who'd been her favorite stylist ever since he'd made her that wig in *National Velvet*, dress her hair for the film. But in October Wanger was forced to tell her that Guilaroff had to depart because Fox had failed to obtain a proper work permit for him. The next day Elizabeth called in sick with a sore throat. Which then became a fever. This went on for nearly two weeks.

The *Daily Mail*, perhaps with a bit of revenge in mind, reported that Elizabeth was hiding out because she was too fat to fit into her costumes. Fox issued a stern denial. Meanwhile, the film's director, Rouben Mamoulian, one of the great old-timers of Hollywood who dated back to Garbo and Dietrich, tried to film around Elizabeth, aiming his cameras at Peter Finch, who played Caesar, and Stephen Boyd, who played Antony, and the "million dollars' worth" of temples, galley ships, and Egyptian buildings that had been erected in the English countryside. But that could suffice for only so long.

By the middle of the month, Elizabeth seemed to be getting better. The problems with Guilaroff had largely been resolved: With Mamoulian's tacit approval, the fussy hairdresser worked his magic in Elizabeth's hotel suite, away from the prying eyes of the British crew. On October 20 the star was feeling well enough to attend the Sophia Loren–Peter Sellers movie *The Millionairess* with Wanger. Everyone agreed that November 1 would be her return-to-work date.

But Elizabeth remained extremely unhappy with the production. The problems extended beyond those with Guilaroff. She didn't care for Mamoulian's stodginess and was distressed by the lack of organization she saw on the set. "She has been around too long not to be aware when a company is muddling—and we are muddling," Wanger admitted in his diary. "She is getting tired of the press laying the blame for our confusion on her. She is especially irked that [Fox chief] Skouras is using her as the scapegoat with the insurance company."

It was then that Elizabeth got sick, just as she did at other fortuitous times during similar stressful filmmaking situations. On October 30, the day before she was to resume work, the star reported to the London Clinic with a temperature of 103. Within forty-eight hours, word had spread all over the city that Elizabeth was suffering from "Malta fever"—a highly contagious bacterial disease spread from animals to humans by consuming undercooked meat or infected milk. The exotic-sounding illness quickly led to headlines around the world. "A tenacious bug that's as hard to shake as it is to diagnose," said the *New York Post*. Convalescence might take three months, Spyros Skouras was warned. So much for finally getting started on *Cleopatra*—which by then had already used up $6 million of the studio's money.

When Elizabeth was once again hospitalized two weeks later, this time by ambulance, there was a free-for-all. Perhaps it wasn't Malta fever, after all; perhaps it was even worse. Word spread that Elizabeth had meningitis. Suddenly the British tabloids had the star fighting for her life. The American press soon picked up the panic. The *New York Journal-American* ran a three-inch headline across its front page: STRICKEN LIZ TAYLOR RUSHED TO HOSPITAL. She was "suffering from piercing head pains and fever," according to the *Los Angeles Times*, and was "semi-conscious under sedation." Whipped up by the alarming coverage, several hundred "shrieking fans" crowded around Elizabeth's hotel, and more gathered at the hospital. That's when Rex Kennamer was summoned from California.

Working with his British counterparts, Kennamer eventually determined that the cause of all of Elizabeth's pain, all her headaches and terrible fevers, was an *abscessed tooth*. This somehow had led to a low-grade virus that doctors diagnosed not as meningitis, but as meningismus, which was very different. But while they made sure to tell the public—and Fox executives—that she was "still a sick girl," they were also satisfied that her condition was "not serious." A short time later, she was released from the hospital.

Again, this shouldn't imply that she was faking. The pain was very real. Meningismus can produce the symptoms of meningitis even if none of the spinal membranes are actually infected. It was perhaps fitting that, since meningismus is a virus "more frequently encountered in children than in adults," Elizabeth, still a child in so many ways, was felled by a childhood disease.

But it was, in fact, more than that. Eddie Fisher would later wonder how much of the illness was brought on by the virus, and how much was the result of the increasing abuse (by both his wife and himself) of drugs and alcohol. "She had become addicted to every pill on the market," he said—and by introducing her to Max Jacobson, he was partly to blame for that. "Pills to help her sleep, pills to keep her awake, pills to dull her pain, pills and more pills." Both of them also drank heavily. "Elizabeth's problems in 1960 were basically the same as they were in 1990," Eddie would later say.

No matter its specifics or the undeniable truth of her pain, her illness—like the one during *Giant* six years before—had certain positive outcomes. And perhaps she had counted on that being the case, at least on some level. The situation that she returned to on the *Cleopatra* set was not the one she had found so intolerable when she had left. With her producers becoming increasingly desperate to finish the picture and stanch the loss of money, she now enjoyed considerably greater clout in getting what she wanted. Skouras agreed to fire Mamoulian if that's what it took for his star to hit the ground running. And who did she want as his replacement? Elizabeth chose Joe Mankiewicz. "I'm here to do whatever you want," Joe said. His star was thrilled.

Shooting was planned to resume after the new year. But the curse of *Cleopatra* had only just begun.

While Elizabeth's illness may have frustrated the Fox brass, over at MGM they were dancing a jig. All that publicity was a bonanza for *Butterfield 8*, which was released at the height of the hospitalization headlines.

"It was always going to be a big film," said Hank Moonjean. "But Elizabeth Taylor with all her publicity—that just meant it was going to get even more attention."

The film's publicity campaign followed the lead of the script, capitalizing on Elizabeth's titillating public image. "Elizabeth Taylor is in a class by herself as a worldwide box-office personality," the *Motion Picture Herald* astutely observed shortly before the film went into general release. The inclusion of Eddie in the film was a smart move, the paper reflected, since it "made headlines from New York to Tokyo and back." But it was Elizabeth's offscreen reputation as a femme fatale that would give *Butterfield 8* "its special status."

MGM's ad campaign played that up to the hilt. Her sexy image, once again showcased in provocative clothing, dominated newspaper advertisements and illustrated the key ad line: "The most desirable woman in town and the easiest to find . . . just call BUtterfield 8." In *Life* magazine, a full-page ad was created out of two adjacent half-pages in the center fold—a novel format that generated considerable industry buzz. That was the goal. In a world where audiences now had many other choices for entertainment, Metro understood that they needed new, innovative ways of drawing attention to its product.

Nowhere was this more important than in distribution. The old formula for the release of an important picture—big premieres in Los Angeles and New York, then general release to the rest of the country a month or so later—was scrapped for *Butterfield 8*. Instead, there were a dozen early openings in Chicago and Washington and other places, then roughly thirty in more provincial cities like Cincinnati and Hartford during the Thanksgiving holiday—since, it was reasoned, people would have more free time to see a movie that weekend. Today such holiday strategy is taken for granted. But in 1960 it was radical. And it's no coincidence that one of the first pictures to utilize such a wide initial release starred Elizabeth Taylor, whose already formidable box-office appeal was only enhanced by the current headlines about her health.

The old studio system was coming to an end; Lana Turner, one of the last MGM contract stars, described her last days there as "working amid the ruins." The fabled wardrobe and prop departments were thinning out, and hundreds of studio workers lost their jobs. The old publicity department, with its constantly ringing telephones and whirring mimeograph machines, fell silent. But with *Butterfield 8,* studio execs showed that they might still have one last hurrah—courtesy of freelance press agents, the heirs of the old studio publicists. These agents were put in charge of various parts of the country to coordinate local campaigns—not so different from what Todd had done with *Around the World in Eighty Days.* Full-size cardboard cutouts of Elizabeth wearing a mink coat over a formfitting slip were distributed to theaters for lobby displays. Radio disc jockeys were coerced into airing "Salutes to Eddie Fisher" with promises of tickets to special screenings of the film for their listeners.

Perhaps the most creative promotion involved the phone company; the film's title, after all, was a phone number. Special telephones were installed in theaters, reachable by dialing BU-8 "no matter what the actual exchange destinations may be." Persuading Ma Bell to go along with the scheme was easy because the company was offered the opportunity to publicize its newest phone equipment in theaters. The scheme was brilliant and simple. Ads in local papers featured Elizabeth in her sexy pose next to an enticement to call BU-8. Curious members of the public would call in, and theater employees would answer with a studio-prepared script describing "Gloria, the most desirable woman in town." The *Motion Picture Herald* was rightly impressed with this "useful exploitation hook." These creative efforts, so successful with *Butterfield 8* and other big pictures like *Ben-Hur*, would anticipate and inspire today's precisely orchestrated promotional campaigns, with their ubiquitous ad placements and broad merchandising tie-ins.

Not surprisingly, *Butterfield 8* was yet another colossal box-office hit for Elizabeth Taylor. And this time she carried the picture entirely on her own. There was no Montgomery Clift or Rock Hudson or Paul Newman or Katharine Hepburn or Tennessee Williams to help her along. *Butterfield 8* was Elizabeth's picture all the way—a throwback to the kind of woman-centered film that Hepburn or Bette Davis or Joan Crawford once made.

And despite her loathing of the script, Elizabeth is exceedingly good. The scene where she describes being sexually abused as a teenager is remarkable. Her coiled emotion bursts forth with just the right amount of horror and shame; it could easily have been a melodramatic moment, but it's not. The beginning of the film is a delight and feels honest—Elizabeth is very good at throwing out bitchy lines. Only with the sappy ending does she turn maudlin and, as a consequence, not as believable.

Still, was it enough to finally win her that Oscar? To win over the bluenoses in the public? It remained to be seen. But change was definitely in the air.

Time magazine scribe Ezra Goodman thought that by the time of *Butterfield 8* more people were taking "long-range stock" of the scandal. He noticed that the fan magazines were "warming up to Liz again." One publication actually scolded its readers: "The true love that exists between Liz and Eddie is the only thing that can make her find forgiveness in her heart for the fans who didn't stick by her when she needed them most." Columnist Earl Wilson observed that Elizabeth's experience set a precedent for the emerging new Hollywood: "It seemed the thing to do . . . was to create such an outlandish personality for yourself that the public had to grant your every exigency. Eventually you would get away with holy hell."

"I think the Bad Girl image was finally starting to lose its stigma," said Gavin Lambert. "After the studios started fading away, the public seemed to change its outlook somewhat toward its movie stars. They could see through manufactured public images ... The remarkable thing about Taylor was that she was always very authentic, and the public came to admire that about her, no matter how many marriages she had."

The repressive fifties were giving way to the rebellious sixties, symbolized by miniskirts and *Playboy* magazine and the young, progressive-thinking family in the White House. Elizabeth's great achievement during this period was that she made the public want her *as she was;* she made being sexy, independent, and defiant of cultural norms the desirable way to be. Some stars gauge what the public seems to want, and become that to sell their movies and their images. Elizabeth did exactly the opposite. By not conforming to the traditional picture of woman or star—by not trying to be Debbie Reynolds—she made the public want to buy what she already had to sell. Given her personality, to smile and fake her way through an artificial public persona would have been intolerable. After all, she never tried to be that ordinary housewife.

Of course, vamps and femme fatales had been popular in Hollywood as far back as Theda Bara. But the ideal woman had always been the devoted wife and mother; consequently, every major female star—from Marlene Dietrich to Joan Crawford to Debbie Reynolds—was portrayed this way in their studio publicity, whether true or not (and it usually wasn't). Elizabeth turned that paradigm on its head. She made the Bad Girl the ideal. No longer did women just secretly envy her; now they wanted to *be* her. And they said so publicly. "If I could be Elizabeth Taylor for just one day," wrote a reader to a fan magazine in 1961, "I'd live the dreams of a lifetime in twenty-four hours." This letter was very different from what the magazines had been publishing just two years before.

Throughout her career, but especially now, Elizabeth Taylor was proving that true stardom depends on a reconciliation of contrasts: that one could be good and bad at the same time, sexy and sweet, loyal and fickle, compassionate and tempestuous. All of those adjectives describe Elizabeth Taylor, and by 1960, the public was finally acknowledging how much they loved that about her.

The furs, the jewels, the yachts, the trips around the world, and yes, even the men and the multiple marriages—Elizabeth's celebrity was like none before, offering a glimpse into an exciting, magical life that no Good Girl, certainly not little Debbie with diaper pins stuck to her blouse, was ever going to achieve. With the possible exception of Kim Novak, no woman who'd broken into the box-office top ten had ever been as notorious in her personal life as Elizabeth—not even Marilyn Monroe. Most of the women who'd made the list over the last ten years had projected wholesome images: Betty Grable, Esther Williams, Doris Day, June Allyson. But "by the time of *Cleopatra*," Tom Mankiewicz observed, "every woman in America wanted to be Elizabeth Taylor. And every man wanted her." She was "the gold standard" for a movie star.

Being bad—or at least a little naughty—was now glamorous, thanks to Elizabeth. *Butterfield 8*, with Gloria waking up in a strange bed in a fabulous apartment and absconding with a mink coat, certainly made it seem that way. The audiences flocking to the film weren't coming to see a morality play; Gloria's death at the end was simply a bone tossed to the killjoys, a concession to the last gasps of the censor. What made the film a box-office smash was its celebration of sexual freedom and self-indulgence, which was sold to the public through those seductive posters and those special telephones. The studio was actually goading the public into pretending that they were calling a prostitute. After all those years of Production Code restraint, who knew being bad could be this much fun?

But the question remained whether the industry would reward such badness. When the Oscar nominations were announced on February 28, 1961, the smart betting was that either Elizabeth or Deborah Kerr (for *The Sundowners*) would go home with the Best Actress prize. Hedda Hopper, extending an olive branch, predicted that it would be Taylor's year: "This is the fourth nomination for

Liz; I believe she'll win. She is the only woman star who can carry a picture alone."

Yet as much as the tide of public opinion seemed to be turning in Elizabeth's favor, she no doubt understood that there were a few things she could still do to help it along.

It was just past midnight on March 4 when the nurse caring for Elizabeth Taylor, who had once again fallen ill, suddenly noticed that her patient had turned blue in the face. Ensconced in the penthouse suite of London's posh Dorchester Hotel, Elizabeth was recovering from the flu that she had picked up after too many late nights at the Munich Carnival. But now the nurse discovered with alarm that the star had stopped breathing.

A doctor was located within the hotel. Immediately he saw the urgency of the situation. "She might have survived fifteen minutes without attention," he recalled, "but no more." To loosen the congestion in her lungs, he resorted to rather unorthodox measures, holding Elizabeth upside down by her ankles, then pushing at her eyeballs and sticking his fingers down her throat. She gagged a little, which meant air was flowing. Then he called her doctor from the London Clinic, who arrived around four o'clock. An oxygen tank was sent over, as well as a portable toilet—the same one, Walter Wanger was told, that was used by Her Majesty when she traveled to "primitive corners of the Commonwealth."

Eddie had just gotten out of the hospital himself. He'd told his doctors that he'd been having chest pain, but what he really wanted was a little rest and detox from all the pills and booze. In Munich he'd had a humdinger of a fight with Elizabeth, after which she'd swallowed too many Seconals and had to have her stomach pumped. It had been this way for months, the Fishers constantly at each other's throats, exchanging sickbeds as they recovered from binges. But this time his wife's illness was serious, her doctors insisted. With her immune system severely depressed from lack of sleep and ingesting too many substances, Elizabeth's flu had turned

into staphylococcus pneumonia, and now her lungs were dangerously congested. She needed to be taken to the London Clinic for
a tracheotomy. Otherwise she could asphyxiate and die. Eddie was
speechless.

Word had leaked outside the hotel, and aggressive photographers were ready to pounce when Elizabeth was carried out on
a stretcher and placed into an ambulance. Their brazenness was
scolded in the House of Lords. But now that the word was out, it
was received with stunned disbelief by the world. Beautiful Elizabeth Taylor, just twenty-nine years old—her lovely throat cut open
and a breathing tube inserted! Would it be permanent? If not, would
it leave a hideous scar? No answers were forthcoming. The statement from the doctors simply said, "Her condition remains grave."

Grave. Standard hospital terminology, but it was a frighten-
ing word for the public, especially in America, where Elizabeth's
condition would probably have been described as "critical." *Grave*
sounded far more serious. Not surprisingly, the headlines on Sunday, March 5, were sensational: MISS TAYLOR HAS SURGERY TO
SAVE LIFE. LIZ AT DEATH'S DOOR IN LONDON. Based on what
little news had been given to the public, it was an overreaction. As
the *Times* of London more soberly reported the next day, "The
condition of Miss Elizabeth Taylor, the film actress . . . had considerably improved last night"—although the paper did add that she
was "not yet out of danger."

Inside the hospital, Elizabeth was in and out of consciousness,
the tube in her throat pumping in oxygen, a drip system feeding
her through her ankle. A throng of reporters took up a vigil around
the clinic, pestering each person who went in or out for news of
Elizabeth Taylor. To keep them satisfied, doctors began issuing
health bulletins every fifteen minutes, even if the news was simply
"no change." These bulletins were then read on the radio as soon
as they came in. In his hotel room, Walter Wanger listened raptly.
He'd written in his diary just days before, "At last everything is going along beautifully. The plan is to start shooting April 4, then to

Egypt for the exteriors." Now he spent a sleepless night with the telephone right next to his bed.

That the situation was indeed grave is undeniable. Wanger's own doctor thought that it was serious enough to prescribe a sedative for the producer so he could be "prepared for the worst." But on Monday, March 6, things spiraled out of control when an American news report allegedly announced that Elizabeth Taylor had died. Just where this report was made has never been determined. No such account was found in any of the voluminous clippings about Elizabeth in any film archive. Perhaps it was a radio or television report. Or perhaps it was just one of those stories that spreads so quickly in Hollywood. Alan Cahan remembered hearing it from a publicist friend. "It'll soon be all over the news," he was told. "Liz Taylor is dead in London!"

Spyros Skouras heard the report, too, and placed a transatlantic call to Wanger. "My God," he cried. "How did it happen?" Wanger assured him that it wasn't true.

But the world couldn't be as easily reassured. The story spread like wildfire. Perhaps it was intended to. "I wouldn't be surprised," Cahan said, "if that story of Liz Taylor suddenly dying in London wasn't planted." Dick Clayton thought that it was possible as well. "Press agents are pretty clever like that," he said. And certainly Elizabeth had some very good ones working for her, both on her own and at Fox. A call might have been made, and then another, and soon all of Hollywood would have been buzzing with the tragic news, and then, of course, it would have zoomed around the globe. "We are all very frightened," Wanger wrote that night in his diary, "and, it appears, so is the world. People are crying. Flowers and gifts and 'cures' are coming in from all over."

Whether they planted the story or not, surely Bill Doll or any of Elizabeth's other press agents remembered the "shrieking fans" who had gathered, quite on their own, when the star, said to be suffering from "Malta fever," had been hospitalized just a few months earlier. Witnessing this latest outpouring of affection for their client, they had to be pleased. And they had to know that such sentiment could be harnessed.

When the account of Elizabeth's famous tracheotomy was previously reported, this part of the story was never told. The reaction to her earlier illness has been treated as incidental, if at all. But, in fact, the narrative of her brush with death and the outpouring of public support was already in place by March 1961, because *it had already happened.* And had any clever press agent been so inclined, it would have been easy to whip it up again by starting a little whisper campaign that Elizabeth had died. The reaction of the press and the public was already known. Crowds would fill the streets and newspapers would banner the latest reports of Elizabeth's condition.

Which is exactly what happened. On March 7, the day after the death rumor, the headlines about Elizabeth moved from below the fold to the top of the page, from regular font size to three inches tall in some instances. Thousands of grief-stricken fans choked the streets around the clinic, depositing flowers in enormous piles on the steps as a sort of shrine—a common enough gesture today for sick or deceased celebrities, but unusual in 1961. Newspaper reports about Elizabeth's condition read almost like obituaries, with photographs of Elizabeth in her greatest films and descriptions of her "once-lithe body" now "linked to medical apparatus around her bed." And surely it was press agents—and not "friends," as reporters described them—who leaked the few precious facts that emerged from the star's hospital room: her constant pain due to lack of sedation (it could weaken her breathing) and her sudden, heartfelt concern about her children, which caused her to sit bolt upright in her hospital bed.

Though doctors were in fact reporting a "slight improvement" in Elizabeth's condition, the press had no interest in quelling the sudden hysteria. They wanted to sell newspapers. So it was the star's anemia (a "setback," it was called) that the reports trumpeted. "Elizabeth Taylor developed dangerous symptoms of anemia today in her fight for life against pneumonia," the *New York Daily News* declared.

No matter how many hospital bulletins insisted that Elizabeth was "breathing quietly and peacefully," the histrionic coverage continued. Reporters trailed Eddie's agent, Milton Blackstone, as he hurried to board a plane for London, allegedly carrying twenty vials of an antipneumonia drug. Just why Elizabeth's doctors would need Eddie Fisher's agent to procure drugs for them in America was never made clear. When a grim-faced Sara and Francis Taylor arrived in London, pursued down Harley Street by a mob of shouting reporters, the public reasoned that things must indeed be dire. They were, of course—just not as dire as the press made them out to be.

And then, suddenly, Elizabeth got better. On March 10 the *Times* announced that she was "out of danger"—even if the tabloids in England and America carried on for another day or two. But on March 12 the breathing tube was removed from her throat. Doctors assured reporters that she was "going along very nicely," and that seemed to be that. London police dispatched a "black maria," or paddy wagon, to disperse the crowds amassed around the clinic. "Go on home," they barked through megaphones. "It's all over."

But the story wasn't over. It was far too profitable to fade away that fast—for both the newspapers and the principals involved. Eddie gave several different interviews, describing how the "dreadful illness" had nearly taken his wife's life "more than once this past week." Even with the crisis over, he stood on the clinic's front steps to have his picture taken and read statements expressing the couple's "limitless gratitude and appreciation to those who made possible her miraculous recovery." Indeed, the "miracle" of Elizabeth's "second chance at life" was heralded in newspapers the world over.

Of course, these statements were written by press agents who knew their audience. And it wasn't just Elizabeth's adoring public. It was also those Academy voters back in Los Angeles who had yet to cast their ballots for Best Actress, and who were following the saga of the star's near-death experience in their morning newspapers. To suggest that there was no awareness of how Elizabeth's health crisis might play out for Academy voters is naïve. "Of course that's what was on their minds," said Dick Clayton. Frank D'Amico, who worked at the time for the publicity firm of Rupert Allen in Hollywood, observed, "A good publicist is always thinking of ways in which an event can be turned around to help his client." That would explain the parade of interviews arranged over the next few weeks, first with Eddie, and then with Elizabeth herself.

The first photos of "Liz on the mend" appeared on March 23. For the occasion, the French hairdresser Alexandre, whom she'd met in Paris, flew to London at her request to give her a new hairdo. "There, in her hospital bed," said Alexandre, "she was held up by three nurses while I created her famous artichoke cut." Above her cashmere sweater, she wore a discreet bandage hiding the wound on her throat. She smiled meekly for photographers, but said nothing, since she was still too weak, according to spokesmen. But not too weak to share champagne with Truman Capote, who came to visit.

And, yet again, that is not meant to trivialize the experience that she'd been through. Elizabeth would tell remarkable stories to her friends, and later to the public, about seeing "the white light" while she'd been unconscious, of feeling "so welcoming and warm"—the classic description of near-death experiences. She'd even seen Mike, she insisted, who told her that she needed to go back, that it wasn't her time yet—though he had promised that he'd be waiting for her when it was. No doubt she fervently believed all of it. That stories such as these only further riveted the public to her drama was immaterial.

A few days later her release from the hospital caused a riot. The door of her Rolls-Royce was nearly ripped off its hinges by eager fans, and Elizabeth had to be moved to another car. This was followed by a much ballyhooed return to America. It wouldn't do for the next Best Actress Academy Award winner to recuperate

outside of her own country. MISS TAYLOR COMES HOME TO RE-
GAIN HEALTH blared the headlines. There was even talk of making *Cleopatra* in Hollywood; in any event, the London shoot now
had to be abandoned, which meant that Peter Finch and Stephen
Boyd couldn't wait around anymore. A new Caesar and Antony
would need to be found. Wanger was thinking Rex Harrison and
Richard Burton, who, though not a big movie star, had recently
been a sensation on Broadway in *Camelot*.

Cleopatra, however, was the furthest thing from Elizabeth's
mind. When she arrived in New York, she told reporters that she
felt "a little better," and then, in a "wan and wispy" voice, thanked
the public for all "their good wishes." The press was also there when
she arrived back in Los Angeles, carried down from her plane by
two TWA attendants and placed in a wheelchair, her left leg covered with bandages from "numerous shots of antibiotics during her
fight for life in England." Dressed in a stylish tan suit, she was
whisked away to a limousine, where, as she petted a little dog in her
lap in the backseat, she spoke a few words out the window to newsmen. They had to lean down and strain to hear her whisper: "I plan
on doing nothing. I won't do anything for at least several months.
I have to do what my doctors tell me."

In every account of her life, Elizabeth Taylor's frail health has
been a recurring motif. It is part of her story, part of her legend.
Even before this latest crisis, *Motion Picture* magazine had tried to
explain her ever-fragile health as a result of that other important
theme of her story: her passion and lust for life. "It is *love* that is
killing Liz Taylor," the fan magazine wrote. "[I]n her brief life [she]
has loved not wisely, but too well, and too many things: men and
beauty, fame and talent, children and travel and money and excitement and love itself." While little more than pop psychology, some
of this may have been on the money, even if the writer didn't fully
realize it. Certainly Elizabeth's headlong embrace of sex, drugs, alcohol, and food did exacerbate her various health issues.

But the stories of struggle and infirmity served a real purpose in
the larger narrative of Elizabeth's life. In an article titled "Can Liz

Ever Be Cured?" written during the "Malta fever" episode, another writer imagined the glamorous star alone in her hospital room, "a beautiful woman of twenty-eight, rich, famous, loved, idolized." But he was sure, if he listened carefully, that he "could hear her sobbing." He imagined her "lying in a simple, unironed hospital nightgown, in a crude, white cot of a bed in a barren room, clutching a pillow, shaking with emotion and weary from weeping."

When chronicling the life of a woman who appeared to have it all, such a narrative was necessary as counterbalance. The public seemed to need to believe that there was *some* hidden misery, that *something* wasn't perfect for this magnificent goddess. Stories about Elizabeth's propensity for illness indulged that suspicion. There were some, of course, who dismissed her health problems as hypochondria or the behavior of a spoiled, pampered movie star, claiming they were nothing "that a good spanking wouldn't cure." But for the most part, the stories generated sympathy for the "poor little rich girl," for the girl who was "too beautiful" or who "loved too much" for her own good.

By now, Elizabeth's handlers—and no doubt the star herself—understood how it worked. They knew how the public responded to her illnesses and accidents. They knew how those posttracheotomy interviews would be received, what effect that bandage on Elizabeth's throat would have on those who saw it. No longer a pariah or a home wrecker, she was a strong, courageous young woman who had returned Lazarus-like from the dead. In Hollywood, fans lined the street waving placards welcoming her home. "This was the ultimate climax," Eddie Fisher said, "the queen rising from her deathbed to receive the love of her court."

Elizabeth may have said that she planned on doing nothing, but armed guards couldn't have kept her away from the Academy Awards presentation on April 17. "Elizabeth Taylor looks tough to beat," predicted veteran Hollywood scribe Bob Thomas, "and not only because of her recent brush with death. She lifted *Butterfield 8* out of the ordinary." But she'd been overlooked three years in a row. Nothing was sure until she held that shiny little gold man in her hands.

That year, due to renovations at the Pantages Theatre, the Oscar show was moved out of Los Angeles for the first time. The closest venue of sufficient size was the Santa Monica Civic Auditorium. But that didn't stop the fans from showing up—twenty-five hundred of them, the largest in Academy history. They congregated along Main Street and Pico Boulevard, waiting for the stars to appear on the red carpet. Many of the nominees and presenters were late, caught in a massive traffic jam that clogged the beachfront city. The curtain had already gone up inside when Elizabeth and Eddie finally arrived. The crowd went wild. Stepping out of the limo in a flowing Dior gown with a mint green bodice and white sheath skirt with a floral pattern, Elizabeth appeared "cool and confident," one reporter observed. But as the clamor around her escalated, she seemed to grow "tense" and gripped Eddie's arm. He escorted her inside, where she composed herself in the lounge before taking her seat.

When the nominees for Best Actress were read, Elizabeth sat emotionless. Yul Brynner, winner of Best Actor for *The King and I* in 1956, unsealed the envelope and read her name as the winner. Applause tore through the auditorium. Elizabeth clapped her hands over her mouth and stared straight ahead in astonishment. For several seconds, she didn't move or say a word. Then she turned to Eddie, who helped her stand. She made her way up to the stage slowly and uncertainly. One emotional observer commented: "Near death two months ago, now at the peak of her career . . . Miss Taylor's victory was one of the most dramatic moments in Oscar's thirty-three years." Eddie Fisher wondered if the Academy had deliberately seated them in the middle of the auditorium instead of close to the stage just to "prolong the drama."

For drama there certainly was. Elizabeth stood at the podium trembling perceptibly, looking out at her peers as they got to their feet, offering a standing ovation in her honor. "A coronation,"

Eddie called it. Those applauding her were people with whom she had lived, worked, and grown up—people who, for the last two years, had seemed to ostracize her. Now, standing there with the scar on her throat visible, everything was forgiven. "I don't really know how to express my gratitude for this and for everything," she whispered into the microphone. "All I can say is thank you with all my heart."

Backstage, she posed for photos with the other winners, Burt Lancaster for Best Actor in *Elmer Gantry* and Billy Wilder as Best Director for *The Apartment*. She went cheek-to-cheek with Eddie in a gesture of triumph. But then she skipped out, avoiding the usual post-show interviews. There was nothing more to say. She had won, and on her terms—by playing the game better than anyone else and by rewriting the rules. She didn't yield; Hollywood did.

Two and a half years earlier, few could have predicted this night. But both of the women who'd been involved in the scandal (which was already being called "quaint" by many) triumphed in the end. Debbie Reynolds, so shrewd, so calculating, would rapidly follow Elizabeth as the second woman to make a million dollars per picture. With her trademark spunk, Debbie elbowed her way right into the box-office top ten. Scandal had been very good for little Debbie.

But she would never quite claim the same exalted place in the pantheon of Hollywood that Elizabeth had achieved. For if stardom was about reconciling differences, there was never any contradiction to the perky and sweet public image of Debbie Reynolds. So controlling was the actual woman behind the façade that she never allowed the real—and far more fascinating—duality that defined her to be glimpsed by anyone outside her private circle. As a consequence, she would never become a star of the rank of Elizabeth Taylor.

Elizabeth understood the position that she occupied, and what it meant, and what it had taken to get there. With Max Lerner, her friend and occasional lover, she talked about writing a memoir: "I'll

do the recalling, you do the heavy thinking." Growing close again
Elizabeth convalesced from her surgery, they tape-recorded son
conversations that eventually led to an article some years later
which Lerner referred to Marilyn Monroe as a "myth"—a crea
ture made and destroyed by Hollywood—but Elizabeth as a "leg
end." Though Lerner intended the distinction as a complimen
Elizabeth took offense, even if much of it was tongue in cheel
"You have a nerve saying that Marilyn was a myth and I'm just
lousy legend," she told him. When Lerner replied, "Both of you ar
forces," she let him off the hook.

"Narcissistic," Lerner called her, looking back. "Self-referential." But that's to be expected; all great stars must be such things
And since Elizabeth's sexuality was the engine of her fame, and
Lerner himself admitted that "a good deal of sexuality comes
from the concentration on self," it's perhaps fortunate—for Hollywood, for the world—that Elizabeth Taylor was as self-referential
as Lerner claimed she was. While she may not have chased fame
simply for fame's sake the way so many others did, from Crawford to Hepburn to Reynolds, Elizabeth understood very well the
power and position that she had achieved in Hollywood, and, indeed, by 1961, around the world. And it was a distinction that she
prized, guarded, and very much enjoyed.

In the end, the only one who would ever pay any real price for
the scandal that had so transfixed the public for two years was its
lone male player—poor, luckless Eddie. That July, he opened an act
at the legendary Cocoanut Grove at the Ambassador Hotel in Los
Angeles. It was to be his big comeback, and Elizabeth's first outing
since she'd had plastic surgery on her neck to remove the tracheotomy scar. Rex Kennamer sat solicitously by her side. The whole
audience glittered: In attendance were John Wayne, Henry Fonda,
Lucille Ball, Kirk Douglas, Danny Thomas, Groucho Marx, Yul
Brynner, and Jerry Lewis. And the Rat Pack, with whom Eddie
was supposed to be pals: Frank Sinatra, Dean Martin, Peter Lawford, Sammy Davis Jr., and Joey Bishop.

Maybe the star-studded crowd intimidated the kid from South

Philly, because he forgot the words to several songs. "Come on, Eddie!" Martin shouted from the audience. Sinatra put his fingers in his mouth and whistled. Eventually Eddie dared them to come up onstage if they thought that they could do a better job, and they did, cocktails in hand, singing a couple of songs and bantering jokes back and forth. Retreating to the bandstand, Eddie smiled gamely, but he was clearly embarrassed to be upstaged by the Sinatra "clan." The next day, the reviews of the show were snarky. Eddie Fisher had become a joke, and his wife, his friends, and his public knew it.

With his television show canceled, his nightclub act withering, and his marriage to the woman of his dreams crumbling before his eyes, Eddie knew only misfortune in the wake of the infamous triangle of 1958. And it would get significantly worse over the next eighteen months when the international spotlight followed him and his wife during the tumultuous filming of *Cleopatra*.

But all that was in the future. For the moment, all that mattered to the Fishers was that Elizabeth had regained the respect of the industry and the love of the public. She was supreme, the greatest star in the world. She could do anything she wanted to do now. Anything.

And so she went to Rome and fell in love with Richard Burton.

Eight

No Deodorant Like Success

April 1962–July 1965

N O MATTER THE STORIES flying across the Atlantic about the scandal on the set of *Cleopatra*—or maybe, in fact, *because* of them—George Stevens wanted one actress and one actress only to play Mary Magdalene in his epic production of *The Greatest Story Ever Told*. Sitting at his desk at Desilu studios in Culver City, he insisted to his associate producers that Elizabeth Taylor was the only one he could see in the role. Thirteen years earlier, planning *A Place in the Sun*, Stevens had held a similar conviction that no one else could better animate the character he had in mind. Now, planning what he hoped would be his magnum opus, he once again wanted Elizabeth. Who better to play the whore who became a saint, the woman of the streets exalted by the Son of God?

Of course, the director expected some naysayers. In his files were letters that had flowed in to him after Hedda Hopper had announced the possibility of Elizabeth's casting in September 1960. One woman from Texas had angrily condemned the idea since Elizabeth was now a Jew—apparently forgetting that Mary herself had been Jewish. From Oregon had come this plea: "Surely you can find an actress of good moral character for the part." And a writer from Iowa had exclaimed, "A woman like Liz Taylor in a story of Christ—never, never, never!"

But then had come Elizabeth's near death in London and the public restoration symbolized by the Academy Award. The letters against her died out. Stevens moved forward with his plan. Elizabeth was intrigued by the idea, but only if the terms were right. Stevens was offering $50,000 a week for five weeks. While that meant a quarter of a million dollars for what was essentially a supporting role, Kurt Frings was not impressed. Elizabeth was now the highest-salaried female star in the world, and would only be satisfied with $3 million at the break-even point. Why not make a film called *Mary Magdalene* that starred Elizabeth, Frings suggested, instead of "this Jesus picture"?

Stevens blew his top. His notes reveal that he thought a deal was close until Frings tried to "spike" it. "Cheapskate agent makes a cheapskate out of G.S." the director scrawled across one page. "[Frings] obviously doesn't want any of his clients in my pictures, and I am astonished at the lengths he will go to keep them out."

His hostility toward the pugnacious agent, however, didn't dampen his enthusiasm for Elizabeth. She remained his first choice for Mary Magdalene even as the filming of *Cleopatra* seemed to drag on forever. According to his notes, Stevens may have been preparing to offer her 10 percent of the gross. But the scandal with Richard Burton, then exploding in Rome, would eventually change everything.

The problem was that the lovers hadn't just gone public. They were *flaunting* their affair, heedless of scandal and seeming to revel in the headlines and round-the-clock publicity. Elizabeth may have developed a new addiction by this point, one that pumped her up even more than vodka or chocolate fudge: the adrenaline-producing rush of public drama. With Eddie Fisher removed from the picture, the front pages of the London and New York tabloids bannered daily developments of what was coming to be known as "Le Scandale." IT'S LIZ OR ME: WIFE TO BURTON. LIZ, BURTON ROMP AS SYBIL WAITS ALONE. LIZ AND BURTON OFF TO PARIS. One moment Burton was cabling Sybil in London to say that he had no plans to divorce her; the next he and Elizabeth were sashaying down the Via Veneto in the wee hours, paparazzi in tow, cameras flashing. Strolling arm in arm, they moved from the posh George's restaurant to the raucous nightclub Pipistrello, famed for its "twist" band. Elizabeth, reporters observed, was in "a gay party mood," wearing a low-cut polka-dot dress and a huge Cossack-style fur hat. With Mankiewicz *père* and *fils* in tow, the couple ended their night at the Little Bar, knocking back shots until three thirty in the morning. "I can choose any man I like," Elizabeth was reported as boasting to a friend. "I don't see why everyone is making such a fuss."

But the world was indeed making a fuss. "Probably no news event in modern times has affected so many people personally," Art Buchwald joked, though the truth lay not far underneath his humor. "Nuclear testing, disarmament, Berlin, Viet Nam and the struggle between Russia and China are nothing comparable to the Elizabeth Taylor story."

If Elizabeth thought that she'd endured the height of public scrutiny during the affair with Eddie, she quickly discovered otherwise. On the night of April 15, five hundred torch-bearing university students packed the road outside her villa, chanting for "Liz." Rumors flew that they wanted to kidnap her. A few nights later Elizabeth broke down in tears when the paparazzi cornered her on the Via Veneto. The constant attention, until now so carefully tended and tolerated, had simply become too much for her.

"Who could really be prepared for that kind of publicity, that level of attention?" Tom Mankiewicz asked. "Not even Elizabeth, who'd grown up with it, who knew better than anybody how to deal with it." Burton, when he wasn't torn by guilt over Sybil and his two daughters, seemed to thoroughly enjoy the ride and the notoriety that it generated for him. He egged Elizabeth along and kept their excursions in front of the cameras. Yet for all their shrewd media manipulation, even "Liz and Dick" didn't fully grasp the powerful response their romance had evoked.

In the hushed and hallowed halls of the Palace of the Governorate of Vatican City, a sandal-wearing Jesuit priest was handed an official bulletin that had been prepared, debated over, and finally approved by the top leaders of the church. As the morning fog lifted, Vatican Radio echoed across the cobblestone streets, decrying those who would treat marriage as "a game which they start and interrupt with the capricious make-believe of children." A week later *L'Osservatore della Domenica,* the weekly magazine supplement of the Vatican newspaper, was even more direct. Though it still refrained from mentioning Elizabeth by name (the open letter was addressed to "Madam"), the unnamed writer criticized the star for adopting a child while living a life of "erotic vagrancy." Some sources speculated that the words were those of Pope John himself; at the very least, they had his approval. "Your motive, madam," the writer continued, "is that when a bigger love comes along you kill the smaller love."

Burton, the "bigger love," laughed off the censure. "He's never been on my party list," he told his brother, referring to the pope. But the Italian papers suddenly found their religion: "We would say that morally she has lost it," declared *Il Giornale d'Italia* of Elizabeth. Even the magazine that had first published the infamous kissing photo, *Lo Specchio,* now pronounced Elizabeth "out of style" in Rome: "No one wants to hear anything more about what she's wearing, her adornments, her illnesses, her scar, her food poisoning, her children, her husbands." The American Catholic press followed the lead of its Vatican counterpart, condemning "the nauseating headlines" coming from Rome and lamenting the disappearance of the old studio morals clause. Nowadays, charged the *Catholic Transcript,* Hollywood rewarded indecency. "Sometimes a star is given the industry's highest honor for portraying a depraved character that calls for hardly any acting at all"—a clear reference to Elizabeth winning the Academy Award for *Butterfield 8.*

Almost exactly one year after that triumphant night, Elizabeth's careful rehabilitation of her image now seemed ready to come undone. She stood once again in the crosshairs of public opprobrium, and this time, the harshest attacks weren't confined to the pages of *Photoplay.* After the Vatican weighed in, the Italian government, in the person of Egidio Ariosto, undersecretary of the interior, warned the star against "self-destruction" due to her "amorous and non-amorous conduct."

Ariosto's statement came in response to a highly publicized episode on the night of April 24. After the lovers shocked the world by spending Easter weekend together in unwedded bliss in a seaside bungalow at Porto Santo Stefano, Elizabeth turned up at the local doctor with a bloody nose. When the doctor couldn't be found, she hurried back to Rome alone, setting off a flurry of rumors. Had Burton hit her in a violent quarrel? Had she taken another overdose of pills when he refused to divorce Sybil? Once more, headlines raged around the world. The Roman police concluded that Elizabeth had simply bumped her nose when her car had made a quick stop and she was thrown forward. Still it was enough for the conservative Italian paper *Il Tempo* to declare that her presence in Rome was now "undesirable." Not long afterward, Elizabeth received an anonymous letter threatening her and her four children with death unless she stopped seeing Burton. Roman police began guarding her round-the-clock.

Over the next few weeks the criticism only escalated from all quarters. In remarks leading up to the dedication of his presidential library in Abilene, Kansas, former president Eisenhower asked: "What has happened to our concept of beauty and decency and morality?" He denounced the "vulgarity, sensuality, indeed, downright filth" that was being used by Hollywood to promote itself. Given the timing of his commentary, he could only have been referring to the scandal in Rome.

Backed up by the words of a former president, one U.S. congresswoman called for Elizabeth and Richard to be barred from returning to the country. Iris Faircloth Blitch, a fifty-year-old, four-term Democratic representative from Georgia, took the podium on the floor of the House of Representatives and launched into a ringing denunciation of the two stars. "Communists chuckle," said Blitch, "because the Roman spectacle seems to prove their thesis that capitalists are unscrupulously depraved, wanton and decadent, and that capitalism breeds these undesirable traits." As her belligerent words tinged by her lilting Southern accent echoed throughout the chamber, Blitch urged Attorney General Robert F. Kennedy to "take the measures necessary to determine whether or not the two are ineligible for re-entry into this country on grounds of undesirability."

Kennedy took no action on Blitch's request. But the outrage of Washington encouraged Elizabeth's Hollywood critics, who once more took up arms against the star. Hedda, no surprise, led the charge. "Her beauty masks a willful, ruthless nature," the columnist declared, pronouncing Elizabeth "sick—very sick." Hedda wrote smugly that she had not spoken with the star since she'd gone to Rome; unlike four years earlier, when Hedda's infamous interview had uncorked the Liz-Eddie-Debbie scandal, Elizabeth had "done it all on her own this time." At the Academy Awards, where just a year before Elizabeth had been anointed queen, she was now reduced to a one-liner from host Bob Hope: "Whoever would have thought the Italians would learn realism from *us*?"

Her cause wasn't helped by yet another scandal erupting around Kurt Frings. This time it was the agent's estranged wife, Ketti, who made the complaint. Hedda Hopper, only too happy to link Frings's behavior to his client's, phoned Ketti to get the scoop. Hedda made sure her readers knew that the wily Frings had managed to have assault charges against him dropped yet again. Frings endured another round of bad publicity when it was revealed that he was seeking visitation rights not to see his children, but to use the steam room in the house that he'd shared with Ketti.

All of it was enough to apparently convince George Stevens to look elsewhere for his Mary Magdalene. Frings's bullheadedness (and his unsavory reputation) may have been the chief reason, but the negative publicity could not have helped. "Liz Taylor will never play the role of Mary Magdalene in *The Greatest Story Ever Told* because George Stevens feels the risk is too great," Mike Connolly's column in the *Hollywood Reporter* revealed that summer. After the story broke, Stevens fired off a letter to Elizabeth saying that he'd been misquoted. "My affection and respect for you are too deep-rooted," the director told the star, "for me to ever say anything unfavorable concerning you."

Elizabeth's reaction is unknown; she seemed to have lost interest in *Greatest Story* by that point. But she was nevertheless annoyed by the latest firestorm that she'd caused in her home country, a place that now seemed hopelessly parochial to her. "I will never go back to America," she said. "I hate America and America hates me."

Those were fighting words. Elizabeth's reaction to this scandal would be very different from four years previous. She would not hide. She would not make nice. No battery of press agents would duel on her behalf for sympathetic coverage in the fan magazines. This time around, Elizabeth said to hell with all that. No matter the high-profile criticism, Le Scandale proceeded without letup or apology. Many, like Hedda, were appalled. But others, like the columnist Ruth Waterbury, felt some grudging admiration. Speaking privately to George Stevens, Waterbury observed that, although the press was "being real vicious towards her now . . . and she has nowhere to hide," Elizabeth was leaving many people impressed with "the courage to be herself." On her own, no longer protected by any studio or any husband's organization, Elizabeth had to trust that such courage would be enough.

From his secluded perch on the volcanic island of Ischia at the northern end of the Gulf of Naples, Elio Sorci trained his telephoto camera at the yacht docked just off the coast. The hot Mediterranean sun beat down on the backs of a sunbathing Richard Burton and Elizabeth Taylor onboard. Sorci snapped a rapid-fire series of shots as the lovers huddled close together, moving in at one point for a quick kiss. The photographer was ecstatic. He knew pictures of Elizabeth Taylor in a bathing suit cuddling with Richard Burton would fetch hundreds of thousands of lire.

Such telephoto pictures by the paparazzi had not yet become commonplace in celebrity culture; they were an immediate sensation when they were published in 1962. "Incendiary," they were called—an extraordinary glimpse into the private moments of the two most written-about people on the planet. After seeing the pictures, Sybil Burton reportedly sent for her lawyer.

But even then the lovers didn't quit each other. Indeed, the times seemed to give them license to continue just as they were. "The Sixties was to pride itself on being a decade of honesty, of openness, an end to hypocrisy," Burton's biographer Melvyn Bragg observed. The "sexual cover-up" was exposed; shame was a thing of the past. "The brave flaunted it and [Taylor and Burton] were the first of the brave. Older generations may have envied them in secret; younger generations openly applauded."

Richard Burton was an unlikely herald of a new age. Born Richard Jenkins in 1925 in Pontrhydyfen, a tiny village near Port Talbot in southeast Wales, he was the twelfth of thirteen children, the son of a coal miner, a "twelve-pints-a-day" man, with whom his son shared much in common. "He looked very much like me," Burton would say of his father. "That is, he was pockmarked, devious, and smiled a great deal when he was in trouble." His mother died before he was two years old and he was raised by his sister and her husband. The working-class life of a mining village meant that Richard began smoking when he was eight and drinking regularly by the time he was twelve. Still, he was a good student, with an affinity for literature—but he was no shrinking intellectual. His skill in the classroom was matched by his ability on the playing field. Many thought that if he hadn't become an actor Richard would have become a rugby star like his brother Ifor. He himself wondered sometimes if he'd chosen the right path: "I would rather have played for Wales at Cardiff Arms Park than Hamlet at Old Vic."

But it was his lively performances in school theatrical productions that really made him stand out from his sooty classmates. One of his teachers, the urbane Philip Burton, himself a child of the coal mines, who'd managed to graduate from the University of Wales and write drama for BBC radio, spotted Richard's potential early on; eventually Burton adopted the teenager as his ward and gave him his name. While eternally grateful to his new father for this lift out of poverty, Richard seemed to believe on some level that he'd been snatched from his natural course and set upon a more elite, effeminate route in life. He'd spend the rest of his days blustering and swaggering to make up for it.

The young Richard Burton was strikingly handsome, with eyes as compelling as Elizabeth's: blue-green and so intense that they gripped audiences over the footlights. He suffered, however, from terrible acne, the scars of which left his face and shoulders pitted for the rest of his life. Yet nothing could blunt his sheer magnetism, his raw sexual energy. "He oozed sexual charm for both men and women," said Hank Moonjean, who got to know Burton well in Rome. "It was very powerful. And he could turn it on and off like a faucet." Richard understood his appeal and how to use it. He wasn't averse to flirting with a man if it meant getting what he wanted; he admitted that one time he actually gave in to a male admirer, although sex with men just wasn't for him. Still, his power over gay men was well known. According to some, Philip Burton was a deeply circumspect homosexual who regarded his teenage ward, at least in the beginning, as an unrequited object of desire. So powerful was Philip's devotion that he never lost his commitment for making Richard a success.

This he accomplished first by keeping the boy in school, when so many others dropped out to work in the mines. He also trained Richard's acting voice and helped him land radio parts on the BBC. Philip discovered that the young man had an insatiable curiosity to learn. Richard was rarely without a sack slung over his shoulder filled with dictionaries, the complete works of Shakespeare, and books of quotations. He discussed the classics of literature, art, and music with ease and passion, thanks to the tutelage of his mentor.

In 1943, when Richard was eighteen, Philip was instrumental in getting him into Exeter College, Oxford, for a special term of six months. At first, the coal miner's son found himself brawling with the sons of aristocrats, those "chaps with posh accents" whom he had always resented. His worldview would be forever imprinted with a sense of his otherness. "It's difficult for somebody," he explained, "who comes from the majority to know quite what it's like to be in a minority, to be a Jew or a Welshman or an Irishman. What it does to a Negro, I shudder to imagine." At Oxford, far from the sooty streets of Pontrhydyfen, Richard taught himself to speak with a standard accent. But still, he admitted, he never quite spoke what might be considered "proper" English.

Again he was saved by an older homosexual man who discerned his potential. Nevill Coghill was a fellow in English literature and director of Oxford's lavish annual undergraduate production, an event that had launched many actors on their way. Coghill gave Richard an audition for *Measure for Measure* in which the young man intoned, "To be or not to be." Coghill was bowled over. "Out came the most perfect rendering I had ever heard," he said. He told colleagues: "The boy is a genius and will be a great actor. He is outstandingly handsome and robust, very masculine and with deep inward fire."

Another of Richard's gurus was Emlyn Williams, in whose play, *The Druid's Rest,* he made his professional debut first in Liverpool and then in London in 1943. He was a natural, instinctive actor, disdaining the kind of training so popular then in New York. "I'm the least Method actor that ever was," he'd declare. For Burton, acting was about summoning his own depths of power and emotion. Following a stint in the Royal Air Force, he began making a name for himself on the stage, appearing with John Gielgud in *The Lady's Not for Burning,* both in the West End and on Broadway. In 1951 he was a sensation as Prince Hal in *Henry IV, Part 1* at Stratford. Critic Kenneth Tynan noted, "His playing of Prince Hal turned interested speculation to awe almost as soon as he started to speak; in the first intermission local critics stood agape in the lobbies. Burton is a still, brimming pool, running disturbingly deep; at twenty-five he commands a repose and can make silence garrulous."

From there it was a series of quick leaps to the top: first *Montserrat* at the Lyric Theatre, Hammersmith, then two memorable seasons of Shakespeare at the Old Vic, where he played Hamlet, Caliban, Henry V, and Othello, among others, and was hailed as the heir of Gielgud and Olivier. And yet he did it all without an abiding interest in the traditions and history of his art. "[Acting] doesn't especially appeal to me," he said. "I hardly ever go to see plays or films, and I've never been much interested in the so-called craft or art of acting." Nonetheless, Alexander Korda signed him to a film contract and sent him on a jaunt to Hollywood in 1952 to make *My Cousin Rachel* with Olivia de Havilland. There, at a party at Stewart Granger's house, he first met Elizabeth Taylor, aged twenty and married to Michael Wilding. While she noticed Burton—and that he had obviously noticed *her*—she thought, "Huh! I'm not going to be a scalp on his belt because he was a terrible flirt." At that first meeting, the sparks were suppressed.

Richard was married to Sybil Williams by this point, an actress of Welsh background who had given up her career after bearing two girls. Richard worshipped Sybil, setting her on such a pedestal that she became almost untouchable, the sanctified mother of his beloved daughters Kate and Jessica. Such a hallowed relationship, however, almost demanded extramarital affairs for a man as carnal as Burton. His womanizing proceeded apace, while Sybil obligingly looked the other way. "Sybil was the good loving bride," her friend, the actress Rachel Roberts, wrote in her journal, "keeping house, making French fries, ignoring his infidelities, perhaps not even accepting them herself." Many felt Sybil, by her denial, ensured the continuance of their marriage. For all her husband's philandering, Sybil trusted that she was first in his heart.

That presumption, held by so many, has served Elizabeth's story well. Only a woman as irresistible as Elizabeth Taylor could possibly tear Richard away from Sybil, the chroniclers insisted; only Elizabeth could have succeeded where so many other women had tried and failed. Yet Richard had fallen head over heels for a woman and contemplated leaving Sybil for her at least once before. "Oh, my lovely girl," he wrote to Claire Bloom, his pretty, spirited Viola from the *Twelfth Night* that ran at the Old Vic in 1954. "I've had a savage attack of flu. It must be 'love pine.'" He apologized for not reading her letters at home, where Sybil might peer over his shoulder. Their next play, he hoped, would be during the winter, because then "my lovely girl [would] be forced to sleep with me because of the cold." (He jokingly advised her to "cooch up to the working class"—meaning himself.) "I haven't looked at another woman," he swore. "This has never happened to me before. You have changed me. I have almost grown up."

Yet not that grown up, because Bloom eventually walked in on him trysting with Susan Strasberg. In the end, the marriage to Sybil endured all of these capers—that is, until Rome. And even then, there were those who still placed their bets on Mrs. Burton. "Not a chance!" Hedda Hopper declared, when asked if Burton would leave his wife for Elizabeth. "Richard has romanced many leading ladies; Sybil has made a career of being the forgiving wife. It's made them millionaires, which they enjoy being."

But those on the ground, the ones watching the affair unfold in Rome, had a rather different perspective. "Richard couldn't believe how attached [to Elizabeth] he'd become," said Tom Mankiewicz. "He tried to end it, but he kept turning around and coming back to her. He just couldn't help himself. He couldn't get enough of her."

When they'd started the film, she'd been "Miss Tits," a silly overhyped Hollywood movie star whom Burton had dismissed to his friends. Now Elizabeth was his sun and his moon. "I have been inordinately lucky all my life but the greatest luck of all has been Elizabeth," he wrote in his diary, lifting some passages from the Welsh poet David Jones. "She is a wildly exciting lover-mistress, she is shy and witty, she is nobody's fool, she is a brilliant actress, she is beautiful beyond the dreams of pornography, she can be arrogant and willful, she is clement and loving, Dulcis Imperatrix, she is Sunday's child, she can tolerate my impossibilities and my drunkenness, she is an ache in the stomach when I am away from her, *and she loves me!* [his emphasis] And I'll love her till I die."

So different from each other in many ways, yet the attraction of opposites is a mighty force. Richard would load himself down with old volumes from obscure bookshops in Rome and London while Elizabeth was off buying furs and shoes. He was an Oxford man, she a graduate of the Little Red Schoolhouse. In terms of acting, she knew what the movies had taught her: that sometimes a look or a turn of the head said it all. For Burton, language was everything. A put-down from Burton was always framed in irony. When the despised director Tony Richardson wanted him for a project, Burton said that he ought to have been "scared witless to approach me to play Scrabble." Elizabeth, on the other hand, just said "Fuck you" when someone ticked her off. Not that Richard didn't resort occasionally to such mundanities himself. He once screamed "Fuck!" at the top of his lungs in the middle of a hotel lobby because "To scream 'fuck' in the lobby was the only possible way to meet the justice of the day," he wrote in his diary.

Yet what truly set the lovers apart was their approach to fame. Elizabeth endured the spotlight without complaint because of the abundance it provided. Burton, by contrast, was left baffled and bemused by such trappings. A few years later, when the *San Francisco Chronicle* columnist Herb Caen asked them both to describe in one word their choice of a way of life, their answers were revealing. Elizabeth said "wealth"; Richard said "adventure." For Elizabeth, the jewels, the yachts, and the villas were valuable for their own sake; for Richard, the wealth only mattered because of the adventure that it made possible.

Indeed, there's no question that Burton enjoyed the excitement his ladylove provided, the international acclaim and jet-set life that was suddenly his to share. In fact, some people charged that his whole courtship of Elizabeth had sprung from a desire to dip into that extraordinary well of celebrity. Old friends would accuse him of sacrificing his great transcendent art for the more temporal fame that Elizabeth promised, of sloughing off his mantle as heir to Olivier for a chance to become a fabulously privileged Hollywood star. Yet while it was true that Elizabeth "redrew the maps of his ambition," as Burton biographer Melvyn Bragg admitted, the fame that Richard truly prized was the world of Dylan Thomas and Evelyn Waugh, great writing and great performances. "Movie fame was dandy," Bragg wrote, "but not in the same league."

In the end, Richard latched onto Elizabeth for far more personal reasons. For a man whom director Mike Nichols described as "temperamentally spectacular," Elizabeth proved to be his one-of-a-kind match, living a life as large as any great character from literature or the stage. And, like Burton, she was also a bit of a freak: so famous, so beautiful, so exceptional, that she lived her life mostly apart from the rest of the world, just as Richard had done ever since Philip Burton had pulled him out of the coal mines and declared him a prodigy and the greats of the British theater had all dropped to their knees before him. "I have this knack," Richard famously, and magnificently, understated to Anthony Quayle. And so the union of Taylor and Burton might have been foretold. "They were two fatally glamorous people," said Mike Nichols, "who became each other's lives."

Looking up into Richard's magnetic eyes as they filmed one of the last scenes for *Cleopatra*, Elizabeth was every bit as transfixed with her costar as he was with her. Lust was the first lure between these two extraordinarily sexual beings. "Richard is a very sexy man," Elizabeth told one reporter. "He's got that sort of jungle essence . . . When we look at each other, it's like our eyes have fingers and they grab ahold." But then lust metamorphosed into love, though the process by which it did so mystified even the lovers themselves. "There's no way of encapsulating it," Elizabeth said. "It would be like trying to describe a sunset. It's ever changing but it's beautiful. It's too large to make a cliché of it. I don't know how to explain it but it's the most wonderful thing that's ever happened to me. Each day is better than the last day."

"It was so intense," Elizabeth said later of falling in love with Richard. "There is something very mystic about all Welsh people. And that sense of poetry and wildness was where I had always wanted to be. I had wanted to be free, running in the rain on the grass, and just nothing to tether me. I just wanted to go."

Like Mike Todd, what Richard offered was a sense of liberation—from the daily grind of moviemaking, from studio control, from the strictures that had dictated how she must behave in the public eye. With the money and notoriety that *Cleopatra* had brought them, Richard and Elizabeth were now rich enough and famous enough to chart their own course. And with Richard at her side, Elizabeth had achieved her holy grail: She was answerable to no one—except, as she enjoyed pointing out, to Richard himself.

There was more about Burton that recalled Todd. His comfort with the many homosexuals in the world of theater and film made him extremely attractive to Elizabeth, whose entourage remained largely gay. And like Todd, Richard was her equal, even if their fame derived from different sources. He might not have yet made it big as a movie star, but he had enjoyed one megahit, *The Robe,* as well as the *succès d'estime* in 1958 with *Look Back in Anger,* one of the first pictures of the British New Wave. But it was the soon-to-be-released World War II epic, *The Longest Day,* filmed shortly before *Cleopatra,* that everyone expected would ratchet up Burton's box-office clout—just in time for his Marc Antony to stride across the world's screens.

For Elizabeth, Richard's most appealing quality was no doubt his decided lack of awe. While Eddie Fisher had spent his days in constant solicitude, Richard, once more like Todd, enjoyed taking good-natured potshots at her in the press. "Elizabeth is a pretty girl," he told Kenneth Tynan, "but she has a double chin and an overdeveloped chest and she's rather short in the leg. So I can hardly describe her as the most beautiful creature I've ever seen." Elizabeth, as always, was ready with a comeback. Referring to her paramour's famous disinterest in attending the theater, she said: "Richard has enormous taste and discretion. He can't stand to watch any other actor but himself."

They bickered, they bantered, they carried on. They snuck off to the Italian coast or partied at their respective homes in Switzerland. Burton proved to be a turning point in Elizabeth's life. For the first time, she was choosing a husband entirely for love, without any professional consideration. This was significant. The choice of every preceding husband, no matter how much passion was involved, had also made sound sense in terms of her career. And while the affair with Burton was looking more and more as if it might actually enhance her stardom—all those paparazzi had made her even more famous than Jackie Kennedy—certainly no one in the middle part of 1962 had any assurance that this would be the case. In fact, there was considerable fear that it might just do the opposite.

Elizabeth, either too much in love or more trusting of the public's response than those around her, paid no attention to such grumblings. But Richard was torn. Despite the euphoria for his Dulcis Imperatrix, his "black moods," as his friends called his depressive episodes, had not disappeared. Some felt, in fact, that his drinking changed after Le Scandale, that it became an escape from the guilt over leaving his family, especially little Jessica, who had by now been diagnosed as autistic. "I generally shut Jess out of my mind," Richard wrote heartbreakingly in his diary, "but sometimes she enters with staggering agony." The only thing that he could do, he wrote, was to "make her rich." And so he did.

But Richard Burton had always had his black moods, what he called his *hiraeth*, a Welsh word best translated as a longing for unnamable things. Elizabeth was all too aware of these moods. "He is a snakepit of ramifications," she admitted. "I tell him, if a frontal lobotomy were performed on his skull, out would fly snakes, frogs, worms, tadpoles, bats . . ." Asked by a reporter if there wasn't "anything better" in Burton's brain, she acknowledged: "Oh, perhaps a grasshopper would leap out at last, with a slim volume of Shakespeare—it would have to be the sonnets—tucked under his arm."

For Richard, the conflict in his mind was essentially existential, the curse of a simple man plucked from humble origins and given to greatness. A deep river of insecurity ran within him. He would tell the producer Ernest Lehman that he believed "all great art comes from people who are either ugly or have a terrible inferiority complex." Lehman was left to wonder how Burton classified himself in that argument. His *hiraeth* could disturb his sleep.

"I sometimes wake up in a cold sweat and I say to myself, 'What's going to happen to me?'" he admitted to Kenneth Tynan. "It's not the fear of death—it's the fear of dying and being forgotten, of being nothing, that keeps me awake."

For the moment, he found distraction from such fears in the embrace of Elizabeth, the most voracious lover he had ever known. As the world watched, fascinated and scandalized, the couple took up residence together in Rex Harrison's villa in Portofino. Sybil Burton, in her only recorded remarks about the affair, said, "This was so that Richard, who was still married to me at the time, should have some place to shelter from the pursuit of Elizabeth and him by the press." According to Sybil, Harrison's wife, Rachel Roberts, always felt "very bad" that her house was "lent to 'that man and his woman' who had broken up my marriage." But while Sybil may have been touched by her friend's loyalty, fewer and fewer people seemed to share Roberts's reservations about the romance. As the spring of 1962 rolled on, no two people in the world were more watched, more envied, or more idolized than "Liz and Dick." Even if no one could predict how their story was going to end, all agreed that it would be one for the ages.

Under the Porta San Sebastiano Mike Nichols whizzed in his little rental car, heading out of the city and into the rolling green of the Roman countryside. He drove along the dusty route of the Appian Way unpursued and unnoticed. He might be the current toast of Broadway, having exploded onto the scene a couple of years earlier with his brilliant comedy improv act with his partner, Elaine May, but his face was not internationally known. No paparazzi chased him the way they did his pal Rich Burton, whom Nichols had met when they were on Broadway at the same time: *Camelot* had played just a block away from *An Evening with Mike Nichols and Elaine May*. After their final curtains, Nichols and Burton had often met for a few drinks, sometimes for more than a few. They became chums. And now, learning that Mike was in Rome, Rich had rung him to ask a favor. He was away and couldn't see him, but would

Nichols be so kind as to take Elizabeth out for an excursion? She was trapped in the house by the paparazzi, Burton said, and was going a bit stir-crazy.

"Take Elizabeth Taylor out for a day?" Nichols recalled. "I jumped at the chance!"

Nichols was a trendsetter. He and May were in the process of rewriting the rules of acting and performance. The pair had helped found an improvisational theater group at the University of Chicago that eventually became the famed Second City company. Then they moved on to television and Broadway, leaving audiences and critics alike in stitches with their fast-paced, largely ad-libbed routines. But what Nichols really hankered to do was direct, both for the stage and the screen. "I want to direct in motion pictures most of all," he told a reporter, "but I figure that I must learn a whole [new] technique or the whole machine can roll over you."

Certainly few people knew those techniques or that machine better than Elizabeth Taylor. And while that's not why Nichols took her out that day in the spring of 1962, the business of movie-making and the idiosyncrasies of fame would inform the conversation they had. Telling Elizabeth to put on a kerchief and sneak out the back door, Nichols met her in his car, unrecognized by the paparazzi, and spirited her off to Villa d'Este in Tivoli. There, strolling anonymously among the terraced gardens and famous fountains of the sixteenth-century villa built for the son of Lucrezia Borgia, Elizabeth opened up to Nichols about her life. She talked about the scandal, about her fears of hurting Sybil and drawing the wrath of the world once again. She talked about falling in love with Richard, and the long, long journey that had taken her from child star to this place of exalted worldwide fame. Nichols was awestruck by her candor. "She never had a life of her own," he said. "Every movement had always been public. But where most people would have developed a shell, for some reason she didn't. She was extraordinary.

"She said a startling thing to me one time during those days in Rome," Nichols continued, "when we were at some horse show in the middle of the city and everyone was walking past her to stare at her. I asked her if it was ever a pain in the ass being so beautiful. And she looked at me and said, 'I can't wait for it to go.'"

Their visits ended with Nichols determined that one day he would work with this remarkable woman. On her part, Elizabeth was resigned to further hassles from the press and public—at least until that blessed day when she could finally put *Cleopatra* in the can. After nearly two years, it looked as if her long ordeal might soon be coming to an end. But several big scenes were still to be shot, including the one where Cleopatra enters Rome on top of a thirty-foot-high Sphinx drawn by three hundred slaves. In the film, it is the moment of Cleopatra's big gamble. If the Romans accept her, she has won. If they do not, she might lose Caesar, and her life. Elizabeth felt that the stakes were just as high for her.

Walter Wanger described her as "nervous and tense" when she was preparing for the scene. For the first time since the scandal had broken, she would be facing seven thousand extras—Roman citizens who had surely heard the Vatican condemnations. Would they jeer her? Would they make obscene gestures? Holding her chin high, Elizabeth strode out in front of the crowd. And to everyone's great surprise, the applause that greeted her was far more than anything Mankiewicz had called for as the director. "Leez, Leez!" the extras chanted. *"Baci, baci!"* ("Kisses, kisses!") Walter Wanger witnessed the "sense of relief" that flooded through Elizabeth's body as a sea of "slave girls, handmaidens, senators, guards, and thousands of others applauded her—personally."

It was a very different public response this time to a very similar scandal. The groundswell of outrage that had occurred in 1958 did not happen again. Fewer letters of indignation flowed in to Hedda Hopper, despite the columnist's best attempts to whip up public sentiment against the lovers, and hardly anyone wrote irate letters to the newspapers.

Of course, the religious conservative base—the same one that had rallied against Elizabeth playing Mary Magdalene—was just as offended as ever. Congresswoman Blitch's mail ran fifty-to-one against Elizabeth, encouraging her to call for a "Congressional investigation of the most serious kind" into the "motion picture industry's lack of sensitivity of good taste and high moral values." But no one was listening. Blitch retired that fall, and the Congress that was elected in November was among the most liberal delegations ever sent to Washington, with little interest in policing the lives of entertainers. When one member, Rep. Michael Feighan (D-Ohio), did attempt to pick up the baton from Blitch by calling for the revocation of Burton's visa, he was quickly slapped down by the U.S. State Department, which concluded that there was nothing that made Burton ineligible to enter the United States. Editorials chided Feighan for reaching "new heights of ridiculosity." In a stark break from the past, much of the press now believed that "people are not concerned with Hollywood morals" when so many other, more pressing issues existed.

The world was changing rapidly. In June 1962 Stanley Kubrick's film of Vladimir Nabokov's sexually charged novel *Lolita* debuted to strong box office. HOW DID THEY EVER MAKE A MOVIE OF LOLITA? read the film's posters, a coy wink at the evolution in cultural mores. On Broadway, Edward Albee's profanity-laden *Who's Afraid of Virginia Woolf?* opened to ecstatic reviews. The long-banned Henry Miller novel *Tropic of Cancer* was finally published in the United States, prompting legal reconsiderations of the definition of obscenity. When photographs of a topless Jayne Mansfield from the film *Promises! Promises!* were published in *Playboy*, publisher Hugh Hefner was arrested, only to be acquitted at his trial, proving just how in flux public sentiment really was.

Elizabeth herself pushed the envelope when she allowed Hefner to publish nude photographs that Roddy McDowall had taken of her on the set of *Cleopatra*. No matter that the photos were tastefully discreet—no nipples or genitals—the very inclusion of a star of Elizabeth's magnitude in a periodical like *Playboy* enflamed moralists across the country. Yet the average fan-magazine reader seemed more titillated than affronted. "Is she modern or immoral?"

Photoplay asked. The answer, given the way Elizabeth was increasingly being portrayed, seemed to be the former.

Indeed, nowhere was the change in the public mood better illustrated than in the way the fan magazines covered the Taylor-Burton affair. To be sure, sensationalism still ruled, but censure and condemnation not so much. THE FINAL ACT THAT SHOOK THE WORLD was showcased in *Modern Screen* with a two-page telephoto spread of Elizabeth and Richard stretched out kissing in bathing suits. In the accompanying story, Elizabeth comes across not as the black-hearted home wrecker of four years earlier but as a fascinating inamorata determined to marry the man she loves.

To the editors' surprise, this new persona delighted readers instead of driving them away. At the height of Le Scandale, *Photoplay* crowned Elizabeth, along with Jackie Kennedy, as one of "America's 2 Queens." Burton benefited, too. Eddie Fisher had been turned into a cad in the public's mind, but Burton was hailed as a sex god. In *Modern Screen*, Radie Harris revealed WHY WOMEN CAN'T RESIST RICHARD BURTON: a "knock 'em between the eyes kind of animal magnetism that makes little girls sigh, 'Thank heaven for little boys who grow up to be big little boys like Richard Burton.'"

Editorial attacks still occurred, but with Helen Gurley Brown's *Sex and the Single Girl* dominating the bestseller lists, they seemed relics of a different era. A new relationship between celebrities, the press, and the public was developing. Tabloids like the *New York Daily News,* which depended on front-page sensationalism, grasped the change quicker and better than most others. While the editorial page might still regurgitate the standard line that the affair in Rome was doing "no good" for the movie industry, the paper also acknowledged the "interesting newspaper copy" the story of "Liz and Dick" had yielded, including the "intriguing telescopic-lens photographs which *The News* has been pleased to present to its fascinated (we hope) readers."

This was the point. Those up-close pictures and stories offered a more uncensored glimpse of celebrity lives than ever before, which in turn allowed the public to form its own opinions about its heroes and heroines without the mediating intervention of publicists or press agents. Such a formula had been unthinkable in the old days; such transparency had been considered fatal to careers. Conventional wisdom had held that such reporting could never work to a star's benefit. Elizabeth Taylor turned that thinking upside down. The more the public was let in on her life, the more it worshipped her.

With celebrity coverage no longer consigned only to fan magazines and gossip columns and now spilling across newspapers, radio, and television, Elizabeth's fans were able to track her every movement, her every nightclub date, her every purchase of Dior furs and diamond wristwatches. Consequently, she became less the shadowy black widow that *Photoplay* had fabricated in 1958 and more like an old familiar—albeit flashy and fabulous—friend. By now people expected Elizabeth Taylor to live like the sexy nymphs of *Cat on a Hot Tin Roof* and *Butterfield 8*. No one but the most rigidly puritanical took offense at her affair with Burton. No one but the most rigidly puritanical would ever turn on Elizabeth Taylor again.

And yet this new paradigm was due as much to the woman herself as it was to any shift in public sentiment or standards of press coverage. Elizabeth's decision not to hide, not to eat humble pie, had paid off. This time there was no skulking around in the back of Roddy's car to avoid the press. Instead, gambling that the world had moved on, she had stepped out unapologetically with Burton on her arm. "If part of the world, unfortunately, has some kind of nasty opinion, maybe it's only to be expected," she said candidly. "But, to me, being honest is all a part of being what one is. I don't try to give any illusion, or delusion, at all. It isn't that I don't care. But what I am is my own business."

Her gamble proved on the money. The public did not turn on her. In fact, her honesty and her sheer likability ensured her continued success. The press, so long accustomed to charades and half-truths, found fresh respect for her. After all, this was a new generation of the fourth estate. Conservative mavens like Hedda and Louella and Walter Winchell were no longer calling the shots. The most influential entertainment writers were increasingly younger and more liberal, people like Pauline Kael and Andrew Sarris and Liz Smith and Rex Reed—the same generation who were chronicling the revolutionary impact of the burgeoning youth culture. Writers like these were far more apt to extol an independent-thinking woman like Elizabeth Taylor than they were to chastise her, a fact that did not go unnoticed by the old guard. "The press has seemed determined to make a heroine out of Elizabeth Taylor," complained one woman in a letter to Iris Blitch, citing a recent issue of *Look* magazine that had praised "her to the skies." But to a new way of thinking, a celebrity who eschewed spin and studio trickery was worth the veneration. She was a heroine indeed.

This was a radically new dynamic. For a star to speak so plainly was unprecedented. "To tell you the truth," Elizabeth told one reporter at the height of the affair with Burton, "I haven't kept track of my so-called 'public image.' I know that, in the American press, I must get *shticklech*, which is a good Jewish word for needles right below the heart . . . [But] why get a heart attack over [such press]? I suppose [the public] rather regards me as a scarlet woman. I guess I seem so scarlet I'm almost purple." She seemed to truly enjoy flouting convention. One magazine showed her sprawled out on a couch drinking champagne with Richard, asking in the caption below: "So what do the papers say about us now?"

Her nonchalance was refreshing—yet how would it all play at the box office? That was still the unanswered question. In June the *New York Times* reported that Fox had launched a "quiet study" to test Elizabeth's "box-office status" in the wake of Le Scandale. Apparently in cooperation with the studios that had produced them, a number of Elizabeth's old pictures were rereleased, with Fox reportedly keeping a close eye on how well they performed. (*Suddenly, Last Summer,* for example, played at New York's Murray Hill Theatre from May 23 to 28.) Fox, however, denied that the pictures had been reissued as any kind of test, but instead as a straightforward means "to garner extra dollars at a time when Miss Taylor's name is before the public via daily headlines."

For once a studio denial seems more believable than the story being denied. Surely Fox knew the advantages of those daily headlines; Elizabeth and Richard had become what Melvyn Bragg called "a self-contained media event," providing the studio with "unpurchasable publicity." Even Hedda Hopper expected the headlines were only going to help *Cleopatra* in the end: "The public wonders if the latest scandal will hurt the picture. Well, the day headlines popped about the Fisher separation, people lined up at the corner of Hollywood and Vine to buy papers. Scandal is not always a drawback."

And yet the lore of *Cleopatra* has always held that Fox officials were opposed to the Taylor-Burton affair. Previously unreleased court depositions do provide some evidence of that view, with Elizabeth admitting that Wanger had told her that Skouras was concerned about "a wave of public opinion ... being developed by reason of [her] conduct." Yet, significantly, the depositions also make clear that no one ever requested that she and Burton end the affair. In fact, Wanger's expressed opinion on the relationship was apparently so innocuous that Elizabeth "forgot about it two minutes after he had given it." Later, it would be in Fox's interest to claim that the studio had opposed the affair; but most of the execs were probably in agreement with Darryl Zanuck, soon to replace Skouras at the helm, who candidly admitted: "I think the Taylor-Burton association is quite constructive for our organization."

On July 14, 1962, after two tumultuous years, Elizabeth finally completed her work in *Cleopatra*. "I told you we would make it, darling," she said to Richard, squeezing his hand. Mankiewicz and his camera crew headed off to Egypt for a few final location shots, then hunkered down in the editing room with thousands of feet of raw footage. Meanwhile, eager fans besieged Fox with requests for advance tickets, offering to pay up to twenty dollars a pop. And Elizabeth and Richard were bombarded with dozens of offers for new film roles, sometimes apart but more often together. There were no more worries about Elizabeth Taylor's bankability.

Life magazine put her on the cover naked (cropped at the shoulders) and immediately sold out at newsstands. Inside, Elizabeth was quoted dramatically: "I have paid and Richard has paid through both of our hearts and our guts. Our brains have bled." But there was no bitterness in her voice, only triumph. "I have learned," she said, "that there's no deodorant like success."

Seventy-seven-year-old Hedda Hopper, stiff with arthritis as she made her way down the airplane steps, was not giving up without one last fight.

On tour to promote her memoir, *The Whole Truth and Nothing But*, Hedda was frequently asked to comment about "Liz and Dick." On this day she paused as she stepped onto the tarmac, turning her sharp features in the direction of the questioner and saying, "They are destroying themselves utterly." Then she adjusted her crazy Eiffel Tower hat and walked with a slightly shaky gait to her waiting limousine.

Her book had quite a bit more to say about the pair. Le Scandale had broken just as the memoir was going to press so Doubleday had asked for some quick updates. Only too glad to comply, Hedda added considerable material about Elizabeth to the front of the book. She seems to have had a rather specific editorial motive. Since she'd been unable to rally the masses this time, Hedda had settled on another tack. She went after the entire Elizabeth Taylor mystique, suggesting that it wasn't worth the newsprint it had been printed on—even though she herself had done much of the printing.

In the first fifteen pages of her book, Hedda willfully exposed Sara's relentless ambition, portrayed Mike Todd as conniving, rehashed the wrongs done to poor little Debbie, and finally divulged what Elizabeth had said to her after Todd's death ("What do you expect me to do? *Sleep alone?*"). Most incendiary of all, however, was her revelation of the scoop she'd sat on back in 1952: that she believed Michael Wilding to be gay and that she had warned Elizabeth against the marriage. *The Whole Truth and Nothing But* amounted to an all-out broadside against Elizabeth. If one thing didn't stick, Hedda seemed to be hoping, then maybe something else would.

The book came out in November 1962 and spent several months on the bestseller lists in early 1963. Elizabeth had no comment about any of it. But Wilding was furious. Hedda could never understand why; what she'd written about him was "just a little stinking bit," she believed. But, in fact, until the tabloids made "outing" a common tactic two decades later, Hedda's strike against Wilding was the most explicit example of gay baiting in Hollywood history. It was also utterly mean-spirited and thoroughly extraneous. Hedda had no beef with Wilding. He was simply a means to "get" Elizabeth. Wilding decided to get Hedda instead. On April 4, 1963, he blindsided her and her publisher with an unexpected libel suit for $3 million.

Why the suit was unexpected is difficult to comprehend. Hopper's editor at Doubleday, the usually astute Kenneth McCormick, had never asked a lawyer to sign off on the material. Another editor, Margaret Cousins, told Hedda, "I would never have let that pass." But pass it had—into several thousand copies that were now causing cash registers to jingle all across the country. Quite understandably, Wilding feared the effect the book might have on the meager career that he still maintained. In his suit, he charged that Hedda had made her statements in "a reckless and wanton disregard of his rights and feelings with intent to injure his feelings." Of course, Wilding's feelings were the furthest thing from Hedda's mind; he was merely collateral damage in her campaign to punish his ex-wife. Still, the book had subjected him to "hatred, contempt, ridicule and humiliation, and was injurious to his reputation as an actor and entertainer." Wilding vowed to friends: "I'm going to fight this battle and I'm going to win."

He may have had some encouragement in that fight. "Hedda

always believed that Liz Taylor was behind Wilding, urging him along," said Hopper legman Robert Shaw. After all, the former spouses had remained friendly, and Wilding enjoyed a good, if often distant, relationship with his two sons. Friends agreed that Elizabeth was infuriated by Hedda's revelations. "She was very protective in some ways of [Wilding]," said one person close to her. "She would have seen this incident for what it was, as an attack on her, and her loyalty to [Wilding] would have rushed to the forefront."

But Hedda dug in her heels, refusing to settle. "She stood by what she had written," said Shaw. "She believed Wilding was a homosexual and figured it would be easy to prove it." She had plenty of connections in the gay world; that's how she'd heard the story in the first place. But despite dispatching an army of assistants to comb for "evidence" in both Hollywood and London, she discovered to her mounting dismay that the first loyalty of her gay friends was not to her but to one another. "No one was willing to testify that Wilding was gay and therefore ruin his career," Shaw said. "If they did that, who's to say somebody else might not do it to them someday?"

In desperation Hedda turned to an unlikely ally: Eddie Fisher. The man whose career she'd played a large part in destroying answered his telephone one day to hear her shrill voice on the other end of the line. "I wanted to hang up," Eddie said. But Hedda invited him over to her house, where she gushed all over him, telling him what a great singer he was and hinting that she could help him make a comeback. But Eddie was wary; he was in the midst of his own legal problems, haggling with Elizabeth over custody of Maria and the financial terms of their upcoming divorce. Hedda hoped that this might make him eager to come over to her side, but Eddie just stared at her blankly when she revealed the real reason she'd called. "I have no idea whether Michael Wilding is a homosexual," he said. Coldly, Hedda told him he could leave. There was no more talk of comebacks.

But Wilding was taking no chances. As his roles dwindled to a couple of television episodes on *Burke's Law* and *The Alfred*

Hitchcock Hour, he announced that he was giving up acting to become a talent agent with the Hugh French Agency. (Among the
clients he'd pick up was Richard Burton—evidence of a continuing close association with his ex-wife during the legal battle with
Hedda.) Bracing himself for a trial, which he no doubt dreaded,
Wilding married the actress Margaret Leighton. His lawyer, Ben
F. Goldman Jr., continued pressing Hedda to settle. They were asking for a monetary figure as well as a public apology. But Hedda
wasn't ready to surrender.

"She was at the end of her career, and she knew it," said Shaw.
"Hollywood had sort of passed her by at this point. So it was her
reputation she was fighting for now. She kept hoping she'd find
someone who'd give her the evidence that she needed, to prove she
hadn't made it all up. If that happened, she could show she was
still relevant. But fewer people seemed to think of her that way
anymore."

There was one person who hadn't completely written Hedda
off yet. As the trial date approached, a memo in her papers reveals that a call came in from Sara Taylor. "All very chatty and
friendly," Hedda's secretary wrote. Sara insisted that it had been
Elizabeth's idea to call, just as a courtesy to update the columnist
about the wonderful family holiday they'd all celebrated. Elizabeth
and Richard had brought Elizabeth's four children, and Howard
Taylor came with his wife and five children. Sara said Elizabeth
had prodded her: "Don't forget, you promised to call Hedda."

It seems extremely unlikely that Elizabeth gave a whit about
Hedda at this point, except perhaps to curse her for the troubles
she'd caused Wilding. A far more likely scenario is that Sara was
still trying to facilitate her daughter's career, hoping to assuage
Hedda's wounded feelings by sharing a story of happy family to-
getherness. Her daughter's embrace of a new, poststudio world order wasn't for Sara; Mrs. Taylor proceeded as if Hedda still wielded
the kind of power she had back in the days of Louis B. Mayer. Her
efforts paid off; Hedda wrote a glowing account of the family's
holiday celebrations and described Elizabeth as feeling sentimen-

tal about their old friendship. "I wish we could be friends again as we used to be," she quoted Elizabeth as saying about her. No doubt that was a lot of malarkey given to her by Sara. But Hedda, pathetically aware of her increasing irrelevancy, wanted very much to believe that it was true.

Currying favor with the Taylors did no good. Three weeks before the trial was to start, a dispirited Hedda finally agreed to settle with Wilding. None of her sources had agreed to back her up. Wilding would receive $100,000. But Hedda steadfastly refused to apologize. Attorney Goldman put the best face on the situation by saying that "the settlement in itself is an apology" and a "complete vindication" of Wilding.

Whether it was or not, Hedda was wiped out. "The suit is settled, but at what a cost!" she wrote to a friend. She'd been counting on her memoir to cushion her retirement, but now, she said bitterly, the roughly $110,000 she'd made (minus $26,500 to her coauthor) would go to "Wilding and his Jew lawyer." Although it seems unbelievable for someone who made her living as a gossip columnist, she didn't have any libel insurance. And despite Doubleday's agreeing to pay half of the settlement, their lawyer had charged Hedda $12,800 on top of her own legal fees of $23,000. "So, you see," she wrote, "I get nothing." She was particularly aggrieved by those Hollywood gays who hadn't come forward to help her out and who, in fact, seemed to take delight in her fall from grace. She singled out *Hollywood Reporter* columnist Mike Connolly—"one of the boys," she wrote sarcastically. "It is sort of precious, isn't it? I don't believe [Connolly] cared much about Wilding, but Mr. Wilding has the last laugh. I hope he will enjoy it."

As Hedda declined, Elizabeth triumphed. She and Richard flitted around Europe, defying traditional values as the most famous unmarried, cohabitating couple in the world. Producer Anatole de Grunwald eagerly snatched them up to be part of his all-star film *The V.I.P.s*, shot in London in December 1962. It was an original Terence Rattigan script about a group of stranded airline passengers whose lives are changed by the unexpected delay. Directed by Anthony Asquith, the picture was rushed out to theaters to capitalize on the still-bubbling interest in the Taylor-Burton affair. Elizabeth was particularly pleased that *The V.I.P.s* was an MGM picture. No longer a contract player forced to accept the studio's terms, she was now a freelancer who commanded $1 million plus 10 percent of the gross. It was "good revenge," she said, for the paltry salary they'd paid her on *Butterfield 8*. "Even I wouldn't have the audacity to ask for more," she said.

Early in 1963 word came that Fox needed her back for a couple of linking shots on *Cleopatra*. For $50,000, she once again donned Egyptian eye makeup and emoted for half a minute, reacting to the Battle of Actium. Later, sitting at the "most conspicuous table" in the cocktail lounge of London's fashionable Dorchester Hotel, she laughed about it with a reporter. "Do you think it will ever be finished?" she asked, referring to *Cleopatra*. "Are the stockholders going to scream and haul it back for a happy ending when they finally see it?"

Looking more curvy than ever—busybodies called her "plump" —and wearing a lavender sweater and slacks, Elizabeth was gesturing dramatically and speaking in a loud voice. Anyone who came in through the swinging doors that led out onto Park Lane would have spotted her immediately—and Burton, too, sitting there in his Marc Antony makeup, having just finished his own last few shots. They were drinking and laughing and carrying on, lighthearted and carefree. The world was theirs. Richard had finally asked Sybil for a divorce. Elizabeth couldn't have been happier.

The same couldn't be said of Joe Mankiewicz. Those stockholders *were* screaming. The previous year Fox had posted a $40 million loss, with *Cleopatra*'s astronomical expenses much of the reason. Skouras, forced to resign as president, had been replaced at the top by former Fox chief Darryl Zanuck, who'd immediately clashed with Mankiewicz. With so much footage, the director had decided to make two two-and-a-half-hour movies, the first one focusing on Cleopatra and Caesar (Rex Harrison), the second on Cleopatra and Antony. Zanuck, however, would have none of it.

"The studio didn't have enough money to make a cartoon at this point," Tom Mankiewicz said. "Zanuck's rationale was: What if these two people [Taylor and Burton] fell out of love between now and the second half? Who'd come to see the picture then?"

Zanuck's goal, understandably, was to get the picture out as soon as possible, while the affair between its two principals was still hot. He was determined that *Cleopatra* not be tagged as a four-hour history lesson, which would have consigned it to the art houses. It had to be a big, sexy, romantic spectacle—the only way it might possibly pay for itself and lift the studio out of the red. And so began what Mankiewicz called the "butchery" of the picture, but what Zanuck would have described as a studio-saving venture. Everything was reshaped and reorganized to centralize the love story between Antony and Cleopatra. When Mankiewicz protested the cuts, he was fired.

Elizabeth was outraged. "Mr. Mankiewicz took *Cleopatra* over when it was nothing—when it was rubbish—and he made something out of it," she told the press. But the director's vision was obliterated in this new version, sliced down from five hours to four. On Zanuck's express order, the whole package, including publicity, was geared to capitalize on Le Scandale. Many of the ads didn't even bother to use the film's title or the stars' names. They simply featured Taylor and Burton in a sexy clinch. But the studio wasn't finished tinkering. After the New York premiere in June 1963, another twenty-one minutes were cut from the film. Elizabeth refused to see the truncated picture, turning her back on an enterprise that had consumed two long years of her life.

Most critics shared her low opinion of the film, and they weren't too impressed with her performance either. "To look at, she is every inch 'a morsel for a monarch,'" observed *Time* magazine, quoting Shakespeare. "But . . . when she plays Cleopatra as a political animal she screeches like a ward heeler's wife at a block party." Indeed, while she's quite good in the passionate scenes—Maggie the Cat in ancient Egypt—when she starts spouting dialogue about the politics of the classical world, she sounds absolutely absurd. Critics derided her reading of such lines as "Did you know that Apollodorus would kill Pothinus?" There was a sense that she'd memorized the names phonetically with no clear idea of what she was talking about. She gave the appearance of a pretty 1960s teenager, complete with flip hairdo, playing dress up as an ancient queen.

Bosley Crowther in the *New York Times* was one of the few voices of praise, calling Elizabeth's Cleopatra "a woman of force and dignity" and the picture itself "brilliant, moving and satisfying." But far more reviewers seemed to agree with Peter Baker in *Films and Filming,* who, despite how much the picture had cost, thought *Cleopatra* never rose above the level of a low-budget "Italian Hercules spectacular."

And yet it was an enormous hit. That, too, is a fact that's been obscured by the legend around the film that has seeped into the public consciousness: that *Cleopatra* was a box-office disaster. But, in truth, with full domestic earnings of $15.7 million, *Cleopatra* was the top-grossing film of 1963; after all those headlines and magazine covers of "Liz and Dick," how could it have been otherwise? *Cleopatra* outgrossed the top film of 1960, *Spartacus,* by $2 million, and beat the second top-grossing picture of the current year (Burton's other starring vehicle, *The Longest Day*) by $3 million. Only a handful of pictures (including *Around the World in Eighty Days*) had ever made more money; *Cleopatra* was by far the biggest grossing picture Elizabeth had ever made. The problem, of course, was that it had cost somewhere around $40 million to produce, so $15.7 million was nowhere near what was needed to turn a profit. Fox was banking on an extraordinarily long run over several years, in which the film might gross, at least according to their estimates, over $200 million.

No matter the studio's problems, Elizabeth was a clear winner. With ten cents of every dollar earmarked for her, that meant an additional million and a half by the end of the year. And no matter what the critics thought, the public loved the picture. One opinion poll asked those who had seen *Cleopatra* to rate it: 53 percent called the film "excellent," 29 percent called it "good," and only 18 percent considered it "fair" or "poor." Once again, public hostility—or the presumption of it—hadn't taken a dime. Elizabeth Taylor was at the height of her fame and power. No star had ever been as big.

An orange fingernail moon hung low over Banderas Bay, one of the deepest, widest, and bluest bays in the world. From the sprawling white-brick-and-stucco house perched amid the vine-hung foothills rising up from the bay, gas lamps cast a soft golden light onto the papaya trees and the creeping red bougainvillea. The cliff-hanging house with its six bedrooms, six baths, and gleaming white-tiled floors was named Casa Kimberley after a previous owner, but from October 1963 forward, it would be known as the place where Elizabeth Taylor and Richard Burton lived when they were the most notorious unmarried lovers in the world.

"Here on the lazy west coast of Mexico," one reporter wrote, "the couple who fell in love on the Rome set of *Cleopatra*—despite prior commitments—are finding a measure of tropical solitude some nineteen months (and no divorces) later." Their notoriety would put the obscure little fishing village of Puerto Vallarta on the map.

Watching from a chaise lounge as Richard ran lines with John Huston—rehearsing for the film *The Night of the Iguana*—Elizabeth was aglow. She adored the peace and lush exotic beauty of Puerto Vallarta. "I can live here," she had told Burton soon after they'd arrived, and so Casa Kimberley had become a little love gift. From their terrace, Elizabeth could look down onto the village where men in wide sombreros rode burros over the cobblestone streets. Just past the house she could see the belfry of the village church, modeled after the crown of the Empress Carlota, and beyond that the moonlit bay, which was close enough that the fierce surf could be heard all through the night. Colorful moths fluttered in through the glassless windows while spirited little geckos ran across the beams overhead. Elizabeth was awakened in the morning by bright green macaws announcing the first rays of the sun reflecting against the red tiles of the roof. She was in heaven.

After the tumult she'd fled, Puerto Vallarta offered a welcome sanctuary. Stopping in Montreal and Toronto on their way from Europe to Mexico, "Liz and Dick" were greeted by a crush of fans and reporters so enthusiastic that Dick Hanley and Jim Benton, Richard's secretary, had to form a protective shield around them as they moved from the plane to the limousine. Richard grabbed a terrified six-year-old Liza Todd and held her above his head to keep her away from the flashing cameras and clutching hands. The Burtons hired a bodyguard for the first time, an ex-boxer named Bobby LaSalle, who, when he wasn't posted at the doorway of Casa Kimberley swatting away mosquitoes, spent his time playing endless games of Ping-Pong with Elizabeth.

The V.I.P.s was a hit; as Elizabeth and Richard were flying down to Mexico, people were flocking to theaters to see them together in modern dress. The film was fluff, but very attractive and entertaining fluff, with Elizabeth playing a wife toying with the idea of leaving her husband (played by Richard) for a playboy lover (played by Louis Jourdan)—a rather ironic twist that audiences loved. They also adored the jewels and furs that Elizabeth wore in the film. With its sparkling cast—Margaret Rutherford would win an Oscar as the eccentric, scene-stealing Duchess of Brighton—*The V.I.P.s* proved that MGM, even in its decline, could still turn out glossy crowd-pleasers.

Puerto Vallarta was far, far away, however, from the world of furs and jewels. In the morning, standing in front of her mirror, Elizabeth tied her hair back and slipped into a plain white gauzy dress. The air was humid and the temperature was edging into the nineties. Packing some cold fried chicken and a bottle of tequila into a basket, she followed Burton down to the bay, where they stepped barefoot through the frothy surf to board the yacht that Elizabeth had insisted upon. Michael Wilding, as Burton's agent, had arranged for the yacht, though it may also have been a bit of a thank-you to Elizabeth for her support in the battle against Hedda. Off through the blue waters the yacht sailed, slicing a path across the bay. Their destination was the isolated cove of Mismaloya, south of the village, a den of lizards and insects where *Night of the Iguana* was being filmed. There were no roads, no phones, no restaurants, no bars. That's why Elizabeth had brought the chicken and the tequila. From the yacht she leapt onto a floating pier, where she and Burton had to wait until the waves brought them closer to shore. Then, basket over her arm, she began the long ascent up the side of the cliff with Burton behind her, climbing the 134 earthen steps to the top where Huston had built his sets.

Elizabeth had experience filming in remote locations. And, just as in Marfa, Texas, the cast and crew drank a lot to pass the time. Burton quickly finished a case of beer, then started in on the tequila. So did everyone else, including Elizabeth. In addition, they discovered a "paralyzingly potent" local agave liquor called raicilla that Richard said he could feel move into each individual intestine. "That's because they left the cactus needles in it," Huston said.

The drinking was fun and convivial; Huston was pleased with the way his cast got along. Some had predicted antagonism between Elizabeth and Ava Gardner, one of Burton's three romantic costars (who also included Deborah Kerr and Sue Lyon, the nymphet from *Lolita*). But the two glamorous graduates of the old studio system adored each other, with Elizabeth diverting the press away from Ava so that she could concentrate on her role. "She's fearless," Gardner said gratefully as Elizabeth posed and waved and threw kisses at the assembled newshounds. Huston quipped that there were "more reporters on the site than iguanas." And as fascinating as the rest of the cast was, everyone knew why the press was really there. They were hoping to catch a glimpse of "Liz and Dick" kissing—or, better yet, fighting.

Reports of trouble in paradise had already reached the gossip columns. Zoe Sallis, Huston's girlfriend and the mother of his son, remembered "a lot of rows" between Elizabeth and Richard. There were numerous reasons for their tension. Together now for nearly two years, the lovers were still prevented from marrying. By continuing to haggle over the terms of their divorce, Eddie Fisher had frustrated Elizabeth's hopes of a picturesque, beachside, Christmastime wedding ceremony in Puerto Vallarta. Yet as furious as she was at Eddie, Elizabeth also blamed Sybil for dragging her feet. And since Richard would truck no criticism of the sainted mother of his daughters, some doozies of fights resulted. All the drinking only exacerbated the tension. Mike Nichols thought that Elizabeth, always a hearty drinker, was imbibing even more than she had in the past simply to keep up with Richard. "It's what she felt she had to do if she was going to be with him," Nichols said.

On November 23 they were in the midst of shooting when word arrived that President Kennedy had been assassinated the day before in Dallas. Huston said a few words, then called for a short break. "But . . . there was nothing we could do," said art director Stephen Grimes. "So we went on shooting."

They finished sometime in early December, though the Burtons hung around Puerto Vallarta to celebrate the holidays because they had fallen in love with the place. They were a little tired of arroz con pollo, however, so Elizabeth had hamburgers imported from the United States that they grilled on their barbecue. They'd also flown in the wife of their London chauffeur because they adored her roast pork. The woman was thrilled to get an all-expenses-paid Mexican holiday just to cook a meal or two.

Finally they headed up to Toronto, where Richard was scheduled to begin rehearsals for *Hamlet* under the direction of John Gielgud. The divorce from Sybil had come through at long last, concluded in a court in Puerto Vallarta, but Eddie was still fighting on, determined not to lose even a penny in the division of profits from the producing company that he'd formed for his wife back in the days when he expected to be piloting her career. Eddie continued to tell the press that Elizabeth was the only woman he "ever really loved," even though he added quickly, and unconvincingly, "I don't love her anymore, of course."

The divorce finally came through on March 5. Elizabeth and Richard were on a plane to Montreal almost immediately, since, unlike Ontario, the province of Quebec didn't quibble over such things as the validities of Mexican divorces. It was there that they were married on March 15, 1964, by a Unitarian minister in Suite 810 of the Ritz-Carlton Hotel. Sara and Francis Taylor flew in to witness their daughter's fifth marriage, the climax of a red-hot, two-year romance that had left two continents scorched in its wake. The beaming bride, her hair braided with white Roman hyacinths, wore a gown of yellow chiffon designed by Irene Sharaff, who'd done her costumes for *Cleopatra*. The previous month, Burton had presented Elizabeth with diamond-and-emerald drop earrings for her thirty-second birthday; now, to her eye-popping delight, he gave her a stunning matching necklace. They planned to repeat their vows at a synagogue in New York, but somehow the plans never materialized. Richard had *Hamlet* to do, after all.

Then it was on to Boston, where fans waited for hours to catch a glimpse of the newly married pair. As the Burtons' Trans-Canada airplane touched down at Logan Airport on March 23, a crowd of people suddenly burst through a line of state troopers and scrambled out onto the tarmac. Despite the efforts of the vastly outnumbered police, the fans swarmed around the plane. Burton peered out from a window and told Elizabeth to sit tight. Along with Alfred Drake, who was playing Claudius to his Hamlet, Burton disembarked from the plane and pushed through the frantic crowd to a waiting limousine. After he had driven off, the fans began chanting "Liz, Liz." Mothers held babies up in their arms, as if asking for her blessing. The police were finally able to part the crowd to allow a truck to move in and tow the plane across the tarmac to an airport hangar. But the throng followed, storming the hangar doors. The police had to use force to push the crowd back and secure the area. Only then was a shaken Elizabeth able to depart from the plane.

But the ordeal wasn't over. As their limousine pulled up to the Sheraton Plaza Hotel in Copley Square, the Burtons were greeted by another thousand screaming fans. Of course, all these people hadn't just materialized. They—and their counterparts at the airport—had been alerted to the arrival of "Liz and Dick" well in advance by regular press releases printed in newspapers and read on radios, as well as by colorful flyers pinned to telephone poles (and preserved today in archives). It was all part of an aggressive campaign by John Springer, the Burtons' new press agent.

At forty-eight, Springer was already something of a legend in the world of entertainment. In the 1940s he'd labored as a publicist at RKO and Fox. In the late 1950s he'd followed the trend and opened his own agency, quickly assembling one of the most stellar client lists in Hollywood: Marilyn Monroe, Judy Garland, Montgomery Clift, Joan Crawford. A master of discretion, Springer was able to work for Elizabeth and Richard while representing Debbie Reynolds and Sybil Burton at the same time. Few publicists were better at selling Hollywood than Springer. Much of the frenzy in Boston was whipped up by his canny crew in an effort to boost the box office of *Hamlet*—with the ancillary benefit of demonstrating that the Burtons, even when respectably married, could still stir up the crowds. "[Springer] was one of the best," said Dick Clayton, a contemporary. "Getting crowds like that was considered a big success."

Boston police would later complain that the Burtons had encouraged the fans' frenzy by driving around the hotel three times, waving and smiling at the crowd. Finally the limousine pulled up to the hotel and Richard and Elizabeth stepped out of the car. A riot broke out as soon as their feet touched the ground. The crowd surged, pushing their idols into the lobby of the hotel. Elizabeth screamed. Hands were everywhere, pulling at her clothes. Someone yanked her hair as others cried, "See if it's a wig." Separated from Burton, Elizabeth was thrust up against a wall, her neck twisted and bolts of pain shooting down her sensitive spine. It was several minutes before the Burtons were rescued by the hotel manager and guided safely into the elevator. A photo of Elizabeth in a white fur coat, her white gloves pressed to her face in terror, was splashed across the front pages of dozens of newspapers the next day.

As harrowing as the experience had been for his clients, Springer had also gotten them tremendous publicity, positioning the Burtons as the most popular stars in the world. "Why, I used to handle Marlene Dietrich and Marilyn Monroe," Springer made it a point to tell the press, "and I never saw anything like this." Yet his outrage at the lack of police protection was largely manufactured. While comparisons to Dietrich and Monroe were fine, it was four considerably younger celebrities to whom Springer most hoped to draw parallels. In the last month, the country had been riveted by the unprecedented public reaction to the Beatles, four mop-topped youths from Liverpool, England, who had arrived at New York's Kennedy Airport on February 7 to the shrieks of three thousand fans. Police barricades had to be erected to keep the hordes of teenagers from reaching their idols. Everywhere the Beatles went, they drew huge crowds who screamed and cried and grabbed at their clothes and hair. An appearance on the *Ed Sullivan Show* on February 9 was intercut with shots of hysterical fans sobbing and clutching the air. It's no surprise that Springer would estimate the number of fans at the airport to be *five thousand*—two thousand more than what the lads from Liverpool had managed to draw. And he was also quick to describe the composition of the crowds as equally divided between teenagers and adults.

Keeping the Burtons relevant when the prevailing youth culture was admonishing its followers not to trust anyone over thirty would take a bit of work, especially now that Elizabeth and Richard were no longer illicit lovers. But at every stop during Richard's tour of *Hamlet,* Springer made sure that the public knew where and when Mr. and Mrs. Burton would appear, and the crowds never failed to show up. The street outside the stage door of the Lunt-Fontanne Theatre in New York was packed with people after every show, with Elizabeth and Richard always appearing at some point to be hustled into a car, a sparkle of diamonds shining from

Elizabeth's throat or hair. Onlookers watched as if "rooted to the spot by some strange, felt presence of history," observed Stanley Elkin, a writer for *Esquire* who moved among the crowd one night. Richard enjoyed the hubbub, the slow inching of their limousine through the crowds as they headed back to their hotel. He laughed at the people pressing their faces to the glass. Elizabeth, more accustomed to it all, was more blasé. "For God's sake, Richard," she said, "don't you realize the only reason this is happening is because they think we're sinners and freaks?"

They could have gone on just being freaks—drawing crowds because of who they were, more famous than nearly anybody else on the planet, more envied and more desired. A play or a movie premiere wasn't needed to draw out their fans. John Springer could just send a press release about their next shopping trip or restaurant visit. Many celebrities today have mastered the art of attracting attention based on nothing more than their own "freakishness"—fame based on fame itself. But in 1964 there was a very different understanding of stardom. "You had to give something back," said Gavin Lambert. "You had to *do* something, act in something, or push yourself somehow in your craft. Otherwise you'd be seen as just one of the Gabor sisters."

Elizabeth and Richard, said one person very close to them, understood that their extraordinary fame was "part of an exchange with the public . . . It didn't come without expectations." Never was there a sense among the Burtons or their entourage that they might merely coast by on sensational headlines. "That's the difference between stars then and now," said Lambert. "Back then, it was understood that they had to give the public something in return for the privilege of being a star."

And so Elizabeth appeared for the first time on stage in June, reciting poetry with her husband as a benefit for Philip Burton's drama school, the American Musical and Dramatic Academy. She was terrified, stumbling at first and feeling her armpits dampen her blue silk dress. Then she steeled herself, as she knew how to do so well, feeling "daring [and] audacious," proceeding from Dorothy

Parker to D. H. Lawrence to Frost, Eliot, and Yeats. Even if poetry snobs insisted that she didn't understand what she was reading, she finished the night to a roar of applause. "Rarely has poetry drawn such a crowd," observed the *New York Times*. Once again, however, Elizabeth was realistic: "I knew that eighty-five percent of them had come and spent a great deal of money for me to fall flat on my face." But where she'd never been excessively proud of her films, she admitted, "I was proud of myself at that poetry reading."

In October it was once more back to MGM. The Burtons flew first to Big Sur, California, and then to Paris to make *The Sandpiper* for Vincente Minnelli, who'd directed Elizabeth fourteen years earlier in *Father of the Bride*. Elizabeth considered the film "a pile of crap," and insisted that she and Richard were making it only for the money. But it's hard not to see *The Sandpiper* as a kind of coda to Le Scandale. Richard plays a minister who, despite a deep respect for his virtuous wife, cannot resist falling in love with the beautiful, free-thinking artist played by Elizabeth. At one point, she says that society might consider their love to be wrong, but questions how it could be wrong when their feelings were so true and so pure. "I never knew it could be like this," she gushes during one of their secret trysts, and the audience is left feeling that Elizabeth might have said something similar during those early days in Rome. "Being with you is like having the whole world in my arms." If that didn't explain why Taylor and Burton had moved heaven and earth to be together, what could?

"The film was not written about her," said Martin Ransohoff, who both produced and wrote the story, "though people thought it was." How could they not? Observers on the set said that Minnelli, who was not fond of the original script, had wisely tweaked the material to reflect the offscreen love affair of Elizabeth and Richard.

There was also a deliberate attempt to appeal to the youth culture. Although *The Sandpiper* was shot predominantly in Paris, the location shooting in Big Sur made the most of the bohemian lifestyle of the California coast. The film features several earthy, sexy parties, and even includes a nude scene for Elizabeth, surely intended to evoke her spread in *Playboy*. Posing for a sculptor who is also her occasional lover, Elizabeth removes her smock, and though the camera is very discreet, the scene still caused audiences to gasp. The sculptor was originally to be played by Sammy Davis Jr.—which, in 1964, would have caused more gasps. "A wild idea," Minnelli thought, but ultimately Davis was vetoed by Ransohoff and replaced with Charles Bronson, much to Elizabeth's regret.

Her character was also styled to suggest a sixties flower child rather than a glamorous movie star. "Don't let Taylor wear much makeup," one studio technician advised. "This is not a standard of beauty anymore. The less she wears makeup-wise, the more the public will like her." Minnelli took this advice, and the result was that Elizabeth looked more beautiful than she had since *Butterfield 8,* her hair long and flowing, her unadorned eyes popping off the screen more brilliantly than ever in the Metrocolor film.

In the months after the film was completed, Springer and Frings spearheaded a campaign to ensure that the Burtons' names remained on the front pages. Elizabeth's reminiscences with Max Lerner were dusted off and expanded into a small memoir published by Harper & Row in 1964. Next it was Richard's turn, waxing poetic about his wife in the March 1965 issue of *Vogue.* The article was later expanded into a slim volume called *Meeting Mrs. Jenkins,* published by William Morrow in 1966 with full-color glossy pages featuring Elizabeth in all her violet-eyed glory.

The effect of both books was to lift the Taylor-Burton story out of its scandalous origins and transform it into a tale of eternal love and fate: "To have found, through trial and error, a tranquility in proud subordination, is so beautiful," Elizabeth wrote. By showing that she was just like any woman—indeed, like her character in *The Sandpiper*—she could hopefully bring any lingering doubters over to her side. Any person with even half a heart would understand that true love explains and conquers all. And while she might be a nonconformist in admitting her love of sex and four-letter words, Elizabeth also reminded the public of her romantic side, the part that was still the dreamy teenager from MGM. When she married Richard, she told her readers, she felt a "golden warmth," and instantly knew that the only way to make up for all the pain and struggle of the past was to "be good to each other and love each other." Only a hard-hearted cynic could fail to appreciate that.

By 1965 the world had once again, almost unanimously, fallen in love with Elizabeth Taylor. In July *The Sandpiper* opened to mixed reviews but frenzied box office, setting the record for the biggest opening day up to that point at Radio City Music Hall in New York. The picture ended up raking in $6.4 million, the seventh highest grossing film of the year. Once again Elizabeth was among the top ten moneymaking stars, having been absent from the list the year before due to the long lapse between *The V.I.P.s* and *The Sandpiper*. And right beside her on the list was Richard, finally a star as big as she was. They could have coasted for a while, flitting between their homes in Switzerland and Mexico, causing uproar wherever they went—but as ever there was that sense of responsibility. What to do next?

That's when they finally had their chance to make a picture with Mike Nichols.

Nine

Rewriting the Rules

July 1965–February 1968

STUCK IN TRAFFIC as he headed toward the Warner Bros. studio in Burbank, Ernest Lehman gripped his steering wheel with one hand and wiped his brow with the other. Normally calm and cool, the urbane producer of *Who's Afraid of Virginia Woolf?*—and acclaimed screenwriter of *North by Northwest, West Side Story,* and *The Sound of Music*—was feeling a bit anxious this morning. The night before, he'd been too excited to sleep, his mind consumed with all the little details that came with the start of a picture. "On a day that I would like to be in top shape," he lamented into the tape recorder on the seat next to him, "I'm weary, and the day hasn't even started yet."

There was a reason for his weariness. Lehman, who got his start working as a legman for Walter Winchell and then served as a Broadway publicist, had a pretty good idea of what he'd face with the stars of his latest picture. "No one," he said, "is bigger than Elizabeth Taylor and Richard Burton." That was why, as both producer and screenwriter for *Virginia Woolf,* he'd been convinced that the only way he could turn Edward Albee's profanity-laden tragicomedy into a box-office smash was to cast the most notorious husband-and-wife team in cinema history. Of course, studio chief Jack Warner had needed some persuading. The Burtons didn't come cheap. But they'd be worth every penny, Lehman promised. He'd do everything to keep them happy.

When he finally made it to Warner Bros., he dashed across

the lot to make sure that his stars' dressing rooms were all set. He'd taken tips from Dick Hanley on what sorts of goodies might put the Burtons in a good humor. For Richard, Lehman had ordered a bottle of Rémy Martin cognac, a bottle of Johnnie Walker Red Label Scotch whisky, and a huge bowl of fruit. Not to be outdone, Jack Warner had sent over six bottles of champagne, a case of Scotch, and a case of gin. Lehman quipped that if anyone got loaded during the production, at least they'd know whom to blame.

For Elizabeth, there were white roses and lilies of the valley that complemented the dressing room's yellow and white decor. Hanley had cautioned Lehman against overdoing the flowers. "Keep it moderate in size and in good taste," he advised. He also suggested a bottle of Dom Pérignon. Lehman made it three bottles. Hanley hadn't cautioned about overdoing the champagne.

A few days before, Hanley, along with the rest of the Burtons' entourage, had come by the studio to inspect their employers' dressing rooms. The designation was hardly apt: They were suites instead of rooms, each with its own kitchen and piano. Elizabeth's suite was airy and feminine; Richard's was wood-paneled and "Old English," which Lehman found "rather fitting." Hanley and John Lee nosed through the kitchens, ensuring that everything was in place, while Michael Wilding and Hugh French, as the Burtons' agents, went down a checklist to make sure that all contractual specifications had been met. Everything was in order. "Elizabeth's dressing room was so beautiful," Lehman recorded, "that they said they would like to stay there and live in it themselves."

A delivery boy arrived with a pound of caviar from Mike Nichols. Hugh French doubled that, just to make sure that his clients had enough.

The "confusion and last-minute running around" at the studio ended when Lehman spotted the Burtons getting out of a car. Everyone tensed for their entrance. Richard sauntered in first, dressed in a white cardigan sweater and a pair of tan slacks. Elizabeth followed in a silk dress and straw hat. Burton was "surprisingly warm," hugging the producer instead of shaking his hand. Elizabeth bestowed a polite kiss.

"Somebody knows what I like," she cooed after spotting the flowers and the champagne in her dressing room.

The studio was a hubbub of activity that morning. It wasn't every day that Elizabeth Taylor and Richard Burton made a picture on the lot. The last time Elizabeth had been at Warners had been for *Giant*, a decade before. Back then she'd been a twenty-three-year-old girl, a popular star but hardly the worldwide phenomenon that she had become. Now secretaries and technicians pushed their way to the windows, trying to catch a glimpse of her, but the attendants that constantly swarmed around her prevented a good look. Arriving with the Burtons were Bob and Sally Wilson, their personal dressers; Irene Sharaff, who was doing Elizabeth's costumes; Hugh French and his son, Robin; and press agent John Springer. Finally Mike Nichols shooed them all away. It was time he, Lehman, and their actors—who also included George Segal and Sandy Dennis—sat around a table in a closed room and read through the script for the first time together.

For Nichols, there was some trepidation. The day before, lounging with Lehman by his pool at his rented house in Brentwood, he'd mused about Elizabeth's ability to play the role of Martha, a woman a decade older than she was, a woman who was out of shape, in decline, trapped by rage and frustration and grief. "It's like asking a chocolate milkshake to do the work of a double martini," he'd lamented to Lehman.

Elizabeth had already been cast when Nichols was hired to direct. She had been chosen despite Edward Albee's expressed desire that Bette Davis and James Mason play Martha and George, the two bitter spouses waging war against each other on a New England college campus. Davis was the right age and fit the character's blowsy, caustic image, but Lehman had gone for "star power first," Nichols said, "and correctness for the part maybe second or third." To prepare for their task, Nichols and Lehman had watched Hitchcock's *Rope*, another film set in real time. The whole time,

Nichols had complained "bitterly" that he wasn't directing Davis in the part of Martha.

But the director wasn't entirely opposed to Elizabeth. He'd been wanting to work with her for years, and he'd seen her in *Suddenly, Last Summer* and *A Place in the Sun*. He knew she could deliver powerful performances. He was just worried that this beautiful creature seated across the table from him could never convince audiences that she was a middle-aged, washed-up shrew.

But yet as the four actors began reading the script—beginning with Martha's splenetic "Jesus H. Christ!"—something magical occurred. "Almost immediately," Lehman said, "Mike and I exchanged very pleased glances at Elizabeth's performance." It was the first time they'd actually heard how she might express the character, and they were thrilled. She possessed the right fire and wasn't the least bit hammy. If anything, it was Richard who was "a bit uneven" in the beginning, though he got "very good indeed" by the end of the day. Bloody Marys were served all around during the reading, keeping everybody's spirits free-flowing. At four thirty, the reading concluded with a line from Elizabeth: Martha's heartbreaking reply to George, who'd been singing the play's catchphrase, "Who's afraid of Virginia Woolf?" Looking up from her script with just the right amount of fear and sadness and grief on her face, Elizabeth said softly, "I am, George. I am." Nichols sat back in his chair, pleased.

Elizabeth let out a whoop. It was the first time in her entire career, she announced, that she'd ever acted out a complete screenplay in one day while seated around a table.

She'd find much that was new and different making a picture with Mike Nichols. There would be two weeks of rehearsals, and his actors could expect no advance direction from him. "I don't like to go into rehearsals with a set plan," Nichols explained. "I would rather that it come from the cast. In that way they have an investment in the outcome."

By now, Nichols's directorial skills were unquestioned, even if *Virginia Woolf* was his first movie. On Broadway, the Nichols-helmed *Barefoot in the Park* had been the biggest comedy hit two seasons ago; *Luv* quickly followed, and this year it was *The Odd Couple* that had everyone talking. Nichols had won the Tony for Best Direction for all three. Just thirty-three, he brought a fresh, innovative style to his projects that made old-timers think twice about what they thought they knew. "His invention is as resourceful as his author's flair for humorous twists in rapid-fire dialogue," the *New York Times* said. Even the way he introduced his characters on stage was novel: "Those entrances could become classics of a kind as exercises for students of advanced acting."

For Elizabeth, Nichols offered a connection to *Giant* that was more than just a return to the same studio. Not since George Stevens had she worked on a project with this kind of artistic fusion: director, material, cast, and chemistry. Not since Stevens had any director set out to kindle such prowess within her, to lure out talents heretofore unsuspected. Certainly Richard Brooks had shrewdly used the well of emotion that she'd felt over Todd's death in *Cat on a Hot Tin Roof*, and Joe Mankiewicz had pushed her to striking extremes in *Suddenly, Last Summer*. But Albee's play—blasphemous, bitter, profane—was a very different kettle of fish. It required her to be shameless and sympathetic, despicable and delightful, abhorrent and alluring, all at the same time. And whereas her physical power was vital to the picture, it could not arise from her beauty, as it always had before. Instead, the audience must be made to forget Elizabeth Taylor while still finding Martha irresistible. Elizabeth would need to summon qualities from within herself that no director had ever asked her to bring forth before.

She'd risen to the occasion in the past, particularly on *A Place in the Sun*. But she'd been a child then, looking up at her director with hero worship in her eyes. Yet Nichols couldn't have been more different from Stevens. Slim, soft-spoken, boyish, he was nearly the same age as Elizabeth. He socialized with her, shared the same friends—hardly the case with Stevens. Indeed, the friendly synergy among the Burtons and their director was like nothing that they'd experienced before.

On those soundstages in Burbank, the three of them were

helping to change Hollywood, and they knew it: *Virginia Woolf* was breaking down the last strictures of the old Production Code. After Jack Warner had gone through the script circling multiple *goddamn*s, a handful of *bastard*s, scattered *sons of bitches,* and the occasional *melons bobbling,* Nichols had agreed to soften Albee's dialogue. But then he suddenly reversed course and announced that the profanity would be retained. The "clean but suggestive phrases" he'd replaced it with had made the script read like "an old Gary Cooper movie when somebody said, 'He's so poor he hasn't got a pot to put flowers in.'"

Nichols insisted that the integrity of Albee's play would not be compromised. Aghast, the Production Code Administration threatened to deny the picture a seal of approval. Jack Warner pressed for "protection shots" in case the censors flat-out rejected certain scenes, but Nichols refused. "Mike's theory," Lehman said, was "that if we ever did shoot the protection stuff, somehow it would find its way into the picture." Nichols had come to the conclusion that a seal from the antiquated PCA wasn't necessary to sell their picture. They had the Burtons, after all.

And so, one more nail was hammered in the coffin of the old way of making movies. Just as she had when she broke the rules about star salaries, Elizabeth was using her enormous celebrity to break down one more vestige of a system that she had so despised as a girl.

Nichols relished being a young turk. Acting out scenes with his stars around the pool of his house, he knew that they were walking on hallowed ground. During the studio era, the house had belonged to Cole Porter and was a gathering place for many of the old greats: the Barrymores, George Cukor, Cary Grant, Bea Lillie, Elsa Maxwell, Clifton Webb. Now the nude marble statue in Porter's garden was adorned with sunglasses and a red-checked bikini, and a hi-fi system played loud music while Nichols's stars swore at the top of their lungs. "I don't know why you want to make a picture like this," sniffed the antediluvian Sydney Guilaroff as he designed Elizabeth's wigs. Nichols and company just laughed him off. Already the director was planning his next picture, *The Graduate,* in which a young college man is seduced by an older woman and then falls in love with her daughter. It was indeed a brave new world.

Elizabeth was not used to rehearsing like this, walking around an empty room as if they were putting on a play. The day was warm, and she kept fanning herself with the script in her hands. She wore a yellow linen dress with a matching yellow hat and yellow high heels. Off to the side sat Mike Nichols, who jumped up every now and then to act out a scene himself, showing his actors how it should be done. Elizabeth just shook her head, clearly ill at ease. To reassure her, Richard walked over to her several times and gave her a kiss. "Somehow she feels that she can't perform this way," Ernest Lehman observed, especially as all three of her costars were "experienced stage actors."

But Nichols laid down the law. They would rehearse in this manner from July 6 to 19. For those two weeks, the Burtons had agreed to take no pay, which may have contributed to Elizabeth's disquiet. After that, of course, it was back to business, with Elizabeth pulling down $100,000 per week for ten weeks, and Richard $75,000 for the same terms. By then they would move out of the stark bare room that made Elizabeth so uncomfortable and commence shooting on Stage 8, where the interior sets of George and Martha's house were being built. Then Elizabeth would feel more at home, as if she were really making a movie. But until that time, she'd be fretful and uneasy.

Arms akimbo, she confronted Nichols during a break. She insisted that her contract stipulated that she was not to be called to the set earlier than 10 in the morning. Nichols replied softly that it most definitely did *not* say that. Well, if it *didn't,* Elizabeth huffed, she'd have to fire her agent, Hugh French. Indeed, for a couple of days after that, she made "very large sounds" about firing French. Burton confided to Lehman that she was feeling "very guilty" about leaving Kurt Frings and was "probably looking unconsciously for some excuse" to dump French and go back to the man Mike Todd had anointed to represent her. Frings had, after all, done so much for her, and now, Burton said, he was rather "hard up." The messy divorce from Ketti had taken its toll.

But Elizabeth didn't fire French. With Lehman's help, her new agent got Jack Warner to agree to the 10 A.M. starting time. Reluctantly Nichols acquiesced. He said they might as well grant her request because otherwise "she'd be impossible to work with." But the "gentleman's agreement" proposed by Warner was completely unacceptable to Elizabeth. "If they agree to it," she told Lehman, "they must put it in writing. I'll be damned if I'll ever expose myself to the possibility of a suit." She'd been making movies far too long to take anyone in Hollywood at his word. "She is not only rich and beautiful," Lehman recorded in his journal, "she is also very shrewd."

Recognizing his star's agitation on the set, Nichols suggested a vocal coach. Elizabeth had been struggling to find the right pitch for Martha, and the director thought that a coach might help bring her voice down an octave. But once again Elizabeth said no. She insisted that working with a coach would only make her self-conscious. How times had changed. Long gone was the contract player who had needed to manipulate her way into getting what she wanted. Now, as Elizabeth Taylor Burton, she just announced what she wanted and she got it. "So I am afraid," Lehman sighed into his tape recorder that night, "we are going to have a relatively high-voiced Martha."

Despite her refusal, Elizabeth really *did* want to be good in the part. In fact, her desire to push herself as an actress was incredibly strong going into *Virginia Woolf.* Like Monty Clift had done a decade ago, Richard impressed and inspired her with his dedication to his craft. As one half of the team known as the Burtons, Elizabeth was aware that she was considered the lightweight in terms of talent. That rankled her. Some of the churlish comments after their poetry reading had no doubt gotten under her skin. So she threw herself into preparing for the film, paging through the script, underlining passages, circling scenes that she thought needed changing.

At one point during rehearsals, she took issue with a line of George's, where he says, "Don't start in on the bit"—a reference to the imaginary son they'd talk about later in the script. She told Nichols that it didn't jibe with the ending, when George says that he has to "kill" the son because she'd mentioned him. The incident sounds, in fact, more like a gripe that had come from Richard, not Elizabeth; she may have volunteered, perhaps strategically, to wage the battle for him. But the line was not changed.

Other quibbles were clearly her own concerns. She was passionately opposed to the scene in the roadhouse where she dances with George Segal. She called it phony, an example of "Hollywood vulgarity." It should not be a set piece, she argued, with the roadhouse looking as empty as an old-time musical soundstage. A "full-scale argument" flared up, with Burton, Nichols, and Lehman all having their say. "We went back and forth on it," Lehman said. Elizabeth's "eyes were really flashing." Lehman told her that he thought her argument was "intellectualized," to which she responded, "Why, thank you, Ernie, for calling me an intellectual." He wasn't sure if she was amused or angry. Though things got "pretty hot," eventually they all settled on a compromise, with Nichols promising as much realism as possible. "It was our first indication that [Elizabeth] is going to have things to say about the script," Lehman recorded.

Of course she was going to have things to say. She knew the risks that she was taking with the part. "When I first read the script," she said, "I didn't think I was the right casting. I was too young and I hope—I trust—I'm unlike Martha myself. Richard read it and he said, 'You're not right for it, but I want you to do it because I don't want any other actress to do it. It's too good a part.'"

It was clear that *Who's Afraid of Virginia Woolf?* was going to be a big, big movie. Anticipation was mounting, and Nichols was cutting no corners. The sets were decorated by George James Hop-kins, an old studio veteran who dated back to Theda Bara and Mary Miles Minter. Nichols insisted that no detail be spared in creating the perfect ambience for the home of a New England aca-demic. Strewn about were novels by Thomas Mann and old copies of the *Kenyon Review*. The glasses at the bar were old jelly jars and containers that had once held pimento cheese. Verisimilitude was the order of the day; Nichols wanted audiences to forget that they were watching a movie. "I want the audience drawn into the lives of these people," he said, "and not be aware of any director's tech-nique, any camera or any cutting."

The script was so carefully guarded that even George Se-gal hadn't seen the final draft until he sat down at the table for the read-through. Everything about the production was carefully shielded from the public in order not to give anything away. And with so much of the studio publicity apparatus gone, it was up to the filmmakers themselves to manage the press. Lehman's re-sponse to a request from *Cosmopolitan* to do a story about the pic-ture shows that they knew how to play the game. "What we haven't decided yet, and hope to do in the next few days," he recorded in his journal, "is select the writer we feel would be right for the role of writing that kind of piece and also who would be acceptable to *Cosmopolitan*." They were casting their journalists just as they had cast their actors.

In June there was "a full-scale publicity strategy meeting" in Lehman's office. Studio publicists like Max Bercutt and Carl Combs were there, along with John Springer, who worked exclu-sively for the Burtons. It was decided that the set would be com-pletely closed to the press. Any interviews with the stars had to take place away from the set, and under no circumstances was Elizabeth ever to be seen in her makeup as Martha. That little shock would be reserved for the premiere.

There was a reason for such secrecy. For the first time in her career, Elizabeth Taylor would not be glamorized. Her beauty, for once, would not be a selling point for the picture. Instead, it was the concealment of her beauty that was generating interest: How would Elizabeth look as Martha?

That was what everyone was asking in the summer of 1965. Cameraman Harry Stradling, like George James Hopkins, had a career stretching back to the silent days; he'd photographed leading ladies from Betty Blythe and Norma Shearer to Carole Lombard and Judy Garland. He knew all the tricks to make stars look as beautiful as possible—but here was Mike Nichols telling him to shoot Elizabeth as pitilessly as he could. It was another clash of old Hollywood values versus the new. "What are those ravishing shadows on Elizabeth's throat?" Nichols asked upon seeing the tests Stradling had made. The cameraman insisted that he was covering her double chin. When Nichols replied that he *wanted* to see her double chin and the circles under her eyes, Stradling grumbled, "Yes, but are you worried at all about what the public might want?"

Stradling would soon depart the film, although Warners insisted that it had nothing to do with how he was shooting Elizabeth. Nichols, however, stated plainly, "He wanted her beautiful. We wanted a certain harshness." Haskell Wexler, younger and more in tune with the times, was hired to replace him. Wexler had just made a documentary about the civil rights movement and had photographed Tony Richardson's avant-garde *The Loved One*, so he had the right sensibility for this more modern assignment. Yet he too had to overcome some ingrained presumptions. "My job is traditionally to make women look good," he explained. "Mike Nichols said, 'I don't want her to look good.'" So Wexler did as he was instructed, letting Elizabeth's double chin waddle freely and the bags under her eyes retain all their unflattering shadows. But he'd admit to a friendly covert agreement with the star not to "uglify her too much."

Indeed, for all of her celebrated courage in deglamorizing herself for the sake of the part, Elizabeth was not at all comfortable with the idea, at least not at first. The publicists quoted her as saying, "If Mike wants me to have a double chin, we'll emphasize it," but in fact she was terribly self-conscious about what it would do to her image. She complained about being forced to consume "a lot of cream and butter and sweets"—though one suspects that she didn't find such gourmandizing as odious as she made out. But it made her nervous. One day, just before shooting was scheduled to begin, Elizabeth buttonholed Lehman and turned on all her power and charm. "Listen, Ernie," she said, eyelashes batting, "you must be sure to tell the press from here on in that you and Mike have *ordered* me to get fat for this picture. I don't want them to get the idea that I'm overweight and sloppy simply because I don't know any better." Lehman was impressed with her skill for public relations. Once again he called her shrewd.

After more than two decades of merchandising her looks, it's understandable that Elizabeth was anxious about appearing as Martha. While it was true that she didn't possess the overweening vanity of many stars, she was smart enough to realize that much of her success heretofore had been bolstered by her appearance. It had been that poster of her in a white bathing suit that had turned *Suddenly, Last Summer* into a box-office smash after all. So it's not surprising that, as she was made up as Martha for the first time, she was cranky and querulous, knocking back vodka after vodka. Striding out of her dressing room wearing the gray wig that Sydney Guilaroff had made for her, she awaited consensus. Lehman thought it made her look chic, "ravishingly beautiful" in fact—which of course pleased Elizabeth but horrified Nichols. The wig was sent back to Guilaroff to obtain the dowdier look that they wanted.

Elizabeth threw a fit. She was suddenly convinced that there was no reason to play Martha as an old harridan. "She felt that the role would work perfectly if she could play her own age, which is thirty-three," Lehman said. He and Nichols made no reply. They did not want to antagonize her. They allowed her to vent her rage and her fear. But they knew there was no way that Martha could be thirty-three. In Albee's play, she is described as a "large, boisterous woman, fifty-two." Uta Hagen had been in her midforties when she'd played the part on Broadway. And Martha was supposed to be older than George; the age difference helped to fuel the conflict between them. Nichols had already surrendered that bit of characterization; there was no way Elizabeth could convincingly look older than Richard, who would be forty in a few months. But the director was certainly not going to allow Martha to turn into a pretty thirty-three-year-old.

Makeup artist Gordon Bau had aged Elizabeth in *Giant.* But then she'd been in the springtime of her beauty. Now when he turned her around in her chair to look at herself as Martha, she nearly burst into tears. Lehman called her "awfully unhappy." It had been a long day; Elizabeth was swearing and demanding that they postpone the start of filming. Lehman felt she had been drinking too much and was far too tired. True enough; but she was also a woman on the edge of middle age, whose beauty had been celebrated around the world since she was an adolescent, and who was now forced to compete with fresh-faced twenty-somethings like Julie Christie and Jane Fonda for magazine covers. Bau's magic had only sped up the aging process. As she stared into the mirror, what likely troubled Elizabeth the most was that Martha's double chin and puffy eyes weren't all cosmetic. No wonder she was so insistent that Lehman spread the word that she had done all this for her art.

The drinking would continue throughout the shoot, sanctioned by the top brass and encouraged by the director; the film, after all, is one marathon binge. Elizabeth was conscious of depicting "the physical progression of drunkenness." Martha "starts out tippling," she explained, "and in the course of the play she has twenty-one or twenty-two straight gins." On the set, she and Burton nearly matched Martha and George shot for shot. There were pills, too, Lehman believed; at one point, when Elizabeth was "exceedingly cheerful" to everyone on the set, the producer had a realization: "For the first time it occurred to me that she might just possibly be taking some sort of medication to 'elevate her mood.'" Watching the dailies, he noted her "highly energetic performance" and became even more convinced that she was "taking something."

He was hardly complaining. A happy Elizabeth meant a happy set. "Whatever the pill is," Lehman told his journal, "I am very much in favor of it."

Filming began on Monday, July 26. Standing beside Wexler and his camera, Nichols waited for Elizabeth to start her scene. When she didn't move for several seconds, he looked over at her as if to ask what was taking her so long.

"I can't *act* until you say *action*," she told him.

Nichols laughed. There were some parts of filmmaking that he still hadn't gotten the hang of—and some parts of the old studio system that Elizabeth was never going to let go. He complied by stuttering, "Ac-ac-ac-ac-ac-action." Elizabeth grimaced, but it was good enough. She went into the scene.

Nichols was awed by her technical virtuosity. "Elizabeth can keep in her mind fourteen dialogue changes, twelve floor marks and ten pauses—so the cutter can get the shears in and still keep the reality," he said. All that MGM training was still paying dividends. Elizabeth was more than just a glamorous star; she was an old pro. In just one weekend she'd learned twenty-six pages of the script and had showed up to work "very well-prepared," Lehman said. The stress of preproduction was evaporating.

Now that the cameras were rolling, Elizabeth was having a ball. She found playing Martha a cinch. "I had a character to grab ahold of and sink my nails into," she said, and the script provided "wonderful words to wrap your lips around." She'd insist that she had needed no specific preparation for the part. "It's a matter of concentration," she told an interviewer. "I read the script over several times. I think about it all the time. I very rarely discuss it. It's an inward process that works itself on me probably even when I'm asleep."

All of her husband's initial doubts about her were banished. "You cannot believe it is her," Burton said in awe. "When I first saw the rushes, I was absolutely astounded. The voice, the accent, the walk. It's so vulgar and oddly poignant." He pointed out that it would have been easy for her just to play an old woman, as she had in *Giant*. "But for a thirty-year-old woman to play a forty-year-old is very difficult."

"I have totally divorced myself from Martha so when I'm doing Martha I completely forget anything else I've ever done, or ever was, or ever will be," Elizabeth explained. "It's almost like a split personality kind of thing. It was difficult in the beginning because I didn't know if I was going overboard or underboard. All the things I had to find for myself, like the voice, and the walk, and the slouch, and the laughter, and the vulnerability. I can turn Martha on now. It's the easiest role I've ever played. It's difficult playing yourself. And Martha is so remote from me."

That would be a continuing refrain in her interviews. She stressed often that she was not like Martha. It didn't matter that those words she found so wonderful to wrap her lips around were the same sort of obscenities that she used so casually in real life, or that she and Richard could snarl and bicker in ways that were not completely dissimilar to Martha and George. It didn't matter that Elizabeth often scuffed around in slippers and a housecoat at home, eating cold fried chicken with her hands—an image not out of character for Martha. Maybe that was why Elizabeth subconsciously took Martha home with her on occasion, keeping the voice and the walk. She and Richard would have people over for dinner, and the next morning Richard would look at her and ask, "Do you know how you spoke to so-and-so last night?" Elizabeth found it quite amusing. In tape-recorded interviews that she made at the time, it's uncanny to hear how easily she could move from her well-modulated speech, containing traces of her childhood English accent, to the shrill, coarse voice of Martha: "What the hell do you want?"

As filming progressed, Nichols and Lehman realized that there were certain things they could do to keep their star happy and cooperative. Little gifts were left for her to find in her dressing room, over which she'd titter and giggle like a child. Of course, giving gifts to Elizabeth Taylor was a tradition that dated back to Stanley

Donen, and perhaps even earlier, to the day when Louis B. Mayer presented her with the stallion from *National Velvet*. But in recent years, the tradition had reached extraordinary heights. Throughout the filming of *Virginia Woolf*, Elizabeth constantly compared (unfavorably) the gift giving of Lehman to his predecessor, Martin Ransohoff. "Ernie," she trilled one day, "I thought you'd be interested to know that Marty has just given me another present." Playing along, Lehman asked what could anyone possibly give to the woman who had everything. "Another husband," Nichols deadpanned. "Hey, now, wait a minute," Burton said, glancing up suddenly from his newspaper.

Elizabeth paid them no mind, slinking over to Lehman to tell him that she'd seen a "fabulous" piece of jewelry designed by David Webb, whose pieces adorned the throats, ears, and wrists of the Duchess of Windsor, Diana Vreeland, and Gloria Vanderbilt. Lehman professed ignorance of the man. "David Webb," Elizabeth repeated forcefully. "Take out your pen and write down that name." Lehman told her that he'd forgotten his pen. But he added that he *had* considered buying her a baby wolf to commemorate the picture. Elizabeth squealed with delight. She'd *love* to have a baby wolf.

A few weeks later, after Ransohoff had dropped off a double rope of nine-and-a-half-millimeter pearls in gratitude for the continued outstanding box office of *The Sandpiper*, Elizabeth reminded Lehman that all *he'd* given her so far were flowers and bottles of champagne. Even Mike Nichols had splurged on some sapphire earrings. Lehman took it in with a noncommittal nod. Watching from the sidelines, Richard found it all very funny. Elizabeth, he said, reminded him of his aunt Tessie, who was "a bit on the greedy side." Dropping his arm around Lehman's shoulders, Richard said, "The wonderful thing about Elizabeth is that she loves jewels so much that she makes even a stingy man like me want to give her jewelry just to see the thrill she gets when she sees it."

Her husband wasn't always so benevolent, however. Mike Todd Jr. stopped by the set on day, and Elizabeth gushed over him, making hay out of the fact that, in her Martha makeup, she finally looked as if she could truly be his stepmother. Later, during a break in a scene, Richard, who'd been drinking, called her a "sourpuss," and said she "was giving a lousy performance." Lehman thought that the two incidents were connected, that the "reminder of one man she really loved so much might have led Richard to say what he said." To assuage any hurt feelings, Nichols encouraged the crew to say kind things to Elizabeth and, indeed, to part with some cash to buy her gifts.

But, in her own way, Elizabeth could be quite generous herself. For Nichols, one anecdote summed up her "very essence." They were getting ready to shoot a particularly long monologue of Martha's. In the course of it, she was supposed to cry. Elizabeth was terrified that she might not be able to bring forth the tears when she needed to. Nichols insisted that she not worry, that he was confident that she could pull it off. But his star wasn't so sure. Nichols called "Action"—he was getting better at that—and the cameras began to turn. With a deep breath, Elizabeth started in on the scene. Her director watched as she summoned all the emotion she could. Her eyes began to glisten. And then, with a groan, Nichols had to call "Cut." There was a technical problem with the camera. Elizabeth deflated like a balloon.

"Okay, so now it's the second take," Nichols described, "and she has to get herself going again. She's really going and she's amazing and the tears suddenly start flowing on cue and she's *great*." But then disaster. Right in the middle of the scene came a very loud snoring sound from overhead. A crew member had fallen asleep. "And he was snoring so loud," Nichols said, "that there was absolutely no way to go on filming." Once again he had to cut the scene. "And the first thing out of Elizabeth's mouth," Nichols said, "right on top of the word 'Cut,' was 'Don't fire him! Please don't fire him!' That was her very first response—her reflex—even after all her worries, even after this guy had ruined her very difficult scene. She said, 'Don't fire him!' There are not a lot of people like that."

Granting his leading lady's wish, Nichols let the errant crew member keep his job. And Elizabeth redid the scene. Brilliantly.

The Burtons were furious. For all their jet-setting, they insisted that they hated flying, especially takeoffs and landings. Why Ernie Lehman had chartered a plane that had to refuel in Chicago was beyond them. As they settled into their seats, they ordered a couple of double vodkas with tonic. Lehman knocked on the cockpit door and pleaded with the crew to change the flight route. Once in the air, the captain announced that due to favorable weather conditions, they could fly straight through to Hartford. Everybody cheered, especially the Burtons, which meant that the whole company could now relax and have a good time. Little Liza Todd, accompanying her parents on the New England location shoot, scrambled out of her seat to play with George Segal's little daughter. The liquor flowed freely. "The spirit in the cabin was marvelous," Lehman said. Nichols mused, "If only we could stay in the plane and never land."

But land they did, touching down at Bradley Field outside Hartford, Connecticut, a little after 5:30 P.M. It was Saturday, August 21. Elizabeth had made it plain that she wanted none of the shenanigans that had greeted their arrival in Boston a year earlier. Bowing to her wishes, John Springer had cleverly informed the press that the flight wasn't due in until seven. In those days before the Internet, it was an easy ruse to pull. All the *Virginia Woolf* company found waiting for them as they debarked from the plane were three buses for the crew and four air-conditioned Cadillacs for the stars, director, and producer. The next day the local press would report that "advance publicity was not calculated to please the many avid fans" who had arrived a half hour after the caravan pulled away.

Well tanned, in a white dress, and with her hair worn in a stylish upsweep, Elizabeth watched from the window of the Cadillac as they headed north on Interstate 91. Their destination was

Northampton, Massachusetts, home of Smith College, where exteriors for the film would be shot. Northampton was an old town on the banks of the Connecticut River, with a wide main street lined with brownstone buildings and a cemetery that dated back to the seventeenth century. Smith was founded in 1871 as a college for women and counted among its former students Margaret Mitchell, Julia Child, Sylvia Plath, Nancy Reagan, and Gloria Steinem. Its hillside campus, ringed with pine and oak trees, included a botanical garden and an arboretum designed by Frederick Law Olmsted. Warner Bros. had settled on Smith to serve as the backdrop for the film after a long search for a suitable campus location in California had proven fruitless. "We finally decided that we could not find New England in the far West," Lehman said. The studio offered to pay the college $5,000. Smith asked for, and got, five times that.

Known for its liberalism, the college nonetheless triggered some dissension among its alumnae by allowing the campus to be used for a movie starring Elizabeth Taylor. "Why should we help support a college that entertains such an unsavory female?" one graduate of the class of 1922 asked in a letter to president Thomas C. Mendenhall. The president's reply was succinct. "The play is about hypocrisy," he wrote, referencing Albee's original. "Personally I find hypocrisy unattractive but considerably less so than jealousy, for instance, which is the central theme of *Othello*, a play doubtless studied in many schools in Northampton and elsewhere. As you well know, it is dangerous for an individual or college to play censor." Still, the college decreed that it not be credited in the film and insisted that the company be off the grounds by the time classes resumed.

Trailed as usual by controversy, the Burtons and company descended upon the campus, just as the skies opened up and poured down torrential sheets of rain. The storm was a surprise; the forecast had only called for clouds. With temperatures hanging in the low seventies, the green woods of western Massachusetts took on an almost tropical glow. As the last bit of daylight disappeared behind the wet trees, everybody hurried off to their various lodgings. Lehman and Nichols were thrilled with the Victorian houses with the large yards that the studio had found for them. But, perhaps not surprisingly, the Burtons were not quite as satisfied with theirs.

Word had leaked out. When Elizabeth and Richard arrived at their lakeside house, they found hundreds of people standing all over the yard and "bothering them with banners and requests for autographs." It was clear that there would be no way to efficiently cordon off the house. Thus began, in the midst of all that rain, what Lehman called a game of "musical houses." Graciously, the producer offered to switch houses with his stars. Back in their limousine, Elizabeth and Richard zipped over to Lehman's and sloshed through puddles to check out the place. Elizabeth declared that it was no better. So they headed off to another house, which was also unsuitable. Finally they found themselves at Mike Nichols's house. After much champagne, Elizabeth decreed that this one would do just fine. Her director very kindly agreed to make the switch.

Walking barefoot with Lehman on the wet grass, Elizabeth blamed no one but herself for all the confusion. She had been the one to select the first house based on its descriptions and photos. "But [she] had never dreamt," Lehman recorded in his journal, "that the residents of Northampton would think that the presence of the Burtons would be worthy of crowds gathering to see them." As she said this, the producer no doubt looked at her closely to see if she was being ironic. She wasn't—or at least she gave no indication that she was. Lehman replied that he thought she underestimated their fame.

Shooting began on August 23 and was frequently interrupted by rain and thunderstorms, fog and humidity. On rainy days the Burtons occasionally slipped away to the Academy of Music downtown, where they watched movies from the balcony. Elizabeth once snuck off with some of the crew to catch *What's New, Pussycat?* at a cinema in nearby West Springfield. Their days were largely free because the entire location shoot was conducted after dark. The action in the film unfolds in the course of one long night, ending with sunrise. Accordingly, the call was for 6:30 every evening, two hours before darkness. "If you want to turn a crew into a tribe of zombies, try having them work at night and sleep during the day," said second-unit director Michael Daves.

But Nichols defended his methods. "It's easy to say you're tired, and you've been drinking a lot, and it's 5:30 in the morning," he explained, "but how do you really feel? We wanted to do it, and we found some things we hadn't thought about."

Their nights would end when everyone stumbled home as the sun rose over the Berkshire mountains. Area farmers eventually would sue Warner Bros., contending that the harsh movie lights shining through the trees had confused their cows and decreased the production of milk.

The first scene shot was the opening scene of the picture, where George and Martha stroll across the campus after a party at the house of the dean, who also happens to be Martha's father. To simulate late fall instead of high summer, dried leaves were blown around by wind machines. Various Smith faculty members served as extras, sauntering out of the house and dispersing across the lawn. Lehman fell in among them, a bit player in his own picture. It was decided that George and Martha knew him, so they exchanged a wave. But Lehman cringed when he heard Elizabeth call over to him, "Good night, Ernie! Up yours!" He hoped that the microphone hadn't picked that up.

The need for secrecy was even greater now that they were shooting out in the open. Northampton residents, with their long history and New England common sense, were not easily impressed. And yet there they were, night after night, gathering in the streets, their cameras popping. The studio had arranged for one hundred guards to encircle the campus, but the police could only keep crowds back, not disperse them, because the house that served as George and Martha's was on a main thoroughfare. People stood three and four deep staring at the house all night waiting for Liz or Dick to come outside. One reporter snuck into the operation by getting hired as a chauffeur, but he was quickly fired.

Such tight controls meant that the filmmakers eventually would butt heads with the Burtons' press agents, whose job, after all, was to maintain public interest in their clients. It was difficult to do that if reporters were banned from location. John Springer caused a stir one night when he tried to sneak in a couple of magazine writers. Lehman blew up. He had no intention of allowing Springer to "start fouling things up in the interests of publicity." Eventually, however, Springer was persuasive. A few writers, like Roy Newquist from *McCall's,* were allowed to visit and interview Elizabeth and Richard, but only if they promised not to reveal anything about Elizabeth's appearance as Martha.

The nights were long. When she wasn't in front of the cameras, Elizabeth was usually drinking a glass of Lancers wine. For much of the shoot, Liza was on the set, falling asleep on the grass or in the waiting room where the actors passed the time between shots. Elizabeth was unhappy about keeping Liza up so late, but Richard enjoyed having her around; he'd bonded tightly with the little girl. ("She has the larceny of her father and seductiveness of her mother," he'd tell friends.) He insisted that Liza stay, causing a row with his wife in front of the crew. Finally Elizabeth was convinced to let her daughter stay because it was too risky to hire a babysitter. Sitters might "turn out to be unofficial newspaper people or unreliable personnel," Lehman said, who'd sell their stories to the magazines. It had happened before in Rome. So eight-year-old Liza remained on the set, staying up until dawn, watching her mother in that crazy gray wig shout obscenities at her beloved stepfather.

Richard had become close with all of Elizabeth's children, something Eddie Fisher had failed to do. Michael and Christopher were now twelve and ten, respectively, and were attending school in England, though they, too, spent some time in Northampton that summer. Little Maria was now almost four. After doctors discovered that she'd been born with a malformed hip, her mother, painfully aware of the difficulties of living with an untreated congenital condition, had paid for all the necessary surgeries needed to correct it. Now Maria could walk and run freely. That summer she was living with Sara and Francis, but like her sister, Maria had formed a fast attachment to the charismatic Richard, who officially adopted her and gave her his last name.

The charisma that emanated from both the Burtons was apparent every morning when the rushes were screened. Nichols and Lehman were unqualified in their praise for their stars. "Both Elizabeth and Richard seem to have a quality of sadness as well as funniness which I think is just right for their roles," Lehman recorded in his journal. Knocking on Elizabeth's door, he peered inside to say that he hoped he wouldn't embarrass her, but he thought that she was simply wonderful in the morning's rushes. "Don't be silly," Elizabeth said, beaming. "There's nothing embarrassing about hearing that."

She had brought something to Martha that only she could bring. "Yes, it would have been very interesting with Bette Davis," Nichols reflected. "But with Elizabeth somehow—even though her light was dimmed with the age makeup—she shone as herself anyway. I think that's one of the things that worked for the film. Instead of just two academics—and one hopes you can accept them as academics as well—you see these two were once very hot people who were now buried in this place." What had originally attracted George to Martha was very clear. "Underneath it all, you could see how sexy Martha had been," Nichols said. "She still had that allure." When George Segal sneaks off to have sex with her, it's not so difficult to fathom, the way it probably would have been with Bette Davis playing the part.

Burton, too, was shining. "It's the most enjoyable—in a funny, perverse way—of any [modern] role I've ever done," he said. With the exception of Jimmy Porter in *Look Back in Anger*, George was "the most brilliantly written" role he'd ever played.

That didn't mean he didn't have his insecurities. With Richard Burton, there were always insecurities. One night in early September, Richard casually asked Lehman if he could cut out early, which meant that he wouldn't finish all of his scheduled scenes. He explained that Elizabeth's sons were leaving for school the next day, and he wanted to spend some time with them. Lehman said that he was sorry, but he couldn't allow it: They needed to finish the crucial scene between George and Sandy Dennis's character. The scene was an emotional one, the moment where George's bravado cracks and he cries, forcing Dennis to look up at the window where her husband is having sex with Martha. Burton seemed resigned to Lehman's refusal for an early dismissal. But a short time later he was making the same request of Nichols.

Eventually the director discovered what was really going on. "We're in trouble," he told Lehman. "The man is in tears. The story about having to get home because Elizabeth's sons are leaving was just a cover-up. He's tired and feels he cannot go on with the scene. He's always been afraid of this scene . . . He gave so much during the early evening that he feels that he just cannot go through with it." There was nothing they could do. They couldn't force him to act. With great reluctance, Nichols called it a night. Burton was extremely apologetic. He promised he would do the scene first thing the following evening. And he did. Masterfully.

Burton's George is the calm in the storm of Elizabeth's Martha. Hers was the showier part; his was, in many ways, the more difficult. He admitted that his "natural ego" wanted to make the character more aggressive and powerful, but that he'd learned to accept being dominated and led around by Elizabeth. His respect for Nichols helped. "I listened absolutely to what he said," Burton revealed. "First time in my life I've ever done so with a director. Whatever he says, I do."

At the Red Basket diner in nearby Southampton, he followed Nichols's directions impeccably. The night was chilly but clear, the moonlight suffusing the gravel parking lot and surrounding trees. Over and over, Nichols instructed Richard and Elizabeth to walk out of the diner, which was serving as the roadhouse in the picture. It was a long trucking shot, and the director wanted to make sure he got them from every angle, not knowing which would look best in the editing room.

Then came the fight between George and Martha in the parking lot. "Elizabeth and Richard were absolutely blood-curdling in their performance," Lehman recorded the following morning. Their struggle was so realistic that the crew winced every time Elizabeth was thrown back and hit her head against the station wagon. At one point tears sprang to her eyes and she had to lie down for a bit, the company doctor looking in on her. Still, she came back again and redid the scene "many times," Lehman said. Even when Nichols finally said that he had what he wanted, Elizabeth requested they do it once more, because she felt she could do it better. "And indeed she did," Lehman said.

"I've never had a better time in my life," Elizabeth would say, looking back on the filming of *Virginia Woolf*. Perhaps to counterweight the sturm und drang of the script, there was considerable laughter and lightheartedness on the set. Elizabeth and Sandy Dennis engaged in belching contests, and for the first time in her life, Elizabeth didn't win. Burton and Nichols played word games, betting each other that they wouldn't know the definitions of odd words like *porbeagle, roup,* or *pleach.* The quarrels that had arisen early in the shooting had been largely replaced by harmony.

Part of the reason Elizabeth would always have such rosy nostalgic memories of *Virginia Woolf* was because, in many ways, this was the pinnacle of her time with Richard. They were truly, deeply, happily in love for these five months. Not long before shooting wrapped, Richard showed Lehman a short poem he'd written about Elizabeth that, in the producer's opinion, was "decidedly erotic." Lehman later asked Elizabeth, "How does your husband do things like that?" She replied simply, "I inspire him."

Passionate for each other and their movie, they took lusty delight in shouting and cursing at each other in front of the cameras and then falling into each other's arms after Nichols called "Cut." It was rather like foreplay. "We both had to pull out all the stops, and throw all the scenery around," Elizabeth said. "That was fun. It was very cathartic, too, because we would get all our shouting and bawling out on the set and go home and cuddle." And probably more than cuddling, too.

As the film neared completion, Burton grew reflective. He told Lehman that the two fears he'd had at the outset had been dispelled. The first was that Elizabeth wouldn't be capable of doing Martha. The second was that the shoot would undermine their relationship. It hadn't, he said. On the contrary, they'd not had one major quarrel the whole time—unusual for them, he said. For one halcyon moment, there was reason to think that maybe all of the drama of their coming together might actually pay off, that despite all the naysayers they might truly have found soul mates in each other, that they might really be together forever.

Then, on September 21, it was time to go back to Los Angeles.

As ever, only aggravation awaited in the movie capital.

Her mother told Elizabeth that Hedda Hopper had called again, desperate for an interview. Largely forgotten, the old woman was still rattling on, turning out columns that weren't all that different from the days when Shirley Temple was the biggest draw in Hollywood. One noticeable difference these days, however, was that she no longer attacked Elizabeth. After the Wilding settlement, Hedda seemed to have considered Elizabeth off-limits, though once in a while she just couldn't resist the temptation. In August she'd given the Burtons some backhanded praise by quoting a source who said they were the only actors who could draw audiences with bad movies.

But now Hedda wanted very much to interview Elizabeth. She was hoping that it might stem the tide of newspapers dropping her column. From her spartan office, attended now by just one loyal secretary, Hedda placed call after call to Sara Taylor, a pathetic reversal of roles from their original interaction. Hedda knew that she stood no chance of getting through to Dick Hanley, who refused to speak to her. But if Sara could arrange something, she'd be eternally grateful. Hedda had done her part to promote *Virginia Woolf,* even if she'd found the material abhorrent. Such language! Such situations! Yet dutifully she'd interviewed Nichols and Lehman and printed up a fluff piece laden with accolades. Now she pleaded with Sara to arrange a sit-down with her daughter. But Elizabeth didn't have the time to take Hedda's call.

Even if they remained in the minority, other columnists weren't as reticent as Hedda to go on the attack. When Elizabeth announced that she would be giving up her U.S. citizenship, there was considerable carping in the American press. Since she'd been born in London, Elizabeth had always had dual British-American nationality. But not since 1959 had she been a permanent resident of the United States; she owned no American real estate. Her decision, she claimed, was based on loyalty to Burton, a British national, and not because she "loved America any less." She just loved her husband more. But cynics thought that tax breaks were her true love. Earlier she'd admitted, "The tax thing is so crippling to Americans living in Europe, especially for those in my bracket." She netted just six cents for every dollar of her phenomenal earnings, she claimed. If she remained a U.S. citizen, those million-dollar salaries would boil down to only sixty thousand. With utter candor she said, "Money is more valuable than citizenship or patriotism. Down in your hearts, you know I'm right."

For the dwindling but still passionate Elizabeth haters, that was like red meat thrown to a pack of wolves. "A lot of grated parmesan about Elizabeth Taylor's 'loyalty,'" snarled Mike Connolly in the *Hollywood Reporter*, who pulled a Joe McCarthy by making hay with the fact that Burton had donated to the left-wing Bertrand Russell Peace Foundation. "This is loyalty? Let her go, quick, now, the soonest—and Burton with her."

But for Elizabeth the worst irritant she found back in California was Eddie Fisher, who'd announced that he was suing for custody of Maria. To interviewers, Elizabeth had frequently revised history, insisting that she'd found Maria on her own, cutting Eddie completely out of the picture. But in the beginning, as letters document, Eddie had been considered the girl's adoptive father.

"How's the new baby?" writer Paddy Chayefsky asked Eddie in a letter dated January 1962. "Did the cast come off properly? How exciting all this must be for you both." But the fact was, not long after that, Eddie had been removed from Maria's life and all communication between them had ended. His attempt to gain custody of her now was, like Hedda's offensive against Wilding, really a volley aimed at Elizabeth.

And there were other ongoing legal battles. Elizabeth had sued Fox for failing to pay all the royalties due from *Cleopatra*. The studio, furious that it was still in the red over the picture while the Burtons made millions from it, launched a countersuit asking for $50 million in damages. The charge: breach of contract. Fox had decided to hit Elizabeth with everything it could. She had not reported for work, or not reported on time, the studio charged; she had not performed "her services with due diligence, care or attention"; she had caused "herself to be held up to scorn, ridicule and unfavorable publicity as a result of her conduct"; she had "become offensive to good taste and morals and [depreciated] the commercial value of *Cleopatra*." Claims against Burton were similar. In other words, Fox was suing them for their affair—the same thing that had garnered all that unpurchasable publicity and turned *Cleopatra* into a box-office bonanza. But when the film failed to earn out, the studio figured on balancing its books by taking back some of the monies it had unwisely signed over to Elizabeth and Richard.

John Springer responded that the suit was "too ludicrous" for comment. But not so ludicrous that the Burtons could avoid giving testimony to a battery of Fox lawyers who grilled them behind closed doors upon their return from Northampton.

As she was peppered with questions, Elizabeth's beautiful eyes flashed with anger. She did not like being interrogated. She wasn't accustomed to people badgering her in this way. She sat beside her lawyer, Aaron Frosch, one of the shrewdest entertainment lawyers in the biz. Brooklyn born, he'd represented John Gielgud when the actor was being blackmailed over his homosexuality and had served as executor of Marilyn Monroe's estate. Frosch knew how to take care of his clients. He routinely surprised Elizabeth with little gifts of jewelry. But try as he could, he'd been unable to forestall this deposition. He did his best to limit Elizabeth's testimony, but Fox's lawyers were determined to wheedle something, anything, out of her.

It was all rather humorous. Frederick W. R. Pride, Fox's legal counsel, was a very serious inquisitor. A Harvard man, Pride was well known in New York society; his daughter had been presented at the debutante cotillion at the Waldorf-Astoria in 1955. Phrasing and rephrasing his questions to Elizabeth, he never cracked a smile. He wanted to know where she'd been on certain days during the making of *Cleopatra,* and where Burton had been. Without any sense of irony or bemusement, he asked questions about where trysts had taken place, and when, and for how long. Much unfolding of maps ensued. When Pride asked Elizabeth to point out where her villa had been in relation to Burton's, she just gave him a withering look, adding that she couldn't read maps. Of course she couldn't.

But Pride was not deterred. "These two defendants," he said, "by their irresponsible, illicit conduct during the production of this picture directly and indirectly brought down upon this company expenses of millions of dollars." He recalled the time when they "sneaked away from Rome to a hideaway over Easter weekend and what happens? This principal character in this picture, Elizabeth Taylor, comes back with a black eye, a cut nose, and becomes unphotographable for two weeks." With her salary and living expenses, Pride charged, "whether the picture went forward or didn't was of no concern to her; the longer it lasted the more weeks she earned this princely amount."

Elizabeth seemed to enjoy making Pride's job as difficult as possible. She repeatedly said she couldn't remember dates, even when Pride showed her pictures of her hairstyles to help jog her memory. When he asked her about where she lived at certain times, she was evasive. She wasn't going to say anything that could be used against her, either by Fox or the Internal Revenue Service.

When Pride pressed her on where she had resided in 1961, she said that she didn't remember if it was New York or Rome or London or California. When he asked about January 1963, she had to admit she was in London; it was a matter of public record.

"And you were not in New York at that time, is that correct?" Pride asked.

Looking at him with utter contempt, Elizabeth said, "Well, I couldn't very well be if I was in London."

When Pride asked if she held any mortgages, Elizabeth turned to her lawyers and asked, "Do my houses have mortgages?" She had no idea about such things.

At times the deposition sounded like an Abbott and Costello routine. Pressed if she had any visas that might show her residency, Elizabeth replied with another question: "Don't you have to have an entry permit to go to Italy?" Pride: "I'm asking that." Elizabeth: "I don't know. I'm asking you."

"Obviously, Mr. Pride," Elizabeth's lawyer chimed in, "Mrs. Burton is not aware of what she does or doesn't have along these lines. These things are taken care of by others." Of course they were.

She was deliciously sarcastic. Asked if the Regency was a transient hotel, she replied, "I imagine most hotels are." Questioned about whether she had business interests in California, she quipped, "I haven't any business interests, period." After admitting to living for several months in Switzerland, she was pushed to define "several." She said that she didn't know the definition. When asked again, she said, "Sweetheart, I said I don't know." "She doesn't know," her counsel echoed, just in case Pride hadn't gotten it.

Frederick W. R. Pride was unable to break down Elizabeth Taylor. He left without getting anything incriminating on her. But the Fox lawsuit wasn't the only legal hassle she faced. A number of exhibitors' groups had also sued the Burtons for turning *Cleopatra* into an "inferior attraction" due to their disregard of "good taste and morals." It didn't help Fox's case against the Burtons that the exhibitors had sued the studio as well, claiming that it shared some of the blame. All of this was merely evidence of yet another precedent Elizabeth Taylor was setting for celebrities in poststudio Hollywood. If one is famous enough, one will be sued. It would become an unavoidable by-product of fame.

Thankfully, she had the final wrap-up of *Virginia Woolf* to distract her. She and Richard agreed to work the two final weeks free of charge. "This picture is too important to Elizabeth and me for anything to happen to it that might interfere with its quality," Burton said. At the eleventh hour, Elizabeth had to reshoot a scene where Nichols felt she'd gone too far emotionally. He feared that it would make her last scene—the crucial moment where she says, "I am, George. I am"—anticlimactic. Elizabeth was "tight-lipped but thoroughly professional" during the retake.

The final scene was shot on December 13. Elizabeth was overjoyed when Lehman presented her with the gift she'd been asking for: a turquoise and gold pendant with a pearl and platinum chain.

It wasn't the only perk she took away from the shoot. Because delays had kept the Burtons from getting back to Europe in time for Christmas, they had to bring the family to Los Angeles, and Warners agreed to reimburse the costs. Michael and Christopher, their nanny, Richard's brother, his sister, and sister-in-law all flew in from England, at a cost to the studio of $5,688.65. Plus there was the $3,000 evening gown that Elizabeth had worn to a dinner in honor of Princess Margaret, because Frosch argued that she'd only gone as "part of her efforts to publicize *Virginia Woolf.*"

At least it had taken her mind off the lawsuits. But now Eddie was harassing her again, claiming that their Mexican divorce wasn't valid and her marriage to Burton wasn't legal. He also was asking for visitation rights to see Liza—not even Maria, but Liza! Elizabeth was beside herself with rage at the man for whom she'd once jeopardized her career. Any compassion she once may have felt for him over what had happened in Rome evaporated. Eddie was a nightmare that just wouldn't go away. This is why Eddie Fisher would always be the lone target of Elizabeth's venom among her numerous former husbands, why even more than three decades later, when asked what she thought of him, she replied: "I wouldn't put it in print. I don't even want to mention his name."

But there was one old adversary she no longer had to worry about. Ten months after the humiliating settlement with Michael Wilding, Hedda Hopper died of double pneumonia on February 1, 1966, at the age of eighty. "The passing of an era," the *Los Angeles Times* proclaimed. Indeed. Movies were no longer the kind of commodities that Hedda had once sold; stars weren't the kind of objects that she'd been able to build and tear down. It could be argued that Hedda's obsessive campaign to topple Elizabeth Taylor had contributed to her own decline. "The Wilding lawsuit kind of finished her off," said Robert Shaw. "She was never the same after that." Her spirit broken, her reputation in tatters, her health rapidly declining, Hedda soldiered on, but she was an anachronism, and she knew it. Her funeral, for all her storied reputation, was sparsely attended. After cremation, Robert Shaw and those few friends who were left sent her "back home to Altoona in a box."

Tossing a vase at her husband and letting out a scream, Elizabeth seemed to be releasing all the pent-up rage and frustration from her long sojourn in America. Richard artfully dodged the vase, and Franco Zeffirelli called "cut."

They were back in Rome, filming *The Taming of the Shrew*. Elizabeth felt liberated, grateful to be out of the country that seemed only to oppress her these days. Richard had long fancied doing Shakespeare with his wife, envisioning her as Lady Macbeth. But Elizabeth had just laughed and asked, "Wouldn't it be better typecasting for me to do *The Taming of the Shrew*?" Indeed it was—and everyone on the set, including Zeffirelli, was amazed at the intelligence and vitality that she brought to the part. She was a force of nature, wild, untamed, and perfectly at ease with the Shakespearean dialogue.

Even after the exertions of *Virginia Woolf,* there was still no thought of coasting. After *Shrew*, there would be a version of *Doctor Faustus* for Richard's mentor Nevill Coghill and the Oxford

University Dramatic Society, in which Elizabeth would essay the nonspeaking part of Helen of Troy. There were also plans to re-unite with Montgomery Clift on a film based on Carson McCullers's novel *Reflections in a Golden Eye*. And Ernest Lehman was seriously pursuing her to star in the film version of *Hello, Dolly!* "Why not?" Richard cracked to his wife. "You're fat and you're Jewish." Elizabeth adored the idea ("I could play it with a real Brooklyn accent") though she worried that Carol Channing, the original Dolly on Broadway, would be "very angry" with her. But somehow no one else saw her in the role.

What everyone was waiting for was Martha. On June 24, 1966, *Who's Afraid of Virginia Woolf?* opened at the Criterion Theatre in New York. Two thousand people pushed through the doors to watch the Burtons spit, snarl, and scrape at each other. At first, the Production Code Administration had refused to grant the film a seal of approval, but then Jack Valenti, the new president of the Motion Picture Association of America, had pressured the group to change its mind. But many theaters, including the Criterion, would allow those under eighteen to attend only with a parent or guardian.

The seal proved irrelevant. By refusing to change a line of the script, Nichols, Lehman, and Warner Bros. had accomplished something tremendous: They had effectively ended three decades of the Production Code's draconian rule. "The Code is dead," the trade paper *Motion Picture Daily* editorialized the week after *Virginia Woolf*'s premiere. Indeed, the PCA was soon obsolete, replaced by the ratings system that would dominate for the next thirty years.

The legacy of *Virginia Woolf* would be a new era, one that, as Vincent Canby described it in the *New York Times*, allowed "the public morality in film to reflect more accurately the state of private morality." Once again, it was Elizabeth Taylor at the center of a moral contest, and once again, she was on the winning side.

In fact, she won more than that. From coast to coast and across the Atlantic, critics were swooning over her bold portrayal of Martha. "The finest performance of her career," crowed the *Motion Pic-*

ture Herald. The *New York Times* agreed, calling Elizabeth's work "sustained and urgent . . . [charged] with the utmost of her powers." *Variety* thought she'd earned "every penny of her million plus," and *Time* declared that she was "loud, sexy, vulgar [and] pungent" while still achieving "moments of astonishing tenderness." Indeed, "astonishing" is the best way to sum up her performance. She slashes her way so fiercely through the film that we can almost see the rips in the celluloid made by her fingernails. She's cruel and cunning, and yet we root for her, too. She inspires compassion as much as revulsion, perhaps even more so. At the end of the picture, one sits back out of breath, heart pounding. It is a remarkable cinematic achievement. The widespread consensus among critics was that the little girl who had started out making pictures with Lassie had surpassed all expectations that anyone ever had for her.

Elizabeth was flabbergasted. She'd expected to be skewered by the critics. As the picture wrapped, she'd told Lehman that reviewers always blasted her. He suggested that maybe she should have someone screen her reviews for her, but she wouldn't hear of it. "I'm not a masochist," she said, "but I do want to read everything that they say about me, even if it's bad." This time, she was pleasantly surprised and deeply gratified.

Who's Afraid of Virginia Woolf? would be the third biggest movie of 1966. Elizabeth was perched atop the list of box-office stars once more, with Julie Andrews her only female rival. So it was with some cockiness that she sauntered onto the set of *Reflections in a Golden Eye* to begin work. When presented with the idea of shooting a television documentary on the set as a promotion for the film, Elizabeth refused out of hand, defending her decision to her furious producer, Ray Stark, by saying, "I am told by a recent report from the motion picture trade papers that none of my pictures have ever lost money. These pictures were made without the benefit of a television documentary." (*Cleopatra* had finally reached its break-even point a few months earlier.)

Despite shooting in Rome and being directed by John Huston, Elizabeth didn't enjoy making *Reflections.* For the first time in four years, she didn't have Richard as a costar. He made sure to stick close by, however, bowing out of *Goodbye, Mr. Chips* in case his wife needed his help. If she'd had her way, Elizabeth would never have made another film without Richard at her side. He pooh-poohed the idea: "We don't want to be seen as Laurel and Hardy." Elizabeth countered, "What's so bad about Laurel and Hardy?"

In many ways, her role in *Reflections* was an old familiar one: the beautiful woman left unfulfilled by a repressed, tormented homosexual. But this time Elizabeth's character acts out on her own, engaging in her own affair and scheming against her husband. It was a tricky part to make sympathetic, and despite Huston's best attempts to direct her, she never really found her way. Part of the problem was that she'd expected to be working opposite Monty. But her old friend had been found dead in his home in July—a personal loss for Elizabeth that was made even worse by the casting of Marlon Brando to replace him. Although she liked her costar personally, Elizabeth found Brando's habit of continually blowing his lines, sometimes on purpose, terribly irritating; it recalled the "Method" madness inflicted on her by James Dean a decade earlier.

On top of that, she resented playing second fiddle to Brando's character. It was enough of a conflict that Stark penned a private memo to Huston: "Please let's at least write in enough scenes for Elizabeth so there can be no doubt about it being the best of costarring parts. We can always either not shoot them or cut them out later."

So it was with some relief that she finished up the picture and hurried off to Dahomey (now Benin) in western Africa to make another picture with Richard, *The Comedians*, directed by Peter Glenville. Meanwhile, a world away, *The Taming of the Shrew* opened in New York on March 8, 1967, to surprisingly good box office; Shakespearean films didn't normally bring in the crowds. But apparently the Burtons still could. In gorgeous pastel Renaissance costumes, Elizabeth is a heaving-bosomed delight. Audiences seemed to consider all the kicking and sparring and jumping

into haystacks as a glimpse into the Burtons' famously tempestuous private lives.

Hollywood was impressed. Elizabeth could still pack them in
after twenty years. But would they reward her for it? She'd been
nominated for an Academy Award for *Who's Afraid of Virginia
Woolf?* No one had doubted that she would be. But the question on people's minds was whether Academy voters—Elizabeth's
peers—felt that she'd already been rewarded enough. Those million-dollar salaries, those jewels, those houses in Switzerland and
Mexico. And she already had one Oscar. Well-known award handicapper Bob Thomas gave the odds to Lynn Redgrave for her engaging performance in *Georgy Girl*, a favorite among young moviegoers. But Marilyn Beck, one of the new breed of writers who'd
appeared in the wake of Hedda and Louella, had a different view,
predicting that Elizabeth and Richard would be the first husband
and wife to take home joint Oscars. "The emotional climate seems
right for this to be the Burtons' year," Beck wrote in her syndicated
column. "For Liz and Richard are now among the filmland's favorites, and don't think that such things don't have a lot to do with se-
lecting a winner."

This was more proof of how times had changed. Elizabeth and
Richard were no longer just tabloid fodder. Now they were "filmland's favorites," causing a sensation wherever they went, spicing
up parties with a dash of old-time glamour in an increasingly blue
jeans–and–T-shirt industry. When Elizabeth's name was read as
the winner on the night of April 10, the applause that thundered
through the Santa Monica Civic Auditorium was heartfelt. Unlike
the night six years earlier when she'd won for a film that she'd respected much less, Elizabeth was not present to receive her award.
She was no longer a denizen of Hollywood; she graced them with
her presence only on rare and special occasions. But the next day
her photo landed on the front pages of newspapers around the
world. Richard didn't win, however, much to her chagrin, and neither did Mike Nichols, but Sandy Dennis did take home the supporting actress trophy.

Despite the slight to her husband, it seemed that in this new world order, Elizabeth Taylor was still queen. She alone had anticipated what was to come. Every criticism made of her, every action taken against her, was eventually proven wrong or overturned. Her way of seeing the world prevailed, as the lawsuits she faced were settled one by one, largely in her favor. When one of the exhibitors suing over *Cleopatra* argued that he'd lost revenues because audiences didn't want their money going to "that woman," Appellate Judge Gilbert H. Jertberg looked at him in disbelief. Undeterred, the exhibitor pressed forward, even if he had no evidence that Elizabeth and Richard had hurt his business. All he had to bolster his argument was his own umbrage. "In this case," he said indignantly before the court, "they were each married to someone else." Jertberg gave him a trenchant look. "But that's no longer very shocking, is it?" the judge asked.

Indeed, it was not.

"We're all *dieting,* so no dessert," Elizabeth told her entourage one night in the royal suite at the Plaza Hotel in Manhattan. "That's why we are ordering lima beans, corn on the cob, steak and kidney pie, and mashed potatoes."

Elizabeth was thirty-five years old and on top of the world. Whatever she wanted, she could have. And tonight she was hungry.

"God, I love food," she gushed to Liz Smith, entertainment editor for *Cosmopolitan,* as the entrées arrived. "And wine, I adore wine." But when she took a gander at the bottles that Richard had ordered, she scrunched up her face. "Really, Agatha," she said, using one of her pet nicknames for her husband. "Are you saving money again? Really, I don't believe you, you are so *cheap.*"

"Quiet, Tubby," Burton responded, "or I shall belt thee in thy tiny chops."

"Listen," Elizabeth said, wagging a finger at the waiter. "I think I'll have a hot fudge sundae."

No one dared remind her about the diet.

Glancing around the hotel suite, Smith pondered what exactly it was that made the Burtons so larger than life. She watched as Alexandre fussed over Elizabeth's hair while the star polished off her sundae. Behind them, a secretary was on the telephone, ordering lingerie from Henri Bendel. "Money, stardom, fame, and married sexual excess were not their gods," Smith observed, "at this point, anyway." It was *food,* she realized, penning a hilarious, notorious piece about the Burtons' culinary intemperance.

And yet while Smith was being funny, she was also quite serious. By the later part of the 1960s, Elizabeth's raison d'être was the voracious acquisition of all that would sustain, fulfill, and satiate her: wine and mashed potatoes and hot fudge sundaes, to be sure, but also Alexandre's elaborate Parisian hairstyles and the lacy slips sent over from Henri Bendel.

And the jewels. Definitely the jewels.

As the Burtons and their crew sailed "unobtrusively" out of the Plaza, Smith hurried to tag along, taking notes all the way. Elizabeth wore a coffee-colored suede coat trimmed with fox. Her eyes were "flashing like 'walk' signs." They climbed into a robin's-egg-blue Rolls-Royce in order to ride two blocks to David Webb's jewelry store. When they walked in, store employees sprang to attention "as if we were wearing stocking masks," Smith wrote.

"I want to see some rings and things," Elizabeth announced. "Nothing over $5,000." Trays of jewelry suddenly materialized around her. Alexandre was nearly orgasmic, slipping rings onto his fingers, but Richard just rolled his eyes. "A steal at $4,000," he said sarcastically, looking at one piece.

Elizabeth shot him a look. "Richard, you don't understand, man. This stuff is not just ordinary diamonds-and-rubies junk. This is *it* now—it's very chic." She already had several of the gold and silver rings jammed onto her short, chubby fingers.

Turning her attention to the sales clerk, she asked sweetly, "What will these pieces be with my *spectacular* discount?" With a grand wave, she indicated several leopard, zebra, and serpent rings. "Never mind," she said quickly. "Send them to the hotel, and these too." She pointed at a $2,500 cigarette lighter and a $29,000 shell purse.

This was Elizabeth's fame now. In October 1967 there were no movies on the immediate horizon. Three had just opened: *Reflections in a Golden Eye* and *The Comedians* in New York and *Doctor Faustus* in London. None were big moneymakers. The cockiness that Elizabeth had displayed to Ray Stark now rang awfully hollow; for the first time, not just *one* Elizabeth Taylor movie, but *three*, failed to cash in at the box office. Not even *Reflections*—which had promoted the latest (and as always discreet) nude shot of La Taylor with a suggestive tagline, "Leave the children home."

Yet in some ways box office didn't matter anymore to Elizabeth. In February 1968 the New York premiere of *Doctor Faustus* brought out the Robert Kennedys and the Peter Lawfords and even Spyros Skouras, who let the past be the past and toasted the Burtons grandly. Outside the theater, another riot broke out. "We just stepped right on one poor man who had fallen," Elizabeth said. "I couldn't help it, the way they were shoving and clawing at us."

"It was Bobby Kennedy who saved us," Richard said, describing the fracas the next day. "He just took over. He turned to those cops and snapped, 'Is there a police car outside? Well, get the Burtons into it.' He is a fantastic person."

"We adore Bobby Kennedy," Elizabeth echoed. "We simply adore him."

Richard couldn't get over the fuss that people still made over them. "Here were these two middle-aged people, Elizabeth and me, merely trying to get into the cinema," he said.

Elizabeth sighed. "I thought we were all through with that sort of thing. I thought we had gone over the popularity hill. The crowd was strange: not the usual types along in years who might hang around to see us, but a young groovy bunch—like hippies almost."

Apparently their appeal knew no bounds. "With Elizabeth around," Burton said by way of explanation, "you always get that sort of excitement."

"Oh, Modesty Blaise," his wife said, throwing him a look, "I hardly know you."

She made that kind of noise often, insisting that the crowds came to see Richard as much as they did her. But her husband was right. It was Mrs. Burton, in her elegant furs and sparkling jewels and daring miniskirts—then all the rage—who really drew the attention. Still, the two of them together provided the glamorous traveling road show that the press covered so eagerly and the public devoured so greedily. As media stars, their only peers were Jackie Kennedy and Aristotle Onassis, but Jackie and Ari, for all their wealth, were never so deliciously conspicuous as the Burtons.

"We get a great giggle out of all our things," Elizabeth said. "The yacht, the Rolls, a sable fur coat." Of course she quickly assured the reporter that she and Richard were "totally unblasé" about it all. Indeed, it was her very enjoyment of extravagance—her sheer, undisguised elation—that made Elizabeth and her lifestyle so appealing. "Some people believe it is vulgar to show their possessions," she said, "but we show ours. In Gstaad, it is fun to look at everything we've collected over the years." And she insisted with utter conviction that she loved the little straw donkey a bartender had given her years before in Rome with as much fervor as she loved the sapphires and emeralds.

She was probably being just a tiny bit disingenuous. Her love of jewels seemed to grow exponentially with every month she stayed away from moviemaking. She had finally achieved what she had always wanted: She could stay home, luxuriate in her bath, play with her animals, and eat chicken straight out of the deep fryer. She was the little girl she'd always wanted to be. And sparkly jewels were her favorite toys.

"What are you doing, Lumpy?" Richard called to her, waiting for her in bed, in a moment he preserved for posterity in his diary.

"Playing with my jewels," she called back cheerfully.

She liked pretty clothes, too. "I'm much more broad-minded about clothes now," she tried telling one reporter. "I used to only go to Dior. Now it's *all* the good French designers." She laughed, aware of the press coverage the Parisians gave her. "I *sort* of try to live on a budget. Richard says I'm the reason for communism in France."

But she *needed* new clothes: Her figure was filling out. By 1968 she was no longer the slim-hipped siren of *Cleopatra* and *The Sandpiper*. It was almost as if she'd taken a look at Martha's padding and extra poundage and not really minded what she saw all that much. To stay slim meant that she couldn't "pig out," an activity at least as enjoyable as playing with her jewels, with her favorite meal consisting of fried chicken, mashed potatoes with "lots of gravy," corn on the cob with "lots of butter," and "something chocolatey for dessert." For all her partiality to Europe, it was common American food that Elizabeth craved most.

"The lazy little bugger ought to lose a few pounds or so to look at her absolute best," Richard wrote in his diary around this time. Looking at her as critically as he could, he saw few signs of aging except for a few gray hairs; the breasts, "despite their largeness and considerable weight," sagged no more than they had when he first met her. "She needs weight off her stomach," he declared, "not so much out of vanity but because all the medical men say it will ease her bad back if she has less weight to carry for'ard."

But still the paparazzi aimed their telephoto lenses at the Burtons' new yacht, a 279-ton, 130-meter vessel christened the *Kalizma*—for Richard's daughter Kate and Elizabeth's daughters Liza and Maria. With six cabins and two staterooms, the *Kalizma* could sleep fourteen and required a crew of five. Columnist Earl Wilson called it a "floating palace." Elizabeth adored the freedom that the *Kalizma* gave them. The yacht meant they could live anywhere, go anywhere. Lounging on its deck of polished Edwardian mahogany and chrome, she could be a citizen of no place, completely on her own, answerable to no one but herself. It was her lifelong dream.

"Hi, Lumpy," Richard called as she arrived onshore from the *Kalizma* by motorboat. They'd moored the yacht off the coast of Sardinia, and Elizabeth was meeting her husband and Earl Wilson for lunch at the Hotel Capo Caccia, perched atop a rocky promontory and surrounded by the crystal blue sea. She wore pink trousers, a white shirt, blue cap, and dark sunglasses, and carried under her arm a spotlessly white poodle named O Fie (one of her favorite oaths from *The Taming of the Shrew*). From her left pinky sparkled a twenty-nine-carat diamond ring, a gift from Mike Todd, and from her wrist an opal-faced, diamond-encircled wristwatch, which came from Burton. But it was mostly emeralds that her husband had been giving her of late, she told Wilson.

Settling down for a quick conversation, Elizabeth was anxious to get back to the yacht. Onboard, John Lee was frying six chickens for the kids. Maybe she was hoping to snag a drumstick. A walkie-talkie kept her in touch with the crew. Throughout the meeting with Wilson, she let Richard do most of the talking. When the columnist observed that they seemed "the happiest, richest husband-and-wife team in show business," Burton quipped, "It's because I happen to have in my wife a remarkable star."

Elizabeth smiled, her eyes dancing in the Mediterranean sun. Then the remarkable star stood, replacing her sunglasses and bidding the men a good afternoon. Trooping down the cliff, she headed back out to the *Kalizma*.

Finally she was going to coast for a while.

She'd earned the right.

Epilogue

How to Stay a Movie Star

AFTER 1968 ELIZABETH TAYLOR didn't need movies to be famous anymore. Other things worked just as well. Diamonds, for instance.

As the world watched, a diamond the size and shape of a small pear was put up for auction at the Parke-Bernet Galleries in New York. At 69.42 carats, one and a half inches long, and an inch deep, the diamond, discovered a few years earlier in a South African mine, was considered flawless. Cut and mounted into a platinum ring by famed New York jeweler Harry Winston, the gem was owned by Harriet Annenberg Ames, sister of Walter Annenberg, the billionaire publisher and current ambassador to the Court of St. James's. The announcement that Mrs. Ames was putting her rock on the block sent diamond lovers around the world into paroxysms of lust and longing. On October 23, 1969, nearly eight hundred dealers, agents, and socialites jammed into the velvet-curtained auction room at Madison Avenue and Seventy-sixth Street. Bidding was frantic. Everyone knew that Al Yugler of Frank Pollack & Sons was representing Elizabeth Taylor Burton, and it was suspected that Robert Kenmore, bidding for Cartier, was working on behalf of Aristotle Onassis. As the bids climbed, people leapt from their chairs, swinging their gazes from Yugler to Kenmore. When Yugler stopped bidding at $1 million—then an unprecedented sum for a precious stone—Cartier acquired the diamond for $1,050,000. "Wowee," said Mrs. Robert Scull, wife of the well-known art collector. "That was something, wasn't it?"

But that wasn't the end of it. Calling from London, Richard

Burton was furious. He ordered Aaron Frosch to get on the line with Cartier. In less than twenty-four hours, the Cartier diamond had become the Taylor-Burton diamond. "It's just a present for my wife," Burton told reporters when they reached him on the phone.

Elizabeth never asked what he had to pay to get the ring, but it would be reported that he paid $1.1 million, providing Cartier a profit of $50,000. For the next several days the diamond was displayed in a breakproof glass case at Cartier's Fifth Avenue store, flanked by two armed security guards. Ten thousand people filed past to see "Liz Taylor's gem," the one they knew her husband had bought for her as a little gift because she'd been disappointed she hadn't gotten it at auction.

"I missed lunch to see this," said Mary Jane Mildenberger, a clerk-typist. "If I had a couple of million I'd spend one of them on a diamond like that, too."

This was now the crux of Elizabeth's fame, not the disappointing box office of her last few pictures or the excruciating reviews for *Boom!*, a wild, psychedelic, ahead-of-its-time film that she'd made with Burton for the director Joseph Losey. Dry attendance totals and pompous reviews tucked away on an inside page of the newspaper didn't count. The shiny Taylor-Burton diamond was smack-dab on the front page, and on *The Ed Sullivan Show,* and on display on Fifth Avenue and later in Chicago, available to thousands to gawk at and sigh over. More people saw the diamond than saw *Boom!* What they were looking at was irrelevant; all that mattered was that they were still looking.

And the Cartier diamond wasn't the only sparkler to grab the public's attention. It came on the heels of Burton's acquisition the year before of yet another oversized stone, the Krupp diamond. Once owned by a German armaments manufacturer, the Krupp prompted Elizabeth's famous quip about how nice it was that the ring should end up on "the nice little Jewish finger" of a girl like her.

Some society matrons sniffed, calling it all just too gaudy. "Nobody I know wants a diamond," said Mrs. Archie Preissman, wife of the Beverly Hills real estate magnate. "They don't look right with the beading on dresses and the jeweled necklines." Mrs. Preissman said that she wasn't wearing her diamonds anymore.

But Elizabeth Taylor was. At a reception with Princess Margaret not long afterward, aware that Her Royal Highness had called the Krupp the most vulgar thing she'd ever seen, Elizabeth asked if she'd liked to try it on. Once the ring had changed hands, its owner asked the princess brightly, "Doesn't look so vulgar now, does it?"

Mrs. Preissman and Princess Margaret were in the minority. Most people were like Mary Jane Mildenberger, gushing in awe. Even at thirty-seven years old, Elizabeth Taylor was still living a fairy tale for the world to follow. Just getting the Krupp from New York to the *Kalizma* in the south of France had provided good copy for the tabloids. Since the diamond wasn't insured between the time it left the auction house and the moment it was slipped onto Elizabeth's hand, Aaron Frosch arranged for five men to leave New York all at the same time with identical boxes. Each arrived in France on different planes. When they finally stood face-to-face with Elizabeth, the men handed her their boxes. One by one, she found them all empty. Richard let out a laugh as he saw his wife's jaw drop. Then Aaron Frosch pulled the ring out of his pocket and presented it to her. There weren't four decoys; there were five. Frosch had had the ring all along.

Elizabeth liked to say that she was merely a temporary "custodian" of her jewels. "You can't own a thing of such rare beauty," she said, flashing the Krupp on her finger to Helen Gurley Brown, "and I take good care of it." But Brown pointed out that when she'd walked through the kitchen earlier that day, she had seen the ring sitting by the sink. "There were people there!" Elizabeth declared defensively.

With stories like these, who needed movies? The films that Elizabeth made after 1968 were almost all made reluctantly. It had been Richard's idea to do *Boom!*, and he'd encouraged her to make *Secret Ceremony*, another flop. Elizabeth was miserable. Even a reunion with George Stevens on *The Only Game in Town,* which she shot in Las Vegas in the spring of 1969, turned out badly. She'd expected to play opposite Frank Sinatra and had little chemistry with his replacement, Warren Beatty. Worst still was Stevens, well past his prime and unable to shape the material. The result was a sorry end to a collaboration that had once produced such magic.

In some ways, Elizabeth was a casualty of the changing times. In the United States, attendance at the movies had plummeted from 38 million in 1966—the last year of Elizabeth's box-office reign—to 18 million a year later. The old generation of moviegoers—those who had first discovered Elizabeth Taylor and turned her into a star—were staying home, replaced by hippies and college kids revved up by pictures like *Midnight Cowboy* and *Easy Rider* and auteurs like Martin Scorsese and Francis Ford Coppola. Never again would one of Elizabeth's pictures break the top twenty.

Richard remained profitable enough if paired with a leading lady younger than his wife, like Geneviève Bujold in *Anne of the Thousand Days.* It was a cold hard fact that every actress of a certain age eventually faces. No matter how good Elizabeth looked in her miniskirts, she was no longer the youngest chick in town. And in Hollywood, growing old is a sin second only to flopping at the box office.

So it wasn't surprising that, at the age of forty, she trudged with terrible reluctance onto a soundstage in Munich to make a film called *Divorce His, Divorce Hers.* It was the autumn of 1972. She would have much preferred staying on the *Kalizma,* moored off Corsica, but Richard had arranged that they make the picture as a favor to Harlech Television, a Welsh station in which he held stock. "It was if by now stardom was a sword of Damocles that hung over her head," observed Waris Hussein, the director of *Divorce His, Divorce Hers.* After thirty years she had lost interest in moviemaking and would have preferred doing almost anything but. She asked no questions about the script; she sent her stand-in to rehearsals with the other actors. But she was still enough of a pro—enough of a movie star—that when she showed up for the actual shoot, she hit all her marks perfectly, even without any rehearsal.

"Movie stardom, real movie stardom, is something that never goes away," said Gavin Lambert, who knew and wrote about many great stars. "Once you have it, you carry it with you all your life, even if you're not making any movies at all."

For *Divorce His, Divorce Hers,* Hussein saw Elizabeth's character as a tasteful East Coast intellectual from old money; and he asked legendary costume designer Edith Head to create Elizabeth's wardrobe for the film with this in mind. Head listened to his description, then arched an eyebrow at him. "You haven't met Elizabeth yet, have you?" she asked. At that point, Hussein had not. Head agreed to design the clothes as he described, but she made no guarantee of his star's approval. Sure enough, when Hussein got the costume sketches back from Elizabeth, she had circled every neckline with a bold red pen and drawn an arrow to indicate that they should drop lower.

Elizabeth Taylor knew how she should appear on the screen. No young upstart director was going to tell her otherwise. Getting ready to shoot one scene, she emerged from her dressing room wearing another famous bauble that Burton had bought for her: La Peregrina, a pearl once owned by King Philip II of Spain, who had given it to his wife, Mary Tudor of England; later it adorned the necks of several Spanish queens. To get it, Richard had had to outbid Prince Alfonso de Bourbon Asturias, who'd hoped to bring La Peregrina back into the family and present it to the aging and exiled Queen Victoria Eugenia. Now Elizabeth appeared on the set with the famous pearl gleaming against her throat. Hussein told her that it was completely out of character. "Who the hell cares?" she snapped. "People want to see Elizabeth Taylor in jewels!" And so they did.

Divorce His, Divorce Hers, of course, could have been the Burtons' own story. The director watched as his stars' marriage disintegrated a little more every day. Shooting a street scene with Richard one night, the filmmakers were suddenly interrupted by "all sorts of sirens and police cars." It could mean only one thing: Mrs. Burton was arriving ahead of schedule. In the midst of all the flashing lights and the commotion of police escorts and frantic reporters, Hussein looked around and saw that Richard was gone. He'd bolted, unable to face the traveling circus that followed his wife wherever she went. Hussein later found him drunk at a bar.

The battles between the Burtons had only gotten worse. On the set of *Boom!*, they'd arrived drunk and screaming at each other. "Absolute hell," Joseph Losey said, but in the morning, their schizophrenic relationship became all "sweetness and light." The Burtons' friend and photographer Gianni Bozzacchi said that the fights between Elizabeth and Richard at the end were very much like those between Martha and George in *Who's Afraid of Virginia Woolf?*—cruel, unrelenting, way below the belt. When he got drunk, Richard got terribly mean, and he was drunk much of the time now. Elizabeth responded the only way she knew how: like a child. She lashed back.

But it broke her heart. "You see, she didn't care about being a star," Bozzacchi said. "She cared about living a certain way. It was what she was used to. And she lived that grand life with Burton and thought they'd have it forever. That's what was most important to her: to have a great companion in her great life. With Burton she felt she'd found her soul mate. It was all about being with him. That's all that really mattered."

Yet for Richard, it went far, far deeper. Elizabeth was indeed his great love; but she was also the world's greatest movie star and that meant he was forever caught in the crosshairs of her fame. More and more, he felt that he'd given up his great literary potential in order to play in soap operas for the masses. "In the beginning," Bozzacchi said, "Richard was fascinated by the whole thing. He liked being part of the big love story of all time. But then it became terribly distracting to what he was all about."

And so the bottle. On the set of *Divorce His, Divorce Hers,* he was drunk and swaying so much that the cameraman couldn't focus. Hussein stopped shooting. He kindly asked Richard what he could do to help. Richard just glared at him. Suddenly he bellowed, "Fuck off! I am Lear! I could play Lear!"

Certainly he was as tragic. "That's what destroyed him," said Mike Nichols. "The thing about Richard was that he was so much more generous to others than he was to himself. He beat himself up over what he thought was his failure as an actor. When he married Elizabeth and became a superstar, he saw himself in a much more cruel way than others did. I think he saw himself as having made the devil's bargain, and you only make the devil's bargain if that's how you think of yourself. He wasn't pleased with himself for the way he ended up as part of an international marriage scandal that was perpetual . . . And so the drinking took over and that was sad and awful to see."

The battles raged. The separations made headlines. The reconciliations did too, though they were increasingly seen as merely delaying the inevitable. Richard was acting out, womanizing, making Elizabeth look bad. Finally they divorced on June 26, 1974, after a decade of marriage. But the long saga of Liz and Dick wasn't over. Largely through Elizabeth's machinations, they remarried on October 10, 1975, in Botswana on the Chobe River with two hippopotamuses as witnesses. But this time the marriage lasted just nine and a half months. The Burtons divorced for the second and final time on August 1, 1976.

When Elizabeth had stepped out of her dressing room in her Martha makeup on the set of *Virginia Woolf,* Richard had looked over at her "quite adoringly." With great affection, he told his wife that he couldn't wait for her to *really* be forty-eight years old; he'd love her just as much as he did right then. "He was looking forward so eagerly to what she would be like in salt-and-pepper gray hair," said Ernest Lehman, who had witnessed the moment. Burton wistfully told Elizabeth that he'd be fifty-four when she was forty-eight. "That is," he said with a smile, "if I can make it to then." He'd be fifty when they divorced for the second time, fifty-eight when he died.

Without Richard, there were fewer old reliables around Elizabeth. Her father had died in 1968, and her children had become adults, leading lives as far outside their mother's orbit as they could. Michael joined a commune for a time, and when his wife gave birth to a little girl in 1971, he turned the thirty-nine-year-old Elizabeth into the "world's most glamorous grandmother." But in many ways the greatest upheaval in Elizabeth's life was the death of Dick Hanley from a massive heart attack on New Year's Day 1971. No one could run the ship quite like Dick.

To fill the void there came a striking, deep-voiced Egyptian woman who proved that she was Hanley, Kurt Frings, and John Springer all rolled into one. Elizabeth first laid eyes on Chenina Samin when she and Burton were in Botswana, right before their second marriage, when Richard had come down with malaria. Samin, a London-educated pharmacologist working for the Botswana Ministry of Health, arrived by helicopter to save the day. Her dark, knee-length hair swinging from side to side, she kept a raving Burton from ripping out his saline drip. As he came around, Richard's eyes focused on the exotic beauty tending to him with such efficient solicitude, and he was enchanted. "Richard persuaded me that I should drop medicine and become his personal publicist," Samin said—an unlikely switch, but Richard Burton was a very persuasive man.

Yet not so persuasive that Samin didn't side with Elizabeth in the divorce. "We're like sisters," she told the press—the sister and best girlfriend Elizabeth never had. Until now, all of her best chums had been men. Samin changed that, becoming aide, confidante, nurse, and champion. "Don't call me a secretary," she snapped at a reporter. Shortening her name to Chen Sam, she styled clothes, did makeup, organized Elizabeth's calendar, and pumped out press releases that *New York* magazine said "shrewdly [kept] Elizabeth Taylor in the spotlight long after the last big movie, whatever that was."

The throaty Egyptian who'd grown up wearing a burka took the media by storm. Swifty Lazar expected "a little Chinese man" when Chen called his secretary to make an appointment. In walked a gorgeous woman instead, throwing out ideas left and right as if she'd been a publicist for decades, and the veteran Hollywood agent was floored. In 1976 Chen helped spearhead a radically new direction for Elizabeth's public life and image: the Elizabeth Taylor Diamond Corporation. It was a much-lower-key effort than her later jewelry businesses, but it still gave clerk-typists the chance to wear gems like Liz. The diamonds started at $124, loose or mounted, and were sold in department stores in tasteful brushed aluminum cases.

More than one columnist observed that Elizabeth's celebrity was becoming more business than show business. She still made the occasional movie, but they were, as critic David Thomson said, "increasingly imprecise and unnecessary." She showed more excitement for the presents she might net on a picture than any acting challenges in the script. "Miss Taylor liked to find gifts in little robin's-egg-blue boxes in her dressing room every morning," said Mart Crowley, the writer of her film *There Must Be a Pony.*

None of her theatrical films went anywhere at the box office; the television films were a mixed bag, some pulling in high ratings, others being ignored. Mostly they served to remind the public that Elizabeth Taylor, even a little plump, still looked fabulous in diamonds and furs. Magazines like *Ladies' Home Journal* and *Woman's Day* knew they could still get a bump in newsstand sales if they splashed her violet eyes on their covers. Elizabeth had successfully parlayed her movie stardom into a post-movie-star life. And in 1978 that stardom would be used to promote a campaign with loftier ambitions than the sale of diamonds in brushed aluminum cases.

A few months after learning of Richard's remarriage to a leggy blond model many years her junior, Elizabeth herself tied the knot for the seventh time. The latest husband was an aristocratic Virginian farmer by the name of John Warner, the former husband of millionaire heiress Catherine Mellon. Washington insiders whispered that Warner had been looking around for the right woman to give his political ambitions a boost. Before meeting Elizabeth, he'd reportedly told the newscaster Barbara Walters, "You are such a terrific woman, you could make me a Senator." Walters demurred, but Elizabeth offered "more positive results," wrote the *New Republic*. The magazine dubbed Warner "the Senator from Elizabeth Taylor."

But where most observers clearly saw what Warner was getting from Elizabeth, only a few really understood what *she* expected out of the deal. *Esquire* picked up on some of it, calling the marriage "Liz Taylor's latest race for the big prize." What Warner was offering was the kind of life she'd been hankering after ever since Mike Todd had first dangled it in front of her twenty years earlier—a life she'd enjoyed all too briefly before Richard's drinking had knocked it all off-kilter. "I thought we would get married, live on the farm, raise horses," Elizabeth admitted. "I thought it would be all very sort of farmish . . . horsey, and I could have animals. I would go out and brand the cattle." She laughed at the memory of it. "Shit, man. It was going to be my dream."

If there were any fears that her Hollywood lifestyle and marital exploits would hurt Warner in the conservative hills and hollows of his state, they were quickly put to rest by the enthusiastic crowds that turned out to greet the couple on campaign stops. "I'm looking forward to a good life here," Elizabeth said, winning over doubters. "John's farm is beautiful. The houses he has remind me of the countryside in England." What she didn't share was the fact that she'd installed a disco in the farmhouse so she could entertain pals from Studio 54 like Andy Warhol and Liza Minnelli and Bianca Jagger.

The stage management of the marriage sometimes seemed obvious. Talking to the writer Aaron Latham, Elizabeth insisted that Warner had proposed to her with a bottle of wine and some caviar. "We didn't have any caviar," Warner corrected her, apparently worried that it might sound too elitist on the campaign trail. Elizabeth laughed. "Too rich for the Republican stomach?" she asked. Ignoring her husband, she told Latham that the caviar had been a gift from Ardeshir Zahedi, an Iranian diplomat she'd once dated briefly. "That's a terrible story," her husband said, even more uncomfortable after the mention of the Iranian. "I have no recollection of any caviar," he insisted.

"Okay," Elizabeth said, her eyes dancing with mischief, "we went up with some ground groundhog meat. A little moonshine. Oh, that's illegal. What do you call that really cheap wine? Oh, a bottle of muscatel. Virginia muscatel. Virginia ham. Anyway, they were all Virginia products." She laughed, as did Latham, but Warner was poker-faced. "Virginia caviar," Elizabeth added. "It's wonderful." Burton had enjoyed such badinage with his wife, but Warner didn't have Richard's wit. Tucked away in the rolling green hills of Virginia, Elizabeth missed her old sparring partner very much. She would never stop loving him, no matter how fondly she smiled at Warner for the cameras.

But she was a trouper. She crisscrossed the Commonwealth with her husband for ten months, putting her shoulder to the wheel of Warner's senate campaign. In one three-day marathon, she shook more than sixteen hundred hands. Elizabeth enjoyed it all, eating fried chicken and ribs at campaign stops, hurling cream pies at charity events, needling her husband in front of the press for not supporting the Equal Rights Amendment. Warner, a Republican, admitted that his wife "leaned left," though, as a British citizen, she couldn't even vote for him. What official Washington didn't know was that, even *before* giving up her U.S. citizenship, Elizabeth had never been a voter; she had "rooted" for candidates, she said in court depositions, but had never actually voted in any election. All Warner's supporters knew was that their candidate had promised that his wife would become a citizen. "Virginia needs her!" they cried.

By all accounts, Elizabeth was a hit on the stump. Once again, it was Chen Sam who orchestrated many of these campaign events. Warner had insisted that John Springer be ousted as Elizabeth's publicist. "John [Warner] wanted very understated work," Chen explained. "No Hollywood types." So she moved into a high-rise apartment complex in Washington to be near her boss. It wasn't long before the Capital learned what Los Angeles and New York already knew, that Chen was a canny architect and fierce protector of Elizabeth's image. She was called "Genghis Khan," said one press agent, "a real barracuda." But all those great shots that she engineered of Elizabeth smiling broadly and kissing babies and wolfing down Virginia ham hocks would pay off nicely.

Warner won the election on November 7, 1978. Almost immediately, however, Elizabeth began to realize that her husband had gotten a far better deal than she had. Once all the inaugural festivities were over, she found herself terribly lonely in Washington, rattling around Warner's drafty Georgetown house in her caftans. She wasn't used to living in cold weather. She missed friends like Roddy McDowall. She had nothing in common with the other senators' wives. "I think they [Washington] thought I was a freak, which is probably true," she said. To pass the time, she ate, drank, and ate some more.

"She was eating and drinking a *lot,*" said one of her assistants from that period. "She'd order cases of Clyde's chili [from the popular Georgetown restaurant] and keep them in a refrigerator in her bedroom. That way she'd only need to take a few steps out of her bed to grab another bowl. She'd take the chili back with her to bed and pull the sheets up over her as she'd give us our marching orders for the day."

At the Republican National Convention, Elizabeth looked even more zaftig sitting next to a rail-thin Nancy Reagan. For something to do, she tried becoming a patron of the Wolf Trap Farm Park, the premier outdoor performing-arts venue for metropolitan Washington in nearby Vienna, Virginia. Though the galas she hosted raised considerable funds for Wolf Trap, they could sometimes be downright tumultuous. At one event, she was determined that she would read a poem onstage with Johnny Cash. "It was the most absurd thing," said the assistant, "about some mother who spun straw into gold, very Rumpelstiltskin or something. It was the strangest sight during rehearsals. There's Elizabeth with her little girl voice, and there's Johnny with his deep drawl, drawing out all his words. Everyone was like, 'Who the fuck thought this was a good idea?' It was just the craziest thing." But on the night of the actual performance, poet Rod McKuen, a friend of Elizabeth's, stayed onstage past his allotted twenty minutes, which meant that the poem had to be cut for time. "Elizabeth was furious," said her assistant. "She *really* wanted to read that poem with Johnny Cash! So she went up to Rod and slapped him across the face. We couldn't believe it. Elizabeth started to leap at him and she would've been rolling around on the floor if Chen hadn't pulled her away."

She was probably drunk. Sitting alone in Georgetown or on Warner's farm, she had started drinking more heavily than ever. She'd also developed an addiction to Percodan, originally prescribed for her back pain but increasingly used to palliate all of her aches and pains and frustrations. The problem was exacerbated when Chen Sam started drinking too much herself; the two women could be spotted at hotel bars knocking back shots together. Married and divorced before she met Elizabeth, Chen had tragically lost a young son, and now found herself entangled in a destructive marriage to a much younger man. It meant that for a time she lost some of her renowned ability to keep her boss on the up-and-up. The result was only deeper chaos for Elizabeth.

At one Wolf Trap function, her assistants could barely get Elizabeth out of her dressing room and onto the stage. "Do you remember that scene in *Lady Sings the Blues* where Diana Ross is doing the lipstick on the mirror?" the assistant asked. "Elizabeth was like that. She was so far gone that night. They'd all been drinking and doing drugs—it was Elizabeth and Halston and Liza Minnelli. It was just mayhem backstage. Liza was walking into walls and Elizabeth was just sitting there, talking loudly to herself, not realizing she needed to go on."

But he admitted that when they finally got her onto the stage, she was "majestic," despite being completely "out of it" an hour earlier. "That's the power of a real movie star," the assistant said.

Still, for all of her power, or perhaps because of it, she was miserable in her country-estate marriage. She'd wanted the good life, so where were the parties? The music? The Mediterranean islands? And she continued to miss Burton terribly. "When I saw her with John Warner," said Gianni Bozzacchi, "she had lost her sparkle, the glow she had with Richard. It was just gone."

Making it all worse was the fun the press was having with her public image. On *Saturday Night Live,* the portly comedian John Belushi played her in drag. No longer did the paparazzi stalk Elizabeth to snare a sexy shot of her in a bathing suit, or kissing lovers on a yacht; now they looked for shots where she was struggling to get out of a car or waddling down the street. "Just like that," Bozzacchi lamented, "the most beautiful woman in the world was gone. It was very sad. After that, I could not sell a photo of Elizabeth where she looked good because [publishers] said, 'Oh, no, that's been retouched.' I had to say, 'No, it hasn't been, this is truly how she looks.' But they wouldn't believe me."

Trapped in Washington and mocked by the press, Elizabeth needed a plan. "Thank God she had Chen," said another assistant. Although Chen continued to struggle with alcohol, she was able to get it together enough to help Elizabeth find her way forward once more. "Together these two women were determined to re-create the image and the legend of Elizabeth Taylor," the assistant said.

"I believe at that point Elizabeth wanted to start a new life for herself," said the actor Dennis Christopher, soon to be her costar, "and to take all that wonderful stardom she had and really make it work for her."

She couldn't go back to making films. She was forty-eight—the age Burton had once wanted to see her at, but not an age that Hollywood had much use for, particularly in women. The marriage to Warner had run its course, failing to deliver what she'd hoped for. So she needed to find something to replace it with, something financially lucrative enough to sustain the lifestyle she required, but also something fulfilling enough, and interesting enough, that it would give her a new place in the world, a world that was post-Burton and post-Warner, and defined only by herself.

Elizabeth was rebuilding her career, her image, and her life without a man for the first time. With Chen at her side, she figured that she could pull it off. If she'd been able to use her movie-star powers to turn her husband into a United States senator, she ought to be able to use that same know-how to turn herself into a success all on her own.

But if not movies—or Washington society—then what?

In September 1980 producer Zev Bufman was previewing his revival of *Brigadoon* at Washington's National Theatre. He was told that his seat mate would be "the wife of a senator who was working late." As the overture ended, he felt someone slam him on the shoulder, as if to say, "Move over!" It was Elizabeth Taylor. When she learned who Bufman was, she became far more charming. At each round of applause, she'd turn to Bufman and whisper that she wanted to go on the stage. By intermission, they'd arrived at a preliminary plan for a partnership. Bufman swore a cast of actors to secrecy and arranged read-throughs of several potential plays. They decided on Lillian Hellman's *The Little Foxes*.

Elizabeth adored the part of the grasping, greedy Regina Giddens. But to her mind, Regina was more vulnerable than vindictive. The Regina she planned to bring to life would be very different from those played by Tallulah Bankhead or Bette Davis in previous incarnations. Departing from Hellman's vision of Regina as coldly manipulative, Elizabeth—with encouragement from director Austin Pendleton—chose to play her closer to her own skin. "What if *The Little Foxes* became about *appetite*," Pendleton wondered, "a healthy appetite for life? Of course it would turn into greed before our eyes, but what if Regina started out as a hearty, hedonistic lady?" He laughed. "And who's better at projecting a healthy appetite than Elizabeth Taylor?"

She would layer facets of her earthy movie-star image onto her portrayal, bringing everything she knew about star charisma and larger-than-life public images to the effort. Her Regina—no matter her crimes—would wring every last possible drop of sympathy from her audiences. It was an undertaking that Elizabeth knew something about, of course, having mastered that same task for herself even as she stole other women's husbands and turned living in sin into just another way to live.

She understood the stakes involved. Where she had been stubborn and churlish on movie sets for much of the past ten years, she was a woman transformed rehearsing for this play. She knew she couldn't afford to fail. Nearly fifty years old, she was aware that she might end up just another old movie star, trotted out for an occasional retrospective or tossed an honorary career award, but without the cash or the clout or the cachet to support the moviestar life that she truly believed she needed to survive—and maybe, in fact, did. So despite her aching back, Elizabeth got down crosslegged on the floor with her fellow actors to run lines with them for as long as she needed to be there.

"She had an enormous work ethic," said Dennis Christopher, cast as her nephew. "She worked her butt off. She never made star demands. She was just an actor on a play who'd gotten the job." The little notes in pencil that she made to herself in her personal script show this: "Sit on sofa." "Look to Ben and Oscar, then sit." "Pause." "Go upstairs." More experienced stage actors might have known such things instinctively, or at least not have felt the need to write them down. But Elizabeth wanted to make sure that she got everything right.

After all those months of boredom and loneliness in Washington, she adored the camaraderie of the company. Elizabeth's lack of airs meant that her cast mates could tease her the way they would anyone else. Practical jokes, like moving props without telling her, left her in hysterics. "Asshole!" she'd bray, drawing the word out, punctuating it with her distinctive cackle. "It's hard not to love her," said Maureen Stapleton, who played her sister-in-law. "You really have to go out of your way not to."

But being one of the gang didn't mean that Elizabeth surrendered one iota of her star power. She summoned all of her mystique to create Regina. Slimming down, toning up, it was as if she were back in the MGM hair and makeup department, being transformed into a goddess. Her hair was elaborately styled. Her costumes were designed by legendary Broadway designer Florence Klotz, who'd dressed Elizabeth for the film adaptation of *A Little Night Music* a few years earlier. Klotz understood the importance of star power and accentuated Elizabeth's famous hourglass figure. By the time of the show's first previews, Miss Taylor looked gorgeous, every inch the glamorous movie star the world had known for so long. "She didn't try *not* to be Elizabeth Taylor," Maureen Stapleton said. "It came naturally to her—she wasn't contrived. She did it instinctively."

But there needed to be some accommodations. At the previews, the cast was mystified when Elizabeth didn't make her entrances on time the way she had during rehearsals. The problem was the red light backstage. In the world of movies, a red light meant that filming was under way. Everyone would fall silent; no one moved a muscle. In the theater, however, the red light was a cue for the actors to enter. "And there's poor Elizabeth," Dennis Christopher said, "conditioned by her mother all those years ago to freeze up when the red light went on. She was all dressed and ready to start her scene, and she just couldn't move." Pendleton had to post a couple of people in the wings to literally push her onto the stage.

The mother who'd taught her about the red light was still there, gazing up at her daughter at nearly every preview of the show in Fort Lauderdale. Sara Taylor was now eighty-six years old, a tiny white-haired woman with enormous eyes. She'd often join the cast and crew for parties after the show. "Elizabeth made a big deal out of her mother," Dennis Christopher said. "It was obvious she really loved her. She took her out and showed her a good time." After Francis had died, Elizabeth became extremely solicitous of Sara. "Despite all [Elizabeth]'s protestations about her mother over the years," Burton wrote in his diary at the time, "like the good girl she is, she now only wants to protect and cherish her."

She did this by covering Sara's small frame with jewelry, always the best way to cherish a Taylor female. There was a diamond platinum wristwatch, a Cartier gold medallion belt inscribed TO MY HIPPY MOTHER, a fourteen-carat gold pendant, a platinum stickpin with twenty-one diamonds, one large cultured pearl, and dozens of others—not to mention a full-length black diamond mink valued at $3,500 and a white ermine at $4,500. Sara was richly repaid for her years of devotion. Until she died at the age of ninety-nine, she'd live in a high style paid for by the daughter for whom she'd worked so hard.

But at the moment Sara Taylor was still very much alive, sitting in the front row and cheering on Elizabeth as always. The extended previews in Fort Lauderdale meant that when the show opened at the Martin Beck Theatre on Broadway on May 7, 1981, Elizabeth would be comfortable and at ease in her part. She no longer froze up when the red light came on. On opening night, she weighed in at just 125 pounds and looked absolutely smashing. Good thing, too. Peering from the curtain, Dennis Christopher spied Liza and Warhol and Halston and Halston's lover, the artist Victor Hugo, sitting in the front row. "All of New York was there, it seemed," he said. They all wanted to see how Elizabeth Taylor, Hollywood star, would fare on Broadway.

For the last couple of days, the news had been filled with reports of a throat infection and doctors' demands that Elizabeth cancel her performance. Some suspected that it was just Chen Sam playing a tried-but-true publicity trick to lower expectations. Elizabeth, of course, insisted to the press that she was determined to carry on. "No matter how sick I am," she said, "I will go on for the opening. I won't cancel it, even if I'm croaking." She was a trouper. And Broadway rewarded troupers.

She didn't miss a beat that first night. Her voice was strong and full. Her magnificent eyes seemed to reach the farthest seat in the theater. "If *The Little Foxes* is Broadway melodrama, it's as good as the genre gets," said Frank Rich, reviewing opening night for the *New York Times*. "Or so it is in the hands of people who know how to milk it for every last gasp, thrill and laugh that it's worth. Count Miss Taylor in that company." Maybe the part of Regina, Rich observed, didn't necessitate great acting or soul searching, but it did require "the tidal force of pure personality." Few phrases have ever summed up Elizabeth Taylor quite so well.

"She had such a power about her that night," said Dennis Christopher. "By the time we opened on Broadway—and I'm really a theater snob, so I don't say this lightly—she was brilliant, indelible, on fire."

She knew she'd done well. The applause after the final curtain went on and on. Backstage Chen Sam was a bundle of ecstatic energy. "So many flowers, nowhere to walk," she said. "Oh, well, press on!" So they did, out onto the street, where hundreds lined the sidewalks waiting for a glimpse, cheering and whistling. Striding into Sardi's, Elizabeth broke into tears when the waiting crowd jumped to its feet, shouting "Bravo!" Floating from table to table in her diamonds and pearls, she was a vision in white, her breasts nearly falling out of her low-cut white Halston gown. So many people were there from so many parts of her life. Her daughter Maria, now a striking beauty of twenty. Warhol, of course, and Liza and Halston and Bill Blass. Swifty Lazar sat with Lee Radziwill. Joan Fontaine reminded reporters that Elizabeth had gotten her start in her picture *Jane Eyre*. And Rock Hudson, to whom Elizabeth made a beeline. As Bick and Leslie Benedict embraced, the crowd cheered again.

Not everyone would be as kind to her as Frank Rich. Elizabeth's new—and in some ways feminist—interpretation of Regina didn't sit well with all the critics, and Broadway elitists nodded in agreement when John Simon of *New York* magazine pronounced Miss Taylor "not yet ready for the legitimate theatre." But who cared? The public adored her and the play. This was their "Liz," in all her sensual lust for life. They had come to see a movie star, the kind that people said didn't exist anymore. Already the media was calling Elizabeth the "greatest" or the "last." *The Little Foxes* would be one of the biggest hits on Broadway that season. Elizabeth received Tony and Drama Desk nominations. Taking the show on the road, she made all the money that she needed to keep the yachts fitted and the diamonds polished. And at every stop, the standing ovations would've gone on all night if she had let them.

The cheers that went up for her weren't only in recognition for her thoroughly enjoyable performance as Regina. The public was applauding all the rest of it as well: for winning the Grand National disguised as a boy, for cradling Montgomery Clift in her arms, for her fairy-tale wedding to Nicky Hilton, for the trips around the world with Mike Todd, for being so alive as Maggie the Cat, for fighting off death without ever mussing her hair, for all the magazine covers, for the late-night strolls on the Via Veneto, for donning Martha's gray wig, for the Cartier diamond and the Peregrine pearl, for the yachts and the furs, for Switzerland and Sardinia, for Portofino and Puerto Vallarta.

She'd divorce Warner in due time. There would be one more husband after that, and one more play, with Burton no less, and more movies and television appearances. There would be rehab, twice. There would be her trailblazing, courageous work on behalf of those with AIDS. There would be perfume businesses and jewelry lines. And every one of those endeavors, wrapped in ermine and decorated with diamonds, would be defined by Elizabeth's unparalleled fame. It would be with a movie star's poise and sense of self that she would address Congressional committees, knowing exactly how to move into the room, how to turn her shoulder for emphasis, how to lift her eyes to the camera. She'd learned those lessons at MGM long ago, and she had learned them well. It would be with a movie star's allure that she sold her perfumes, and with a movie star's passion that she spoke of her recovery from addictions. It would be with a movie star's presence that she would continue to draw the cameras, even from a wheelchair. Elizabeth did indeed know how to milk every gasp and every thrill.

The night of her Broadway triumph, as the cheers and the

whistles for her echoed up into the rafters, if anyone in the audience had wondered how she had done it, how Elizabeth Taylor had so transfixed the world, all they would have had to do was look inside one of the *Playbill*s that were scattered across the floor. There was just one word underneath her photo, one word that described and explained everything.

That word was STAR.

Acknowledgments

★

My thanks to the many people who spoke with me about this project, enlightening me about Elizabeth Taylor, movies, Hollywood, the media, and the enterprise of fame: Henry Baron, Joseph Bottoms, Gianni Bozzacchi, Michael Childers, Dennis Christopher, Dick Clayton, Mart Crowley, Elinor Donahue, Dominick Dunne, Clarence "Doc" Ericksen, Eddie Fisher, Anne Francis, Waris Hussein, Jack Larson, Shirley MacLaine, Tom Mankiewicz, Kevin McCarthy, Mark Miller, Hank Moonjean, Mike Nichols, Austin Pendleton, Gilberto Petrucci, James Prideaux, Martin Ransohoff, William Richert, Noel Taylor, Susan McCarthy Todd, and Susannah York. I am also grateful to those who spoke to me off the record, particularly two people who are very close to my subject. The background information they shared proved vital in understanding Elizabeth's story and the celebrity expedition that she navigated so well.

Interviews with subjects now deceased, conducted for previous projects, often proved germane as well. Among them: Alan Cahan, Frank D'Amico, Gavin Lambert, Elliott Morgan, John Schlesinger, Robert Shaw, Emily Torchia, and Miles White.

As always, the most telling information came from primary sources such as letters, journals, ledgers, production memos, and medical records. My deepest appreciation to those archivists who helped me unearth this material: Barbara Hall at the Margaret Herrick Library at the Academy of Motion Picture Arts and Sciences; Ned Comstock at the University of Southern California Cinematic Arts Library; Sandra Joy Lee at the Warner Bros. Archives, USC; J. C. Johnson at the Howard Gotlieb Archival Research Center at Boston University; Randy Thompson at the National Archives and Records Administration, Pacific Region; Jan Levinson at the Richard B. Russell Library for Political Research and Studies, University of Georgia; Nicolette A. Schneider, Syracuse University Library; Nancy Schwartz, Sonoma County Library; Debbie DeJonker-Berry, Provincetown Public Library, Massachusetts; and the largely anonymous but always helpful staff of the New York Public Library for the Performing Arts.

Colleagues and friends provided information, tips, leads, advice, photos, articles, and encouragement: Clark Bason, Jay Blotcher, Andrew Budgell (www.dameelizabethtaylor.com), Craig Chester, C. David Heymann, Peter Howe, Wayne Lawson, Vince Lodato, Patrick McGilligan, Gary Shaw, Sam Staggs, and Allan Trivette (www.taylortribute.com).

My assistants, Maggie Cadman in New York and Monica Trasandes in Los Angeles, were tireless and deserve a round of applause.

Thanks also to my parents, William and Carol Mann, for their ever-present support (and for all those items about Elizabeth clipped from the *Daily News*!).

Finally, my gratitude to my agent, Malaga Baldi, for her sense and foresight; to my astute copy editor, David Hough; to Michaela Sullivan, for her gorgeous cover design; to my editors, Andrea Schulz in New York, Walter Donohue in London, and especially George Hodgman, who conceived this idea with me and came up with the title, and who helped ensure that every page was the best it could be; and to my husband, Dr. Timothy Huber, always my first and best critic.

Notes

Abbreviations

AMPAS = Margaret Herrick Library, Academy of Motion Picture Arts and
    Sciences
GSC = George Stevens Collection
HCSBU = C. David Heymann Collection, Stony Brook University
HHC = Hedda Hopper Collection
JWC = Jack Warner Collection
LAT = *Los Angeles Times*
NYPL = Billy Rose Theatre Collection, New York Public Library for the
    Performing Arts
NYT = *New York Times*
USC = Performing Arts Archives, University of Southern California

Where not cited, quotes are taken from personal interviews with the author.
On occasion, quotes from printed sources have had grammar adjusted and/
or ellipses discarded, but only if by doing so the original intent, meaning, or
accuracy of the quote was not altered.

Prologue: How to Be a Movie Star

2   Getting into that shark cage: Private interviews, as well as the *Daily Mail,*
    August 24 and September 20, 2006.
2   "To be in that cage": *Interview,* February 2007.
4   "At her best": Camille Paglia, *Sex, Art, and American Culture* (Vintage,
    1997).
5   "I started it": Interview on *Larry King Live,* May 30, 2006, CNN tran-
    scripts.

5   "questioning old values": O'Neil was quoted by Lester David and Jhan Robbins in *Richard and Elizabeth* (Ballantine Books, 1978).

5   "the Madame Curie": Maureen Orth, *The Importance of Being Famous: Behind the Scenes of the Celebrity-Industrial Complex* (Henry Holt, 2004).

6   by the reconciliation of contradictions: Richard Dyer, *Stars* (British Film Institute, 1979).

6   "the most beautiful": Sarris quoted by Patricia Bosworth in *Montgomery Clift: A Biography* (Harcourt Brace Jovanovich, 1978).

6   the ordinary and the extraordinary: Adrienne McLean, "The Cinderella Princess and the Instrument of Evil" in Adrienne L. McLean and David A. Cook, eds., *Headline Hollywood: A Century of Film Scandal* (Rutgers University Press, 2001).

6   "Who is this person?": *Cosmopolitan,* July 1973.

7   "that rarest of virtues": George Cukor to Elizabeth Taylor, July 24, 1973, George Cukor Collection, AMPAS.

7   "I try not to live a lie": *Look,* May 7, 1963.

7   "movie queen with no ego": Memo from Gloria Steinem to Ray Stark, [nd] 1966, John Huston Collection, AMPAS.

7   "She is the good-bad girl": *McCall's,* September 1974.

8   "no deodorant like success": *Life,* December 18, 1964.

8   "The most ambitious of them all": David Thomson, *The Whole Equation: A History of Hollywood* (Little, Brown, 2005).

8   "Taylor seems more to co-exist": Ethan Mordden, *Movie Star: A Look at the Women Who Made Hollywood* (St. Martin's Press, 1983).

9   "without an iota of braggadocio": *Vanity Fair,* March 2007.

9   "But what do I *do* with them?": The breakfast anecdote was told to me by Hank Moonjean, who was on the set.

1. When in Rome

13   in her own lively fashion: Interviews with Tom Mankiewicz and Gilberto Petrucci, as well as Eddie Fisher, *Eddie: My Life, My Loves* (Harper & Row, 1981); and Elizabeth Taylor, *Elizabeth Taylor: An Informal Memoir* (Harper & Row, 1964); and various newspaper articles (NYPL, AMPAS).

14   "It is important": Paddy Chayefsky to Martin Goldblatt, December 13, 1960, Paddy Chayefsky papers, NYPL.

14   Her $1 million salary: LAT, December 29, 1961.

15   she was lost among them: *New York World-Telegram,* September 29, 1961.

17   The term *paparazzi*: Peter Howe, *Paparazzi* (Artisan, 2005); Diego Mormorio, *Tazio Secchiaroli: Greatest of the Paparazzi* (Harry N. Abrams,

1999); catalog for *A Flash of Art: Action Photography in Rome 1953–1973,* an exhibition organized in 2005 by Photology in association with the city of Rome; NYT, May 3, 1959; May 18, 1962.

18 "We discovered that by creating": Mormorio, *Tazio Secchiaroli.*

18 "You'll see photographs": *Photoplay,* January 1962.

19 to bring her the dirt: Interview with Robert Shaw; also Hedda Hopper, *The Whole Truth and Nothing But* (Doubleday, 1963).

21 "Now a palazza in Rome": LAT, January 4, 1962.

21 Hedda was cheering Jack Warner: LAT, January 24, 1962.

21 "What's left for Liz": Hopper, *The Whole Truth and Nothing But.*

21 two Virginia baked hams: LAT, January 10, 1962, and an interview with Tom Mankiewicz.

22 "He was the most important nobody": HCSBU.

22 "on the Appian Way": Her address was confirmed by letters written to her and Eddie Fisher by Paddy Chayefsky on January 23 and February 27, 1962, located in the Chayefsky Collection, NYPL.

23 the incongruous name of Fred Oates: *Photoplay,* July 1962, and Taylor, *Elizabeth Taylor.*

25 the lead in a play by Sartre: Paul Ferris, *Richard Burton: The Actor, the Lover, the Star* (Berkley Books, 1982).

26 "an irresistible force": *New York Journal-American,* March 12, 1962.

26 "Elizabeth and Richard are": From an interview with Tom Mankiewicz.

26 "To keep Elizabeth happy": Eddie Fisher with David Fisher, *Been There, Done That* (St. Martin's Press, 2000).

27 Elizabeth's shopping expedition: Various newspaper accounts, including the *New York Daily News,* February 6, 1962, and the *Hartford Courant* (Associated Press wire report), February 5, 1962.

27 an overdose of sleeping pills: I based my account on interviews with Tom Mankiewicz, Hank Moonjean, and Eddie Fisher. Also see Jack Brodsky and Nathan Weiss, *The Cleopatra Papers: A Private Correspondence* (Simon & Schuster, 1963); Walter Wanger and Joe Hyams, *My Life with Cleopatra* (Bantam Books, 1963); Fisher's two memoirs; as well as the *New York Daily News,* February 18 and 19, 1962; LAT, February 18, 1962; *The Times,* February 18 and 19, 1962; and the Associated Press and other wire reports.

28 so the star could have a little rest: Interestingly, George Stevens also seemed disinclined to believe the suicide theory. Discussing Elizabeth and the *Cleopatra* brouhaha with journalist Ruth Waterbury, he discounted the idea of a female star wanting to escape the pressure of movie-making by taking "too many sleeping pills" because that meant "putting the whole cast out of work . . . hurting the labor unions . . . destroying

the industry." Although he did not specifically name Elizabeth, Stevens's point seems clear: He did not feel she had made a conscious, deliberate attempt to kill herself. (Transcript of an unpublished interview with George Stevens by Ruth Waterbury, September 7, 1962, GSC, AMPAS.)

29 "*here I am*": Interview on *Larry King Live,* January 15, 2001, CNN transcripts.

29 "It was very, very embarrassing": Audio commentary to *Cleopatra* DVD.

29 "behaved like a man": Fisher, *Been There, Done That.*

29 "upset about her life": Wanger, *My Life with Cleopatra.*

29 "scenes missing": Alexander Walker, *Elizabeth: The Life of Elizabeth Taylor* (Grove Press, 1997).

31 "never [to] do anything": *New York Daily News,* February 20, 1962; various wire reports.

31 "all the preliminary details": *New York Journal-American,* February 19, 1962.

31 "the fall guy": *Los Angeles Herald-Examiner,* February 21, 1962.

31 she screamed nonstop for hours: Interview with Hank Moonjean, as well as Melvyn Bragg, *Richard Burton: A Life* (Warner Books, 1990).

31 offered Jack Brodsky 100,000 lire: Brodsky, *The Cleopatra Papers.*

32 Elizabeth's thirtieth birthday: *Los Angeles Herald-Examiner,* February 28, 1962; various UPI and AP reports.

32 "Sheer horror": *Cosmopolitan,* September 1987.

34 "bottle it up": Brodsky, *The Cleopatra Papers.*

34 "appreciate the invaluable publicity": *New York Journal-American,* February 21, 1962.

35 "very much in love": LAT, March 12, 1962, and elsewhere.

35 *The Gouffe Case:* Memo from William Orr, September 11, 1961; memo to Jack L. Warner from P. D. Knecht, November 15, 1961; Jack L. Warner Collection, USC (hereafter, JWC, USC).

35 "Eddie's friends think": *New York Journal-American,* March 11, 1962.

36 "a neat stroke of public relations": *New York Journal-American,* March 28, 1962.

36 Gracie Square Hospital: Fisher, *Been There, Done That.*

36 the bizarre press conference: Various newspaper accounts, including the *New York Journal-American,* March 30, 1962; *Daily News* (New York), March 30 and 31, 1962; LAT, March 31, 1962; as well as Fisher's two memoirs.

37 the banner headline: *New York Daily News,* March 31, 1962.

37 "The 'kissing picture'": *New York Journal-American,* April 1, 1962.

38 "I was, I suppose, behaving wrongly": ET, *Elizabeth Taylor.*

39 through the windows of the villa: Interviews with Tom Mankiewicz and Hank Moonjean.

40 "I don't remember ever not being famous": *Vanity Fair*, March 2007.

40 "half asleep from being stared at": David Thomson, *A Biographical Dictionary of Film* (Alfred A. Knopf, 1975).

40 "They want pictures": Graham Jenkins, *Richard Burton, My Brother* (Michael Joseph Ltd., 1988).

40 Striding down the Via Veneto on Burton's arm: Various newspaper accounts, including the *Los Angeles Herald-Examiner*, March 31 and April 1, 1962; the *New York Herald Tribune*, April 1, 1962; LAT, April 1, 1962.

41 "baroque and jocular": Ennio Flaiano, *Opere. Scritti postumi* (Bompiani, 1988), quoted in Mormorio.

41 "nuzzle over their vino": Dorothy Kilgallen's column, *New York Journal-American*, April 4, 1962.

41 "Miss Taylor and Burton": *Los Angeles Herald-Examiner*, March 31, 1962; various wire reports.

42 "How did I know": Brodsky, *The Cleopatra Papers*.

42 "Elizabeth Taylor and her three children": *New York Daily News*, April 2, 1962.

42 they all went off to the beach: Various newspaper accounts, including LAT, April 2, 1962, and the *Daily Mirror*, April 2, 1962.

43 "an official military": *New York Herald Tribune*, April 3, 1962.

43 "Elizabeth Taylor is going to have": *New York Mirror*, April 1, 1962.

43–44 sexual intercourse was invented in 1963: This comes from the poem "Annus Mirabilis," in Larkin's collection *High Windows* (Faber and Faber, 1974).

44 the latest trend for women: Throughout late February and most of March various newspapers ran syndicated fashion articles about Elizabeth and *Cleopatra*. See, for example, *Hartford Courant*, February 24, 26, 27, and 28, 1962.

44 "Will her new Cleopatra look": *Look*, February 27, 1962.

2. Educating a Movie Star

46 At the studio gates: This description is taken from a careful consideration of various recollections of both Elizabeth and her mother, as well as a transcript of an interview between Clarence Brown and C. David Heymann, HCSBU. See also C. David Heymann, *Liz: An Intimate Biography of Elizabeth Taylor* (Birch Lane Press, 1995).

47 "Two diminutive": HCSBU.

48 "I was terrifically impressed": ET, *Elizabeth Taylor*.

48 "It was a complete city," "I think people don't": Jeanine Basinger, *The Star Machine* (Vintage Books, 2009).

49 "What impressed me": HCSBU.

49 "spiritual affinity": *Photoplay*, December 1945.

50 "clamoring for bits": Channing Pollock, *Harvest of My Years: An Autobiography* (Bobbs-Merrill Company, 1943).

50 born Sarah Warmbrodt: U.S. Census, 1900, 1910, 1920.

50 "She was afraid": LAT, May 29, 1921.

51 from ingénues to vamps: LAT, May 29, 1921; October 26, 1922; LAT online database; Internet Broadway Database. Sara was in Los Angeles at the Majestic at least by December 7, 1920 (not July 1922 as has been written), when an article in the LAT mentions her appearance in *Clarence*. Far from being in only a handful of productions, as has usually been presumed, Sara enjoyed quite a varied stage career that lasted more than a decade. Herewith is an incomplete list of her stage credits: *Fair and Warmer*, 1917, probably in a touring company; *Upstairs and Down*, 1920, Los Angeles; *The Naughty Wife*, 1920, Los Angeles; *Clarence*, 1920, Los Angeles; *The Remnant*, 1920 or 1921, Los Angeles; *Parlor, Bedroom and Bath*, 1921, Los Angeles; *Turn to the Right*, 1921, Los Angeles; *The Ruined Lady*, 1922, Los Angeles; *My Lady Friends*, 1922, Los Angeles; *The Sign on the Door*, 1922, Los Angeles; *The Fool*, 1922, Los Angeles, Broadway, London; *The Dagger*, 1925, Broadway; *Arabesque*, 1925, Broadway; *Fool's Bells*, 1925, Broadway; *Mama Loves Papa*, 1926, Broadway; *The Little Spitfire*, 1926, Broadway.

51 Franklin Pangborn was known: LAT, May 29, 1921; various articles, NYPL.

52 "hectic" (read: sexy) bathing suit: LAT, June 8, 1922.

52 "brilliant first-night audience": LAT, July 14, 1922.

52 Alla Nazimova: Pollock, *Harvest of My Years*.

52 "their fair Sara": LAT, August 22, 1922.

53 "creditable but not startling": *Theatre*, November 1922.

53 "A complete triumph": This was quoted in the LAT, October 22, 1924, under the headline CALIFORNIA GIRL MAKES HIT ABROAD. Sara's parents had by now moved to Lawndale, south of Los Angeles near Manhattan Beach.

53 "the size of a belt buckle": Pollock, *Harvest of My Years*.

53 Her return to the United States: U.S. Ship Passenger Lists, RMS *Mauretania*, departing Southampton March 21, 1925, arriving New York March 27, 1925, National Archives.

53 the waiting room: Elinor Donahue recalled this place for me, where the mothers would "sit and knit and gossip with each other."

54 on Hedda's nerves: Interview with Robert Shaw.

54 From the windows of her office: I have taken this from an interview with Robert Shaw, as well as a detailed description by the columnist's copy editor that was published in the LAT, March 13, 1940 (it might have been written by Hedda herself). A profile of Hopper in *Time*, July 28, 1947, was also an important source, including Hedda's greeting of "Hello, slaves."

54 that Hedda found her true calling: U.S. Census, 1900, 1910. See also Hedda Hopper, *From Under My Hat* (MacFadden Books, 1964) and George Eells, *Hedda and Louella: A Dual Biography of Hedda Hopper and Louella Parsons* (Putnam, 1972).

54, 55 "A few words from Hedda," "Wake up," "On that day": *Time*, July 28, 1947.

56 "a Quaker," said Dema Harshbarger: *Time* (July 28, 1947) quoted "a friend" of Hedda's as saying she was "a Quaker from the mouth down." Anthony Slide, who knew many of Hedda's legmen, identified the friend as Dema Harshbarger and used the wording I have included here. Personal interview with Slide; see also Slide, "Hedda Hopper," *Stallion*, June 1986.

56 *Gone With the Wind:* In *Elizabeth Taylor*, Taylor writes: "I guess the first serious thought about my acting came when they were casting *Gone With the Wind*," and she then recounted the tales of people stopping them on the street. Sara had first told this story in print in a three-part article for *Ladies' Home Journal*, February–April 1954. She wrote, disingenuously, that Elizabeth "wasn't the least scrap interested. Neither was I." Robert Shaw confirmed stories that Sara had been eager for Elizabeth's casting and that Hedda had pushed for Elizabeth behind the scenes.

56 child star Deanna Durbin: In her December 2, 1940, column, three months before Elizabeth signed a contract with Universal, Hedda wrote: "Deanna Durbin's teacher, de Segurola, has a new find—8-year-old Elizabeth Taylor." Andrés de Segurola, at one time basso of the Metropolitan Opera Company, was working at Universal as a vocal coach for Durbin. Whether or not Elizabeth ever actually trained with de Segurola is unknown (and unlikely), but Hedda's comparison of the two girls at this juncture could only have helped Sara's negotiations with the studio, where Durbin was the reigning child star.

56 "one of the most painful": Hopper, *The Whole Truth and Nothing But*.

56 "walks off with": LAT, September 26, 1941.

56 "one of the most beautiful children": LAT, October 21, 1942.

56 "so good": LAT, April 2, 1943.

57 Hedda had first met the Taylors: She wrote this in her column on October 21, 1942.

57 a letter of (re)introduction: *Ladies' Home Journal,* March 1954.

57 "When I was called": Hopper, *From Under My Hat.*

58 "denoting Miss Hopper's": LAT, March 13, 1940.

58 "people who wanted": Interview with Robert Shaw.

58 "Gossip has become": *Time,* July 28, 1947.

59 "x factor": Basinger, *The Star Machine.*

59 "Remind me to be around": Secondary quote, no primary attribution, used in Ellis Amburn, *The Most Beautiful Woman in the World: The Obsessions, Passions, and Courage of Elizabeth Taylor* (Cliff Street Books, 2000).

59 "Her eyes are too old": This is a quote that has been used in many accounts, including Walker, *Elizabeth.* There appears to be no primary source, however, so it may be apocryphal. But among many in Elizabeth's inner circle, it is accepted as the attitude Universal held toward the child actress.

59 "accurate memory": Sheridan Morley, *Elizabeth Taylor* (Applause Books, 1999).

59 "casting glances," "Being in films": ET, *Elizabeth Taylor.*

60 "in a cocoon": *Good Housekeeping,* April 1974.

60 with his family to Arkansas City: In 1910 the family had already left Illinois and was living in Cherokee City, Oklahoma (U.S. Census, 1910). In 1915 they were in Arkansas City, Kansas (Kansas State Census, 1915).

61 the draft during World War I: No record of him exists in the very extensive draft registration files at the National Archives.

61 Howard Young Galleries: Francis Taylor's uncle was a self-made man. Leaving home at age ten to set up a laundry business, he was selling lithographs throughout the Midwest by the time he was fifteen. By the age of eighteen, Young had amassed a fortune of $400,000, losing it all in the Panic of 1896. He started over with a get-rich-quick scheme. Watching the newspapers for obituaries of wealthy men, he'd hire a painter to render oil portraits from photographs, then sell the paintings to the grieving families for $2,000 each. In his early twenties he began investing in fine art; by 1919 he was one of New York's most prominent dealers. Young could be a miser, but he clearly had a soft spot for his nephew. Uncle Howard could always be counted on for a loan whenever Francis and his young family needed it most. Obituary, NYT, June 24, 1972.

61 remembered her from Kansas: According to a note Howard Young filed with Francis's passport application on April 1, 1921: "This is to certify that Francis Taylor has been in the service of the Howard Young Galleries for

a period of six years as a salesman of art objects" (U.S. passport applications, National Archives). Since Francis didn't arrive in Ark City until some point after 1910, then the most he and Sara overlapped would have been about four years.

61 "permanent retirement": LAT, November 4, 1926.

61 "her present intention": NYT, December 26, 1926. Sara's marriage to Francis took place a little more than a week after she'd relinquished the part of Gypsy in *The Little Spitfire;* she'd been considered a disappointing successor to Sylvia Field, who'd originated the part. NYT, September 1 and 12, 1926; October 12, 1926; various newspaper accounts, NYPL.

61 The Taylors settled in London: To consider the various ways in which Sara, Elizabeth, and others presented these years, see the *Ladies' Home Journal,* February–April 1954; ET, *Elizabeth Taylor* and *Elizabeth Taylor's Nibbles and Me* (Duell, Sloan & Pearce, 1946); Thelma Cazalet-Keir, *From the Wings* (Bodley Head, 1967).

62 a clandestine affair: C. David Heymann interviewed Kurt Stempler, who admitted to an affair with Francis. J. Randy Taraborrelli in his *Elizabeth* (Warner Books, 2006) interviewed Francis's friends Marshall Baldridge and Stefan Verkaufen, who did not acknowledge physical relationships with him but did disclose other details of their extraordinarily close friendships. In one anecdote relayed by Baldridge, it was clear that Sara resented the intimacy he shared with her husband.

62 "all the girls thought": Letter from Mrs. Nona Smith to Hedda Hopper, January 27, 1964, HHC, AMPAS.

62–63 Sara sailed with her two children: U.S. Ship Passenger Lists, National Archive. This wasn't the first time Elizabeth had been to America. On July 26, 1934, at the age of two, she'd arrived with her parents and brother to visit her grandparents; they made a return visit on November 20, 1936, when Elizabeth was four.

63 "In that inbred": ET, *Elizabeth Taylor.*

63 "a lovely, sweet kind man": Draft of a column, dated March 20, 1965, HHC, AMPAS.

63 a dinner in honor of Victor Cazalet: LAT, May 18, 1941. Two years later Cazalet would be killed in a plane crash with General Wladyslaw Sikorski, prime minister of the Polish government in exile. It was a shock that left both Francis and Sara grief-stricken for months.

64 "[She] had absolutely": HCSBU.

64 "You'd never have known": *Look,* June 26, 1956.

64 a wooden ruler across her knuckles: Elizabeth would recall this in several accounts, and a source close to her reported that she told him the same story.

65   to run the MGM schoolhouse in 1932: U.S. Census, 1920, 1930.

65   "The Little Red Schoolhouse": LAT, October 17, 1926; July 18, 1934; September 12, 1937; September 9, 1948; MGM Collection, AMPAS.

65   "Muzzie . . . was someone": Jean Porter oral history, Southern Methodist University Oral History Collection (SMU).

66   "She didn't teach me shit": Quoted in Dick Moore, *Twinkle Twinkle, Little Star: And Don't Have Sex or Take the Car* (HarperCollins, 1984).

66   "Between camera takes": ET, *Elizabeth Taylor*.

67   "kids . . . out of place": Moore, *Twinkle Twinkle, Little Star*.

67   "I paid the bills": *Interview*, February 2007.

67   "I was in constant rebellion": ET, *Elizabeth Taylor*.

67   Dorothy Mullen would remember Elizabeth: Walker, *Elizabeth*.

67–68 "I wouldn't put her": HCSBU.

68   "to come out sounding": Kitty Kelley, *Elizabeth Taylor: The Last Star* (Simon & Schuster, 1981).

68   "Americanese": *Interview*, February 2007.

69   Pan Berman took over from Mervyn LeRoy: The NYT reported on June 26, 1943, that Berman had taken over from LeRoy.

69   measured her against the wall: This was told in Sara Taylor's seminal article in *Ladies' Home Journal*, March 1954, where many of the legends of her daughter's career were first codified. Elizabeth repeated it in *Elizabeth Taylor*.

70   "There was this place Tip's": ET, *Elizabeth Taylor*.

70   "It was high time": *Ladies' Home Journal*, February 1954.

70   "Something quite magical": HCSBU.

70   She burst into tears: This description is culled from several sources, including the interview with Clarence Brown in HCSBU; Alexander Walker's interview with Pandro Berman, relayed in Walker, *Elizabeth*; and various accounts given by Elizabeth and Sara over the years.

71   "rocket to stardom": Syndicated, see *Hartford Courant*, November 14, 1943.

71   "the biggest kid part": NYT, October 10, 1943.

71   "the bluest of blue": Photo caption, undated press release (1943), NYPL.

71   "Mr. Strickling didn't pay": Emily Torchia oral history, SMU.

72   The lifeblood of the publicity department: Various memos and other papers in the MGM Collection, AMPAS, painted a picture of the workings of the publicity department. I also consulted Peter Hay, *MGM: When the Lion Roars* (Turner Publishing, 1991) and Ronald L. Davis, *The Glamour Factory: Inside Hollywood's Big Studio System* (Southern Methodist University Press, 1993). For the distinction between East Coast and West

Coast movie reporting, see Neal Gabler, *Winchell: Gossip, Power and the Culture of Celebrity* (Alfred A. Knopf, 1994).

72 "Young Elizabeth loves animals": MGM press release, carbon copy, no date [circa 1943–1944], NYPL.

72 "absolutely native": *Ladies' Home Journal,* February 1954.

73 CHILD LITERALLY GROWS: LAT, February 27, 1944. A press release with the same headline and virtually the same copy was found in the collections at NYPL.

73 "The child puts a spell": *Photoplay,* December 1945.

73–74 Dick was thirty-five years old: U.S. Census 1900, 1910, 1920, 1930.

75 "the iron lung," "stars were born," "He looked rather": ET, *Elizabeth Taylor.*

75 Francis Taylor's brother: John Taylor was quoted in Heymann, *Liz.*

76 "Big Daddy Mayer": ET, *Elizabeth Taylor.*

76 Guilaroff worked around the clock: Sydney Guilaroff, *Crowning Glory: Reflections of Hollywood's Favorite Confidant* (General Publishing Group, 1996). Guilaroff's claim, sometimes echoed by Elizabeth, that Brown was fooled by the wig might be discredited by a memo from the legal department quoted in Kelley, *Elizabeth Taylor,* that concluded the studio did not have a contractual right to order Elizabeth to alter her appearance. However, I could not locate this memo among the MGM Collection at AMPAS.

77 "She was thirteen," Hirshberg said: Notes from the Jack Hirshberg Collection, AMPAS.

77 "her charms to perfection": Hopper, *The Whole Truth and Nothing But.*

78 "Oh, don't end it that way": HCSBU.

78 "She never knew": Kelley, *Elizabeth Taylor.*

78 the chipmunk leaped onto Hedda's arm: Hopper, *The Whole Truth and Nothing But.*

78 "Aunt Hedda": This comes from an interview with Robert Shaw and is also referenced by Hopper herself in an article that she penned about Elizabeth in *Photoplay,* August 1951.

78 "I haven't yet seen *National Velvet*": LAT, October 27, 1944.

78 "Elizabeth gets a star rating": LAT, November 11, 1944.

79 "plan into action": LAT, December 13, 1944.

79 "face is alive": NYT, December 15, 1944.

79 "one of the screen's most lovable characters": *New York Sun,* December 15, 1944.

79 "as natural and excellent a little actress": *New York Post,* December 15, 1944.

79 among the top ten most profitable pictures of the year: Accurate earnings are difficult to come by before 1950. The National Board of Review calculated *Velvet* as one of the top ten most profitable films (NYT, December 22, 1945). The Gallup Poll also listed it as one of the top ten "most popular films" of 1945 (LAT, December 24, 1945). Although it was released in Los Angeles and New York in December 1944, it did not go into general release until January 1945.

80 "Now if you can love a child": Sheilah Graham syndicated column, as in the *Hartford Courant*, January 30, 1945.

80 posing with two puppies: These shots ran in various newspapers, including the *Hartford Courant*, September 30, 1945.

80 *Nibbles and Me:* The book was published by Duell, Sloane & Pearce, Inc., in 1946, and reissued by Simon & Schuster in 2002.

81 gave the story lots of ink: LAT, June 11, 1946.

81 plus a $15,000 bonus: MGM studio ledgers, MGM Collection, AMPAS.

81 "Oh, I'm quite comfortable here": Interview with Anne Francis.

82 the studio's "chattel": ET, *Elizabeth Taylor.*

82 "We were so surprised": ET, *Elizabeth Taylor.*

82 "a china doll.": *Photoplay,* September 1951.

3. The Most Exciting Girl

83 "The edge had gone off": Interview with Frank Capra by George Stevens, Jr., included in the George Stevens Collection (GSC), AMPAS.

83 out of sync with his prewar films: I based much of this on Marilyn Ann Moss, *Giant: George Stevens, A Life on Film* (University of Wisconsin Press, 2004); various interviews collected in Paul Cronin, ed., *George Stevens: Interviews* (University Press of Mississippi, 2004); and various interviews and notes in the GSC, AMPAS.

83–84 "The kind of girl," "It might appear": George Stevens to William Meiklejohn, May 24, 1949, GSC, AMPAS.

84 from $20.8 million to $6.6 million: These figures were taken from various sources, notably the *Motion Picture Herald.* Cobbett Steinberg, *Reel Facts: The Movie Book of Records* (Vintage, 1982) was also a helpful compendium of data and charts.

85 "very male member of society": Transcript of an interview with Hepburn by George Stevens, Jr., notes for "George Stevens: A Filmmaker's Journey," GSC, AMPAS.

85 Stevens actually prepared two lawsuits: These are discussed in Moss, *Giant*.

85 Dropping out of Wilder's *Sunset Boulevard:* Most accounts seem to have confused the timing of this. William Holden was announced as a replacement for Clift on *Sunset Boulevar*d in the NYT, March 19, 1949. According to records in Stevens's files, Clift was signed for *An American Tragedy* just a few days later on March 23, 1949.

85 So Stevens insisted they do everything: In a memo dated June 15, 1949, Stevens described a meeting with Henry Ginsberg of Paramount about the importance of obtaining Elizabeth and asked for assurances "that all had been done that was possible to bring this about." GCS, AMPAS.

85 "She was this extraordinary child": Transcript of an unpublished interview with George Stevens by Ruth Waterbury, September 7, 1962 (hereafter Waterbury transcript), GSC, AMPAS.

86 If she played this part: Memos dated May 23, 24, and June 15, 1949, GCS, AMPAS.

86 Metro had turned down the request: Hedda Hopper reported in early July: "George Stevens still hopes to get Elizabeth Taylor for *An American Tragedy*. Her studio turned down a loan-out after they'd read the wrong part. Now they've got the right one, and George expects to have a yes within the week" (*Hartford Courant,* July 4, 1949). In fact, Elizabeth had already been signed by the time the item ran.

87 "The big surprise": *New York Herald Tribune,* August 7, 1948.

87 "You have bosoms!": Elizabeth Taylor, *Elizabeth Takes Off: On Weight Gain, Weight Loss, Self-Image, and Self-Esteem* (G. P. Putnam's Sons, 1987).

87 "No longer do her worries": *Photoplay,* June 1948.

87–88 "I learned how to look sultry": ET, *Elizabeth Takes Off.*

88 "Truly a most remarkable machine": ET, *Elizabeth Taylor.*

89 "drifting out through the walls": Ann Rutherford oral history (SMU).

89 paint her mouth "way over,": *Cosmopolitan,* September 1987.

89 "No woman": Elizabeth, rather immodestly, tells this story herself in ET, *Elizabeth Takes Off.*

90 Glenn was twenty-three and Elizabeth just sixteen: NYT, July 19, 1948; LAT, July 19, 1948; September 13, 1948; various articles, NYPL, AMPAS.

90 "spontaneous combustion": *Hartford Courant,* October 7, 1948.

90 "the romance was largely a studio directive": *Hartford Courant,* April 30, 1950.

90 "It was so childish": ET, *Elizabeth Taylor.*

90–91 a live, supposedly authentic radio interview: This extraordinary document is dated July 13, 1947, and is part of the Louella Parsons Collection, USC.

91 "didn't need skates": LAT, April 25, 1949.

91 "The luscious, long-lashed lass of love": Unsourced article, May 10, 1949, NYPL.

91 "deep-set pools of blue": *Hartford Courant,* August 29, 1948.

91–92 "famous violet eyes": Ellen Gatti's short stories about Lily Thorndyke ran in the *Los Angeles Times* from 1946 through 1949. The first instance of Elizabeth's being described as having violet eyes that I could find was in the LAT, March 23, 1949.

92 her lord and master: Much of my conception of Mayer, his times, and his place at MGM comes from Scott Eyman, *Lion of Hollywood: The Life and Legend of Louis B. Mayer* (Simon & Schuster, 2005). See also Charles Higham, *Merchant of Dreams: Louis B. Mayer, MGM, and the Secret Hollywood* (Dutton, 1993).

92 "foaming at the mouth": Interview on *Larry King Live,* January 15, 2001, CNN transcripts. Elizabeth tried a bit of whitewashing in that interview, making herself appear more innocent than she was by saying that she had never heard such words before.

92 "You and your studio can both go to hell": Elizabeth told the story of her contretemps with Mayer in both of her memoirs, in slightly different versions.

94 "I began to see myself": ET, *Elizabeth Takes Off.*

94 "A little red schoolhouse": Waterbury transcript, GSC, AMPAS.

94 "I would get up early": Interview on *Larry King Live,* January 15, 2001, CNN transcripts.

94 "no football games to go to": Interview on *Larry King Live,* February 3, 2003, CNN transcripts.

95 Extramarital affairs were whispered about: Francis Taylor was rumored to have had an affair with MGM chief costumer Adrian. C. David Heymann heard this claimed by at least two sources, one of whom was the longtime Hollywood reporter Doris Lilly. See Heymann, *Liz.* Sara was said to have had a fling with director Michael Curtiz while he directed Elizabeth in *Life with Father;* she would have been forty-nine years old at the time, Curtiz, fifty-nine. This was claimed by Irene Dunne in an interview with Heymann, HCSBU.

95 "idyllic, happy little family": *Interview,* February 2007.

95 "no special loss": These are the words of *Look* reporter Eleanor Harris, who interviewed ET for a three-part story beginning in the June 26, 1956, issue. They are not ET's words, as Kitty Kelley made them seem. Still, it

can be assumed that ET said something similar in the course of her interview with Harris.

95 Benny Thau remained her surrogate father: *Look,* June 26, 1956. ET would name Jules Goldstone, her agent, as another surrogate father. She didn't emotionally reconnect with her real father until later. She told Helen Gurley Brown that she didn't really become close to Francis until after she'd left home. *Cosmopolitan,* September 1987.

95 "It didn't show up at the time": *Look,* July 10, 1956.

95 "point of contention": HCSBU.

96 Hopper, happy as ever to help: *Hartford Courant* (syndicated column), May 16, 1949.

96 the happy couple's engagement: LAT, June 6, 1949.

97 "to announce the," "Elizabeth saw the pattern": *Ladies' Home Journal,* April 1954.

98 When profits began ticking upward: Various articles, *Hollywood Reporter, Variety,* January–June 1949; see also Hay, *MGM,* and Eyman, *Lion of Hollywood.*

98 "She leaves a trail of broken hearts": Unsourced article, October 1, 1949, Elizabeth Taylor file, NYPL.

98 "a series of resounding smacks": *Sunday Pictorial,* September 25, 1949.

98 "Besides taking billions": LAT, September 28, 1949.

98 "If I were the kind of person": LAT, September 28, 1949.

98, 99 "We went well together," "an emotional child": ET, *Elizabeth Taylor.*

99 "Elizabeth isn't just any little girl": Hedda Hopper syndicated column, as in *Hartford Courant,* April 30, 1950.

99 "welfare worker": Memo in the George Stevens Collection, AMPAS, October 2, 1949. Elizabeth, in *Elizabeth Taylor,* would use the description "social worker."

100 "noble sheet of blue water": From Twain's *Roughing It* and included in a travel piece on Lake Tahoe in the NYT, May 15, 1949. Might Stevens have read this as he planned the shoot?

100 "long flannels": LAT, October 4, 1949.

100 "very much the inadequate teenage Hollywood sort": Filmed interview with ET, George Stevens Collection, AMPAS.

101 liked the "ring" to it: Cronin, *George Stevens Interviews.*

101 the cover of *Time* magazine: Elizabeth's face graced the cover of the 101 22, 1949, issue. She had been slated to appear several months earlier, but when *Quo Vadis,* the picture in which she was set to star, was temporarily shelved, *Time* lost its news hook and dropped plans for the Taylor cover. Intrepid press agents, however, kept after *Time,* pushing Elizabeth again

and again, and finally scored their coup. See Hedda Hopper's column, *Hartford Courant*, May 26, 1949.

101 "The Most Exciting Girl in Hollywood": *Photoplay*, January 1950. This was in part a response to the criticisms from the British press, as Maxwell makes mention of it and defends Elizabeth as simply being unafraid "to act her age"—that is, like a teenager.

101 Principal photography began on Tuesday: Daily production log, George Stevens Collection, AMPAS.

102 waiting on the sidelines with a blanket: Sara supposedly complained that the exposure to the cold water affected Elizabeth's menstrual cycles, a story that is often told in the Taylor legend. Alexander Walker sourced the story to "private information" in his book *Elizabeth*. Although Walker is generally a reliable source, production records do not bear out his claim that Sara kept Elizabeth confined to her room for three days. The log shows that Elizabeth reported to work every day that she was called during the location shooting in Tahoe (GCS, AMPAS).

102 "I use the camera": Cronin, *George Stevens Interviews*.

103 she was not charmed by it; Ava Gardner was her idea of beautiful: *Cosmopolitan*, July 1973.

103 "too many freckles": Interview on *Larry King Live*, January 15, 2001, CNN transcripts.

103 "I've just got to take off ten pounds": *Photoplay*, September 1947.

103 costume budget of $6,600: Production notes, *A Place in the Sun*, GCS, AMPAS. Wardrobe costs for Shelley Winters were $1,655 and $1,320 for Montgomery Clift.

103 "with a sort of benign tyranny": NYT, April 2, 1950.

103 "hero worship": ET, *Elizabeth Taylor*.

103–4 he decided that everything was all wrong: Clift was upset with the slant that Stevens was bringing to the script, which downplayed Dreiser's social criticisms and made the main character less ambitious and more sympathetic. Consequently, the factory girl (Winters) who drowns needed to be less likeable. Anne Revere, who played Clift's mother, seemed to feel that Stevens toned down the original script so that it wouldn't be branded as leftist or worse—the movie was being shot when the House Committee on Un-American Activities was attempting to expose Communists in Hollywood. Revere, soon to be blacklisted for her liberal associations, may have been overly sensitive to any perceived political changes, because Stevens was not afraid, a year later, to offer his resignation from the Directors' Guild after it proposed that its members adopt a non-Communist loyalty oath (NYT, October 29, 1950). Also see Bosworth, *Montgomery Clift*.

104 "Downbeat, blubbery, irritating": Bosworth, *Montgomery Clift.*

104 "I'm not called an actor out there": Bosworth, *Montgomery Clift.*

104 Clift was moody, dark, and sultry: I have based my description of Clift's life and outlook on conversations with Jack Larson, Miles White, and Tom Mankiewicz, as well as Bosworth, *Montgomery Clift,* and Robert LaGuardia, *Monty: A Biography of Montgomery Clift* (W. H. Allen, 1977).

104 "pantywaist": LAT, November 21, 1949.

105 "Bartending": Bosworth, *Montgomery Clift.*

105 the premiere of his film *The Heiress:* I based my account on Bosworth, newspaper accounts, and conversations with Jack Larson and Kevin McCarthy.

106 "already being linked together": Russell Holman to J. H. Karp, October 27, 1949, GSC, AMPAS.

107 "those boy boys": Waterbury transcript, GSC, AMPAS.

107 "Liz did the old Garbo trick": Hedda Hopper syndicated column, as in the *Hartford Courant,* November 25, 1949. Hedda also cleverly let on that she knew the truth wasn't quite so simple. In the same column, she mentions Mira Rostova as Monty's "girlfriend." She knew very well that Rostova was not his girlfriend, but by using the term she indicated that she knew Elizabeth wasn't either.

107 So good was the publicity in 1949–1950: For a wide assortment of obviously studio-generated stories, see the articles files at NYPL.

107 "He was my best friend": Interview on *Larry King Live,* January 15, 2001, CNN transcripts.

107 "a loving and lasting friendship": ET, *Elizabeth Takes Off.* Elizabeth has also stated that she was a virgin when she married Nicky Hilton, and there's no reason to disbelieve her. So that would seem to preclude a sexual relationship with Clift.

107 "I was a virgin": *The Advocate,* October 15, 1996. In this interview, Elizabeth also claimed that she helped Monty "realize" he was gay—a statement most of his friends discount. As supportive as Elizabeth was, "Monty was already very comfortable with himself," said Jack Larson. Part of Clift's legend has him being deeply conflicted over his homosexuality. While he did indeed have some turmoil as a gay man living in the spotlight, most of his friends insist that he was not as miserable or as conflicted as he has been portrayed.

108 "might have suggested fancies": Waterbury transcript, GSC, AMPAS.

108 with Monty and Roddy McDowall at the Park Plaza: ET, *Elizabeth Taylor.*

109 "copious notes": Heymann, *Liz.*

109 "work at it": Waterbury transcript, GSC, AMPAS.

110 "Tell Mama all": For this important moment in Elizabeth's career, I have synthesized several accounts given by the director. See the American Film Institute's *Dialogue on Film* (May–June 1975), as well as Cronin and Moss.

111 Bob Precht: Syndicated UPI story, *Hartford Courant,* December 12, 1949. Ironically, Precht would go on to marry Betty Sullivan, daughter of columnist Ed Sullivan and a bridesmaid at Elizabeth's wedding to Nicky Hilton.

112 Ralph Kiner: *Hartford Courant,* December 23, 1949.

112 "a real guy": Hedda Hopper syndicated column, as in the *Hartford Courant,* December 26, 1949.

113 Enter Conrad Nicholson Hilton, Jr.: See Thomas Ewing Dabney, *The Man Who Bought the Waldorf: The Life of Conrad N. Hilton* (Duell, Sloan and Pearce, 1950) and Whitney Bolton, *The Silver Spade: The Conrad Hilton Story* (Farrar, Straus and Young, 1954).

114 "He won't be annoyed": *Photoplay,* June 1950.

114 "With all this 'bride' talk": LAT, February 18, 1950.

114 "I wish you'd seen the wedding": Hedda Hopper syndicated column, as in the *Hartford Courant,* February 8, 1950.

115 "I won't have cold fish": *Photoplay,* August 1950.

115 "something nice": *Photoplay,* August 1950.

116 The Metro wardrobe girls pitched in: LAT, April 13, 1950.

116 calling the union "ideal": Hedda Hopper syndicated column, as in the *Hartford Courant,* April 30, 1950.

116 "Let's hear it for the bride": Walker, *Elizabeth*. Walker sources this quote to "private information."

117 "It's about as plunging": *Los Angeles Citizen-News,* May 5, 1950.

117–18 "It was as the soft rays of the setting sun": *Photoplay,* June 1950.

118 "I'd prefer a gang war": Walker, *Elizabeth*. He does not source this.

118 "I think this is the best thing I've done": NYT, April 2, 1950.

119 "all set to give her a verbal slugging": *Photoplay,* August 1951.

120 "Nick kind of got a kick": *Larry King Live,* January 15, 2001, CNN transcripts.

120 "I was naïve": *Cosmopolitan,* September 1987.

120 "It scarred me," "Divorcing Nick": ET, *Elizabeth Taylor*.

121 "The fairy tale's over": *Photoplay,* May 1951.

121 "gambling and playing around": *Los Angeles Examiner,* December 8, 1950.

122 to stalk Elizabeth again: ET, *Elizabeth Taylor*.

123 "Here was this gorgeous damsel": Stephen M. Silverman, *Dancing on the Ceiling: Stanley Donen and His Movies* (Alfred A. Knopf, 1996).

123 "should be run out of town": Silverman, *Dancing on the Ceiling*.

123 "movie-minded mother," "high time": This, as well as the description of Elizabeth's apartment and the conversation she had with Hopper there, comes from *Photoplay*, August 1951.

124 "You're growing up fast": LAT, May 20, 1951.

125 "The surprise of the evening": Lindsay Durand to George Stevens, May 22, 1951, GSC, AMPAS.

125 "I sincerely believe": Irving Asher to George Stevens, May 25, 1951, GSC, AMPAS.

125 held at the Fine Arts Theatre: There are extensive memos, reports, and seating charts contained in the GSC, AMPAS.

126 "Here is a heroine": LAT, August 15, 1951.

126 "the top effort of her career": NYT, August 29, 1951.

126 "so far beyond anything she has done previously": *Variety*, August 17, 1951.

4. Acting Out

127 "no longer take the embarrassment": Memo from Eric Stacey to Jack L. Warner, June 20, 1955, *Giant* production papers, JWC, USC.

127, 128 "explosive," "far more capable men": Memo from R. Gordon Bau to Henry Ginsberg, June 14, 1955, JWC, USC.

129 "I followed him around": From "George Stevens: A Filmmaker's Journey," GSC, AMPAS.

129 "Cut, I fucked up": Stevens told this to Alexander Walker. See Walker, *Elizabeth*.

129 "She'd had the MGM training": *Memories of Giant*, from the Special Edition DVD edition of *Giant* (2001). Other Baker quotes also come from this source.

129 he'd begin shouting: ET, *Elizabeth Taylor*.

130 why tempers boiled over: This is attested to in the JWC, USC. See also the various biographies of Dean, especially Val Holley, *James Dean: The Biography* (St. Martin's Press, 1996).

130 Their drinking had become legendary: See Rock Hudson and Sara Davidson, *Rock Hudson: His Story* (William Morrow and Company, 1986). These anecdotes were all confirmed to me by Mark Miller.

132 "Dearest George": ET to George Stevens, May 19, 1955, GSC, AMPAS.

133 "more than just glib dialogue": NYT, April 12, 1964.

133 "We are not royalty": Michael Wilding with Pamela Wilcox, *The Wilding Way: The Story of My Life* (St. Martin's Press, 1982). Various newspaper

articles, NYPL and AMPAS, gave accounts of the wedding of ET and Wilding.

134 "I just want to be with Michael": *Daily Express,* February 17, 1952.

134 "everything a doctor could have ordered": *Look,* July 10, 1956.

134 the etiology of the Wilding marriage: This has been reconstructed by carefully reading everything that has been previously written about this period, including Elizabeth's own recollections and contemporary newspaper reports. It became very apparent that some degree of calculation was going on behind the scenes when the tone of Elizabeth's press changed considerably from the summer of 1951 to the fall as the scoldings she was frequently given were replaced once again by accolades. (This is separate from the near-unanimous critical praise for *A Place in the Sun* and is specific to reports on her personal life.) The decision to back out of the proposed idea for an independent company and to sign up again with MGM is also better understood when Wilding is factored into the account. The scenario as presented here—of career calculation playing a part in the Wilding marriage—fits with what was told to me by Robert Shaw, who remembered Hedda Hopper's take on it, and was deemed credible when run by such observers as Dick Clayton, Tom Mankiewicz, Henry Baron, Hank Moonjean, and Kevin McCarthy.

135 ring was paid for not by him: This comes from Walker, who interviewed many of those around during that period, including Anna Neagle.

135 Kay Young filed for divorce: See, among many sources, *Los Angeles Herald-Express,* November 13, 1951.

135 "They were married": *New York Daily News,* November 24, 1960.

136 "cornball sentimental about Benny Thau": *Look,* July 24, 1956.

136 "fishing trip": *Hollywood Citizen-News,* December 12, 1951.

136 "I don't think you know": Hopper, *The Whole Truth and Nothing But.*

137 the idolization of Judy Garland: Wilding, *The Wilding Way.*

137 "sophisticated": *Photoplay,* January 1952. Of course, sophisticated often suggested "bisexual," and indeed Wilding may have enjoyed relations with both sexes. He described himself (and Stewart Granger) as "womanizers" in *The Wilding Way.* Yet what's apparent from reading his memoir is that his cowriter, Pamela Wilcox (the daughter of his mentor Herbert Wilcox), probably wrote most of it (the book is described "as told to"). The frequent references to Elizabeth as "Liz" don't sound like a man who was her husband for several years and who surely knew her abhorrence for the nickname. The book contains many factual errors, not least of which is saying that Hedda published her accusation in her column years before she actually did so. Given Pamela Wilcox's family connection to Wilding, she may have been attempting to whitewash

his life. Wilcox also downplayed the homosexuality of the man she lived with for many years, the director Robert Hamer, in the book she wrote about him, *Between Hell and Charing Cross* (Allen and Unwin, 1977). For more, see Charles Drazin, *The Finest Years: British Cinema of the 1940s* (André Deutsch, 1998). "Womanizer" was another word often used for circumspect homosexuals, who, after all, were often escorts to glamorous women. Consider the cases outlined in my *Behind the Screen: How Gays and Lesbians Shaped Hollywood* (Viking, 2001) and *Kate: The Woman Who Was Hepburn* (Henry Holt, 2006).

138 "Whom does he think": Hedda Hopper to Mike Cowles, Hedda Hopper Collection, AMPAS. For more, see Anthony Slide's discussion of this in *Stallion,* June 1986, and my *Behind the Screen.*

138 "Oh, Mikey": HCSBU.

138 "an oasis": ET, *Elizabeth Taylor.*

138 Hedda could be counted on: This is seen in a letter she wrote to the actor Raymond Burr, who costarred with her son on TV's *Perry Mason.* Confronted with evidence of Burr's homosexuality, Hedda wrote that his secret was safe with her. All he had to do was "call on the mother of Paul Drake [her son's role on *Perry Mason*] and I will stand up and swear anything for you." (Hedda Hopper to Raymond Burr, September 16, 1963, HHC, AMPAS.)

138 Wilding's career would have been ruined: Wilding himself (or his cowriter, Pamela Wilcox) alleged in *The Wilding Way* that Hedda published the charges about him and Granger around the time of his marriage to Elizabeth under a two-column headline with a photo of the two of them "larking about" on Granger's boat. He even has Humphrey Bogart calling him to alert him about the story. But it is not true. An exhaustive computerized check of Hedda's columns and the pages of the *Los Angeles Times,* as well as a thorough search of all articles collections at NYPL, USC, and AMPAS, failed to turn up any such piece. The story never appeared until Hedda's 1963 memoir *The Whole Truth and Nothing But.* It was only then that Wilding launched a lawsuit, not a decade earlier as some accounts imply. Stewart Granger compounded Wilding's error in an interview he gave to C. David Heymann by claiming that he wasn't part of the story until he called Hopper to tell the "frigging bitch" exactly what he thought of her. In Granger's version, Hedda inserted him into the story to retaliate. It seems as if both Wilding and Granger were doing their best to spin the stories to their advantage years later. Their distortions unfortunately made it into official accounts of Elizabeth's life, not only in Heymann's, but also in Donald Spoto, *A Passion for Life: The Biography of Elizabeth Taylor* (HarperCollins, 1995).

138 "as fond of Stewart Granger": LAT, February 23, 1952.

139 "holding hands": HCSBU.

139 "like drunken sailors": Wilding, *The Wilding Way*.

139 "Walt Disney, *Snow White* setting": ET, *Elizabeth Taylor*.

140 "Elizabeth Taylor is an example": *Hartford Courant*, July 18, 1955.

140 "a born mother": *Ladies' Home Journal*, April 1954.

142 On July 9 a convoy of Warner Bros. trucks: Most previous accounts have reported that Elizabeth and the cast and crew spent the entire summer—or three months—in Marfa. The *Giant* production materials in the Jack Warner Collection, USC, disprove this. A small film crew did remain for at least another week, getting some additional location footage.

142 "guarantee Liz Taylor": LAT, September 12, 1955.

142 "My tastebuds get in an uproar": *Look*, July 24, 1956.

143 "He became very introspective": Interview on *Larry King Live*, January 15, 2001, CNN transcripts.

143 "It was a very liquid evening": From "George Stevens: A Filmmaker's Journey," GSC, AMPAS.

144 "causing acute pain": Memo dated July 15, 1955, GSC, AMPAS.

144 "she must have medication": Eric Stacey to J. L. Warner and Steve Trilling, July 16, 1955, JWC, USC.

144 a few hours for wardrobe talks: Memo from Eric Stacey to J. L. Warner and Steve Trilling, July 21, 1955, JWC, USC.

144 "caused by wearing very tight breeches": Report of John H. Davis, MD, to A. Morgan Maree and Associates, March 12, 1956, GSC, AMPAS.

144 didn't return until August 8: Memo from Eric Stacey to J. L. Warner and Steve Trilling, August 8, 1955, JWC, USC.

145 both of them were stung by a bee: *Ladies' Home Journal*, September 1990.

145 "If she opens a beer can": *Look*, July 24, 1956.

145 "Elizabeth Taylor might be facing blindness": unsourced, undated article, NYPL.

145 "I couldn't wear it": *Look*, July 24, 1956.

145 ruptured intervertebral disc: Report of John H. Davis, MD, to A. Morgan Maree and Associates, March 12, 1956, GSC, AMPAS.

145 Meticorten and Demerol: Letter from Paul E. McMaster, MD, "to whom it may concern," dated September 23, 1955, GSC, AMPAS.

145 caused the *Giant* company to shoot around her: Memo from Tom Andre to Eric Stacey, August 8, 1955, GSC, AMPAS. This is also described in a memo from Eric Stacey to J. L. Warner and Steve Trilling, August 11, 1955, JWC, USC.

146 "If she felt well enough": Memo from Tom Andre to Eric Stacey, August 11, 1955, GSC, AMPAS.

146 "Dr. McMasters recommended": Memo from Tom Andre to Eric Stacey, August 12, 1955, GSC, AMPAS.

146 "Hey, wait for me!": *Look*, July 24, 1956.

146 "very bad headache": Memo, August 31, 1955, GSC, AMPAS.

147 her temperature was found to be 99.6: Memo from Tom Andre to Eric Stacey, September 26, 1955, GSC, AMPAS.

147 "remain in bed": Memo from Eric Stacey to J. L. Warner and Steve Trilling, September 27, 1955, JWC, USC.

147 "losing her breakfast": Memo dated October 4, 1955, GSC, AMPAS.

147 distress over Dean's death: "We felt she was upset over James Dean's death," reads a memo found in the GSC dated October 4, 1955.

147 she'd sustained some serious damage: Memo dated October 3, 1955, GSC, AMPAS.

147 "more ill than she had ever been": Memo dated October 3, 1955, GSC, AMPAS.

147 MGM agreeing to release Warners: Memo from Hoyt Bowers to Henry Ginsberg, October 3, 1955, JWC, USC.

148 "exploratory operations," "to finish the picture": Memo from Tom Andre to Eric Stacey, October 3, 1955, GSC, AMPAS.

148 "following completion of the picture": Memo from Tom Andre to Eric Stacey, October 4, 1955, GSC, AMPAS.

148 "the extreme mental duress": Report of John H. Davis, MD, to A. Morgan Maree and Associates, March 12, 1956, GSC, AMPAS.

148 the primary diagnosis was volvulus: These were written up in a letter sent to Stevens, found in the GSC. It's important to remember, especially with the very unusual volvulus diagnosis, that Elizabeth was trying to insist that her illnesses were work-related for insurance purposes, hence the blame being put on Stevens.

148 "obstruction in her intestine": Memo from Tom Andre to Eric Stacey, October 5, 1955, GSC, AMPAS.

148 "he saw no reason": Memo from Tom Andre to Eric Stacey, October 8, 1955, GSC, AMPAS.

148 "the Taylor situation": Memo from Eric Stacey to J. L. Warner and Steve Trilling, October 7, 1955, JWC, USC.

149 "she had been a very sick girl": Memo from Tom Andre to Eric Stacey, October 8, 1955, GSC, AMPAS.

149 "Then why do I feel this terrible pain?": *Look*, July 24, 1956.

149 totaled $44,309.40: Letter from Charles Mackie, certified public accountant, to the Fireman's Fund Insurance Company, December 26, 1955, GSC, AMPAS.

149 "and she's forgotten all about illness": LAT, November 11, 1955.

149 rated as a "good" risk: Insurance folder, *Giant,* memo dated May 13, 1955, GSC, AMPAS.

150 Strip City: Various sources allowed me to describe this long-running, popular club, including ads in the *Los Angeles Mirror* and online interviews with jazz patrons. The NYT noted on July 13, 1960, that many delegates to the Democratic National Convention, held that year in Los Angeles, visited Strip City. See also Roy Porter and David Keller, *There and Back: The Roy Porter Story* (Continuum Publishing, 1991) and Rachel Shteir, *Striptease: The Untold History of the Girlie Show* (Oxford University Press, 2005).

150 Jennie Lee: LAT, July 19, 26, August 23, 1955; May 31, 1956; April 30, 1957; *Adam* magazine, Vol. 1, No. 11, 1957; *San Bernadino Sun,* July 8, 2007. Her fame would be immortalized in the debut single of the pop duo Jan and Dean, aptly called "Jennie Lee."

151 "fond of his Scotch": *Beverly Hills [213]* magazine, January 11, 2006.

151 "strip movie": *Confidential,* November, 1955.

152 Robert Harrison: I based my account of Harrison and *Confidential* on various sources, including Harold Conrad, *Dear Muffo: 35 Years in the Fast Lane* (Stein and Day, 1982); *American Film,* February 1990; Sam Kashner and Jennifer MacNair, *The Bad and the Beautiful: Hollywood in the Fifties* (W. W. Norton, 2002); Robert Hofler, *The Man Who Invented Rock Hudson: The Pretty Boys and Dirty Deals of Henry Willson* (Carroll & Graf, 2005); and Samuel Bernstein, *Mr. Confidential: The Man, His Magazine and the Movieland Massacre That Changed Hollywood Forever* (Walford Press, 2006).

153 "The progressive coming of age": Memo prepared for Dorothy Manners, *Giant* Collection, Warner Bros. Archives, USC.

153 "What *Confidential* proved": Ezra Goodman, *The Fifty Year Decline and Fall of Hollywood* (Macfadden Books, 1962).

153 "to flipping over": *American Film,* February 1990.

155 "A neighbor of Liz Taylor": LAT, September 21, 1955.

155 "Whether it's true or not": *Look,* July 24, 1956.

155 "brother and sister": ET, *Elizabeth Taylor.* She also made this comment to Larry King in an interview on CNN that aired February 3, 2003.

155 "typical row": Wilding, *The Wilding Way.*

156 "It does something to a man": Interview on *Larry King Live,* February 3, 2003, CNN transcripts.

156 she and Mature carried on an affair: Fisher, *Been There, Done That.* There may also have been an affair with Frank Sinatra; Fisher would report that Elizabeth told him that she'd gotten pregnant by Sinatra and had an abortion. Elizabeth has denied the story.

156 WHEN MIKE WILDING CAUGHT: *Confidential*, July 1956.

157 about actress Kim Novak: This is based on revelations from the *Confidential* trial in Los Angeles. See Bernstein, *Mr. Confidential*.

157 months earlier than has ever been reported: Hank Moonjean believed that Todd may have even been present at Elizabeth's house the night of Montgomery Clift's accident in May 1956. Moonjean, who was not present, claimed that Elizabeth told him Todd paid the ambulance driver. However, there are no other reports of Todd being present that night; Kevin McCarthy, who was there, insisted Todd was *not* present.

159 "the beautiful wife": unsourced fan magazine, August 1956, NYPL.

159 all-night romp through Paris: *Look*, July 24, 1956.

159 Sammy was having an affair with Ava Gardner: Kashner and MacNair, *The Bad and the Beautiful*.

159 "I know how to pose for a picture": The quote comes from J. Randy Taraborrelli, *Elizabeth* (Warner Books, 2006), although specific original attribution is not given.

160 "I feared it": Wilding, *The Wilding Way*.

160 "restless to be back": *Photoplay*, January 1957.

160 Kevin McClory and Elizabeth Taylor: Information comes from interviews with Shirley MacLaine and Susan McCarthy Todd, as well as Michael Todd Jr. and Susan McCarthy Todd, *A Valuable Property: The Life Story of Michael Todd* (Arbor House, 1983).

162 "who kept the factory humming": Basinger, *The Star Machine*.

163 "swathed in a turquoise blue robe": Shirley MacLaine, *You Can Get There from Here* (W. W. Norton, 1975).

164 not counting the cost of extras: Memo from Joe Finn to J. J. Cohn, July 5, 1956, *Raintree County* file, MGM Collection, USC.

164–65 "soap opera with elephantitis": Bosworth, *Montgomery Clift*.

165 Father George Long: Bosworth wrote about the priest who said "fuck," but did not name him. Kevin McClory admitted to Mike Todd Jr. that Long covered for his affair with Elizabeth. See Mike Todd Jr. and Susan McCarthy Todd, *A Valuable Property*. Eddie Fisher also wrote of a priest who was having an affair with Monty Clift (Fisher, *Been There, Done That*).

165–66 "cork-twister": ET, *Elizabeth Taylor*.

166 a serious car accident: I have based my account on interviews with Kevin McCarthy and Jack Larson. I also attempted to reconcile various accounts given by Elizabeth in several different tellings of the story. Also see Bosworth, *Montgomery Clift*.

166 "accordion-pleated mess," "Adrenaline does something": Interview on *Larry King Live,* January 15, 2001, CNN transcripts.

166, 167 "All my revulsion," "It would come up": ET, *Elizabeth Taylor*.

168 for *Moby Dick* at Mocambo: *Photoplay,* January 1957.

168 cautioning McClory against being seen with Elizabeth: My descriptions are based on conversations with Susan McCarthy Todd, Shirley Mac-Laine, and Henry Baron, as well as Todd, *A Valuable Property.*

168–69 "I've never really been": LAT, October 31, 1956.

169 "It must have set him": Todd, *A Valuable Property.*

169 *Giant* premiere: Notes in *Giant* file, JWC, USC.

170 "She got hold of that": Waterbury transcript, GSC, AMPAS.

170 "a new artistry": *Motion Picture Herald,* October 11, 1956.

170 "a woman of spirit": NYT, October 11, 1956.

170 "Miss Taylor, whose talent": *Variety,* October 10, 1956.

170 launched a campaign: *Giant* promotional files, JWC, USC.

5. Over the Top

172–73 Dick jetted from Hollywood to New York: Pan Am passenger lists, August 16, 1955; September 13, 1955; various newspaper articles.

173 "the hottest man in show business": Vincent X. Flaherty's column, *Los Angeles Examiner,* February 5, 1957.

173 "Imagine, a duchess on a bus": Associated Press wire reports; see, for example, *Hartford Courant,* July 3, 1957.

174 "An openhanded sort": *Time,* July 15, 1957.

174 "My wife is pregnant": This story has been reported in several different ways. Todd's defense of Elizabeth was used as an example of his quick temper in various articles and columns. In some versions, it's Todd who says that the world isn't ready for another one of him. But this seems to be the most accurate account. See, for example, *Time,* July 15, 1957.

175 "There must be $10,000": This comes from Walker, *Elizabeth,* sourced to "private information."

175 "Call the American Embassy": LAT, July 5, 1957. Also see various Associated Press reports, Mike Todd Collection, NYPL.

177 "He was sort of the top": Katharine Hepburn, *Me: Stories of My Life* (Alfred A. Knopf, 1991). For more on the Hepburn-Hughes relationship see my *Kate: The Woman Who Was Hepburn.*

177 "Mike and I hope": *Screen Album,* August 1957.

177 "I've been an actress": LAT, March 16, 1958.

178 *South Pacific:* LAT, October 31, 1956.

178 the Todds had bantered with reporters: *Photoplay,* March 1958; various articles, NYPL.

178 "I love him madly,": *Motion Picture,* July 1957.

178–79 "There's no such thing": LAT, January 5, 1957.

179 "Thirty carats": Todd, *A Valuable Property*.

179 the glove was left behind: Bosworth, *Montgomery Clift*.

179, 180 "pacing through the rooms," "For the first time in weeks": *Modern Screen*, [nd] 1957, part of the Constance McCormick Collection, USC.

180 "Hollywood is in the business of lying": *Confidential*, September 1957.

180–81 "a marriage of equals": *New York Mirror*, March 9, 1961.

181 "They go off": Walker, *Elizabeth*. Apparently this comment was made directly to Walker by Todd.

181 "Glamour dames": *New York Daily News*, November 24, 1960.

181 "It's nice to be married": quoted in Cy Rice, *Cleopatra in Mink* (Paperback Library, 1962), no original source given.

181 "I loved it when": ET, *Elizabeth Taylor*.

182 "I don't profess": *New York Mirror*, March 9, 1961.

182 Todd carried her up to the balcony: LAT, February 4, 1957.

182 reported to have cost $80,000: *New York Daily News*, November 24, 1960. See also Elizabeth Taylor, *My Love Affair with Jewelry* (Simon & Schuster, 2003).

183 "Life in Europe": LAT, June 13, 1957.

183 "scattering Yankee dollars": *Photoplay*, October 1957.

183 missed their flight to Nice: This was covered extensively, as the various articles in the Elizabeth Taylor file at NYPL show. See, for example, LAT, June 22, 1957, and the *Hartford Courant*, June 23, 1957.

183–84 "There's no doubt": ET, *Elizabeth Taylor*.

184 "Sure Mike and I fight": *New York Post*, July 3, 1957.

184 "[Mike] really hit her": Debbie Reynolds with David Patrick Columbia, *Debbie: My Life* (William Morrow & Co., 1988).

184 "just horsing around": *Photoplay*, March 1958.

184 "We scream at each other": *New York Daily News*, July 11, 1957.

184–85 "Elizabeth's beautiful mouth": James Bacon, *Hollywood Is a Four Letter Town* (Avon Books, 1977).

185 "She told me I was wonderful": *Daily Express*, September 7, 1956.

185 "No deep-breathing declarations": *New York Mirror*, March 9, 1961.

185 "My choice is both of them": *Photoplay*, March 1958.

186 "Talk about dull days": Hedda Hopper to Mike Todd, May 27, 1957, HHC.

187 "Dad felt that the films": Interview with Mike Todd Jr. by Roy Frumkes, former editor of *Films in Review* (hereafter Frumkes interview). The interview was originally intended for that magazine but was never published because *Films in Review* folded. It has since been published online at www.in7omm.com.

187 "Mike thought food": Interview with Glenda Jensen, www.in7omm.com.

187 "By the time most movies": Todd, *A Valuable Property*.

188 "I burned up four girls": Todd, *A Valuable Property*.

188 publicity wizard Bill Doll: Bill Doll clipping collection, NYPL; NYT, May 9, 1943, and March 3, 1979.

189 *Call Me Ziggy:* NYT, February 15, 1937.

189 "so it must be the producer": Letter from Mike Todd to cast and crew of *January Thaw,* dated March 9, 1946, William and Audrey Roos Collection, Howard Gotlieb Archival Research Center, Boston University.

189 a declaration of bankruptcy: *The American Weekly,* January 28, 1951, a copy of which is in Todd's FBI file.

190 "the fact that few books": FBI file on Michael Todd, file number 49-3518, December 5, 1950.

190 "No specific assets": FBI file number 49-3518, August 27, 1951.

190 "he'd kept his mouth shut": Frumkes interview.

191 "showmanship and excitement": NYT, March 23, 1958.

191 "standing room only": Hedda Hopper to Michael Todd, May 27, 1957, HHC.

192 "This is for us": *Hartford Courant,* July 11, 1957.

192 "renting Spain": *Photoplay,* March 1958.

193 Mike Todd liked things his way: I based my account on conversations with Susan McCarthy Todd, Miles White, Mark Miller, Dick Clayton, and others. Also see Todd, *A Valuable Property* and Art Cohn, *The Nine Lives of Michael Todd* (Random House, 1958).

193 "Dad's attitude was": Frumkes interview.

193 "very much a part": Interview with Glenda Jensen, www.in7omm.com.

193 "He'd have ten different ideas": ET, *Elizabeth Taylor.*

194 "Those guys were nuts": Interview with Shirley Herz by the Association of Theatrical Press Agents and Managers, 2000, at www.atpam.com (hereafter Herz interview).

195 "become his own brand": Unsourced article, possibly *Variety,* [nd] 1957, Mike Todd file, NYPL.

196 "needless extravagance": Todd, *A Valuable Property.*

196 "roughed it": *Photoplay,* March 1958.

196 "I've often been broke": This line of Todd's was printed many times, including in several of his obituaries. It is also found in his FBI file.

196 "brashness and cunning": Brooks Atkinson's observations were contained in a review he wrote of Art Cohn's biography of Todd, NYT, October 26, 1958.

197 "I'm spending all my time": LAT, July 28, 1957.

197 The baby was due: *Hartford Courant,* July 29, 1957.

198 "would go the full nine months": LAT, August 12, 1957.

198–99 Enter Kurt Frings: U.S. Ship Passenger Lists, August 30, 1933; October 21, 1933; April 24, 1934; January 31, 1936. Mexico-U.S. Border Crossings, May 24, 1939. Also interviews with Dick Clayton, Hank Moonjean, and Mark Miller. Also transcript of interview between Hedda Hopper and Ketti Frings, February 19, 1963, HHC.

199 "A notorious international character": H. J. Anslinger, Commissioner of Narcotics, to Kenneth Clark of the Motion Picture Producers and Directors Association, October 11, 1940, Production Code Administration Collection, AMPAS.

199 Cukor would eventually terminate: Kurt Frings file, George Cukor Collection, AMPAS.

199 Cronyn was peeved: A 1952 holiday greeting card addressed to "Mr. and Mrs. Hume Croninger" had prompted a stinging rebuke. "I don't mind having my name spelled with an 'I,' or even a 'K,' but I draw the line at the enclosed. This, coming on top of such a long silence, adds insult to injury." Hume Cronyn to Kurt Frings, December 29, 1952, Hume Cronyn Collection, Manuscript Division, Library of Congress.

200 "For Christ's sake": Walker, Elizabeth, from the author's interview with Brooks.

201 Cukor's idea had been: Cat on a Hot Tin Roof file in Cukor Collection, AMPAS; see also Patrick McGilligan, George Cukor: A Double Life (HarperPerennial, 1991).

202 the film's premiere at the Strand Theatre: Hartford Courant, July 1–31, 1957.

202 a Renoir, a Pissarro, and a Monet: LAT, September 28, 1957.

202 "Private Little Party": See various articles, invitations, program books, menus, and other memorabilia in the Mike Todd Collection, NYPL. Some specific newspaper accounts were: Hartford Courant, October 13, 17, 21, 1957 (Associated Press reports); NYT, October 13, 18, 1957; Variety, October 23, 1957. Also see Frumkes interview with Mike Todd Jr.

203 invite 1,000 wonderful people: George Stevens received an invitation and (luckily for us) never sent back his reply, keeping the whole package in his files. GSC, AMPAS.

206 "Dad [became] the unexpected": Frumkes interview.

206–7 she'd told Hubert Humphrey: Todd, A Valuable Property.

207 "make him president": New York Post, August 29, 1968.

207 "Off! Off!": Todd, A Valuable Property.

207 "openly and boldly hijacked": Variety, October 23, 1957.

207 "My God, the sight": ET, Elizabeth Taylor.

208 "All hell's breaking loose": Todd, A Valuable Property.

208 "[Mike Todd] gave the public bread crumbs": *New York Daily News,* October 18, 1957.

208 "New York fiddling": *New York Herald Tribune,* October 18, 1957.

208 "It looked on the whole like a bad circus parade": *Hartford Courant,* October 21, 1957.

209 "It was just to poke a little fun": Frumkes interview.

209 In Moscow Elizabeth was: Various newspaper accounts, Elizabeth Taylor and Mike Todd files, NYPL, including NYT, January 26, 1958; *Hartford Courant,* January 16, 1958; *Daily Mirror,* January 28, 1958; *Daily Mail,* January 18, 1958.

209 "the only place in the world": *Daily Mirror,* January 28, 1958.

209 "People were staring at me": Todd, *A Valuable Property.*

210 "For some persons, the film star": NYT, January 26, 1958.

210 "I would be a phony": Associated Press report; for example, *Hartford Courant,* November 11, 1957.

210 "canceling the rest of their world tour": NYT, November 19, 1957.

210 "Come on, Liz, get out.": LAT, November 27, 1957.

211 "This will be her last time": Associated Press report; for example, *Hartford Courant,* December 23, 1957.

211 "purely a vacation": LAT, November 27, 1957.

212 "bring the people": Todd, *A Valuable Property.*

212 "association by Michael Todd": Memo from J. Edgar Hoover, Mike Todd FBI file, dated April 13, 1956.

212 "no subversive info": Mike Todd FBI file, memo dated April 6, 1956.

213 "expressed great admiration": Mike Todd FBI file, memo dated April 20, 1956.

213 outside "artistic control": Department of State memorandum of conversation, April 3, 1956, Mike Todd FBI file.

213 likening Khrushchev to a Hollywood movie magnate: NYT, February 3, 1958.

213–14 "best secret weapon": This is quoted in Dick Sheppard, *Elizabeth: The Life and Career of Elizabeth Taylor* (Warner Books, 1975), although no specific attribution is given.

214 a summit meeting between East and West: NYT, January 28, 1958.

214 "only had to utter": *Photoplay,* October 1958.

214, 215 rehearsals for *Cat on a Hot Tin Roof:* Richard Brooks papers, AMPAS.

215 "dogged it": HCSBU.

215 "Once the camera begins to roll": Heymann, *Liz.*

215 "Liz is blissfully happy": *Photoplay,* March 1958.

217–18 seeing a plane go down over the mountains: I have assembled this account by using various newspaper articles from the New Mexico area where the crash occurred, which offered considerably more details than the national press. The Associated Press compiled many of these reports for an article that was syndicated in some papers, such as the Abilene, Texas, *Reporter-News,* on March 23, 1958. I also used the detailed report of the Civil Aeronautics Administration, dated April 17, 1959, after it had concluded the investigation of the crash.

218 George Hight: This comes from the interview with Glenda Jensen, www .in7omm.com.

6. Protecting Interests

220 "old harpy": Interview with Robert Shaw.

220 "she would be hiding," "squeezing producers dry": Hopper, *The Whole Truth and Nothing But.*

221 "Good News": *Modern Screen,* [nd] 1958, Constance McCormick Collection of scrapbooks, USC.

221 "a small figure": *Photoplay,* June 1958.

221 "The goddess Todd had built": *Motion Picture,* March 1960.

222 extravagantly crossed out: Richard Brooks Collection, AMPAS.

223 "a lost lamb": *Photoplay,* June 1958.

223 "beauty, talent and youth": LAT, September 1, 1958.

223 "Elizabeth Taylor and Eddie Fisher": *New York Post,* August 29, 1958.

224 The limited Los Angeles opening: Philip K. Scheuer described her performance: "Elizabeth Taylor, proud in her humility as Maggie, cat of the title, and surpassing all her previous portrayals." LAT, August 30, 1958.

224 "The ready-made market": *Boxoffice,* August 18, 1958.

224 "couldn't get enough": My description of Elizabeth's affair with Eddie Fisher comes from an interview with Fisher, as well as his memoir, *Been There, Done That.*

224 "Eddie Fisher says Debbie's home": *Hartford Courant,* September 9, 1958.

225 EDDIE FISHER IS DATING: *Los Angeles Herald Express,* September 8, 1958.

225 When the phone rang: She didn't mention it in her memoir, but in Hedda's column, dated September 13, 1958—two days *after* her explosive front-page interview with Elizabeth—she reported, rather innocuously, that she "couldn't have been more surprised when Liz Taylor phoned to say, 'I'm home.'" When Hedda replied she thought the star was heading for Europe, Elizabeth said she'd caught a cold in New York and was "homesick, so here I am." Columns were written a few days ahead of

publication, so perhaps after this phone call, Hedda tried ringing Elizabeth back at Frings's house, and it was then that the heated conversation about Fisher took place. Or maybe both conversations were part of the same phone call, but Hedda intended to reveal the juicier parts of it in her next day's column—only to have the *Times* editors decide to turn it into a front-page story. But the most likely possibility is that the September 13 quote was *made up*—perhaps with Elizabeth's publicists' approval—once word was sent out that the star was returning to Los Angeles. If so, it wouldn't have been the first time one of Hedda's columns was written ahead of time using publicist-supplied anecdotes that hadn't yet occurred (or might never occur). Her remark on September 10 that *Cat on a Hot Tin Roof* was doing better business in New York than even *Gone With the Wind* had one major problem: *Cat* had not yet opened in New York on September 10.

225 "Level with me": Hopper, *The Whole Truth.*

225 "Elizabeth lived by her own rule": Fisher, *Been There, Done That.*

226 "I don't go about breaking up": I have based my account of Elizabeth's conflict with Hopper on interviews with Eddie Fisher, Robert Shaw, and others, as well as Hopper's personal papers, held at AMPAS, and her memoir, *The Whole Truth and Nothing But.* The quotes from the published story come from LAT, September 11, 1958. This was also edited into various syndicated versions that appeared over the next few days in papers around the country.

227 photographers rushed her plane: *Photoplay,* December 1958; LAT, September 10, 1958; various articles, Elizabeth Taylor microfiche, AMPAS, and file, NYPL.

230 Mike's estate . . . had been worth just $1 million: Will and probate file, Michael Todd, 1958, Surrogate Court, New York.

230 *Busman's Holiday:* NYT, June 19, 1958.

231 "All I can say": *Cosmopolitan,* July 1973.

231 "I guess it's in my genes": *Cosmopolitan,* September 1987.

231 "the face of an angel": Fisher, *Been There, Done That.*

231–32 "My father consoled Elizabeth": Interview with Craig Ferguson, *The Late Late Show,* CBS, April 11, 2006.

232 "I sang to the ladies": *Wall Street Journal,* October 8, 1999.

232 Born in South Philadelphia: I have based my description on an interview with Fisher, as well as his two memoirs, and the U.S. Census for Philadelphia. The family evidently moved around so much they were missed by census takers in 1930, but in 1920 the just-married Joseph Fisher was living with his wife's family, headed by parents Zelig and Ida Winokur, on Marshall Street. The neighborhood was almost entirely Jewish.

233 "Somewhere deep inside": Reynolds, *Debbie: My Life.*

233–34 "Believe me": Fisher, *Been There, Done That.*

235 "You betrayed me!": The phone conversation between Elizabeth and Hedda comes from Hopper, *The Whole Truth.*

235 "Whoever invented Capri pants": Hopper, *The Whole Truth.*

235 "This will hurt you": LAT, September 11, 1958.

236 "I must say": Hopper, *The Whole Truth.*

237 lima bean soup: Fisher, *Been There, Done That.*

238 "It doesn't look good": Sidney Skolsky's column, *New York Post*, September 9, 1958.

238 "a great guy": *Motion Picture*, March 1960. It was reported that Debbie's call came on September 11—obviously *before* she had seen Hedda's piece.

238 "Eddie left Debbie": Secondary quote, no primary attribution, used in Amburn, *The Most Beautiful Woman in the World.*

238 MGM "flacks" going in and out: LAT, September 10, 1958.

238 visit a marriage counselor: Fisher, *Been There, Done That.* The LAT reported the "over the wall" anecdote on September 10, but gave the reason as Debbie being so distraught she needed to see a doctor.

239 "We have never been happier": LAT, September 12, 1958.

239 DEBBIE: I LOVE EDDIE: *New York Herald Tribune*, September 12, 1958.

239 "untenable positions": *New York Morning Telegraph*, September 19, 1958.

239 "He isn't coming home": *Los Angeles Examiner*, Setember 12, 1958.

240 "wasn't quite the 'little darling'": HCSBU.

240 "forget them": Reynolds, *My Story.*

240 "protect her own interests": Heymann, *Liz.*

241 "still very much in love": The *Hartford Courant* reported on the story that ran in the *Chester Times* on September 14, 1958.

241 "I'm the heavy": *Los Angeles Examiner*, September 12, 1958.

241 "full responsibility": *New York Daily News*, September 13, 1958.

241 "how blind love can be": LAT, September 13, 1958.

242 "Insiders know": UPI syndicated column, *Middletown* (Connecticut) *Press*, September 13, 1958.

242 "It seems unbelievable": AP syndicated report, *Hartford Courant*, September 14, 1958.

242 "For many years": Mrs. G.L.H. to Hedda Hopper, September 11, 1958, HHC.

243 "I consider the show people": Mrs. Betty Reifel to Hedda Hopper, October 7, 1958, HHC.

243 "I am so disgusted": Mrs. Marion D. Sparks to Hedda Hopper, October 1, 1958, HHC.

243 "There is *so* much feeling": Mrs. A. L. Wood to Hedda Hopper, September 16, 1958, HHC.

243 "As far back as I can": Mrs. E. R. Gross to Hedda Hopper, October 14, 1958, HHC.

243–44 "I had little respect": B.M.S. to Hedda Hopper, September 12, 1958, HHC.

244 "not to the acting profession": Mrs. John La Peire to Hedda Hopper, September 30, 1958, HHC.

244 "rat she trapped": Anonymous to Hedda Hopper, [nd], HHC. The foil remains in the Hedda Hopper Collection, though the cheese, thankfully, has been discarded.

244 "I always feel": Kathy Hammer to Hedda Hopper, October 1, 1958, HHC.

244 "the blame should be placed": Mrs. W. Doolittle to Hedda Hopper, [nd] 1958, HHC.

244 "Imagine a woman": "Fanny's Column," *The Evanston Review,* [nd] 1958, HHC.

244 "Randy and I": Pat Scott to Hedda Hopper, [nd] 1958, HHC.

244–45 "beautiful job of reporting": "Jack" to Hedda Hopper, [nd] 1958, HHC.

245 "one of the finest jobs": Corinne Griffith to Hedda Hopper, September 12, 1958, HHC.

245 "gutsy and slashing piece": Florabel Muir to Hedda Hopper, September 11, 1958, HHC.

245 "one of the best pieces": Sammy Fuller to Hedda Hopper, September 11, 1958, HHC.

245 "Please do something": Anonymous to Hedda Hopper, September 12, 1958, HHC.

245 "Keep the Catholic": Mrs. Preston Miller to Hedda Hopper, October 6, 1958, HHC.

245–46 "mess of pottage": Lucy Davis to Hedda Hopper, September 26, 1958, HHC.

246 "multiple marriages": Dr. Ida Mary Trask to Hedda Hopper, September 13, 1958, HHC.

246 "the devil's daughter": Anonymous to Hedda Hopper, [nd] 1959, HHC.

246 "God bless you": Mary L. Jenkisson to Hedda Hopper, September 12, 1958, HHC.

246 "The die was cast": J. Frank Smith to Hedda Hopper, [nd] 1958, HHC.

246 "just another beak-nosed Jew": Mrs. Celeste Davey to Hedda Hopper, September 12, 1958, HHC.

246 "Gone are the days": Unsourced article, October 2, 1958, Lana Turner file, NYPL.

246–47 "I was so thoroughly": Theresa Dzriham to Hedda Hopper, [nd] 1958, HHC.

247 "Taylor is even worse": Anonymous to Hedda Hopper, [nd] 1958, HHC.

247 "You play by the rules": Anonymous to Hedda Hopper, September 11, 1958, HHC.

247 "So the Eddie Fisher sponsor": Mrs. Preston Miller to Hedda Hopper, September 25, 1958, HHC.

247 Various petitions were received: These are preserved in the HHC.

247 "never to see": Richard Brooks Collection, AMPAS.

247–48 "I am more than a little shocked": Mary Grant to Liggett & Myers Tobacco, October 1, 1958, a copy of which was mailed to Hedda Hopper and kept in her files, HHC.

248 "7,000 nasty letters": Fisher, *Been There, Done That.*

248 if Eddie and his sponsor could: LAT, September 28, 1958.

248 "the season debut of Eddie's show": Associated Press report; see *Hartford Courant,* October 3, 1958.

248 He sang "Moonlight Becomes You": My description of his show comes from the TV preview listings, *Hartford Courant,* September 30, 1958.

248 "those appearing with Fisher": unsigned letter, unsourced, HHC.

249 "better if Eddie didn't appear": Walker, *Elizabeth.*

249 "Some cautious ad men": Unsourced article, September 20, 1958, Eddie Fisher microfiche, AMPAS.

249 "war whoop": This is quoted in McLean, "The Cinderella Princess and the Instrument of Evil," in McLean and Cook, *Headline Hollywood.* I have been unable to locate the original reference in *Variety.*

249 "In their profession": Edward Hoyt to Hedda Hopper, September 26, 1958, HHC.

249 "We spent most of our time": Fisher, *Been There, Done That.*

250 "siding with Elizabeth": Heymann, *Liz.*

250 "oriented toward short-term profit": For a fascinating consideration of Hollywood scandals and how they played out in the press, see McLean and Cook, *Headline Hollywood.*

251 "the greatest binge": Ezra Goodman, *The Fifty-Year Decline and Fall of Hollywood* (MacFadden Books, 1962).

251 "the Church of Latter-Day Debbie": Carrie Fisher, *Wishful Drinking* (Simon & Schuster, 2008).

252 "Dear Debbie": *Photoplay,* June 1958.

252 "Judas Iscariot": Joanna Walsh to Hedda Hopper, September 25, 1958, HHC.

252 "A no-good mother": Pat Ryan to Hedda Hopper, September 11, 1958, HHC.

252 "excuses for her neglect": Mrs. A. L. Wood to Hedda Hopper, September 16, 1958, HHC.

252 "Does she not even have": Mrs. E. R. Gross to Hedda Hopper, October 14, 1958, HHC.

252 "It makes me furious": "A Texas housewife" to Hedda Hopper, September 30, 1958, HHC.

252 "for her recent role": *New York Daily News,* September 17, 1958.

253 "Debbie loved Eddie": *Motion Picture,* May 1960.

253 "Debbie Reynolds—her hair": *Motion Picture,* March 1960.

253 "Elizabeth Taylor may discover": *Motion Picture,* March 1960.

253 "No sweeter girl": Unsourced magazine, January 1959, Debbie Reynolds file, NYPL.

253–54 "Debbie is a thousand times": Eileen Casper to Hedda Hopper, [nd] 1958, HHC.

254 "an intelligence far above": Janet Wilson to Hedda Hopper, [nd] 1958, HHC.

254 "*Tammy* gave enjoyment": Annabelle Barnett to Hedda Hopper, September 25, 1958, HHC.

254 "Debbie has more beauty": Anonymous to Hedda Hopper, [nd] 1958, HHC.

254 "In Hollywood": Goodman, *The Fifty Year Decline and Fall of Hollywood.*

254 "You know who those friends": *Motion Picture,* May 1960.

254 "[Their] whole relationship": LAT, August 13, 1995.

254 "That's how [stars]": *Outsmart Magazine,* August 1998.

254–55 "I had no control": Fisher, *Been There, Done That.*

255 "strong personality": *Motion Picture,* March 1960.

255 "but only if you lived": Fisher, *Been There, Done That.*

256 "frigid and sexually unresponsive": World Entertainment News Network, wenn.com, May 14, 2001.

256 "My father's story": *The Advocate,* February 3, 2004.

256 "on whose slender shoulder": Charles Denton syndicated column, *Hartford Courant,* September 6, 1959.

256 "all except the light": *Los Angeles Examiner,* September 12, 1958.

256 Camille had been Miss Burbank: LAT, May 4, 1949; June 8, 1956; December 30, 1956; March 1, 1958.

256 "voluptuous": *Outsmart Magazine,* August 1998.

256 elude all offers of marriage: Not for another six years, after Debbie had married for the second time, would Camille finally wed; her husband was Debbie's friend, the well-known film composer Jerry Fielding.

256 Dan Dailey's Vegas act: *Confidential*, January 1957; *Uncensored*, September 1955; see also my *Behind the Screen: How Gays and Lesbians Shaped Hollywood* (Viking, 2001).

256 "very close friend," "who had become": Fisher, *Been There, Done That.*

256 Whatever the truth of Debbie's sexuality: A few years later, she would also forge a close emotional bond with actress Agnes Moorehead. When Moorehead died in 1974, she left Debbie as executor of her estate. "My brilliant, witty, intelligent friend," Debbie eulogized. "Funny as can be, a great teacher, a great friend. And now she was gone forever from my life." In her memoir, Debbie would acknowledge, without officially denying, the persistent Hollywood rumors that she and Moorehead had been lovers. For an in-depth study of Moorehead's representation on- and off-screen as a lesbian, and how Reynolds fit into that narrative, see Patricia White, *Uninvited: Classical Hollywood Cinema and Lesbian Representability* (Indiana University Press, 1999).

257 "I'm not taking anything away": LAT, September 11, 1958.

257 "Although Liz and I": *Motion Picture*, March 1960.

257 "The legend that": *Photoplay*, December 1959.

258 "Ferocious and fascinating": NYT, September 19, 1958.

258 "well-accented": *Variety*, September 10, 1958.

258 "surprising sureness": *Time*, September 15, 1958.

259 Quigley poll: LAT, December 24, 1958.

259 "Year's most popular actress!": *Middletown Press*, April 5, 1959.

260 *Two for the Seesaw:* NYT, September 22, 1958.

261 "People keep stopping me": Hedda Hopper column, as in the *Hartford Courant*, October 8, 1959.

261 seen hugging the star: Unsourced article in HHC. There is no date, but the occasion was a party celebrating Romanoff's U.S. citizenship, bestowed on him by an act of Congress. This was in November 1958.

261 at Romanoff's, Elizabeth took the next step: LAT, December 5, 1958.

261 "the only event he and Liz": *Inside Story*, July 1959.

262 "If Taylor was not": *Esquire*, March 1967.

262 WHAT'S HAPPENING: *Photoplay*, May 1959.

262 Academy Awards ceremony: AP press report, as in *Hartford Courant*, April 7, 1959.

263 "There's nothing blue": *Photoplay*, August 1959.

263 "A traitor to Jesus Christ": Mrs. P. Steffen to Hedda Hopper, April 30, 1959, HHC.

263 "Jewess": This was told to me by Robert Wheaton, a close friend of director George Cukor's, in an interview for my book *Behind the Screen.*

264 "swastika epidemic": *Social Problems*, Volume 9, Number 3, Winter 1962.

264 "What the hell": Heymann, *Liz*.

264 "It's a double act": *Photoplay*, August 1959.

265 "It will be the last time": *Daily Express*, May 13, 1959.

7. A Second Chance on Life

266 "I'm so happy": *Hartford Courant*, May 17, 1959. Elizabeth's honeymoon might have been written off as a business expense, since she made time to do an unbilled walk-on in Mike Todd Jr.'s film, *Scent of Mystery*, shot in Spain and developed around a gimmick that would have made Papa proud. Smell-O-Vision came with a machine that spewed forth various aromas as the film unwound, including a floral perfume when Elizabeth, her face hidden, walks across the screen.

267 "The old moguls": MacLaine, *You Can Get There From Here*.

267–68 "Are you planning": HCSBU.

268 The actor Martin Landau: He made this remark in the commentary for the DVD of *Cleopatra*.

268 "Hell, no!": Dorothy Kilgallen's column, *New York Journal-American*, April 4, 1962.

268 the much-older political columnist Max Lerner: He wrote about his friendship with Elizabeth in *McCall's*, September 1974, but gave far more personal details in an interview with Alexander Walker for Walker's book *Elizabeth*.

269 "Her name is *Mrs. Fisher*": AP report, as in the *Hartford Courant*, May 27, 1959.

269 "songs that meant something": Fisher, *Been There, Done That*.

270 "There's not a decent stone here": Interview with John Valva by C. David Heymann, HCSBU.

270 "An unheard-of price": Wanger, *My Life With Cleopatra*.

271 Fox's 1960–61 production schedule was budgeted: NYT, September 13, 1959.

272 "a fight between the older generation and the younger": NYT, October 25, 1959.

272 "clammy coils": *Time*, January 11, 1960.

272 "possibly the most bizarre film": *Variety*, December 10, 1959.

272 "rightly roiled": NYT, December 23, 1959.

272–73 Even Hepburn hated the film: See my *Kate: The Woman Who Was Hepburn*.

273 "Sam Spiegel expects": *Hartford Courant*, July 17, 1959.

273 the movie poster that would dominate Hollywood: Interview with Tom Mankiewicz, as well as Kenneth L. Geist, *Pictures Will Talk: The Life and Films of Joseph L. Mankiewicz* (Da Capo Press, 1983).

274 "Finds men the source": Notes to shooting script of *Butterfield 8*, Daniel Mann Collection, AMPAS.

275 "normally be clear": Pandro Berman to John Michael Hayes, May 11, 1960, Daniel Mann Collection, AMPAS.

275 "A walking time bomb": Hank Moonjean, *Bring in the Peacocks: Memoirs of a Hollywood Producer* (AuthorHouse, 2004). Other Moonjean quotes are from my interview with him.

276 Screen Actors Guild called a strike: NYT, March 8, 1960.

276–77 Actress Mary Murphy: *Los Angeles Examiner*, June 12, 1959.

277 "A lot of citizens": *Hartford Courant*, October 21, 1959.

277 how cold Elizabeth was in person: *Motion Picture*, March 1960.

277 WHAT I TELL MY CHILDREN: *Photoplay*, April 1962.

277 EXCLUSIVE! DEBBIE THREATENED!: *Motion Picture*, October 1960.

278 HOW MUCH CAN EDDIE: *Screen Stars*, August 1960.

278 She's showcased as a doting mother: *Photoplay*, October 1960.

278 "I've never been America's sweetheart": *Photoplay*, December 1959.

278 "My ambition is to win an Oscar": *New York Post*, October 26, 1959.

278 Reporter James Bacon: *Hartford Courant*, March 27, 1960.

279 yellow chiffon gown: *Hartford Courant*, April 4, 1960.

279 "The crowd ooh'd and aah'd": *Hartford Courant*, April 5, 1960.

280 "There are very few actresses": Wanger, *My Life With Cleopatra*.

281 Elizabeth was hiding out because she was too fat: *Daily Mail*, October 13, 1960. Elizabeth sued them for saying so and won.

281 "million dollars' worth": Wanger, *My Life With Cleopatra*.

281 the fussy hairdresser worked his magic: Guilaroff, *Crowning Glory*.

282 "She has been around too long": Wanger, *My Life With Cleopatra*.

282 "Malta fever": Various articles, including LAT, November 2, 1960; *New York Post*, November 2, 1960; *Daily Mail*, November 1, 1960.

282 "A tenacious bug": *New York Post*, November 2, 1960.

282 STRICKEN LIZ TAYLOR: *New York Journal-American*, November 14, 1960.

283 "still a sick girl": *New York Post*, November 15, 1960.

283 "more frequently encountered": LAT, November 16, 1960.

283 "She had become addicted": Eddie said a version of this quote in both his memoirs, but this comes from his interview with C. David Heymann, for *Liz*.

283 "I'm here to do whatever": Fisher, *My Life, My Loves*.

284 "Elizabeth Taylor is in a class": *Motion Picture Herald*, October 8, 1960.

The trade paper offers a fascinating, detailed account of the studio's marketing and distribution plans for *Butterfield 8*.

285 "working amid the ruins": Lana Turner, *Lana: The Lady, the Legend, the Truth* (Dutton, 1982).

286 "long-range stock": Goodman, *The Fifty Year Decline and Fall of Hollywood*.

286 "The true love that exists": This is from the fan magazine *Movie Stars TV Closeups*, quoted by Goodman.

286 "It seemed the thing to do": Quoted in Heymann, *Liz*. See also Earl Wilson, *Hot Times: True Tales of Hollywood and Broadway* (Contemporary Books, 1984).

287 "If I could be": *Movie Mirror*, [nd] 1961, Elizabeth Taylor file, NYPL.

288–89 "This is the fourth nomination": Syndicated column, as in the *Hartford Courant*, March 8, 1961.

289 "She might have survived": Alexander Walker interviewed the first doctor on the scene, but did not identify him, for his book *Elizabeth*.

289 "primitive corners": Wanger, *My Life With Cleopatra*.

290 House of Lords: Lord Mancroft "wondered whether the freedom of the press would have been seriously endangered if [the public] had not been shown photographs of Miss Elizabeth Taylor lying unconscious on a stretcher and being carried to an ambulance." *The Times*, March 14, 1961.

290 "Her condition remains grave": Various reports, including LAT, March 5, 1961.

290 "The condition of": *The Times*, March 6, 1961.

290–91 "At last everything is going": Wanger, *My Life With Cleopatra*.

292 "once-lithe body": *New York Daily News*, March 7, 1961. For the press coverage of Elizabeth's hospitalization, I read dozens of newspaper articles in her files at both AMPAS and NYPL.

293 "out of danger": *The Times*, March 10, 1961.

293 "going along very nicely": LAT, March 13, 1961.

293 "black maria," "Go on home": Unsourced article, possibly the *Daily Mail*, March 13, 1961, ET file, NYPL.

293 "dreadful illness": LAT, March 13, 1961.

294 "There, in her hospital bed": *The Times*, January 22, 2008.

294 champagne with Truman Capote: Wanger.

294 "the white light": Interview on *Larry King Live*, January 15, 2001, CNN transcripts. The stories did tend to become more grandiose as time went by. In a later interview with King, aired on May 30, 2006, she'd say that she'd been pronounced dead four times and that doctors had tried everything to save her, including giving dog distemper shots to her.

295 MISS TAYLOR COMES HOME: LAT, March 29, 1961.

295 "a little better": *New York Post*, March 28, 1961.

295 "numerous shots of antibiotics": LAT, March 29, 1961.

295 "It is *love* that is killing": *Motion Picture*, March 1960.

296 "a beautiful woman of twenty-eight," "that a good spanking wouldn't cure": *Motion Picture*, February 1961.

296 "This was the ultimate climax": Fisher, *Been There, Done That*.

296 "Elizabeth Taylor looks tough": *Hartford Courant*, April 16, 1961.

297 "cool and confident": AP report, as in the *Hartford Courant*, April 18, 1961.

297 When the nominees for Best Actress: My description of the night and the ceremony comes from the AP reports, April 16, 17, 18, 1961.

297 "prolong the drama": Fisher, *Been There, Done That*.

298–99 With Max Lerner: See *McCall's*, September 1974, as well as Walker, *Elizabeth*, and Kelley, *Elizabeth Taylor*.

299 an act at the legendary Cocoanut Grove: Various, including *New York Post*, July 26, 1961; *Hollywood Citizen-News*, July 26 and 27, 1961; *Los Angeles Examiner*, July 27, 1961; Sidney Skolsky's column, July 28, 1961.

8. No Deodorant Like Success

301 Hedda Hopper had announced the possibility: Syndicated column, as in the *Hartford Courant*, September 19, 1960. Louella Parsons confirmed the casting in the *Los Angeles Examiner* on December 16, 1960.

301 since Elizabeth was now a Jew: Mrs. Velda Fulcher to George Stevens, December 27, 1960, GSC.

301 "Surely you can find": Mrs. Florence S. Chipman to George Stevens, January 3, 1961, GSC.

301 "A woman like Liz Taylor": Mrs. Sidney Myers to George Stevens, December 28, 1960, GSC.

302 Kurt Frings was not impressed: Stevens's handwritten notes, as well as typewritten summaries and annotations possibly made by George Stevens Jr., an associate producer on the film, *The Greatest Story Ever Told* file, GSC.

302 sashaying down the Via Veneto: Various articles, including the *Los Angeles Herald-Examiner*, April 4, 1962; *Daily Mail*, April 4, 1962; *New York Daily News*, April 5 and 7, 1962; UPI reports, as in the *Middletown Press*, April 7, 1962; *Los Angeles Herald-Examiner*, April 8, 1962; *New York Post*, April 8, 1962.

303 "Probably no news event": *Los Angeles Herald-Tribune*, April 14, 1962.

303 five hundred torch-bearing university students: *New York Daily News,* April 16, 1962.

303 Elizabeth broke down in tears: *New York Journal-American,* April 19, 1962.

304 "a game which they start": NYT, April 5, 1962.

304 "erotic vagrancy": *New York Daily News,* April 13, 1962.

304 "He's never been": Graham Jenkins, *Richard Burton: My Brother.*

304 But the Italian papers: UPI report, as in the *Middletown Press,* April 4, 1962.

304 "the nauseating headlines": *The Connecticut Catholic Transcript,* April 12, 1962.

304–5 "self-destruction": AP report, as in the *Hartford Courant,* April 28, 1962.

305 seaside bungalow at Porto Santo Stefano: *Hollywood Citizen-News,* April 25, 1962; *Los Angeles Herald-Examiner,* April 25, 26, 1962; LAT, April 25, 26, 1962; *New York Daily News,* April 22, 23, 25, 26, 1962; *New York Mirror,* April 25, 1962.

305 anonymous letter threatening her: LAT, May 21, 1962; *New York Daily News,* May 21, 1963.

305 "What has happened to our concept": *Catholic Transcript,* April 26, 1962.

305 Iris Faircloth Blitch: See the *Congressional Record,* Volume 108. Also LAT, May 23, 1962; *Variety,* May 23, 1962; AP report, as in the *Hartford Courant,* May 23, 1962. Eight years earlier, on November 7, 1954, Rep. Blitch had made an appearance on the television show *What's My Line?* Available online, the program reveals her charm and Southern accent.

306 "Her beauty masks": Hopper syndicated column, as in the *Hartford Courant,* April 10, 1962.

306 "sick—very sick": Hopper syndicated column, as in the *Hartford Courant,* May 11, 1962.

306 "Whoever would have thought the Italians": *Hartford Courant,* April 10, 1962.

306 another scandal erupting around Kurt Frings: See transcript of conversation between Hedda Hopper and Ketti Frings, dated February 19, 1963, HHC; Hopper's syndicated column, as in the *Hartford Courant,* February 6 and 16, 1963; LAT, April 22, 1963; *Hartford Courant,* April 20, 1963.

306 This time it was the agent's estranged wife: LAT, April 5, 1962.

306 "Liz Taylor will never play": *Hollywood Reporter,* July 30, 1962. According to Stevens's files, Connolly's column that day was ghostwritten by John Bradford, but the director was convinced the item had come from Connolly himself, since the columnist had just recently paid him a visit.

307 "My affection": George Stevens to ET, August 2, 1962, GSC.

307 "I will never go back to America": Bragg, *Richard Burton.*

307 "being real vicious": Waterbury transcript, GSC.

308 "The Sixties was to pride itself": Bragg, *Richard Burton.*

308 "He looked very much like me": Hollis Alpert, *Burton* (G. P. Putnam's Sons, 1986).

308 "I would rather have played": Bragg, *Richard Burton.*

309 he admitted that one time he actually gave in: Bragg, *Richard Burton.*

309 an unrequited object of desire: This was the perception of the director John Schlesinger, who was a fellow Oxford man and also close with Nevill Coghill. The producer Frank Taylor described Philip's attraction to Richard as "unrequited," but said the older man "didn't have sex of any kind." Amburn, *The Most Beautiful Woman in the World.*

309 "chaps with posh accents": *Playboy,* September 1963.

310 "Out came the most perfect rendering": Bragg, *Richard Burton.*

310 "I'm the least Method actor": Richard Burton to Roy Newquist, tape-recorded interview used as basis for article in *McCall's,* June 1966, and aired on WCBS radio, May 1966 (hereafter Newquist interview).

310 "His playing of Prince Hal": Kenneth Tynan was the critic for the *Evening Standard.* Quoted in Bragg, *Richard Burton.*

311 "[Acting] doesn't especially appeal": *Playboy,* September 1963.

311 "Huh! I'm not going to be": Interview on *Larry King Live,* January 15, 2001, CNN transcripts.

311 "Sybil was the good loving bride": Alexander Walker, ed., *No Bells on Sunday: The Journals of Rachel Roberts* (McGraw-Hill, 1985).

311 "Oh, my lovely girl": Richard Burton to Claire Bloom, October 7, 1954, Claire Bloom Collection, Howard Gotlieb Archival Research Center, Boston University.

312 "my lovely girl [would] be forced to sleep": Richard Burton to Claire Bloom, November 5, 1954, Claire Bloom Collection, Howard Gotlieb Archival Research Center, Boston University.

312 "Not a chance!": *Hartford Courant,* October 15, 1962.

312 "I have been inordinately lucky": Richard Burton diary, November 19, 1968, quoted in Bragg.

313 "scared witless to approach me": Richard Burton diary, November 20, 1970, quoted in Bragg.

313 "To scream 'fuck' in the lobby": Richard Burton diary, August 11, 1967, quoted in Bragg.

313 columnist Herb Caen: Lawrence Grobel, *The Hustons: The Life and Times of a Hollywood Dynasty* (Cooper Square Press, 2000).

313–14 Elizabeth "redrew the maps of his ambition": Bragg, *Richard Burton.*

314 "Richard is a very sexy man": *Life,* December 18, 1964.

314 "There's no way": Newquist interview.

314 "It was so intense": Interview on *Larry King Live,* January 15, 2001, CNN transcripts.

315 "Elizabeth is a pretty girl": *Playboy,* September 1963.

315 "Richard has enormous taste": *Look,* May 7, 1963.

316 "I generally shut Jess": Richard Burton diary, quoted in Bragg.

316 "He is a snakepit": *Look,* May 7, 1963.

316 "all great art": Ernest Lehman, unpublished memoir, "Fun and Games With George and Martha: The Virginia Woolf Papers," Ernest Lehman Collection, USC.

317 "I sometimes wake up": *Playboy,* September 1963.

317 "This was so that Richard": Walker, *No Bells on Sunday.*

318 "I want to direct in motion pictures": AP interview, syndicated, as in the *Hartford Courant,* September 20, 1964.

319 "nervous and tense": Wanger, *My Life With Cleopatra.*

319–20 "Congressional investigation": Letter from Rep. Iris F. Blitch to constituents, May 29, 1962, Iris Faircloth Blitch Collection.

320 When one member, Rep. Michael Feighan: NYT, February 4 and 14, 1964.

320 "new heights of ridiculosity": *Hartford Courant,* February 6, 1964.

320 photographs of a topless Jayne Mansfield: *Playboy,* June 1963.

320–21 "Is she modern": *Photoplay,* April 1963.

321 THE FINAL ACT THAT SHOOK: *Modern Screen,* [nd] 1962, Constance McCormick Collection, USC.

321 "America's 2 Queens": *Photoplay,* June 1962.

321 WHY WOMEN CAN'T RESIST: *Modern Screen,* August 1962.

321 "no good," "interesting newspaper copy": *New York Daily News,* April 3, 1962.

322 "If part of the world": *Look,* May 7, 1963.

323 "The press has seemed determined": Anne Ritchie to Iris Blitch, May 25, 1962, Iris Faircloth Blitch Collection.

323 "To tell you the truth," "So what do the papers say": *Look,* May 7, 1963.

323 "quiet study": NYT, June 1, 1962.

324 "to garner extra dollars": NYT, June 2, 1962.

324 "a self-contained media event": Bragg, *Richard Burton.*

324 "The public wonders": Hopper syndicated column; see *Hartford Courant,* March 21, 1962.

324 "a wave of public opinion," "forgot about it": Civil Case No. 66-73, *Twentieth Century-Fox Film Corporation vs. Elizabeth Taylor and Richard Burton,* January 20, 1966, U.S. District Court, Southern District of California, National Archives and Records Administration, Pacific Region.

324 "I told you": *New York Daily News,* July 15, 1962.

325 "I have paid": *Life,* December 18, 1964.

326 "just a little stinking bit": Hedda Hopper to Mildred Cram, February 3, 1964, HHC.

326 the usually astute Kenneth McCormick . . . editor, Margaret Cousins: Details of Hedda's relationship with her publisher come from a letter Hopper wrote to attorney Howard Ellis, March 29, 1965, HHC.

326 "a reckless and wanton disregard": *Variety,* April 5, 1963.

326 "I'm going to fight this battle": Wilding, *The Wilding Way.* Here again, it is clear that either Wilding did not write his memoir himself or he was very, very confused, for the description of the libel suit is set circa 1952, ten years earlier than it actually occurred. So any statements from this account must be considered very carefully.

328 "All very chatty": Memo, January 10, 1964, HHC.

329 "I wish we could be friends": Hopper syndicated column, as in the *Hartford Courant,* January 27, 1964.

329 a dispirited Hedda finally agreed to settle with Wilding: *Los Angeles Herald-Express,* March 25, 1965; *Hollywood Citizen-News,* March 26, 1965; LAT, March 26, 1965; *Variety,* March 31, 1965.

329 "The suit is settled": Hedda's feelings about the settlement of the Wilding lawsuit, as well as her comments about Mike Connolly, come from a letter she wrote to Howard Ellis, March 29, 1965, HHC.

330 "good revenge": *Look,* May 7, 1963.

330 "Do you think it will": *Look,* May 7, 1963.

331 "butchery": *Variety,* October 31, 1962.

331 "Mr. Mankiewicz took *Cleopatra* over": NYT, October 24, 1962.

331 "To look at": *Time,* June 21, 1963.

332 "a woman of force and dignity": NYT, June 13, 1963.

332 "Italian Hercules spectacular": Quoted in Jerry Vermilye and Mark Ricci, *The Films of Elizabeth Taylor* (Carol Publishing Corporation, 1989).

332 Fox was banking on an extraordinarily long run: See Dorothy Kilgallen's column, *New York Journal-American,* February 29, 1962.

332–33 One opinion poll: LAT, June 26, 1963.

333 "Here on the lazy west coast": LAT, October 13, 1963.

333 "I can live here": Richard Burton to Alexander Walker, quoted in Walker, *Elizabeth.*

335 "paralyzingly potent": William F. Nolan, *John Huston: King Rebel* (Sherbourne Press, 1965).

335 "She's fearless": Grobel, *The Hustons.*

335 "more reporters on the site": John Huston, *An Open Book* (Da Capo Press, 1994).

335 "a lot of rows": Grobel, *The Hustons.*

336 "But . . . there was nothing": Grobel, *The Hustons.*

336 they'd also flown in the wife: LAT, October 15, 1963.

336 "ever really loved": AP report, as in the *Hartford Courant,* February 5, 1964.

337 fans waited for hours: *Record American,* March 23, 1964; *New York Journal-American,* March 23, 1964; various articles, Richard Burton, John Springer files, NYPL.

337 a crowd of people suddenly burst through: *Boston Globe,* March 24, 1964; AP reports, as in the *Hartford Courant,* March 24, 1964.

339 "Why, I used to handle": *Record American,* March 23, 1964.

340 "rooted to the spot": *Esquire,* November 1964.

340 "For God's sake": *Ladies' Home Journal,* December 1974.

341 "Rarely has poetry drawn": NYT, June 22, 1964.

341 "I knew that eighty-five percent": Taylor, *Elizabeth Taylor.*

341 "a pile of crap": Ernest Lehman unpublished memoir, "Fun and Games With George and Martha: The Virginia Woolf Papers," Ernest Lehman Collection, USC.

342 "A wild idea," "Don't let Taylor": Unpublished memoir by Vincente Minnelli, Minnelli Collection, AMPAS.

342 "To have found": Taylor, *Elizabeth Taylor.*

9. Rewriting the Rules

344 "On a day": Unless otherwise noted, Ernest Lehman's observations of the making of *Who's Afraid of Virginia Woolf?* come from his unpublished journal, "Fun and Games With George and Martha: The Virginia Woolf Papers," Ernest Lehman Collection, USC, hereafter Lehman journal.

346 "star power first": To be clear, this quote came from a personal interview with Nichols.

346–47 Nichols had complained "bitterly": Lehman journal.

347 "I don't like to go into rehearsals": Associated Press report, as in the *Hartford Courant,* September 20, 1964.

348 "His invention is as resourceful": NYT, October 24, 1963.

349 *Virginia Woolf* was breaking down the last strictures: See files in the Production Code Administration Collection, AMPAS. Also Leonard J. Leff and Jerold L. Simmons, *The Dame in the Kimono: Hollywood, Censorship, and the Production Code* (University Press of Kentucky, 2001).

349 "I don't know why you want": Lehman journal.

350 Elizabeth pulling down $100,000 per week: Interoffice Warner Bros.

memo from P. D. Knecht to Hal Holman, November 1, 1965, JWC, USC.

352 "When I first read the script": Interview with Roy Newquist that was used as part of a *McCall's* magazine article in June 1966. The interviews, much of which did not make it into the article, were played separately on Kenneth Banghart's CBS radio program. This quote is taken from a recording of that program. (Hereafter Newquist-Banghart.)

353 "I want the audience drawn": *Saturday Evening Post*, October 9, 1965.

354 "What are those ravishing shadows": LAT, July 28, 1965.

354 "Yes, but are you worried": Lehman journal.

354 "My job is": *Hartford Courant*, March 29, 2006.

354–55 "If Mike wants me": LAT, July 28, 1965.

355 "a lot of cream": Lehman journal.

356 "the physical progression": Newquist-Banghart.

357 "I can't *act* until you say": *Saturday Evening Post*, October 9, 1965.

357 "Elizabeth can keep in her mind": *Saturday Evening Post*, October 9, 1965.

357 "I had a character": Interview on *Larry King Live*, January 15, 2001, CNN transcripts.

357 "wonderful words to wrap": Interview on *Larry King Live*, May 30, 2006, CNN transcripts.

357 "It's a matter," "You cannot believe": Newquist-Banghart.

361 "advance publicity was not calculated": *Hartford Courant*, August 22, 1965.

362 "We finally decided": *McCall's*, June 1966.

362 "Why should we help support": *Hartford Courant*, March 29, 2006.

363 "bothering them": Lehman journal.

364 "If you want to turn": Interview with Michael Daves by Stephen Bogart, Icons Radio Hour, available online.

364 "It's easy to say you're tired": *Saturday Evening Post*, October 9, 1965.

365 "She has the larceny": *New York Post*, September 1, 1967.

366 "It's the most enjoyable": Newquist-Banghart.

367 "We're in trouble": Lehman journal.

367 "natural ego": Newquist-Banghart.

368 "I never had a better time": Interview on *Larry King Live*, May 30, 2006, CNN transcripts.

368 "decidedly erotic": Lehman journal.

368–69 "We both had to pull out all the stops": Interview on *Larry King Live*, May 30, 2006, CNN transcripts.

369 they were the only actors who could draw audiences: *Hartford Courant*, August 3, 1965.

370 "The tax thing": *Look,* May 7, 1963.

370 "Money is more valuable": *Hollywood Citizen News,* January 15, 1965.

370 "A lot of grated parmesan": *Hollywood Reporter,* January 11, 1965.

371 "How's the new baby?": Paddy Chayefsky to Eddie Fisher, January 23, 1962, Paddy Chavefsky papers, NYPL.

371 royalties due from *Cleopatra:* NYT, April 23, 1964; LAT, April 22 and 23, 1964; Civil Case No. 66-73 and Civil Case No. 66-2066, *Twentieth Century-Fox Film Corporation vs. Elizabeth Taylor and Richard Burton,* U.S. District Court, Southern District of California, National Archives and Records Administration, Pacific Region (hereafter Fox lawsuit, NARA).

371 "too ludicrous": NYT, April 24, 1964.

372 "These two defendants": Case 66-73, Fox lawsuit, NARA.

374 "This picture is too important": Lehman journal.

374 Warners agreed to reimburse the costs: Memo from Mickey Rudin to Walter MacEwan, December 1, 1965, JWC, USC.

374 "part of her efforts": Mickey Rudin to Peter D. Knecht, January 19, 1966, JWC, USC.

374–75 "I wouldn't put it in print": Interview on *Larry King Live,* January 15, 2001, CNN transcripts.

375 "Wouldn't it be better": *Look,* May 7, 1963.

376 the film version of *Hello, Dolly!:* Lehman journal.

376 Production Code Administration had refused: Leff and Simmons, *The Dame in the Kimono;* NYT, June 25, 1966.

376 "The Code is dead": *Motion Picture Daily,* June 27, 1966.

376 "the public morality in film": NYT, June 25, 1966.

377 "I'm not a masochist": Lehman journal.

377 "I am told": ET to Ray Stark, November 1967, John Huston Collection, AMPAS.

378 "Please let's at least write": Ray Stark to John Huston, April 25, 1966, Huston Collection, AMPAS.

379 "The emotional climate": Marilyn Beck syndicated column, as in the *Hartford Courant,* April 4, 1967.

380 "that woman": LAT, June 17, 1967.

380 she gushed to Liz Smith: The article first ran in *Cosmopolitan* in September 1968 and was reprinted in the NYT, April 29, 2001, as well as Liz Smith, *Dishing* (Simon & Schuster, 2005).

382 "We just stepped": NYT, March 3, 1968.

383 "We get a great giggle": *Look,* May 7, 1963.

383 "What are you doing": Bragg, *Richard Burton.*

383–84 "I'm much more broad-minded": *Look,* May 7, 1963.

384 "pig out": *Cosmopolitan,* September 1987.

384 "The lazy little bugger": Bragg, *Richard Burton.*

384–85 off the coast of Sardinia: *New York Post,* August 30, 31, September 1, 1967.

Epilogue: How to Stay a Movie Star

387 the Cartier diamond had become the Taylor-Burton diamond: NYT, October 24, 25, 27, 31, 1969; UPI report, as in the *Hartford Courant,* October 28, 1969. See also Taylor, *My Love Affair with Jewelry.*

387 "the nice little": Alexander Walker sourced this as "private information" in his book *Elizabeth.*

387–88 "Nobody I know": NYT, October 24, 1969.

388 "Doesn't look so vulgar": Walker, *Elizabeth.*

388 "You can't own a thing": *Cosmopolitan,* September 1987.

390 Richard had had to outbid Prince Alfonso: NYT, January 26, 1969.

391 "Absolute hell": Michel Ciment, *Conversations with Losey* (Methuen, 1985).

392 "quite adoringly": Lehman journal.

393 "Don't call me a secretary": LAT, December 16, 1976.

393 Chen Sam: *New York,* August 8, 1994; *Variety,* September 2, 1996; *Parade,* October 13, 1996.

393 "shrewdly [kept] Elizabeth": *New York,* August 8, 1994.

393 Elizabeth Taylor Diamond Corporation: LAT, December 16, 1976.

394 "increasingly imprecise": Thomson, *A Biographical Dictionary of Film.*

395 "You are such a terrific woman": *The New Republic,* February 7, 1983.

395 "Liz Taylor's latest race": *Esquire,* November 1977.

395 "I thought we would get married": Interview on *Larry King Live,* January 15, 2001, CNN transcripts.

395 "I'm looking forward": *McCall's,* January 1977.

395 "We didn't have any caviar": *Esquire,* November 1977.

396 ET had never been a voter: Case 66-73, Fox lawsuit, NARA.

396 "Virginia needs her!": *McCall's,* January 1977.

396 "John [Warner] wanted": *New York,* August 8, 1994.

397 "Genghis Khan": Harriet Meth, quoted in C. David Heymann, *Liz.*

397 "I think they [Washington]": Interview on *Larry King Live,* January 15, 2001, CNN transcripts.

400 producer Zev Bufman: Heymann, *Liz.*

401 "It's hard not to love her": *Mandate,* June 1983.

402 "Despite all [Elizabeth]'s": Bragg, *Richard Burton*.

403 covering Sara's small frame with jewelry: Probate file, Sara Sothern Taylor, Case 068723, Superior Court, Riverside County, July 11, 1995.

403 "No matter how sick": NYT, May 6, 1981.

403–4 "If *The Little Foxes*": NYT, May 8, 1981.

Index